American Snobs

Edinburgh Critical Studies in Atlantic Literatures and Cultures
Series Editors: Laura Doyle, Colleen Glenney Boggs and Maria Cristina Fumagalli

Available titles
Sensational Internationalism: The Paris Commune and the Remapping of American Memory in the Long Nineteenth Century
J. Michelle Coghlan

American Travel Literature, Gendered Aesthetics, and the Italian Tour, 1824–1862
Brigitte Bailey

American Snobs: Transatlantic Novelists, Liberal Culture and the Genteel Tradition
Emily Coit

Forthcoming titles
Emily Dickinson and Her British Contemporaries: Victorian Poetry in Nineteenth-Century America
Páraic Finnerty

Following the Middle Passage: Currents in Literature Since 1945
Carl Plasa

Yankee Yarns: Storytelling and the Invention of the National Body in Nineteenth-Century American Culture
Stefanie Schäfer

Reverberations of Revolution: Transnational Perspectives, 1750–1850
Elizabeth Amann and Michael Boyden

The Atlantic Dilemma: Reform or Revolution Across the Long Nineteenth Century
Kelvin Black

Scottish Colonial Literature: Writing the Atlantic, 1603–1707
Kirsten Sandrock

www.edinburghuniversitypress.com/series/ECSALC

American Snobs

Transatlantic Novelists, Liberal Culture and the Genteel Tradition

Emily Coit

EDINBURGH
University Press

Edinburgh University Press is one of the leading university presses in the UK. We publish academic books and journals in our selected subject areas across the humanities and social sciences, combining cutting-edge scholarship with high editorial and production values to produce academic works of lasting importance. For more information visit our website: edinburghuniversitypress.com

© Emily Coit, 2021, 2022

Edinburgh University Press Ltd
The Tun – Holyrood Road
12 (2f) Jackson's Entry
Edinburgh EH8 8PJ

First published in hardback by Edinburgh University Press 2021

Typeset in 11/13 Adobe Sabon by
IDSUK (DataConnection) Ltd

A CIP record for this book is available from the British Library

ISBN 978 1 4744 7540 2 (hardback)
ISBN 978 1 4744 7541 9 (paperback)
ISBN 978 1 4744 7542 6 (webready PDF)
ISBN 978 1 4744 7543 3 (epub)

The right of Emily Coit to be identified as the author of this work has been asserted in accordance with the Copyright, Designs and Patents Act 1988, and the Copyright and Related Rights Regulations 2003 (SI No. 2498).

Contents

Acknowledgements	vii
Series Editors' Preface	ix
Introduction	1

Part I: Cultivation After Reconstruction: Impossible Educations

1. Slavery, Subjection and Culture in Adams's *Democracy* and *Esther* — 23
   - The Virgin and the Favourite — 26
   - Beasts and Things that Crawl — 33
   - Struggle for Mastery: Pedagogies, Marriage Plots — 40

2. The Education of the People in James's *The Bostonians* and *The Princess Casamassima* — 49
   - The People and the Freedmen — 54
   - The Schoolmarm and the Southerner — 61
   - The Happier Few and the Miserable Many — 68

3. The Professor and the Mob in Wharton's *The Valley of Decision* — 80
   - Born Readers: Race and the Reading Citizenry — 84
   - Idealism and Realism — 92
   - The Learned Lady — 100

Part II: The Remnant at Harvard: Whiteness, Higher Education and Democracy

4. Universal White: Discrimination and Selection in James's American Scene — 113
   - Numbers and the Remnant — 123

Diversity, Distinction and the Note of the Exclusive	134
Serene Puritan *Crânerie*: James and the Genteel Tradition	151
5. The Tenth Mind: Adams and the Action of the Remnant	162
Better Men: The Talented Tenth and the Remnant at Harvard	168
Bostonian Calm and the Action of the Scholar	176
Education and Power: Schools, Schoolmasters, Truants	182
The Type of Passivity: Adams and the Genteel Tradition	193
6. Pure English: Wharton and the Elect	196
Aristocracies: The Value of Duration	201
Doctrines of Election: The Puritan Liberal and the Last Calvinist	211
Purement Anglo-Saxonne: Puritans and Patroons	216
Colonial Mansions: Wharton and the Genteel Tradition	224
Conclusion: The Reign of the Genteel	233
Notes	252
Bibliography	283
Index	306

Acknowledgements

Finishing a book during a pandemic lockdown presents specific challenges, and I thank everyone who helped me tackle them, but most especially Andy Eggers, who supported this project from its earliest stages. Looking farther back, I want to thank my teachers, especially Nicole Fandel, the late Ronald Richardson, Stephen Teichgraeber, Thomas Nolden, Margery Sabin, the late Nathalie Buchet Ritchey, Catherine Labio, Ruth Bernard Yeazell and Jonathan Freedman.

The Princeton Writing Program was crucial to the genesis of this project; I thank its director, Amanda Irwin Wilkins, as well as my colleagues there. In Britain, Laura Ashe has been a sterling mentor and champion. The University of Bristol made it possible for me to write by funding research leave, and Helen Fulton has been an unfailingly supportive department chair. Rowena Kennedy-Epstein, Jane Wright and Siân Harris have been especially kind colleagues. Michelle Coghlan, Michael James Collins, Erin Forbes, Rachel Galvin, Oliver Herford and Michèle Mendelssohn all read and commented on chapter drafts; Erica McAlpine and Kathryn Murphy also gave helpful feedback. I am deeply grateful to each of these generous thinkers. Stephanie Kelley has been a helpful research assistant, persisting intrepidly even as libraries closed. Zachary Seager and Adriana Jacobs kindly assisted with Wharton's French. At Edinburgh University Press, Ersev Ersoy and Michelle Houston have my profound thanks, as do the series editors and anonymous readers who helped to shape this project. I also thank Wendy Lee for assiduous copyediting.

I am grateful to Adrienne Sharpe of the Beineke Library, Kyle DeCicco-Carey of Harvard's Property Information Resource Center, and the staff of the Houghton Library and the Harvard University Archives. Quotations from the Records of the President of Harvard University, Charles W. Eliot, appear courtesy of the Harvard University Archives. Quotations from Edith Wharton are reprinted by permission of the Estate of Edith Wharton and the Watkins/Loomis

Agency. Quotations from *The Collected Works of John Stuart Mill*, copyright © University of Toronto Press, 1965, 1977, 1981 and 1984, are reproduced with permission of the publisher. Quotations from George Santayana's 'The Genteel Tradition in American Philosophy,' copyright © 2009 Yale University, are reproduced with permission of the Licensor through PLSclear. An early version of Chapter 2 first appeared as an article in *The Henry James Review*, Volume 36, Issue 2, Spring 2015, pages 177–98, copyright © 2015 Johns Hopkins University Press; I am grateful to Johns Hopkins University Press for permission to publish a later version here.

Finally, to close out these acknowledgements, I'd like to acknowledge my own relation to the story *American Snobs* tells. It's conventional to name and thank the persons and institutions that enable a book to exist, but I want to say here: I've had the opportunity to write this book partly because of my own place in exactly – and I do mean exactly – the structures of power and sites of privilege that it examines. I became interested in studying certain elitisms and racisms because I'd always lived with them; this book is an effort to learn more about how these ways of thinking developed before I met them in their latter-day forms.

Series Editors' Preface

Modern global culture makes it clear that literary study can no longer operate on nation-based or exceptionalist models. In practice, American literatures have always been understood and defined in relation to the literatures of Europe and Asia. The books in this series work within a broad comparative framework to question place-based identities and monocular visions, in historical contexts from the earliest European settlements to contemporary affairs, and across all literary genres. They explore the multiple ways in which ideas, texts, objects and bodies travel across spatial and temporal borders, generating powerful forms of contrast and affinity. The Edinburgh Critical Studies in Atlantic Literatures and Cultures series fosters new paradigms of exchange, circulation and transformation for Atlantic literary studies, expanding the critical and theoretical work of this rapidly developing field.

Laura Doyle, Colleen Glenney Boggs and
Maria Cristina Fumagalli

Introduction

In the summer of 1915, Henry James wrote commemorative essays about two august American periodicals, *The Atlantic Monthly* and *The Nation*. Recalling his youthful years in Boston and Cambridge, James fondly remembers 'the American, or at least the Northern, state of mind and of life that began to develop just after the Civil War'. Pointing to 'the deep illusions and fallacies in which the great glare of the present seems to show us as then steeped', he relishes the memory of a 'complacency' that believes war and violence over for good. James describes a deluded 'golden age' peopled by, among others, Charles Eliot Norton, professor of art history at Harvard, editor and friend to Ralph Waldo Emerson and Thomas Carlyle, and preeminent scholar and translator of Dante. Looking back from the terrible wartime present, James reminds himself that 'the whole scene and the whole time . . . *were*, they flourished, they temporarily triumphed, that scene, that time, those conditions; they are not a dream that we drug ourselves to enjoy, but a chapter, and the most copious, of experience'.[1] James may be responding here to his friend Henry Adams. Upon reading James's 1914 memoir, Adams had suggested that it did in fact portray a dream: he wrote to another friend, 'Poor Henry James thinks it all real, I believe, and actually still lives in that dreamy, stuffy Newport and Cambridge, with papa James and Charles Norton – and me!'[2] Adams had already pointed to Boston's complacency in his *Education*, and he and James had already discussed whether or not the atmosphere of their mutual Bostonian and expatriate history was 'golden': in 1903, as in 1914, Adams had seen emptiness where James sought to portray a 'golden glow'.[3] The 'golden age' that James evokes in 1915 is golden partly because of its brightly optimistic deludedness. He gazes into the past, 'with the air turning more and more to the golden as space recedes, turning to the clearness of all the sovereign exemptions, the serenity of all the fond assurances'. This serenity is a 'complacency', which is also an 'innocence' and a 'confidence' – and all of it is wrong. This golden time must be remembered, James writes, 'as the Age of the Mistake'.[4]

James is not the only one to observe a 'Mistake' made by Norton and his peers: Adams and Edith Wharton too see error in Boston. These three authors articulate their political thought in response to the liberalism that belongs to this New England milieu. Their responses have not been seen clearly because that liberalism has been widely misrecognised; disparaged as 'genteel', its idealism was long cast as a grim old force triumphantly conquered by a democratic realism. But in fact, this liberalism's idealism is itself quite democratic, and the early iterations of the realist critique against it are not. This book identifies those early iterations in the work of Adams, James, Wharton and other conservative thinkers. Their critical responses to Boston liberalism feed into later iterations of the narrative about the genteel, which are progressive and democratic; and which, paradoxically, sometimes serve to derogate these authors themselves.

By the time James wrote about 'the golden age' in 1915, he had already treated Norton in commemorative prose twice, first in an elegiac essay of 1909, and then in his memoir, where he had given a key role to Norton and his famous library. James describes that space as itself serenely charged with golden optimism: 'I was to grow fond of regarding as a positive consecration to letters that half-hour in the long library at Shady Hill, where the winter sunshine touched serene bookshelves and arrayed pictures, the whole embrowned composition of objects in my view, with I knew not what golden light of promise, what assurance of things to come.'[5] Wharton would write of Norton's library too:

> In his prime Charles Norton, to be really known, had to be seen in the Shady Hill library, at Cambridge, where the ripest years of his intellectual life were lived. Against that noble background of books his frail presence, the low voice, the ascetic features so full of scholarly distinction, acquired their full meaning, and his talk was at its richest and happiest.

Recalling Norton in his 'serene old age', Wharton writes that when she visited Boston, she 'never failed . . . to make the pilgrimage to Shady Hill'. Like James, Wharton remembers Norton ushering her kindly into the world of letters. 'Norton', she recalls, 'was supremely gifted as an awakener': 'his animating influence on my generation in America was exerted through what he himself was, and what he made his pupils see and feel under him. Among those of my intimate friends who came under Norton's influence at Harvard there was none who did not regard the encounter as a turning point in his own growth.'⁶ Adams, though he leaves no affectionate golden picture of pilgrimage or consecration, also pursued his career as writer with Norton's assistance.

In James's and Wharton's reminiscences, Norton belongs to a Harvard, a Boston and a New England characterised by a specific set of tendencies: serenity, certainty, idealism, asceticism and 'Puritanism'. Their accounts thus chime with Adams's portrait of the self-satisfied Unitarian orthodoxy of Harvard and Boston, which is above all 'calm'. This specific set of tendencies reappears in the work of influential twentieth-century scholars. Vernon Louis Parrington, for example, describes, in his *Main Currents in American Thought* (1927–30), 'the serenity of the Brahmin mind', and observes these Brahmins manifest a 'Victorianism of a more maidenly purity than the English strain, so carefully filtered by passing through the close Puritan mesh that the smallest impurities were removed'. 'The Brahmins', he writes, 'conceived the great business of life to be the erection of barriers against the intrusion of the unpleasant.'⁷ During the twentieth century, Norton rises as an emblem of this exhausted, effeminate prudishness, and becomes specifically associated with such 'barriers', which, over time, come to be understood as barriers not just against unpleasantness, but also against immigrants and other democratic hordes. For Parrington and other twentieth-century thinkers, the prudish snobbery of the Brahmins belongs to a sterile, vapid, moribund thing called 'the genteel tradition'.

Parrington's invocation of the 'genteel' in *Main Currents* offers a good example of the words and tropes typically associated with it: the 'Victorian', the 'Puritan' and an objectionably unsexual femininity. Here that unsexual femininity is 'maidenly'; more often it takes the grotesque or ridiculous forms of the spinster, the schoolmarm, the grandmother or the aged aunt. In Parrington's work, as elsewhere, the 'genteel tradition' originates in a declining New England but casts a broader pall over cultural production in the United States. Describing the 'New England in Decay' of the 1870s, Parrington explains: 'The days of high thinking were over and the familiar home of humanitarian causes was inhabited by other tenants. All that remained of the golden forties was the quiet atmosphere of good breeding.' Formerly 'open-minded and militant', Unitarianism becomes a 'staid and respectable orthodoxy'. Transcendentalism fades, and 'the ardor of reform, that had burned fiercely in the Puritan heart, subsided into a well-bred interest in negro schools and foreign missions'. In short: 'The New England conscience was tired.'⁸

Parrington invokes a tale of declining New England that many others too recite, both before and after him. Broadly speaking, this story of decline usually refers to a shift from Calvinism to Unitarianism, and it is often told in gendered terms. Kenyon Gradert shows that even thinkers whose time would be hailed as a golden age felt themselves in a moment of decline from a sharper Puritan intensity into something softer, weaker and more sentimental; he points to Harriet Beecher Stowe's critical comments in 'New England Ministers' (1858) and Henry James Sr's remark in *Substance and Shadow* (1863) that 'religion in the old virile sense of the word has disappeared . . . and become replaced by a feeble Unitarian sentimentality'. As Gradert's account suggests, this narrative of decline extends in variant forms right up into twentieth-century scholarship, perhaps most saliently in Ann Douglas's *The Feminization of American Culture*.[9]

Henry James Jr too invokes this narrative of decline. Surveying American letters in 1898, he looks to New England and notes recent publications on Stowe and Emerson that 'mark strikingly how the Puritan culture both used and exhausted its opportunity, how its place knows it no longer with any approach to the same intensity'. Weeks later, he refers to that lost 'intensity' again as considers the memoir of Thomas Wentworth Higginson, 'a conspicuous figure in almost all the many New England reforms and radicalisms'. Higginson's book recalls for James an old Harvard, the founding of *The Atlantic*, and 'the storm and stress of the war, the agitations on behalf of everything, almost, but especially of the negroes and the ladies'; it is 'redolent of a New England in general and a Boston in particular that will always be interesting to the moralist'.[10] Whether those places are also interesting to the aesthete or the sybarite is a question that James notably leaves open here. He does address that question, however, in *The Bostonians* (1886). With its declining Boston, its quavering old women reformers and its picture of a spinster who undertakes a project of culture, *The Bostonians* provides rich materials for the thinkers who later develop the narrative about the genteel.

Here, however, we can pull a thread and begin a long unravelling: notice that the golden moments of Parrington's *Main Currents* and James's 1915 essays do not fall at the same time. For Parrington, gold suffuses New England air during the agitation and fire of the antebellum period – the 'golden forties' – and Brahmin complacency poisons that air during the 1870s and after.[11] In his 1915 essays, James describes a mode 'that began to develop just after the Civil War' and recalls a 'golden age' that he experienced personally when his family lived in Boston and Cambridge during the later 1860s; his 'Age of the Mistake' runs from 1865 to World War I.[12] And in James's account, the complacency does not follow the golden age: the gold and the complacency are simultaneous. Both Parrington and James suggest that Bostonian complacency is a mistake, but their Bostonians are not necessarily complacent about the same things.

Parrington's Brahmins are complacent in their prudish conservatism, but the complacency James evokes is something different: it is a dogmatic faith in progress, human perfectibility, education and democracy. Their mutual emphasis on a declining New England invites the assumption that both are simply recounting the same true history. But that assumption blurs the divergent political orientations of their respective tellings and also obscures the extent to which tellings like Parrington's draw from tellings like James's. This book works to trace the complex, messy genealogy of ideas that explains the relation between these two invocations of a golden age, a decline and a serene complacency. This tracing shows that although the narrative about the genteel serves progressive, democratic agendas in twentieth-century scholarship about US literature and culture, it has key sources in a body of thought that critically interrogates democratic ideals.

The phrase 'genteel tradition' comes from George Santayana, but the ideas that circulate under this label precede him and, as he himself recognises, vastly exceed his own definition of it. Boston and, more specifically, early twentieth-century Harvard elicit Santayana's arguments about the genteel and also those of Van Wyck Brooks, which are similarly influential; both of these early iterations of the narrative about the genteel feed into that of Parrington, who also draws from the broader body of source material from which Brooks and Santayana draw. That broader body of material includes the work of Harvard Professor of English Barrett Wendell, who taught both Brooks and Parrington; and it also includes the work of Adams, James and Wharton, who themselves respond critically to that same Boston and Harvard.

In their critical responses, they target a Bostonian liberalism fervently committed to the interlinked ideals of democracy, culture, education, perfectibility and progress. Adams, James and Wharton help to develop a conservative realist critique of this liberalism. That realist critique, like other elements of the narrative about the genteel, later serves agendas that are democratic and progressive. But in the earlier body of thought to which these authors contribute, realism is not democratic: seeing clearly and with attention to local particulars, it recognises that humans are not in fact perfectible, progress not in fact sure, and democracy not in fact feasible or even necessarily desirable.

The Boston liberalism on which this realist critique sets its sights is historically specific. 'Liberalism' is a slippery grenade of a word, so I want to be clear: this book is about a liberalism expressed in and around Boston during the nineteenth century and early twentieth century, centred institutionally at Harvard and in periodicals like *The Atlantic* and *The Nation*. Bringing together New England's Unitarian tradition with its exhortations to 'self-culture', Emerson's arguments about culture, and also the thought of Matthew Arnold and John Stuart Mill, this liberalism is particularly committed to education, or 'cultivation', or 'culture', which it understands as practices or processes of development. Since the turn of the millennium, the story of this liberalism has been rewritten by historians, most especially Leslie Butler. Her *Critical Americans* (2007) offers a fresh description of the historical referent that corresponds with the 'complacency' that James observes in the North after the Civil War.[13] She identifies Norton, Higginson, George William Curtis and James Russell Lowell as core members of a fluid cohort of liberal thinkers, one that over time and more broadly includes Norton's cousin, Harvard President Charles William Eliot, and also Richard Watson Gilder, William Dean Howells and William James, among others. Butler identifies these Americans as participants in a transatlantic liberal discourse; she also shows the extent to which the Civil War shapes their thought throughout their lives and the extent to which they prize democratic ideals.

These ideals consolidate especially during the early part of the period that James describes as 'the Age of the Mistake'. In an optimistic moment immediately following the Civil War, Butler shows, Union victory, the abolition of slavery and the expansion of the British franchise together seemed to portend the global triumph of democracy. The liberalism of these thinkers, she notes, 'blended quite easily with other seemingly incompatible political traditions, chief among them republicanism'; they 'embraced not only liberalism but democracy', and 'saw no contradiction in emphasizing both private rights and public duties or in insisting that government be both broadly representative and elevated'.[14] Within the body of thought to which these liberal thinkers contribute, Butler documents two repeated emphases that I show Adams, James and Wharton interrogate repeatedly over the years: a vision of a broadly cultivated democratic people, or 'reading citizenry'; and a vision for leadership by a still more cultivated minority within that population.

Butler's study complements a surge of work on liberalism by Victorianists.[15] Arguments about Arnold and Mill within that body of work help to complicate our understanding of the political thought of the Bostonians who espouse and adapt their ideas. Invocations of a 'genteel tradition' committed to retreat from rough reality frequently implicate Arnold, his 'sweetness and light' and his 'culture' as instruments or accomplices. To this day, 'Arnoldian' still too often functions as a convenient shorthand for exclusionary high culture, the best that has been thought and said in the worst possible sense. As Eric Aronoff observes, however, the relationship between Arnold's 'culture' and the 'culture' invoked by literary and anthropological thinkers in the early twentieth century is complex – and less cleanly oppositional than one might expect.[16] What simplified accounts of Mill's and Arnold's liberalisms tend to obscure are their arguments for the practice of culture and their sense that culture and politics are inseparably connected. That sense is, of course, typically Victorian. Among the most egregious absurdities implied by the broader narrative about the genteel is the notion that to be 'Victorian' is to be politically conservative, to retreat from politics and to insist on a separation of 'culture' from life.

The individual Victorian most extensively slandered by recitations of the narrative about the genteel is Norton. That slandering has been corrected by the work of James Turner and Linda Dowling; more recently, Norton appeared as the adorable object of Elizabeth Gaskell's unrequited love in a work of creative non-fiction based loosely on the actual correspondence between the two.[17] But we do not have to go too far back to find representations of the professor that are remarkable for their strangely personal venom: Norton functions as a figurehead for all the evils associated with the genteel, and then some. Dowling notes that antagonistic accounts cast him in a 'curious sociological melodrama' where he serves as 'a stock character or a necessary villain'.[18] This is especially odd given that Wendell, who is not cast in this manner, is actually guilty of all the sins later attributed to his friend and colleague. It is a problem to name the wrong villain, but it is also a problem to need a villain at all. When Norton's elitism and racism are individual and melodramatically exceptional – rather than systemic and commonplace – it becomes easier for his professional heirs in the academy to see that elitism and racism as remote and alien, and thus disavow him as an antecedent. But in fact, his elitism and racism are part of a liberalism that venerates democracy, and that liberalism is the close kin of the liberalisms that inform much educational work right up through the present. In studying a Norton who is not a villain, we confront elitism and racism that are unspectacular, cordial, full of good intentions and perhaps quite familiar.

Rather than accepting the story that makes Norton and his peers villainous representatives of a genteel tradition that is vapidly Arnoldian, Victorian, Puritanical and schoolmarmish, this book examines the formation and development of that story. In doing so, it points to certain connotations that this set of words can carry during the nineteenth century, connotations that fade and get forgotten as those same words become easy slurs for twentieth-century thinkers. This book also traces democratic twentieth-century arguments for rough realism and vital, fecund sexiness to sources in which that sexiness belongs to white supremacist fantasies of Anglo-Saxon regeneration, and that realism is one that sees clearly the beastliness or depravity of the masses. More broadly, this book recognises that what comes to be called genteel is often more helpfully described as liberal. That truth was always hiding in plain sight, and noted by some; once recognised, it opens up new ways of understanding how Adams, James and Wharton engage in the political conversations of their moment. When we adopt a fresh perspective on the ideas to which these authors respond, their responses too appear in a new light.

The glare of this new light dissolves certain assumptions and perceived alliances. My readings here push back against a tendency to conflate radical or emancipatory thinking about sex and gender with thinking that is democratic. They also resist the impulse to define 'democracy' normatively, as antiracist, rather than historically, as a political formation profoundly committed to racism both in practice and in theory – most obviously, in Anglo-Saxonism and the Teutonic origins thesis that makes democracy the special talent of white people. More locally, my readings here push back against accounts of James and Wharton as anachronistic progressives, not least by associating them with the more overtly unprogressive and notoriously anti-Semitic Adams.[19] Such accounts tend to conflate the radical potential of these authors' texts with radicalism on the part of the authors themselves.[20] We can embrace that radical potential even as we recognise that the evidence against that radicalism is ample and explicit.

A villainous Norton serves as a fine foil to a queerer, cleverer, more modern James or a heroically feminist Wharton.[21] But among these thinkers – who are all elitists, and all in the most basic sense conservative – it is Norton and his fellow Victorian liberals who venerate a democratic ideal, while James, Wharton and Adams have graver doubts about democracy. In pointing this out, I don't wish simply to redistribute the costumes in a reductive drama of villains and heroes. My aim, rather, has been to avoid the simplifications of such casting and costuming. Just about everyone in this book is a snob: in its pages, racism and elitism are not scandals to be exposed, but already recognised norms. My project is to disambiguate the varied elitisms and racisms of a privileged white community.

* * *

'Some American snobs adopt England; others adopt France. Mrs. Wharton has adopted France.'[22] So declared a chilly review in 1919. Eliding expatriation and elitism, this derisive aside gestures towards the social and political resonances of living abroad. For American writers, those resonances can range widely. This book's story of flight from modern American democracy speaks to several other stories of literary expatriation: it tweaks the tale of male modernists that groups James and Adams with Ezra Pound and T. S. Eliot; it complements narratives of avant-garde Americans in Paris, shifting the centre of action from Gertrude Stein's salon at rue de Fleurus to Wharton's rather different one at rue de Varenne. And it sets up a stark contrast to the tradition of African–American writers who go abroad in search of a more egalitarian, less racist democracy.[23] That is not what Adams, James and Wharton seek when they leave the US. But leave they do: James settles permanently in Britain, Wharton in France; Adams spends his formative youthful years in Britain, travels widely, and later in life spends part of each year in Paris, where he frequents Wharton's salon, as does James when he is in town.

These authors are linked not just by their departures from American ground, but by their place in the moneyed white Northeastern elite. Phillip Horne notes the 'extraordinarily dense social texture of the upper class' to which these authors belong: their relationships with each other are overdetermined, and their mutual acquaintances numerous.[24] Each of these authors expresses distaste for Boston but is nevertheless linked to it. Adams and his family are Bostonians, but he flees New England gleefully, making his American life in Washington, DC. James's wildly itinerant New York family settles in Boston and then Cambridge; after spending most of his youth abroad, he lives there after the Civil War and briefly in the early 1880s. Later, after he has settled in England, his brother William's employment at Harvard gives him a lasting link to Cambridge. Wharton too has family in the city, in her case through her unhappy marriage; she maintains friendships there, and, prior to her expatriation, chooses to make her summer home not far from Norton's own in western Massachusetts.

For each of these authors, distaste for Boston and Cambridge is also a distaste for the liberalism that flourishes there. Especially for Adams and Wharton, antipathy towards the joyless, boring, grimly snowbound bastion of the Anglo-Saxons extends into an affinity for its contraries: races that are not Anglo-Saxon (for Wharton, just the superlatively civilised Latinate ones; for Adams, those that linger in savagery), the warmer, softer South, and the lush sensuousness of France or the tropics. Along with the idea that 'Victorian' implies 'conservative', the other great absurdity embedded in the narrative about the genteel is the notion that affinities for a sexier, warmer sensuousness — less icy, less uptight, not so tediously sincere and serious — somehow imply emancipatory politics. As this book will observe, these affinities often imply exactly the opposite.

Harvard is a central node in the elite social web that links these writers. Wharton did not attend the college, but many men in her circle did; and, just as James is good friends with Norton's sister Grace, she is good friends with his daughter Sally.[25] James briefly attends the Law School in 1862; straying from law, he attends Lowell's lectures on literature. During the same wave of recruitment in the early seventies, President Eliot (Harvard '53) hires not just Norton (Harvard '46) and Adams (Harvard '58), but also James's brother William (Harvard MD '69). Adams, Norton and William James all teach Wendell (Harvard '77). Later, as Professor of English, Wendell is friendly not just with these former teachers but also with Henry James, and most especially with Wharton. As Claudia Stokes notes, with reference to Wendell and Harvard: 'Institutional affiliation remains one of the most potent and unremarked-upon contexts for the production of knowledge.'[26] Adams, James and Wharton play a role in the disciplinary history of English partly because their elite networks link them personally to the literary men at Harvard, who, because of their own elite position, wield disproportionate influence.[27]

In a 1908 letter, Adams compares Wharton's Paris salon to that of Mme Récamier and pictures himself and James at her side as the Baron de Barante and the Vicomte de Chateaubriand, respectively. The conspicuously Gallic, aristocratic quality of this tableau is indicative: these authors are self-conscious about their distance from America and Americans. Adams deprecates to James their mutual itinerant set as 'improvised Europeans'. James deplores the ugliness of the US when he visits in 1904; by that time, it had been over two decades since he had declared 'My choice is the old world – my choice, my need, my life.'²⁸ Writing before her permanent move to France to Norton's daughter Sally, who was then in London, Wharton despairs at 'the wild, dishevelled backwoods look of everything' in the US and points to 'the contrast between the old & the new, between the stored beauty & tradition & amenity over there, & the crassness here'. She continues:

> the tastes I am cursed with are all of a kind that cannot be gratified here, & I am not enough in sympathy with our 'gros public' to make up for the lack on the aesthetic side. One's friends are delightful; but *we* are none of us Americans, we don't think or feel as the Americans do, we are the wretched exotics produced in a European glass-house, the most déplacé and useless class on earth!²⁹

This is the sort of comment that lends credibility to Parrington's judgement that Wharton herself is 'the last of our literary aristocrats of the genteel tradition', part of a snobbish cohort that retreats from the rough, vital reality of US democracy.³⁰ In Parrington's iteration of the narrative about the genteel, as in others, this retreat from reality is gendered: an effeminate, primly glassed-in, idealising 'culture' blights the US until a cadre of hard, manly, rough-and-tumble realists arrive to represent the real working life of the democracy. Scholars such as Stokes and Nancy Glazener have done brilliant work to help us understand the sources and the extensions of this gendered binary in the literary history of the US.³¹ But that work does not always acknowledge the overlap between the gendered binary expressed by Parrington and the gendered binary that drives the narrative about the genteel tradition; nor does it fully recognise the importance of thinking about race in development of that narrative. No thorough historiography of the genteel has been published, partly because its literary-historical applications and its political-historical applications diverge. A number of scholars have offered helpful partial accounts, taking widely varying degrees of critical distance, but these accounts often contradict each other; they do so because each looks at just part of a phenomenon that is vast and multifarious.³²

To seek a neat understanding of 'the genteel tradition' by looking to the origins of that phrase in Santayana's work is to adopt a narrow definition that ignores most of the phrase's actual usage, as well as relations between that actual usage and the body of existing thought from which Santayana himself draws as he develops his ideas. After Santayana offers up 'the genteel tradition' in a 1911 address, the adaptable term and its versatile misogyny take on a life of their own. Already in 1942, Alfred Kazin observed that 'Santayana's well-worn phrase, the "Genteel Tradition"' had become a 'dead horse', facilitating the redundant beating of 'everything Mencken's iconoclastic generation disliked in late nineteenth-century life'. Lionel Trilling nevertheless remarks in 1956: 'what the academic historian of American culture would do without Santayana's term "the genteel tradition" is impossible to imagine'.[33]

During the twentieth century, usage of 'genteel' and 'the genteel tradition' is inconsistent, opportunistic and generative. Though 'genteel' often carries generic meanings roughly equivalent to 'refined', 'stuffy' or 'prudish', it also refers more specifically to a cluster of publications (usually including *The Atlantic*, *Harper's*, *The Century* and *The Nation*) and to two loosely defined, sometimes overlapping groups of people linked to those publications. The first of these two groups is literary: it sometimes consists of the New York School of poets that includes Richard Henry Stoddard, Edmund Clarence Stedman and Thomas Bailey Aldrich. But Norton, Curtis and Gilder are also sometimes included in this group, as are James, Adams and Wharton; and invocations of the genteel also sometimes look farther back, to the Fireside Poets and Emerson. Along with Emerson and Howells, Adams and James are sometimes associated with the genteel but also sometimes named among its opponents. The second large grouping of the genteel is made up of the political thinkers and politicians who are called genteel reformers, liberal reformers, liberal republicans, liberal Republicans, or mugwumps. Norton and Curtis usually figure in this group too, along with Edwin Lawrence Godkin, President Eliot, and Adams and his brothers.

For both the literary and the political group, 'genteel' serves to deride. The genteel literary men are the bloodless, elitist, conservative idealists against whom the new generation of real artists of real American life can gloriously revolt, ushering in a sexier, grittier, more authentic, more vital, more democratic modernity. Later iterations of this story of moribund decline and triumphant rupture tend to emphasise racist, antidemocratic tendencies on the part of the genteel and the rich diversity of the modern US they resist. The genteel liberal reformers, whose community overlaps in some accounts with the genteel literary cohort, also find themselves eclipsed and thwarted by modernity. They are an old Anglo-Saxon elite that finds they have lost their power to rising numbers of immigrants and new-money plutocrats. In one version of the story, they retreat from public life, decadent and bitter; in another (and this is where they tend to merge with the literary wing of the 'genteel'), they try to maintain a grip on public life through 'cultural custodianship'.

Given this remarkable sprawl, it is not surprising that the narrative about the genteel has long had critics, questioners and nuancers – as is evident in the work of, for example, Geoffrey Blodgett, Donald Hall, Jackson Lears, Henry May, Joan Shelley Rubin and Matthew Schneirov.[34] Critical responses to the narrative about the genteel also emerge in the larger body of historical scholarship that revises Richard Hofstadter's account of the genteel reformers. Lears observes that there are useful functions to the 'leitmotif of loss' that runs through early twentieth-century narratives of elite decline: 'established elites', he notes, had long 'sustained their power by declaring that it was in decline, or had already disappeared'.[35] Lears does not extend this observation to the narratives of racial decline and dispossession that drive white supremacism, but certain source materials for the narrative about the genteel invoke those narratives explicitly.

Amongst literary scholars, examinations and iterations of the narrative about the genteel tend to participate in the never-ending project of explaining the relationship between the (often gendered) modes of sentimentalism, idealism and realism in nineteenth-century US literature, as well as the related project of describing the political orientations and effects of those modes. Important recent arguments about the relationship between gender and realism implicitly challenge the premises of the narrative about the genteel: Jennifer Fleissner offers a revisionist account of the imagined encounter between a naturalist masculinity and a domestic, morbid, nervous New England femininity; David Ball offers a similarly suggestive reassessment of the (false) binary between an 'oppositional, masculine modernity' and 'a fashionable and feminized sentimentality'.[36]

These arguments build upon the later twentieth-century scholarship that reconsiders the relationship between realism and democracy, including Nancy Glazener's study of '*Atlantic* group' periodicals and Kenneth W. Warren's work on James, both of which inform this book.[37] Reading James's *Bostonians* alongside *Uncle Tom's Cabin* (1852), Warren noticed the repetition of a certain New England schoolmarm type, and discerned in the realist critique of sentimentalism 'an inadvertent alliance between Northern realism and Southern romance in an assault on the political idealism of the New England tradition'.[38] The later narrative about the genteel tends to describe an idealism that is literary, rather than political, and thus obscure this sort of political idealism – which is not synonymous with sentimentalism, though it is linked to and sometimes expressed by it. The mutually misogynist imagery of attacks on sentimentalism and attacks on this idealism can blur the distinctiveness of the latter, but Warren detects it, and his analysis points to the conservative realist critique that is my subject.

Though later twentieth-century scholarship severs a presumed link between democracy and realism, and thus revises certain elements of the narrative about the genteel, it sometimes effectively produces a reinforced version of that narrative. As critical theory and sociology offer new insights about how and where power operates, the moribund Bostonian entity described in earlier versions of the narrative becomes a more insidious and potent force: what had been a story about a prudish stuffiness becomes a story about a bourgeois elite that uses culture to consolidate and perpetuate its hegemony. The recognition of the aesthetic as a site for exercising power allows for a retelling in which aesthetic oppressiveness becomes political and social oppression. This retelling both draws from and informs a fresh awareness of liberal culture's embeddedness in economic liberalism. So, though the 'custodians of culture' described by May in 1959 are relatively benign, 'cultural custodianship' later becomes a more sinister phrase, as scholars more fully recognise the operations of power in culture and education.[39]

Lately, however, both Victorianists and Americanists have been reconsidering the political and social possibilities of culture, the liberal aesthetic and the liberal classroom. Nancy Bentley has offered a sensitive reconsideration of cultural custodianship; still more recently, in studies that speak to questions about democracy and citizenship in the US, Tova Cooper, Laura R. Fisher, Jesse Raber and Allison Speicher have brought fresh attention to the uses of culture, the fiction of development and learning, and the unpredictable variety of educational practice and experience.[40] Some of these studies might be seen to participate in a larger shift away from the hermeneutics of suspicion. If *American Snobs* seems to participate in such a shift, that is partly because the relationship between my trio of authors and Boston liberalism becomes clearly legible only with a bit of unsuspicious reading. In these pages, that kind of reading nevertheless rests on the bedrock of the critical scholarship that explains the political functions of liberal culture and exposes Anglo-American liberalism's bloody record of colonialism and genocide.[41]

That body of scholarship reads liberal claims suspiciously. So too do Adams, James and Wharton: they work to expose Boston liberalism's smug hypocrisies and covert complicities. Rather than extending that project of exposure, this book attends to that liberalism's explicit statements – most specifically, its statements about democracy and education – because those explicit statements are what Adams, Wharton and James interrogate. The realist critique to which these authors contribute finds Boston liberalism not just too hypocritical, but also too emancipatory and too democratic; accounts that read suspiciously to describe this liberalism as simply oppressive and antidemocratic make this critique less legible because they eliminate its object.

In trying to make that object more visible, this book leaves out a great deal. Its omissions reproduce the exclusivities and exclusions it studies: the thinkers who populate these pages are almost universally male, white, rich, Protestant and Harvard-affiliated. In focusing on this privileged group, and naming it as such, I have tried to illumine an important part of the history of thinking about democracy, education, citizenship and race in the US. Though there are long, voluminous traditions of scholarship on Adams, James and Wharton, the vast majority of that work neither calls them white nor contemplates how whiteness operates in their work. More recent Americanist literary-historical scholarship on democracy, education and citizenship has tended – for very good reasons – to turn away from abundantly studied and comfortably moneyed white writers. Such scholarship has often deliberately attended to progressive, democratic or radical thought, or worked to recover progressive democratic political theory in the writing, cultural production and practices of 'common' or disenfranchised Americans. Books by Ivy Wilson, Nick Bromell, Stacey Margolis, Dana Nelson, Gregory Laski and Lloyd Pratt contribute to this body of work, which tends to seek ideas from the past that might be useful for confronting the crises of democracy now, and point to scholarship's progressive political utility in the present.[42] Rather than contributing to this project, I draw attention to the disciplinary history into which it fits, a history in which scholars, critics and intellectuals grapple with the question of their own political duties and powers.

Part I of *American Snobs* shows that, in early or mid-career novels, Adams, James and Wharton stage the embodiment and education, or 'cultivation' of the liberal subject. They do so in the aftermath of Reconstruction's failure, when questions about education and capacity for learning figure centrally in debates about citizenship and enfranchisement – and inform policies that exclude and disenfranchise.[43] Addressing such debates and policies, these novels test out liberal cultivations in bodies that are not white and male. All of these tests fail, producing by the end of this section a remarkable stack of corpses, figurative and real. Collectively, the five potential embodiments tested out by these novels result in two figurative suicides, one figurative assassination, one actual suicide and one actual assassination. All of these liberal educations, like these embodiments of the liberal subject, prove to be impossible, and that impossibility expresses a realist critique of liberal idealism. This critique interrogates liberalism's 'human' and also suggests that its attempts to educate are, in reality, attempts to control; although later leftist, democratic, and antiracist critiques of liberalism will make these same moves, the critique expressed by these novels does not share their aims.

Chapter 1 argues that Adams's *Democracy* (1880) and *Esther* (1883) interrogate Mill's arguments for egalitarian reciprocity in marriage and in education. In response to those arguments, Adams suggests that such egalitarian reciprocity is unfeasible because humans are actually savage creatures who naturally seek domination; the novels express an attraction to such savagery, locating in womanhood and Blackness the primitive vitality and absence of intellect that Adams will later venerate in his Virgin. Attending to the serialisation of James's political novels of 1886, Chapter 2 shows how these texts engage with a post-Reconstruction conversation about the prospective education and citizenship of the freedmen. Olive Chancellor of *The Bostonians* conforms to the New England schoolmarm type who figures in that conversation; like her counterpart Christina Light in *The Princess Casamassima*, Olive undertakes a liberal project of education that is foolish, impossible and fundamentally self-serving. Associating such projects with Mill and Emerson, the novels express a qualified preference for the opposing arguments of Carlyle. Against the claims of Bostonian educators like Olive and Norton, James pleads for cultivation that emphasises pleasure rather than morality or politics. Chapter 3 observes Wharton adapting the New England schoolmarm type in *Valley of Decision* (1902), where the idealist liberal woman educator is murdered by the masses she has attempted to educate and enfranchise. Wharton's novel is not realist, but by engaging critically with the liberal idealism of her mentor, Norton, it articulates sharply for the first time the realist conservatism that characterises her thinking for the rest of her life.

Part II shows that in non-fiction prose from later in their careers, Adams, James and Wharton all interrogate the liberal ideal of leadership by a cultivated minority, or what Arnold calls 'the remnant'. That ideal has a history that goes farther back and is not contained within liberalism, but in Harvard circles around the turn of the century, the conversation about it amongst liberal thinkers intensifies:

they engage with earlier arguments from Arnold, Emerson, Curtis and others to make claims about the role of scholars, the 'college-bred' and the university itself in a modern democracy. A range of thinkers participate in this conversation, including Norton, President Eliot, William James, Theodore Roosevelt, Godkin and W. E. B. Du Bois, whose argument about a 'Talented Tenth' is probably the best-remembered sally in this debate.

Against liberal arguments for a remnant that serves to save American democracy, Adams, James and Wharton imagine a cultivated elite that turns away from such service. All three position themselves against the dour, cold, serene certainty of a tradition associated with Harvard, Boston, New England and Puritanism. Both the proponents and the critics of this tradition associate it with liberalism, democracy, education, the Union cause, and various forms of antislavery activism. Against the grimly inflexible, relentlessly sincere moralism of that Puritan tradition, Adams, James and Wharton take up modes of play, irony, indeterminacy and doubt. Perhaps partly because these modes are ones that literary critics often practise and admire, scholarship has pointed to their subversively emancipatory political agency. I attend instead to the ways that these modes exercise and thus consolidate privilege and power.

Chapter 4 reads James's 1898 essays on American Letters, *The American Scene* (1907), 'The Question of Our Speech' (1905) and 'Charles Eliot Norton' (1909) alongside writing by Norton and Eliot, among others. I show that James responds to liberal arguments for the political agency of the cultivated elite by shifting attention from that elite's duties to its pleasures. Noting that the walls and gates of Harvard Yard elicit from James a remarkable articulation of an aesthetic of distinction, differentiation, discrimination, enclosure and exclusion, I juxtapose that articulation with Norton and Eliot's statements about difference, discrimination and inclusion at Harvard and in the US as a whole. I argue that James's celebration of heterogeneity and difference locates those properties not in multicultural democracy but in the preserved hierarchies of the Old World; and that his negative portrayal of white homogeneity can function to criticise not racism or nativism but rather the sort of democracy with which that whiteness is so closely associated. The last section of the chapter reconsiders James's account of his difference from Norton's New England type by examining the changing connotations of 'serene' and 'Puritan'.

Chapter 5 examines Adams's hostile response to the New England liberalism of Eliot and the young Du Bois; arguing that *The Education* (1907) opposes the forms of action they both propose for the remnant, I show how Adams aggressively rewrites ideas that figure centrally in Du Bois's *Souls of Black Folk* (1903). *The Education* enacts the alternative forms of action that it advocates, which are exercised most safely by those who already have power; in doing so, it offers a breath-taking performance of privilege. The chapter closes by noting how Van Wyck Brooks and Richard Hofstadter adopt Adams's ideas about intellectuals' passivity and agency in their iterations of the narrative about the genteel.

Chapter 6 shows that Wharton's wartime ambassadorial writing in *French Ways and Their Meaning* (1919) and 'Amérique en Guerre' (1918) replicates the project that her friend Wendell undertakes as a visiting professor at the Sorbonne. Reading those texts, as well as *Backward Glance* (1934), in the context of Wendell's perennial antagonism with Eliot, I compare the theories of inequality expressed by each of these thinkers, and then show how Wharton and Wendell align themselves with a Dutch, cavalier lineage that contrasts against the ascetic 'Puritan liberal' heritage associated with Eliot. Eliot's whiteness emphatically claims democracy as its own special inheritance; theirs does not. The final section of the chapter, which focuses on Wendell and Wharton's shared investment in the idea of Old New England, discusses the ways that thinkers like Brooks and Parrington draw from texts by Adams, James, Wharton and Wendell – along with better-remembered contributions from Santayana – as they develop the narrative about the genteel.

The conclusion extends that discussion, showing how Brooks adopts Wendell's ideas and paints a distorted picture of Norton. The book then closes with a brief examination of the gaunt, unsexy femininity that so frequently figures the genteel, tracing it back to the New England schoolmarm figure and the sterile white woman who looms in white supremacist narratives of Anglo-Saxon racial decline. That unsexy femininity serves democratic, progressive agendas in writing by Brooks, Parrington and others, but – like the realist critique of idealism that also animates their work – it has significant origins in profoundly conservative and sometimes viciously racist thinking.

The traces of these origins linger: the disdain for 'Puritanism', the tale of decline, the dispossessed impotence, the sterile white woman. As 'Puritan' comes to connote merely opposition to sex and pleasure, the repellent sterility of that woman usefully represents the deadness of the American cultural landscape, and her vapidity sums up the character of New England idealism. Its associations with liberalism, liberal education, democracy, Unitarianism, the Union cause and abolitionism mostly effaced, this New England idealism appears as an aesthetic idealism utterly disconnected from political idealism. 'Genteel', prudish, Victorian and remote from public life, it readily takes the role of the conservative old thing to be superseded in progressive narratives of American cultural history: figured by aged, unsexy femininity, it exists in order to be cast aside by young, masculine modernity in a triumph for democracy. But earlier derogations of this unsexy femininity and its Bostonian mode of serene complacency do not necessarily express the same outlook as later ones. Before this complacency is simply a vapid prudery, it is an inflexible certainty about the moral obligation to strive for democratic ideals by learning and educating. In their critical accounts of that certainty, Adams, James and Wharton contribute to a tradition of antidemocratic elitism, and also play their part in shaping the way scholars of US culture would think for years to come.

Part I

Cultivation After Reconstruction: Impossible Educations

Chapter 1

Slavery, Subjection and Culture in Adams's *Democracy* and *Esther*

Henry Adams is Bostonian liberalism's greatest apostate. Born into a political dynasty, the young Adams studies John Stuart Mill and Alexis de Tocqueville; self-consciously fashioning himself as part of a leading elite, he tries out the vocations of journalist, editor and teacher. But the public that is his prospective audience proves dully unmovable, or simply inattentive; government itself persists in corruption, and the people seem not to care. With increasing contempt, Adams adopts publication strategies that subject his public to tests of competence: pseudonymous publication, anonymous publication with no advertising, delayed or selective publication, circulation to a coterie, and then, ultimately, posthumous release.[1] The story of Adams's frustrations with audience is also the story of his long slide away from the liberalism that thrives in Boston. As his career develops, Adams interrogates the interlocking principles of that liberalism: sternly inflexible certainty about the value of education, 'culture' or 'cultivation'; a commitment to leadership and service among the cultivated elite; a sense that people are teachable and progress expected; and, thus, a faith in democracy.

Categories of race and sex help Adams to articulate and enact his apostasy. Broadly speaking, nineteenth-century liberalism posits a white male liberal subject, valorises rational intellect, and prizes development at the level of the individual and the race alike. Adams comes to value instead development's absence: he both identifies with and desires what is primitive, savage, undeveloped and therefore intellectually vacant.[2] The savage, undeveloped qualities that fascinate Adams belong to specific types: female, non-white and animal. Primitive, unthinking, instinctive, fecund, physical and raw, they are what the cultivated white male liberal subject is not. This chapter argues that Adams's two novels portray women who meet dead ends because they cannot embody at once that primitive vitality and the cultivated liberal subjectivity that is its opposite.

Adams is a historian and journalist, but he goes to the genre of the novel twice, publishing *Democracy* (1880) anonymously and *Esther* (1884) under the name Frances Snow Compton. Arch and relentlessly knowing, these books take up great questions of their moment: *Democracy* scrutinises power and corruption; *Esther* portrays a battle between art, religion and science for moral and epistemological supremacy. Adams also develops arguments against the principles of Bostonian liberalism in these books, and their genre offers him specific resources for doing so. The novel is the genre par excellence for representing real modern persons – especially real modern women – and the novel is also home to the marriage plot. Adams goes to this genre to write stories of failed embodiment and failed courtship: both of his prospective brides end in figurative suicide. By representing these failures, I want to suggest, *Democracy* and *Esther* interrogate one of the most important documents of liberal thought, Mill's *Subjection of Women* (1869), which draws from the arguments of Harriet Taylor Mill.

Subjection is a polemic about marriage, sex, equality and learning. Pushing back against the idea that women are innately inferior intellectually, it questions the determining force of sexual difference; it insists upon the fundamental pliancy and perfectibility of human nature; and it makes that pliancy a mechanism for progress towards a modernity of emancipations. Mill's vision for that modernity proposes a practice of egalitarian reciprocity for teachers and students, as well as husbands and wives. Adams's novels question *Subjection*'s account of human nature and its visions of pedagogy and marriage. Rejecting Mill's trajectory of progress, *Democracy* and *Esther* entertain visions of decline and atavism. Alluding repeatedly to the continuity between animals and humans posited by Darwin and Darwinian evolutionary science, the novels counter Mill's arguments by suggesting that learning and sex are really sites of competition and domination, not egalitarian reciprocity.

These novels' critique of liberalism shares emphases and insights with subsequent critiques that are democratic, progressive, leftist, decolonial or antiracist. Like those critiques, these novels expose liberal projects of education, culture or civilisation as projects of domination that are often brutally violent; and these novels interrogate liberalism's 'human', which those critiques identify as a device for exclusion and oppression. Lisa Lowe puts it succinctly: 'the modern distinction between definitions of the human and those to whom such definitions do not extend is the condition of possibility for Western liberalism, and not its particular exception'; 'the social inequalities our time', she adds, 'are a legacy of these processes through which "the human" is "freed" by liberal forms, while other subjects, practices, and geographies are placed at a distance from "the human."' For Lowe and for others, Mill figures centrally in this account of liberalism, which rightly gives particular attention to his relationship with colonialism and his remarks on despotism in *Considerations on Representative Government* (1861). With reference to that text, Lowe observes: 'Mill consistently defined liberty by distinguishing those "incapable of self-government" from those with the capacity for liberty.'[3]

Adams too interrogates Mill's 'human'. His novels engage most substantially not with *Considerations*, but with *Subjection*, a text in which Mill proposes a more inclusive definition of human. *Subjection* does not propose that all humans are equal in their capacities, but it does suggest that race and sex cannot reliably predict what any given human might accomplish. Adams counters these claims by inverting them: in response to Mill's suggestion that white women may be just as capable of citizenship as white men, Adams suggests that white men and women may be just as savage as animals and Africans. While critiques like Lowe's expose the murderously exclusionary force of liberalism's 'human', Adams points to its fanciful inaccuracy. Mill's work is part of the apparatus of colonialism, but it also makes a powerful argument for education and freedom, and that is the argument that Adams's novels question. In order to see what Adams opposes, we need to focus on precisely the emancipatory claims that critical accounts of liberalism designate as hypocritical or implicitly selective. Adams too sees them as hypocritical or implicitly selective; but unlike later critics, he also suggests that these claims are wrong.

Neither Adams's thinking nor the liberalism he questions is a fixed thing: as Adams slides away from it, that liberalism itself finds new articulations. Thus the attack Adams mounts against Mill's *Subjection* in the early 1880s has different emphases from his early twentieth-century assault on the orthodoxy of President Charles William Eliot's Harvard, which is the subject of Chapter 5. It would be a mistake to understand Mill's 'civilisation' and 'barbarism' as identical to Eliot's. But Mill and Eliot share commitments to freedom, competition, development and progress. Mill's *Subjection* offers an especially radical statement about the possibilities of education: though it does not say that the material body has no role in determining capacity, it does say that we cannot draw conclusions about the innate capacities of a category of people based on existing knowledge, because that knowledge is drawn from observation within specific historical conditions. *Subjection* focuses this statement on sex, but also extends its implications to race, even as it deploys the standard liberal rhetoric that makes African and Middle Eastern societies the sign and site of unfreedom.

In watching Adams cast off his youthful liberalism, we might expect to observe him adopt a racist biological materialism symptomatic of grimly incipient fin de siècle tendencies, while Mill, earlier in the century, invokes an abstract ideal liberal subject that is only implicitly embodied in white male flesh. But, as recent scholarship has emphasised, biological materialism is ideologically multivalent; and nineteenth-century liberalism, far from working with unbodied abstractions, usually thinks in terms of bodies. As Kyla Schuller's recent work suggests, liberalism's core ideas about development, progress and 'capacity for liberty' draw from (and feed into) arguments of evolutionary science, and steadily implicate race and sex.[4] The liberal discourses that imagine development from barbarism to civilisation and from ignorance to cultivation tend to imagine these processes of learning undertaken by bodies in specific categories: if we seek a prior, unbodied learner who is only implicitly white and male, we do not necessarily find one. Far from proposing a bodiless educability, liberal arguments tend to imagine bodily material that is pliant. Liberal thinkers, like their less liberal counterparts, can subscribe to views about race that are hereditarian and materialist; they simply understand biological material itself to be plastic and teachable over time. And they expect pliancy, teachability and speed of acquisition to differ not just across individuals but also across races. As the nineteenth century closes and the twentieth opens, this vision of differentiated development into civilisation is central to the narrative of progress that informs liberal advocacy of education and eugenics alike. Adams's liberal antagonists understand the pliancy of humans as an opportunity for learning, development, cultivation and progress. Adams, in contrast, questions the value of those things, and considers the attractions of their contraries.

The Virgin and the Favourite

Embodiment is a key problem in conversations about liberalism's human and US citizenship; it is also a key problem in the scholarly conversation about Adams's feminism or lack thereof. One body in particular looms over that conversation: Adams's wife, Marion 'Clover' Adams, was apparently the model for Esther, and she killed herself in 1885. Esther's fictional, figurative, failed embodiment eerily anticipates Clover's, which was real. Scholars recognise that *Democracy* and *Esther* sit on a trajectory of thinking about women that runs from Adams's early essay on Pocahontas up through his early twentieth-century writing about the Virgin; many read the novels' female protagonists as forerunners of the Virgin that emerges more fully in his later work. What that emergence means for actual women is, however, a question about which scholars have disagreed.[5]

Eric Rauchway's reading of *Esther* contends that 'Adams believed that no true democratic civilization could flourish that did not include women – not merely a mystical feminine principle, but actual living breathing women.' Kim Moreland, in contrast, argues that the novels stifle that breath by annihilating their female protagonists: 'Adams kills these New Women off by having them kill themselves, at least metaphorically.' Ultimately, she writes, Adams has a 'sense of women as limited creatures who would do well to aspire only to certain traditional roles and who attempt to transform these roles – to become New Woman (as Marion Adams had done) – only at their mortal peril'. As Cindy Weinstein notes, the Virgin's 'fecundity has nothing to do with her biological body': 'Like the dynamo, which creates force without sexuality, so too the Virgin produces children and forces with little, if any, help from the body.'[6]

A Virgin does not belong in a novel, which is the genre not just of marriage plots but of real modern people. The novel forms an ideal device for Adams to skewer Mill's marriage plot, and it also offers up a good site for eliminating the body of the real modern woman so that the bodiless Virgin can rise. The racial categorisations of the real bodies in these novels matter: although it has gone mostly undiscussed, the novels' thinking about race is integral to its thinking about sex and gender. If we pay more attention to race, we see more clearly how incipient elements of the Virgin take shape in *Democracy*; attending to these elements in turn raises questions about the role of race in the portrait of the Virgin that crystallises many years later.

Adams's work engages conspicuously with 'the discourse of civilization', in which race and sex are central and inextricably intertangled. As Gail Bederman explains: 'in the context of the late nineteenth century's popularized Darwinism, civilization was seen as an explicitly racial concept': "civilization"', she explains, 'denoted a precise stage in human racial evolution – the one following the more primitive stages of "savagery" and "barbarism"'. Within this discourse, sexual differentiation is a sign of advanced development; thus, Bederman notes, '"civilization," as turn-of-the-century Americans understood it, simultaneously denoted attributes of race and gender'.[7] The discourse of civilisation is not monolithic or constant: when, for example, Adams's friend Theodore Roosevelt invokes 'civilisation' and 'barbarism' as he constructs strenuous masculinity and advocates imperialism, he is not replicating President Eliot's invocations of the same terms, nor Mill's, though those invocations too undergird accounts of manliness and of empire.

In the years leading up to the writing of his novels, Adams engages with the broad and varied discourse of civilisation in his teaching at Eliot's Harvard. Adams and his students plunge into Anglo-Saxonism and the Teutonic origins theory, which understands freedom and democracy as the racial inheritances and special capacities of the Anglo-Saxon race. With characteristic energy and irreverence, Adams would interrogate and revise the theory's assumptions, shifting its arguments from parliaments to law and from Anglo-Saxons to Normans.[8] In collaboration with his students (including Henry Cabot Lodge), Adams authored *Essays in Anglo-Saxon Law* (1876), a scholarly volume dedicated to President Eliot. During the year of that volume's publication, he delivered a Lowell Institute lecture titled 'The Rights of Women in History', later published in 1891 as 'The Primitive Rights of Women', which conspicuously draws from his work at Harvard.[9]

The Boston *Evening Transcript* printed its story on Adams's lecture immediately below another on a lecture given the following day by Susan B. Anthony, who, the paper notes, 'reviewed at much length the history of the enfranchisement of the laboring classes in England and of the blacks in this country, to show that the possession of the suffrage had everything to do with their status in the community and their power to successfully demand the rights that directly concerned their comfort and happiness in daily life'. As for 'Professor Henry Adams of Cambridge': 'All accounts agree, he said, that the earliest position of woman was one of slavery, not slavery, however, in the modern sense, not the slavery of superior force, but a species of slavery legalized and sanctioned by custom – that is to say, women were recognized as second to men in the scheme of humanity.'[10] This focus on the distinction between 'the earliest position of women' and the 'modern', on 'slavery', 'superior force' and 'custom', is suggestive, for these are exactly the subjects, and the words, of Mill's *Subjection*.

As Rauchway points out, Adams's 'Primitive Rights' describes the 'construction' of a 'women's sphere', thus denying that sphere 'the authority of immemorial custom and biology alike'.[11] That is also Mill's project in *Subjection*. Adams's biographer, Ernest Samuels, notes that in 'Primitive Rights' Adams pushes back against his friend Henry Maine's 'The Early History of the Property of Married Women' (1873). But it is hard to see how Adams, the straying acolyte of Mill, would not also have been thinking of the most notorious recent work to undertake the project of considering women's status in historical perspective.[12] Samuels perhaps neglects to identify *Subjection* as a source text because of a broader inattentiveness to feminist thought. He suggests that Adams and Mill agree on the Woman Question, noting that Adams 'did not need Mill's essay to prove to him that the degradation of women grew out of convenient myth and not out of the nature of woman. As a descendent of Abigail Adams he knew woman's capacity for greatness within her sphere' and similarly respected his mother and sister.[13] But Mill's deeply subversive work is not about woman's capacity for greatness within her sphere. It is about the socially constructed nature of that sphere, the way that sphere systematically compromises greatness and – most explosively – the unknown extent of that capacity.

Mill defines 'the peculiar character of modern world' as the fact 'that human beings are no longer born to their place in life, and chained down by an inexorable bond to the place they are born to, but are free to employ their faculties, and such favourable chances as offer, to achieve the lot which may appear to them most desirable'.[14] Such a modernity would decline 'to ordain that to be born a girl instead of a boy, any more than to be born black instead of white, or commoner instead of nobleman, shall decide the person's position through all life'.[15] 'It is', he says, 'felt to be an overstepping of the proper bounds of authority to fix beforehand, on some general presumption, that certain persons are not fit to do certain things.' Rather than such general presumptions, 'freedom and competition' determine what each person can and should do: 'it is not that all processes are supposed to be equally good, or all persons to be equally qualified for everything; but that freedom of individual choice is now known to be the only thing which procures the adoption of the best processes, and throws each operation into the hands of those who are best qualified for it'.[16]

Adams in 'Primitive Rights' and Mill in *Subjection* both consider the history of women's power, but their histories of women differ: Adams emphasises that women of certain races had some rights in the primitive past; Mill emphasises that women, like other classes of humans, have been enslaved, and that their continuing enslavement in the present is an anomaly in a modernity otherwise characterised by emancipations. While Adams gazes backward and ponders what has been lost, Mill looks forward to a modernity of continuing progress. The concept of 'slavery' figures crucially in the expression of both these perspectives. The thrust of Mill's whole work is that modernity is a time of progress and equality, and that the past is the era of the rule of force. The status of women is a salient exception: their present state of dependence, Mill argues, 'is the primitive state of slavery lasting on, through successive mitigations and modifications'. In order to show that this is true, *Subjection* considers the history of women's rights and women's educations. In doing so, it considers 'primitive' and 'Christian' contexts, as Maine and Adams subsequently do. Mill suggests that Christianity and modern progress have eliminated many forms of slavery, but the enslavement of women in the home persists anomalously. 'We are continually told', Mill writes, 'that civilization and Christianity have restored to the woman her just rights. Meanwhile the wife is the actual bond-servant of her husband: no less so, as far as legal obligation goes, than slaves commonly so called.'[17]

Working from a commonplace analogy, Mill compares women's status to that of slaves not just metaphorically but literally, pointing to features of legal status that are the same for married women and for enslaved persons. As Stefan Collini notes, 'the whole of *The Subjection of Women* could be regarded as one long elaboration of the basic analogy between the historical position of slaves and the present position of women'.[18] Mill repeatedly equates domestic tyranny with political tyranny, and both with slavery. Why should women wish to marry, he asks, when 'marrying is giving themselves a master, and a master too of all their earthly possessions?' Men are apparently 'determined that the law of marriage shall be a law of despotism'. Thus a married woman is analogous to a 'Sultan's favourite slave'; and in these conditions it is 'wrong to bring women up with any acquirements but those of an odalisque or of a domestic servant'. Mill is especially interested in the figure of the 'favourite', the willing or eager female slave. Noting that women are acquiescent to the power of men, rather than rebellious, he attributes this to their educations and observes that it is a logical response to existing structures of power. As for men, Mill observes, all of them, 'except the most brutish, desire to have, in the woman most nearly connected with them, not a forced slave but a willing one, not a slave merely, but a favourite. They have therefore put everything in practice to enslave their minds.'[19]

Democracy specifically revises Mill's governing analogy comparing women and slaves; like Mill, Adams gives particular attention to the figure of the favourite. *Subjection* associates oppression and slavery with non-European societies, but also points to slavery in the US; *Democracy* instead locates slavery in an African society. The novel makes several scattered references to Black people in the US who may be the descendants of enslaved people, or themselves formerly enslaved. These people figure on the peripheries, as part of the scenery, and are often in positions of servitude. When Sybil dresses for the ball, among the servants allowed to admire her toilette is 'the leading "girl," who was the cook, a colored widow of some sixty winters, whose admiration was irrepressible'.[20] This woman's race, her possible former enslavement and the sexual experience announced by her widowhood are all relevant details, for the extraordinary passage in which she figures also clothes the white virgin Sybil in the garb of an African favourite.

Sybil wears to the ball an exceptionally exquisite gown: she has ordered from Mr Worth 'an entirely original ball-dress – unlike any other sent to America', and the master delivers. But her dress is actually a copy. The original was commissioned by 'the reigning favorite of the King of Dahomey'. Mr Worth designs for this concubine a breath-taking concoction called 'L'Aube, Mois de Juin'. He struggles initially with the commission: 'Visions of flesh-colored tints shot with blood-red perturbed his brain, but he fought against and dismissed them; that combination would be commonplace in Dahomey' (158–9). The 'flesh-colored tints' here raise the questions: what colour, whose flesh? Worth's perturbed imaginings draw from a specific mythology: 'Dahomey epitomized everything negative that the Euro-American imagination of the nineteenth and twentieth centuries wanted to believe about Africa.' Pointing to the importance of the idea of Dahomey in 'the racist imagination' of the period, Edna G. Bay notes that stories about Dahomey typically featured images of great wealth from the slave trade, Amazon warriors, brutal slaughter, cannibalism, and the king on a throne of human skulls, possessed of a harem of thousands; these racist images circulate widely in both proslavery and antislavery writing. Thus, later, in the 1893 World's Columbian Exposition in Chicago, the savage, barbarous 'Dahomey Village' serves as foil to the civilisation of the White City. And thus, earlier, in an abolitionist address delivered at Harvard in 1862, George William Curtis refers to 'the rule of the King of Dahomey, of the pirate-ship, of the slave-market' as that which 'the human instinct' rejects, the opposite of what is 'right, justifiable, humane'.[21]

Adams too uses the idea of Dahomey to address the question of which instincts are human and which are not. In his account, African savagery bleeds into American whiteness. Splendid in Worth's soft tints of green, blue and pink, Sybil manifests 'unutterable freshness', embodying 'maidenhood in her awakening innocence'. Adams's extended lyrical description of the astonishing dress itself and Sybil's beauty as she wears it draws attention away from the fact that this tableau of the pristine white virgin standing in her silken toilette also includes two sexually experienced Black women: the remote African favourite whose dress she unwittingly wears, and the 'colored widow' who gazes on her with admiration. Sybil and the woman in Dahomey have more than just the gown in common. They both wear it with sexual rivalry in mind: the African favourite orders 'a ball-dress that should annihilate and utterly destroy with jealousy and despair the hearts of her seventy-five rivals', just as Sybil, albeit with more politesse, tells her friend that 'the pangs of envy will rankle' once she sees the dress (158–60). The apparently decorous ballroom in the nation's capital resembles the African king's harem in that both host the sexual competition of young females. Here, as elsewhere in Adams's novels, the boundary between savage and civilised blurs.

Democracy rewrites *Subjection*'s discussion of the favourite by crudely literalising and extending its logic. Although Mill affirms that the legal status of women is literally like that of slaves, his 'Sultan's favorite slave' functions as metaphor and imagery.[22] Adams, however, brings an actual enslaved African favourite into his pages – she is remote, but contemporary and real – and suggests that the DC debutante is just like her. Neither the white girl nor the woman in Dahomey is troubled by what Mill describes as an enslavement of mind. The favourite lives in a luxurious, comfortable sexual servitude. Sybil, wearing an exact duplicate of her dress, is equally content. And finally, there is the other woman glad of her subjection: the sixty-year-old Black woman, 'the leading "girl"', overwhelmed with admiration for her white mistress (160). This cluster of three female figures includes elements that will later cohere in the figure of the Virgin, after their misogyny finds a comfortable home and a useful set of tropes within Christian typology and narrative. Here, these elements are diffused and inchoate, but they are perceptible: a pristine virginity; the whiteness in which that purity resides; the unbound vitality of sex; the savagery in which that vitality inheres. All of this cannot fit neatly into any one living body: here, the provisional solution to that impossibility is distribution across multiple bodies. Later, the problem is solved by the elimination of the body altogether.

The tableau of contented subjection that includes the virgin, the favourite and the widow also includes another female figure: the widow is joined by her fellow servant, who happens to be a 'New

England spinster'. Imagery evoking such spinsters, along with similarly unsexy aunts, schoolmarms and grandmothers, will figure prominently in negative accounts of an idealist 'genteel tradition' during the twentieth century; here, we can see one example of how this unsexy New England femininity earlier functions in texts that attack an idealism that is not 'genteel', but liberal. The spinster who admires Sybil performs the hypocrisy that Adams locates in Boston liberalism, and liberalism more broadly. We read that she 'paid in her heart secret homage to their gowns and bonnets which her sterner lips refused': her 'conscience wrestled with her instincts' (160).

Adams suggests that liberalism's heart and instincts yearn for all its stern conscience decries: the spinster dismisses the sexy glory of girlish ornament, as well as the animal sexual rivalries that such ornament manifests – but deep down, in spite of all her self-righteous sterility, she too feels their pull. Like Mill in *Subjection*, New England liberals propose a bright modernity of emancipations and enfranchisements. Adams suggests that both they and those they would enfranchise are actually rather bestial. He also seems to find that bright vision of modernity vacant and unsexy. For him, beastliness has its allure. And he can fetishise it and profess his identification with it from the perfect safety and power of his own body: embodying *contre soi* the citizen and the liberal subject, and finding that rather banal, he loses nothing by hailing womanhood and Blackness as the sites of everything the liberal subject is not.

Beasts and Things that Crawl

As the nineteenth century nears its close, it is not at all unusual for writers to prod at the boundary between animal and human, or point to animalistic qualities in people. In Adams's published and unpublished writing, diction about animals is common, and often embedded in evolutionary thinking that also refers to undeveloped savagery. In letters of the 1890s, for example, he refers to 'the human animal, the superstitious and ignorant savage within us, that has instincts and no reason', and 'the helplessness of insects and polyps like us'.[23] In spite of the ubiquity of this sort of remark, I want to suggest that the pattern of reference to animals in *Democracy* and *Esther* conveys specific meanings, meanings that operate in concert with the novels' allusions to Darwinian science. Such allusions might signify in a wide range of ways: during the nineteenth and early twentieth centuries (as after), political arguments of all sorts find resources in the broad body of thought that is evolutionary science. Abolitionists and antiracists point to monogenesis; white supremacists see Anglo-Saxons manifesting fitness for survival. In Adams's novels, allusions to Darwin, evolutionary science and the continuity between humans and animals express resistance to the ideas that Mill endorses in *Subjection*.[24]

By repeatedly invoking a Darwinian continuity between the human species and other species of animals, these novels take aim at a particular instability within liberal thought. Animals, as Colleen Glenney Boggs has shown, are 'integral to liberalism, as a structuring force that destabilizes the liberal subject at its core'. 'Subjectivity', she asserts, 'emerges in and remains unhinged by cross-species encounters.'[25] The figurative language of Adams's novels stages such encounters relentlessly, producing an unsettling that extends across both texts. Still more overtly, Adams's references to animals and to Darwinian science resist Mill's liberal vision of modernity and progress by invoking degeneration and retrogression. As Dana Seitler shows, Darwin's work provokes fears of 'atavism', especially later in the century: 'instead of a progression toward physical and intellectual superiority as posited by the more ameliorative adaptations of evolutionary theory, atavism signalled a retrogressive animalism'. Pointing to several texts that represent this sort of animalism, Seitler observes that 'each confronts the nineteenth-century classificatory systems separating the human from the animal and therefore blurs a series of boundaries between spirit and body, whites and non-whites, men and women, reproductive virtue and sexual pathology'. Atavism, she shows, produces 'a body that could act as a site of racialized and sexualized primitivism cordoned off from the "modern" body'.[26]

To see how Darwinian ideas operate as part of Adams's interrogation of *Subjection*'s arguments, it is helpful to recall that Darwin himself apparently disliked that book, though he otherwise agreed with Mill about a great deal. Along with other notable scientists, Darwin subscribed to Mill's Jamaica Committee, and sided with him on the issues of slavery and the Civil War in the US. Although they agreed on these questions, Darwin questioned Mill's emphasis on education over innate traits, and also his views on sexual difference. 'Darwin may have admired Mill and been a sometime ally, but he clearly disliked *Subjection*, and he contested its arguments in his own book,' note Diane B. Paul and Benjamin Day, who add: 'some sections of the *Descent*, which was published two years after *Subjection*, could even be read as a rejoinder to Mill'.[27] Darwin argued that sexual selection made women intellectually inferior by nature.

The broader body of scientific and medical discourse that drew from Darwin's arguments included authors like Herbert Spencer and Edward Clarke; within this discourse, during the 1870s, scientific authority had mustered behind the idea that sexual differentiation meant not just female intellectual inferiority, but females' physical incompetence for the rigors of education: schooling might threaten girls' fertility.[28] In emphasising the determining force of the body in matters of education, Darwin and his followers pushed back against the argument Mill made in *Subjection*.

Subjection does not deny that some bodies are more capable than others; but it does insist that we cannot predict the extent of a person's capacity based upon the kind of body she has, given that our only knowledge of bodies' capacities comes from observing them in specific social and historical circumstances. Mill asks: 'was there ever any domination which did not appear natural to those who possessed it?' 'Unnatural', he argues, 'generally means only uncustomary ... everything which is usual appears natural. The subjection of women to men being a universal custom, any departure from it quite naturally appears unnatural.' History shows 'the extraordinary susceptibility of human nature to external influences, and the extreme variableness of those of its manifestations which are supposed to be the most universal and uniform'. Thus, 'that most difficult question, what are the natural differences between the two sexes [is] a subject on which it is impossible in the present state of society to obtain complete and correct knowledge'.[29]

Mill argues, not just in *Subjection* but also elsewhere in his œuvre, that environment and education (everywhere, not just in school) are what shape humans. He writes in the first edition of *Principles of Political Economy* (1848): 'Of all vulgar modes of escaping from the consideration of the effect of social and moral influences on the human mind, the most vulgar is that of attributing the diversities of conduct and character to inherent natural differences.'[30] Many years later, in his *Autobiography* (1873), he reiterates:

> I have long felt that the prevailing tendency to regard all the marked distinctions of human character as innate, and in the main indelible, and to ignore the irresistible proofs that by far the greater part of those differences, whether between individuals, races, or sexes, are such as not only might but naturally would be produced by differences in circumstances, is one of the chief hindrances to the rational treatment of great social questions and one of the greatest stumbling blocks to human improvement.[31]

Here, as in *Subjection,* Mill points to what seems entirely known, fixed, immutable, universal and natural, and shows that it is in fact contingent, local and mutable – wide open to change, and still far from known in the fullness of its possibilities. Of course, the essential pliancy of humans (among other species) and actual mutability of what seems fixed are also emphases in Darwinian evolutionary science, and indeed, liberal thinkers often refer to that kind of science as they describe educational possibility. But divergences on the meaning of sexual difference and its implications for relations between men and women form notable exceptions to the broader agreement between Mill and Darwin.

Adams knew Darwinian science well, so it is especially interesting that his novels offer up distortions and misapplications of it. The putative voice for Darwinian science in *Esther* is George Strong, whose agnosticism figures within the novel's religious drama: 'the professor', a hostile gossip observes, 'is a full fledged German Darwinist'.[32] The model for Strong was apparently Clarence King. When Adams later praises King in a 1904 memorial essay, he recalls his deceased friend's 'famous aphorism': 'Nature never made more than one mistake, but that was fatal; it was when she differentiated the sexes.' Adams remembers fondly Strong's disdain for intellect, which is male, and preference instead for 'the female', which is 'rich in the inheritance of every animated energy back to the polyps and the crystals'.[33] This invocation of sex is also an invocation of race, which is itself embedded in a racially differentiated timeline of progressions into modernity. Adams writes of King: 'It was not the modern woman that interested him; it was the archaic female, with instincts and without intellect,' and 'if he had a choice among women, it was in favor of Indians and negroes'. For King, and for Adams via King, bodies that are neither white nor male offer an escape into the premodern and the instinctual. When he makes King's avatar in *Esther* a perceived 'Darwinist', Adams associates Darwinism with an especially enthusiastic dedication to the belief that intellect resides in white male bodies.

Strong the Darwinist interprets the events of *Esther*'s marriage plot as instances of a competitive struggle for dominance and survival. He observes of Wharton's apparent attraction to Catherine, 'he looks at her as though he would eat her', and notes that 'if she took him, he would make her a slave within a week'. Esther replies that Catherine 'is a practical young savage', and reports: 'the moment she saw how unfit she was for such a man, she gave it up without a pang'. Strong replies, 'I don't see her unfitness [. . .] I should say it was he who wanted fitness' (156). He calls the prospective marriage between Esther and Hazard 'a case of survival of the fittest', a contest in which one religious perspective will dominate and convert the other (103). This is a strange thing for a full-fledged Darwinist to say, for Darwin's insistence upon sexual difference resulting from sexual selection emphasises competition within each sex, not competition between a male and a female who are about to mate with each other. The advocate of competition within marriage is Mill, who sees it as a means of sharpening the intellect of both parties, an opportunity for mutual development.[34] In antifeminist writings of the period, the spectre of men and women – or, worse still, husband and wife – competing with each other is a standard negative trope: it is what will happen if the truth of sexual difference is disregarded. The prospective contest between Esther and Hazard might be imagined as a mutually mind-sharpening one in keeping with Mill's vision; but by using Darwinian language to describe competition within marriage, Strong instead refers to that familiar body of antifeminist thought.

Democracy's play with Darwinian thought portrays atavisms within that body of thought itself, pointing to contradictions and hypocrisies within the modern, liberal perspective that knows its Darwin well. Madeleine borrows one of Darwin's works (the novel does not specify which) from the Library of Congress. Ratcliffe sneers and demands to know why she pursues this material, asking 'Do you think you are descended from monkeys?' They banter along, and Madeleine comments, 'you are very hard on the monkeys', adding: 'the monkeys never did you any harm; they are not in public life; they are not even voters' (59). Here the continuity that Darwin's theory posits between animals and humans serves simply to figure forth, in the course of flirtatious jesting, the racist trope of the voting monkey; far from serving a forward-thinking agenda of expanding the franchise, it works against that agenda. When Ratcliffe hears that Madeleine is reading Darwin, he becomes 'senatorial and Websterian', and declares:

> Such books . . . disgrace our civilization; they degrade and stultify our divine nature; they are only suited for Asiatic despotisms where men are reduced to the level of brutes; that they should be accepted by a man like Baron Jacobi, I can understand; he and his masters have nothing to do in the world but trample on human rights. Mr Carrington, of course, would approve these ideas; he believes in the divine doctrine of flogging Negroes; but that you, who profess philanthropy and free principles, should go with them, is astonishing . . . (58–59).

Ratcliffe names among the likely advocates of Darwin's arguments the Continental roué Baron Jacobi, emissary of an Old World in which inequality is a given and 'human rights' a curious artefact of modernity; and Carrington, the old Virginian, a dispossessed planter. The Senator thus counterfactually associates Darwinian thought with the opponents of liberal thought: slave-owners, conservatives, advocates of paternalistic feudalism, and the tyrannies of the East, beyond the pale of 'civilisation' as imagined by liberal thinkers. As we have seen, Darwin (along with other scientists) falls on the liberal, anti-slavery side of these questions. Darwinism is not old-fashioned, nor is it associated with ancient hierarchies; indeed, Gore names among the 'new dogmas' of the era 'faith in human nature; faith in science; faith in survival of the fittest' (45). Darwinism is associated with progress, modernity and 'philanthropy and free principles', far more than with the Southern slavocracy and with the hierarchies of old Europe. But Ratcliffe's admonition here strangely reverses this set of affiliations. One way to read this is to infer that 'senatorial and Websterian' simply means 'with total disregard for fact'; and the novel's distaste for politicians and their amoral, power-hungry grandstanding would encourage that reading. But it is also the case that, in associating belief in Darwinian evolution with old-school brutality, Adams makes a move we see him make repeatedly: he suggests that what professes to be modern and progressive is, in fact, in its heart, not so. Either deluded or hypocritical, it is actually just as beastly as what it presumes to supersede and rule over.

Such beastliness is amply represented in *Democracy*'s pages, which host a herd of fauna, some appearing via common idioms, others in more unusual figures of speech. Characters are incessantly compared to animals, both by the narration and by each other. In a climactic moment, Madeleine wonders in frustration: 'Where did the public good enter at all into this maze of personal intrigue, this wilderness of stunted natures where no straight road was to be found, but only the torturous and aimless tracks of beasts and things that crawl?' (97). Just such a beast is the politician who seeks her hand, about whom she asks, when she has fully recognised the extent of his corruption: 'What was to be done with such an animal?' (192). In this, their final scene, she recoils from him 'as though he were a reptile' (197).

The novel's abundant animal metaphors and similes invoke a specific account of animal behaviour, one that emphasises violence and competition. The animals here are creatures fighting for dominance or hunting and eating each other; sometimes, their fights are with human animals. In a vivid example, Madeleine is the human fisher and Ratcliffe the caught fish: 'the Senator from Illinois rose to this gaudy fly like a huge, two-hundred pound salmon; his white waistcoat gave out a mild silver reflection as he slowly came to the surface and gorged the hook' (20). Madeleine wants 'to experiment on him and use him as young physiologists use frogs and kittens' (21). No longer just a fisherman, she becomes a sadistic scientist–child: this is not a survival of the fittest in which one animal dominates another in order to eat it and thus stay alive – here, the more powerful animal dominates the other not in order to survive, but in order to play. Precisely by taking the role of the human in relation to that animal, Madeleine becomes more cruel and less compassionate.[35]

Esther does not simply extend *Democracy*'s pervasive pattern of diction: it makes it into a matter of jest between characters, who play overtly with the boundary between animal and human. Much dry hilarity results from the conceit that Catherine is a 'sage hen' (28). The animal and the 'savage' are linked in both novels and, in each, diction about animals leads into diction that refers to Native Americans. In *Esther*, comparisons to the animal lead directly into comparisons with 'Sioux' or 'Indians'. Along with the running joke about Catherine being a sage hen or a beetle, there is Strong's running joke about her being a Sioux, which is the source of the Sage Hen idea. They joke about her name in Sioux (Laughing Strawberry, Jumping Turtle – and finally, Sage Hen) (28), and about her unfamiliarity with culture: having noted, 'The Sioux don't read Dickens!', Strong the scientist adds, 'I would like to know what the effect of the "Old Curiosity Shop" would be on a full-blooded Indian squaw' (51–52). This squaw shows up in *Democracy* too, when Madeleine finds, as she dominates Ratcliffe, that 'to tie a prominent statesman to her train and to lead him about like a tame bear, is for a young and vivacious woman a more certain amusement than to tie herself to him and to be dragged about like an Indian squaw' (49). Ratcliffe, however, has 'the instincts of a wild Indian in their sharpness and quickness of perception' (97). Later, such wildness leads into violence: Carrington tells Sybil of Ratcliffe, 'we will have his scalp if necessary, but I rather think he will commit harikiri himself if we leave him alone' (126). All this light repartee dances around the lines between animal and savage, savage and civilised; imagining the crossing of these lines is, for these characters and for the texts themselves, a great source of amusement.

In *Esther*, as the gathered friends gaze at Niagara Falls, Esther remarks that 'A woman feels most the kind of human life in it', which Strong affirms paradoxically by saying, yes, 'a big rollicking, Newfoundland dog sort of humanity' (147).[36] Esther finds in Niagara a 'tremendous, rushing, roaring companion, which thundered and smoked under her window, as though she had tamed a tornado'. Her 'huge playmate' or 'confidant' speaks in a voice 'so frank and sympathetic that she had no choice but to like it'. 'And its dress!', Esther says to herself, 'What a complexion, to stand dazzling white and diamonds in the full sunlight!' She takes 'infinite pains with her toilet in order to honor her colossal host whose own toilet was sparkling with all the jewels of nature'. Given this ready intimacy and this sparkling toilet, we might assume Esther's confidant is female. But the narrator's next simile suggests otherwise: this host is 'like an Indian prince whose robes are crusted with diamonds and pearls' (143–144). And indeed, the narrator presents Niagara as Hazard's 'rival'. Wharton, for his part, aestheticises the spectacle: 'Think what the Greeks would have done with it!' Catherine insists:

> the fall is a woman, and she is as self-conscious this morning as if she were at church. Look at the coquetry of the pretty curve where the water falls over, and the lace on the skirt where it breaks into foam! Only a woman could do that and look so pretty when she might just as easily be hideous. (147–148)

She finds in the falls a source for 'the design of a dress which should have the soul of Niagara in its folds.' But Esther objects: 'It is not a woman! It is a man! . . . No woman ever had a voice like that!' (148).

Catherine's perception of the falls as a feminine spectacle of gorgeously begowned whiteness opposes contesting perceptions that make the same falls either masculine, Indian or canine. The waterfall is a gorgeous coquette; it is an Indian prince in sparkling diamonds, a rival who will beat out Hazard; it is an enormous, romping dog. At Niagara, and also in Sybil's dressing room as she dons 'L'Aube, Mois de Juin', the question remains unsettled: what is inside this frothy, exquisite dress? The novels delight in the idea that appearances might deceive: what is white may be like what is black; the animal might pervade the human; savagery might linger within the civilised; and, as in the thundering sparkle of these indeterminate waters, the energies of the female might sometimes make a dazzling show in the male of the species.

Struggle for Mastery: Pedagogies, Marriage Plots

Subjection repeatedly describes marriage as a 'school'. Here and elsewhere in his œuvre, Mill's perspective is notable for the way it understands all of life as a site for education: he proposes a radical receptivity to knowledge, questions and ideas, and he models that receptivity in his own life and work (especially as described in his *Autobiography*). In this context, the domestic sphere, as well as the public sphere, is a crucial place for learning, and the quality of the intimate relations that play out in the domestic realm has significant consequences for an individual's development. Marriage, Mill writes, should function for men as a 'school of conscientious and affectionate forbearance', but instead it currently inculcates the worst in them, functioning as an 'Academy or Gymnasium for training them in arrogance and overbearingness'. From boyhood, the relationship between the sexes has adverse effects on his character: 'all the selfish propensities ... which exist among mankind, have their source and root in ... the present constitution of the relation between men and women'. For Mill, the adverse effects of this arrangement are not just moral, but intellectual: 'If the wife does not push the husband forward, she always holds him back.' When one of two married persons is inferior, 'the whole influence of the connexion upon the development of the superior of the two is deteriorating ... Even a really superior man almost always begins to deteriorate when he is habitually ... king of his company'. Mill asks readers to imagine, if women were allowed rights, the 'benefit of the stimulus that would be given to the intellect of men by the competition; or ... by the necessity that would be imposed on them of deserving precedency before they could expect to obtain it'.[37]

Though unequal partnership is 'deteriorating' in its adverse effects on the development of the morality and intellect, there is an alternative, one that Mill takes pains to sketch. Equal partnerships yield development for both partners, he suggests: a domestic world that is not a tyranny is a much better site for learning. 'Family in best forms', he says, is 'a school of sympathy, tenderness, loving forgetfulness of self.' In such contexts 'the daily life of mankind' is 'a school of moral cultivation'. Domestically or politically, he affirms, tyranny precludes these conditions: 'the only school of genuine moral sentiment is society between equals'. Equality is the rule in progressive modernity; it is less advanced states that rely on hierarchy and force. 'The true virtue of human beings', Mill declares, 'is fitness to live together as equals ... preferring, whenever possible, the society of those with whom leading and following can be alternate and reciprocal.' But, he observes, 'to these virtues, nothing in life as at present constituted gives cultivation by exercise. The family is a school of despotism.' It might instead be a site for learning: 'the family, justly constituted, would be the real school of the virtues of freedom', just as 'citizenship, in free countries, is partly a school of society in equality'.[38]

Arguing for such 'a school of sympathy in equality, of living together in love, without power on one side or obedience on the other', Mill works to help his readers imagine a different kind of marriage, comparing the relationship to one 'between two friends of the same sex' or between two partners in business, insisting 'it is not true that in all voluntary association between two people, one of them must be absolute master'. Building upon his earlier mention of 'leading and following' that is 'alternate and reciprocal', Mill offers a passionate endorsement of companionate marriage between equals:

> What marriage may be in the case of two persons of cultivated faculties, identical in opinions and purposes, between whom there exists that best kind of equality, similarity of powers and capacities with reciprocal superiority in them – so that each can enjoy the luxury of looking up to the other, and can have alternately the pleasure of leading and being led in the path of development – I will not attempt to describe . . . But I maintain . . . that this, and this only, is the ideal of marriage; and that all opinions, customs, and institutions which favour any other notion of it, or turn the conceptions and aspirations connected with it into any other direction . . . are relics of primitive barbarism. The moral regeneration of mankind will only really commence, when the most fundamental of the social relations is placed under the rule of equal justice, and when human beings learn to cultivate their strongest sympathy with an equal in rights and cultivation.[39]

Making marriage a key site for cultivation, Mill argues that mutual reciprocity between equals is the criterion for success in cultivation and in marriage alike. His declaration of omission ('I will not attempt to describe') reminds us that, in addition to being an argument about how to learn and teach, this statement about power relations between husbands and wives is a statement about power relations between sexual partners: comparisons to business partners aside, one of the things *Subjection* quietly proposes is an egalitarian, reciprocal approach to sex.

Mill's argument for egalitarian reciprocity in *Subjection* is consistent with the pedagogy he advocates in his 'Inaugural Address' (1867). Mill disparages 'the old notion of education, that it consists in the dogmatic inculcation from authority, of what the teacher deems true'. In moral and religious education, he says, 'it is not the teacher's business to impose his own judgment, but to inform and discipline that of his pupil'. The 'conscientious teacher', Mill warns,

> has no right to impose his opinion authoritatively upon a youthful mind. His teaching should not be in the spirit of dogmatism, but in that of enquiry [. . .] we should not consent to be restricted to a one-sided teaching, which informs us of what a particular teacher or association of teachers receive as true doctrine and sound argument, but of nothing more.

Mill suggests that politics in particular is a subject in which teachers must not exert mastery over students: 'What we require to be taught on that subject, is to be our own teachers. It is a subject on which we have no masters to follow; each must explore for himself, and exercise an independent judgment.' The function of education on this subject, Mill explains, is to 'supply the student with materials for his own mind, and helps to use them. It can make him acquainted with the best speculations on the subject, taken from different points of view.' Similarly, the study of history, he declares, should 'introduce us to the principal facts which have a direct bearing on the subject, namely the different modes or stages of civilization that have been found among mankind, and the characteristic properties of each'. This subject, he adds, is 'quite unfit to be taught dogmatically': the teacher's job is to 'lead the student to attend to' unresolved questions and let that student do his own thinking.[40]

When Adams teaches history at Eliot's Harvard from 1870 to 1877, he conspicuously adopts Mill's egalitarian pedagogy of reciprocity and mutual development. Echoing 'Inaugural Address', he writes to his student Lodge in 1873, 'I propose no more to the fellows who are kind enough to think my teaching worth their listening to . . . than to teach them how to do their work [. . .] it makes little difference what one teaches; the great thing is to train scholars for work.'[41] The preceding year, Adams had reviewed two books about Harvard's history; his review, like his letter to Lodge, echoes Mill. Harvard did well, Adams observes, when it began 'to concede and act upon the principle that the student was in all respects the social equal of the instructor, entitled to every courtesy due to equals'. Adams's review gives particular attention to the power dynamics between teachers and students, and disparages pedagogies that depend on mastery and control. These pedagogies, he suggests, have thus far prevailed at the university. Teachers and students have engaged in a struggle for dominance, and learning has suffered as a result. Adams explains,

'The duty of giving instruction, and the duty of judging offenses and inflicting punishment, are in their nature discordant, and can never be intrusted to the same hands, without the most serious injury to the usefulness of the instructor.' Such a teacher becomes a mere tyrant: 'the habit of instruction and the incessant consciousness of authority tends to develop extremely disagreeable traits in human character, especially wherever character naturally inclines towards selfishness'. These traits include 'not only the consciousness of social superiority, but the consciousness of power to enforce obedience'. Just as this disciplinary, hierarchical system of domination makes tyrants of the teachers, it makes rebels of the students, fostering 'a spirit of opposition' in their minds.[42] For Adams, as for Mill, 'opposition' in the context of inequality distorts and hinders the mind of both the dominator and the dominated: both thinkers see learning come instead from the kind of 'opposition' that inheres in (as Adams later puts it in *The Education*) 'conflict, competition, contradiction' between equals.[43]

Mill is interested in the possibility of extending this egalitarian pedagogy outward to more people; Adams suggests that such attempts end up replicating exactly the sort of domination they presume to thwart. Adams observes, not just at Harvard but also in Boston and New England more broadly, a tendency to undertake projects of education that are, in practice, projects of domination. For Adams, as for later critics of liberalism, 'culture' is a fraud and a ruse. A cluster of bilious, bored letters in 1875 anticipates the attack on Boston conformity and veneration for education that his *Education* will develop more fully. Adams writes with venom about universities, Boston prigs and 'Culture' at Harvard: 'I am preaching a crusade against Culture with a big C. I hope to excite the hatred of my entire community, every soul of whom adores that big C. I mean to irritate every one about me to frenzy by ridiculing all the idols of the University and declaring university education to be a swindle.'[44]

In another letter, having derogated the attempts of 'our young women . . . "to improve their minds"', Adams goes on: 'Our men in the same devoted temper talk "culture" till the word makes me foam at the mouth. They cram themselves with second-hand facts and theories till they bust, and then they lecture at Harvard College and think they are the aristocracy of intellect and are doing true heroic work by exploding themselves all over a younger generation.'[45] Clover's biographer, Eugenia Kaledin, points to 'the vague sexual suggestiveness of the imagery' in this passage.[46] Vague or not, this imagery suggests a specific kind of sex: domination itself is a turn-on here, and this masturbatory climax belongs to the master who explodes himself all over the mastered. Needless to say, this is not the erotics of leading and being led. Adams criticises the sort of mastering he observes at Harvard, but his novels suggest that seeking mastery is what humans naturally do, especially in relations between the sexes.

Democracy extends the critique of 'Culture with a big C' that Adams airs in 1875. Charles Vandersee points to the similarities in the language of Adams's 1875 letters and the passages of that novel that describe Madeleine's pursuit of culture.[47] Adams represents that pursuit as a project of imperial domination. Madeleine engages in a *mission civilisatrice* of redecoration: she exerts herself to correct 'the curious barbarism of the curtains and the wall papers' in her newly rented house; when she is finished, 'a new era, a nobler conception of duty and existence, had dawned upon that benighted and heathen residence' (9). Sybil, surveying her sister's work, says archly, 'You haven't a plate or a fan or coloured scarf left. You must send out and buy some of these old Negro-women's bandannas if you are going to cover anything else. What *is* the use? Do you suppose any human being in Washington will like it?' (10). This casual remark about human beings derides Madeleine's liberal project of culture and civilisation by suggesting the stuff of its culture is indistinguishable from the stuff of negro women: in presuming to correct 'barbarism', Madeleine has simply piled on more of it. Sybil's comment also quietly excepts 'old Negro-women' from the category of human beings, or at least human beings in Washington.

In *Esther*, as in *Democracy*, culture is a device for domination, not a site for emancipation. The men of *Esther* are educated and confident in their practice of culture: they are people of universities, scholarship, travel, art, literature and libraries. Their easy knowledge and connoisseurship contrast against the more meagre resources of the novel's women. Here, men serve as teachers, and the women as students. Catherine the Westerner is a special project. The narrator observes, 'a quick girl soon picks up ideas when she hears clever men talking about matters which they understand' (49). Mrs Murray concurs with the narrator when she asserts, 'girls must have an education, and the only way they can get a good one is from clever men'. After they marry, she jokes, 'The business of educating their husbands will take all the rest of their lives' (146). This light banter casually travesties Mill's ideas about marriage and relations between the sexes as a site for mutual education.

One of the salient events in the novel's plot is the translation of a sonnet by Petrarch.[48] Hazard and Wharton apparently spent time in France obsessively translating Petrarch; they know 'by heart scores of the sonnets' (66). Catherine, who reads no literature at all, boldly asserts that she and Esther can translate too. Esther pleads: 'Don't make me ridiculous!' (62–3). When Catherine persists, Esther protests: 'It is one of her Colorado jokes. She does not know what a sonnet is. She thinks it some kind of cattle punching' (63). But the game is on nevertheless: the women do produce a translation, but only with substantial help from Esther's father. Catherine memorises the translation and 'when she thought herself perfect she told Mr. Hazard, as she would have told a schoolmaster, that she was ready with her sonnet' (65).

Painting, like literature, is a site for the novel's men to exert mastery over its women. Although painting is Esther's realm of greatest mastery and she has 'studied under good masters both abroad and at home', she solicits advice from Hazard, for whom the visual arts are a mere side-line. The novel represents his advice-giving about art as a form of domination: 'she began at length to be conscious of this impalpable tyranny, and submitted to it only because she felt her own dependence' (38–9). Wharton too is a tutor whose teaching is tyranny, and his is more overtly cruel. He instructs Esther with a pedagogy that is quite overtly about mastering the student. Later, when Wharton is in love with Catherine, his domineering via culture continues. He advises her about a European journey she is about to take, telling her she must see the Elgin Marbles because she is like them, quoting the *Iliad* and speaking to her in Greek, which she does not understand. Thus, the novel tells us, 'ended for the time their struggle for mastery' (155).

Both of Adams's novels suggest that these power struggles between teachers and students play out between the sexes, but Adams does not always make the more cultured party the male one. Culture is also a device that Easterners use to exercise power over Westerners: in *Esther*, the men magisterially tutor Catherine; in *Democracy*, culture offers Madeleine a way to outmanœuvre her suitor, Ratcliffe. Readings of Adams's novels often point to similarities between Madeleine and Esther, noting that they are both intense, intelligent women frustrated by not having an outlet for their intelligence and intensity. But these protagonists differ significantly in that Madeleine practises culture much more confidently; in addition to being older and more experienced than Esther, she has travelled more and, it would seem, read a great deal more. Even so, Carrington appears to curate her intellectual life in Washington to a significant extent: he chooses her books for her and marks out passages for her to read, and also directs Sybil's reading. In this sense, Madeleine is able to use culture as a device for dominating one man partly because she so effectively secures access to culture through another.

Democracy and *Esther* attack the liberal argument that education emancipates and civilises by representing education, or 'culture', as just another means of domination. This attack hits hard at the arguments of *Subjection* by locating these practices of domination within relations between men and women: the novels' courtship plots are plots of the 'struggle for mastery'. This is all quite explicit. The central suspense of *Esther* – about whether the marriage between Esther and Hazard will happen – is not about whether she loves him, but about whether she will submit to his dominion, whether he has power over her, or she over him. In this respect, their hypothetical marriage closely resembles Madeleine and Ratcliffe's. Like that hypothetical marriage, this one will never happen, because the woman rejects the man in an assertion of her own power, such as it is. Esther asks Hazard, 'Are all men so tyrannical with women?' He replies, 'I own it! . . . I am tyrannical! I want your whole life, and even more. I will be put off with nothing else' (161). Esther sees the cost of submitting to such a tyrant: 'She seemed to feel now . . . the restraint which would be put upon her the moment she should submit to his will' (162). And she will not place herself in such a harness, so the marriage remains off.

The divergence from Mill's model is even more pronounced earlier in the story, as we read that Hazard and Wharton 'lured her on, by assumed gentleness, in the path of bric-à-brac and sermons' (34). This path replicates derisively the 'path of development' on which Mill sees husband and wife 'leading and being led' in a mutual, reciprocal process of cultivation. Here that path is corrupted into the relation of tyrant and slave that Mill deprecates: the men, possessors of culture, teach tyrannically the uncultured woman. 'Bric-à-brac' degrades culture into acquisitive collecting, and 'sermons' disrupts Mill's model not just in its odour of religiosity but in its denial of reciprocity: he in the pulpit speaks with authority, and the silent congregation listens.

What Adams's archly knowing novels presume to know is that ideas like Mill's are not realistic. Realism is one of the resources that the genre of the novel offers Adams's interrogation of liberal thought: he opposes Mill's account of perfectibility and progress with books that suggest those things are fanciful and implausible. What is real, these novels affirm, is the generally savage beastliness of the human species. We will see this realist critique of liberalism repeatedly:

democracy is a lovely idea, as is a broadly cultivated body of citizens, but given the actual nature of humans, these are optimistic fantasies, not feasible political agendas. It is dangerous, this critique warns, to enfranchise monkeys or other unteachable creatures. Henry James offers his version of this realist conservative critique with empathetic regret, Edith Wharton hers with brusque remove; both James and Wharton are especially concerned about an exquisite realm of art, beauty and leisure that democracy might destroy.

Among these three, Adams's realist critique of liberalism is distinctive for its relish: he imagines the opposite of the liberal subject not with fear but with fascination and desire. Adams's opposition to Boston liberalism will emerge, especially in his *Education*, as the most overt and the most boldly brutal of this trio. This is partly because Adams is far more interested in political questions as such than either James or Wharton. It is also perhaps because neither James nor Wharton is an apostate. Unlike Adams, they do not belong to this liberalism before turning against it, and never really need to sever themselves from it. But further reasons for this brutality suggest themselves too – not least, Adams's self-professed affinity for conflict, and also his sense, expressed throughout these novels, that the line between humans and brutes is neither clear nor fixed. The aggressiveness of his apostasy enacts not just his argument that intelligence and action must be rebelliously individualist, but also his implication that humans are generally rather base creatures, seeking dominance and spoiling for a fight.

Chapter 2

The Education of the People in James's *The Bostonians* and *The Princess Casamassima*

The 'We the People' that begins the Preamble to the US Constitution notoriously designates an unstable and contested category: who is a person, and who are 'the People'? Who can claim personhood and thus citizenship, and who remains excluded from that inner circle of competence and rights? Liberalism's answers to these questions have often pointed to liberal education: any person, the theory goes, might become one of 'the People', if only that person becomes educated enough, and thus prepared for the responsibilities of citizenship. During Reconstruction and its aftermath, these issues take on immediate urgency, as public debates grapple with the question of whether freedmen and white women have the physical and mental capacity to develop into competent citizens. On both sides of the Atlantic, thinkers ask: if democracy enfranchises a broadly inclusive 'People', what happens?

In his anomalously political novels of 1886, *The Bostonians* and *The Princess Casamassima*, Henry James takes up these issues directly. Both books treat the concept of 'the people' with irony and suspicion. That tone is already evident in an 1883 letter from James to Thomas Sergeant Perry, who had written an article on American literature mentioning 'the core of democracy . . . the people, of the present, by the side of which all traces of aristocracy, of the past, are valueless'.[1] In response, James protests to his friend: 'Who are "the people"? I think it odious for any class to arrogate that title more than another . . . I pretend to be one "of the people", moi. And I can imagine no coterie-literature more coterie than a class of novel devoted to the portrayal of the professional democrat.'[2]

James's French-accented reply points to the Old-World, revolutionary connotations of *le peuple*; in his novels of 1886, as in his letter, he uses 'the people' not in the elevated, specifically American sense evoked by the Preamble, but rather in an Anglo-European sense that designates the poor or the working class. At the same time, however, he objects to the assumptions implicit in that usage: as a term for common folk, he suggests, 'the people' simply claims the exclusionary prerogative of the elite coterie for a different crowd.

Though James's letter disparages novels about 'the professional democrat', each of the novels he was shortly to write might be seen to take up just this subject in its portrait of a wealthy woman dedicated to an emancipatory cause. Each of these women more or less adopts someone whom she considers one of 'the people'. These parallel portrayals do not flatter. In *The Bostonians* and *The Princess Casamassima*, democracy is synonymous with revolution, which is synonymous with the destruction of all the sensory and aesthetic glories that civilisation nourishes. Arguing for the conservation of that civilisation and its pleasures, James makes an ambivalent plea for what democracy, according to Perry's article, devalues: aristocracy, the past, hierarchy, preservation.

In each novel, the member of 'the people' adopted by the revolutionary woman undergoes a kind of education under her guidance. In their representations of these educations, these books engage critically with the body of liberal political thought that pervaded both James's intellectual milieu and the pages of the 'genteel' periodicals in which these novels were first serialised, *The Century* and *The Atlantic*. This body of thought emphasises the importance of liberal education, or cultivation, in forming a capable democratic citizenry: one becomes one of the People by practising cultivation and developing into a richly competent liberal subject. The extent to which these novels engage with these ideas has gone unnoticed because the self-professed educational agenda of these magazines has been understood as project of 'cultural custodianship' in which the overt aim of education masks a covert project of exclusion and discipline. This understanding has prevailed partly because it comports with the larger history of liberalism's failures to live up to its own emancipatory rhetoric. But James's novels in fact plead for a more complex account of the 'genteel' project: specifically, they insist upon a difference between the oppressions of liberal education and the oppressions of illiberal tyranny.

That insistence does not emerge sharply in the scholarship on James's politics produced during the late twentieth century, perhaps because that scholarship often sought specifically to expose similarity between these two different modes of oppression. And yet, that late twentieth-century moment remains the last time the scholarly conversation on James focused so energetically on his thinking about democracy. The studies of *The Bostonians* and *The Princess Casamassima* that consider their original publication venues have often focused on those periodicals' repressive effects or complicity in defining exclusionary racial and national identities.³ My analyses here complement that work by giving more sustained attention to the inclusive, democratic aims that these periodicals and their editors claimed for themselves, and by situating those aims within the discourse of transatlantic liberalism.⁴ When we view these magazines' mission – successful or not – as a project of cultivating a people capable of practising democracy, we can see more clearly how these novels interrogate that mission.

That interrogation has been especially easy to miss in the case of *The Bostonians* because the novel is a key source text for the twentieth-century narrative about the 'genteel'. That narrative describes a New England declining from the activism and energy of the antebellum period into a complacent, moribund aridity in the later nineteenth century; the recurrent embodiment of this New England desiccation is an unsexy and unsexual white woman (a schoolmarm, a spinster, an aunt). In its twentieth-century iterations, this narrative makes a progressive, democratic argument for realism. Seeing the source material of this narrative of decline in *The Bostonians*, one might see the novel too express a progressive, democratic perspective, especially if one enjoys finding in Henry James an enlightened thinker whose politics are rather like one's own. But this is to read twentieth-century elements of the narrative back into their nineteenth-century sources, where those elements do not yet carry those connotations securely. James's early portrait of a complacent, declining Boston and a dour New England schoolmarm type does anticipate the progressive argumentation of later thinkers like Van Wyck Brooks and Vernon Louis Parrington. But these tropes do not necessarily signal progressive democratic thought until well after *The Bostonians* is published. And those progressive scholars are not the only ones who offer a realist critique of New England idealism; conservatives like Irving Babbitt do so too. Babbitt's critique, like Brooks's and Parrington's, draws from the earlier work of the reactionary Barrett Wendell, with whom James was friendly. James's own iteration of the realist critique of New England idealism resembles that of the conservatives more than that of the progressives: like Wendell (though not to the same extent), he has doubts about democracy.

During the first half of the 1880s, there was much to draw James's attention to questions about culture and citizenship. The deaths of his parents in the early years of the decade brought him back to Boston, the epicentre of transatlantic liberalism in the US; it is from his room there that he writes to Perry about 'the people' in 1883. Matthew Arnold's tour of the US during in the winter of 1883–4 resulted in a new extension of Arnold's ongoing commentary on culture in democratic societies; his writings on the US notably take up Bostonians, Harvard and *The Atlantic*. James was attentive to this tour and to the writings that emerged from it.[5] The year 1883 also saw the publication of Charles Eliot Norton's edition of the Carlyle–Emerson correspondence, which James reviewed, and in which he observed the clash of a democratising optimism and an antidemocratic pessimism: the long, amicable collision between these two thinkers pitted Emerson's liberalism against Carlyle's illiberal thought. In the larger Anglo-American political arena, moreover, tensions within liberalism rose to the fore with the 1883 Supreme Court *Civil Rights Cases* and the 1884 Mugwump revolt in the US, and, in Britain, with the 1884–5 Reform Act, as well as controversies regarding Ireland and India.

Public debates on both sides of the Atlantic posed questions about the receptivity to cultivation of groups seeking the franchise, and thus about the readiness of those groups for suffrage and citizenship. The brighter optimism of the years around the Civil War had dissipated: regarding the question of 'American institutions, social or political', Norton had written to James in 1873, 'I believe in a distant future not in the present as I used to do.'[6] But this belief in a longer trajectory of progress continued to drive the work of Norton and his colleagues even as they saw their democratic ideal repeatedly checked and baffled by party politics, the intensification of consumer culture, the sensationalism of the popular press, and the large number of Americans who apparently had neither access to nor interest in the practice of cultivation.

For Norton and his fellow American liberals, print periodicals figure centrally in visions of functioning democracy and competent citizenship. Leslie Butler notes: 'the educative dimensions of democratic citizenship required access to discussion, argument, and opinion, all of which now occurred in print and without which liberals believed voters were effectively disenfranchised (as well as dangerous)'; pointing to the 'common ground' that these American liberals share with Mill, she observes that 'the transatlantic faith in educative democracy all but assured that their primary public influence would come through print . . . the print media would give wide airing to their pleas for national cultivation'.[7] Richard Watson Gilder's New York-based *Century*, which featured *The Bostonians*, enjoyed an enormous circulation and was thus particularly well positioned to pursue this agenda of cultivating the broader public. The more prestigious and distinctly Bostonian *Atlantic*, where *The Princess Casamassima* appeared, had far fewer readers, and its editor from 1881 to 1890, Thomas Bailey Aldrich, did not share the democratic aspirations of his predecessors; yet *The Atlantic* had been and would remain an important institution of democratic liberalism in America.[8]

As they seek to constitute a public sphere of learning and debate, these periodicals host discussions about who belongs in such a sphere – or, in other words, who the People might be. For both of them, Reconstruction and its failure structure these discussions: along with white women, the most prominent prospective candidates for education and citizenship are the freedmen of the South. When *The Bostonians* runs in *The Century*, it appears alongside an important debate about the capacity of freedmen to engage in cultivation and thus practise citizenship, as well as that magazine's reconciliationist Civil War series. Later, *The Atlantic*, under the editorship of Bliss Perry, would ask related questions about education and citizenship when it ran its own series on Reconstruction and then on race and disenfranchisement; these series include contributions from white supremacist supporters of the Confederacy, as well as the essays by W. E. B. Du Bois about education and the Freedmen's Bureau that later become part of *Souls of Black Folk*.[9] Not least because they appear in these periodicals, we should read James's political novels about 'the people' as part of this larger conversation about American citizenship and belonging.

James's novels do not participate in this conversation by taking a position. Perhaps the strongest indication that we should not attempt to read either *The Bostonians* or *The Princess Casamassima* as a simple endorsement or condemnation of any political formation is the diversity of political readings that they have elicited over the years. Like much Jamesian scholarship attentive to political questions, readings of these novels have often attempted either to enlist James anachronistically for progressive causes or to expose his unremarkable conservatism as a scandal. But analyses that seek a strident political stance in these novels tend to understate their complexity. If we want to observe James expressing a personal view about the competence of 'the people' as citizens, we might turn to a letter he wrote in 1884: explaining to Grace Norton (Charles's sister), that he will never marry, he remarks, 'I don't think all the world has a right to it any more than I think all the world has a right to vote.'[10] Albeit casually, for the eyes of a particular reader, and in the course of saying something else, this comment states a position on the question of universal suffrage. The novels accomplish something vaster and more ambivalent. As Amanda Claybaugh argues, James 'is less interested in arguing against reform than in pursuing realism'.[11]

Both books provocatively propose a mode of liberal cultivation that takes as much from Walter Pater as it does from Matthew Arnold or John Stuart Mill; but both in the end deny their protagonists access to such cultivation. *The Bostonians* represents a liberal cultivation first corrupted by a demagogue and then crushed altogether by a tyrant; *The Princess Casamassima* literalises the democratic liberal premise that the uncultivated poor can be cultivated, only to fold back on itself by assimilating democracy with anarchy and assuming that cultivation on a large scale causes the destruction of culture itself. Even as they recognise the possible value of broadly diffused culture, these novels suggest that such diffusion, in practice, may destroy that which it disseminates, or may suffer the corruption of the market. Still more sharply, they ask whether 'the people' are in fact capable of cultivation and thus of citizenship.

By embodying liberal subjecthood in the flesh of his charismatic learners – a pretty, middling girl of tawdry parents and a brilliant but poor young man – James evokes a transatlantic contemporary conversation about the embodiment of liberal subjecthood in women, working-class men, colonial subjects, and the freedmen of the American South. These are groups variously excluded from the original 'People' of the Preamble to the Constitution, viewed as a teeming unlettered mass, or denied personhood altogether. *The Bostonians* and *The Princess Casamassima* ask whether they might become a part of the elevated 'We' that inaugurates and defines the US: might they practise cultivation and thus become competent democratic liberal citizens? Neither novel answers this question with a confident yes.

The People and the Freedmen

James's parallel revolutionary women share a dual infatuation with asceticism and with 'the people'. Olive Chancellor and the Princess Casamassima are both readily recognisable versions of the 'slumming' lady philanthropist, and a passion for self-denial governs their political commitments. Starving and abusing their aesthetic senses – or, as Olive thinks of it, trying to 'kill that nerve' – is for these women a keenly pleasurable political act. The Princess believes 'that the right way to acquaint one's self with the sensations of the wretched was to suffer the anguish of exasperated taste'. Olive embraces a similar aesthetic masochism: 'her most poignant suffering', we read, 'came from the injury of her taste'.[12]

For mostly selfish reasons, each of these women adopts a young individual whom she perceives as a member of 'the people'. In keeping with the tone and thrust of his comment about 'the people' to Perry, James represents these adoptions and the desires that drive them with heavy irony. Olive, we read, 'had long been preoccupied with the romance of the people. She had an immense desire to know intimately some *very* poor girl' (32). Her relationship with Verena Tarrant realises this fantasy: for Olive, James writes, the girl's vulgar past has 'the merit of having initiated Verena (and her patroness, through her agency) into the miseries and mysteries of the People'. Savouring the lowness of Verena's father's birth 'in some unheard-of place in Pennsylvania', Olive views the girl as 'a flower of the great Democracy' and relishes the deprivations involved in such a blossoming: 'She liked to think that Verena, in her childhood, had known almost the extremity of poverty, and there was a kind of ferocity in the joy with which she reflected that there had been moments when this delicate creature came near (if the pinch had only lasted a little longer) to literally going without food' (98).

Similar desires shape the Princess Casamassima's fascination with Hyacinth Robinson: 'she wanted to know the *people*, and know them intimately – the toilers and strugglers and sufferers – because she was convinced they were the most interesting portion of society' (175). Like *The Bostonians*, *The Princess Casamassima* treats these desires with irony, but its attack on the concept of 'the people' hits still more directly. The polyglot, cross-class, cosmopolite cast of the novel provides occasion for a critique via comedic misunderstandings. When Lady Aurora makes passing reference to 'the people', Hyacinth asks, 'What people do you mean?' She answers, 'Oh, the upper class, the people that have got all the things', to which he replies: 'We don't call them the people' (80). Later, in explaining the wishes of the Princess to her estranged husband, Madame Grandoni states, 'It is the common people that please her . . . It is the lower orders, the *basso popolo*.' Amazed, he replies, 'The *basso popolo*?' Madame Grandoni clarifies: 'The *povera gente*.' He presses: 'The London mob – the most horrible, the most brutal – ?' (167). It is Mr Vetch, finally, who gives voice to the sentiment that James himself expresses in his letter to Perry. He says to the Princess, 'The people – the people? That is a vague term.' When she elaborates, 'those who are underneath every one, every thing, and have the whole social mass crushing them', he objects: 'The way certain classes arrogate to themselves the title of the people has never pleased me. Why are some human beings the people, and the people only, and others not?' (368).

The periodicals in which these ironic treatments of 'the people' initially appear see education or cultivation as the means by which an unreflective, gullible common folk can become a body of competent citizens. James's ironic treatment of this category calls the possibility of that transformation into question, and his representations of Verena and Hyacinth do the same. In novels that conspicuously deploy naturalist tactics, these adoptees disrupt the naturalist logic of determinism by displaying exceptional characteristics that are not predicted in simple ways by their respective heredities and environments. The inexplicability and unpredictability of their capacities put pressure on the democratic liberal ideal that posits widespread educability. The cultivations of these young learners plucked from 'the people' differ considerably from each other, but neither ends well.

When *The Bostonians* was first published in *The Century*, its representation of liberal cultivation appeared alongside closely related subject matter. During the months of the novel's serialisation, the magazine hosted a controversial debate initiated by George Washington Cable's 'The Freedman's Case in Equity'.[13] Starting a month before the novel's serialisation began and continuing until shortly before its conclusion, this sequence of articles participated in *The Century*'s larger project of sectional reconciliation, which also included its massive Civil War retrospective and a good deal of plantation-myth fiction. The magazine thus intervened in a larger American conversation about what Cable called 'the agonies of reconstruction'; in the course of doing so, it took up questions specifically about the capacity of freedmen to be citizens.[14]

Scholars of US racism identify this debate on the pages of *The Century* as an important event. Ibram X. Kendi sees in Henry Grady's contribution the origins of 'the New South's defense of racial segregation'. David Blight points to the role of the exchange, as well as the Civil War series, in disputes between emancipationist, reconciliationist and white supremacist narratives of national history. Most importantly for our purposes here, Saidiya V. Hartman notes that Cable's 'description of black citizenship as a foreign appendage grafted onto the national body bespeaks the anxieties about amalgamation attendant to the enfranchisement of blacks'. 'The body', she shows, 'was pivotal in representing the transformation of the nation-state and citizenship instituted by the Civil War and Reconstruction.'[15] *The Bostonians* is, among other things, a fiction of impossible embodiment and impossible citizenship. As such, it speaks to this adjacent discussion about the capacity and rights of freedmen, in which Cable's arguments give voice to core principles of liberalism. But, as Barbara Hochman notes in her reading of the novel as serialised, 'James's fiction is especially difficult to reduce to a political message'; in that sense, she suggests, *The Bostonians* upset the 'conventions of discourse for controversial issues: gender, slavery, and national reconciliation'.[16]

Cable, in contrast, is very happy to offer 'a political message'. In 'Freedman's Case', he argues: 'the one thing we cannot afford to tolerate at large is a class of people less than citizens . . . every interest in the land demands that the freedman be free to become . . . the same sort of American citizen he would be if, with the same intellectual and moral caliber, he were white'.[17] A rebuttal from Grady equates desegregation and civil rights with miscegenation. Two months later, Bishop T. U. Dudley examines the view 'that the negro is incapable of development, and that he is utterly incapable of the proper performance of the citizen's duty'; rejecting this view, he asserts, 'the Federal Government which added this great number to our roll of citizens should . . . do all that it may do to help them to the attainment of civic capacity'.[18] He asserts that they are not 'lacking the capacity for development'.[19] 'Capacity is not lacking', he continues, 'but help is needed': 'the superior race' must assist these 'ignorant and untaught neighbors', and protect them from 'demagogues'.[20] Three months after that, Cable's counter-rebuttal to Grady repeats his call for civil rights while decrying miscegenation and disavowing any call for social rights. Letters and editorials extend the discussion, contending, 'we owe the colored man an education . . . we have made him a citizen, and as such he is entitled to an education'; and asserting that 'the negro' was given the franchise 'as a weapon of defense', but 'if the class thus armed be ignorant and poor its weapon will be an inadequate protection'.[21]

On the pages of *The Century*, the 'untaught' Verena's expansion through education stands in a suggestive relation with that of the freedmen discussed by Cable and others, and not just because her 'capacity for development' remains unproven.[22] The analogy between the oppression of women and of enslaved peoples was already commonplace. Verena's chance to develop depends upon her becoming a chattel: Olive essentially buys the girl from her father. Noting that *The Bostonians* comments on 'the function of both the independent-minded New Woman and the politically enfranchised African American in the postbellum imagination', Aaron Shaheen shows that James's representation of Verena includes imagery that marks her as racially other, offering indicators of Irish, Jewish and African–American identity. Shaheen also notes that Olive's project is one of 'uplift' and that her decision to take Verena on a speaking tour replicates 'the white patron/escaped slave narrative'.[23]

James had apparently noticed fiction about the education of freedmen; he wrote approvingly in 1887 of Constance Fenimore Woolson's *Rodman the Keeper* (1880), which includes 'King David', her tale of a New England schoolmaster who attempts, with the aid of the Freedmen's Bureau, to educate a formerly enslaved Black community. Competing against a dispossessed planter and an opportunistic huckster, the schoolmaster fails because his students are too stupid and lazy; they prefer his rivals, who are ready to recognise and exploit that stupidity and laziness. James praises in particular Woolson's 'singularly expert familiarity with the "natural objects" of the region, including the negro of reality'.[24] *The Bostonians* echoes 'King David' in several respects, not least in juxtaposing the 'reality' of a weak student against the ideal of a Yankee educator's hopes.

But Olive is no schoolmaster, and this matters: James's Bostonian conforms to the type of the New England schoolmarm. In portraying Olive, James draws from a foundational antebellum iteration of this type, Harriet Beecher Stowe's Aunt Ophelia. Ophelia's plot is mostly about her frustrated attempts to educate Topsy: initially unteachable, Topsy later becomes a teacher herself. Stowe's narrator reports that Ophelia was 'tall, square-formed, and angular. Her face was thin, and rather sharp in its outlines; the lips compressed, like those of a person who is in the habit of making up her mind definitely on all subjects.' In descriptions of regional character during the nineteenth and early twentieth centuries, Ophelia's habit of inflexible certainty, reflex to educate, commitment to duty over pleasure, and opposition to leisure (which she calls 'shiftlessness') are the defining traits of a 'Puritan' New England mode.[25] James invokes this type again as he writes on Emerson in 1887: he refers to 'old Miss Mary Emerson, our author's aunt', and registers his 'impression that she was a very remarkable specimen of the transatlantic Puritan stock', a 'grim intellectual virgin and daughter of a hundred ministers'.[26]

Ophelia's thin-lipped angularity, like Mary Moody Emerson's grim intellectual virginity, typifies an unsexy New England femininity that is sometimes associated derisively with sentimentalism. But Stowe's sentimental novel distances itself critically from Ophelia's unfeeling educational work; and, as Faye Halpern shows, the 'sentimental orator' in *The Bostonians* is not Olive but Verena.[27] Olive's New England educational project – like Ophelia's – stands adjacent to a sentimental project of persuasion, but is much more stern and bookish. Especially in the aftermath of Reconstruction, this sternly bookish, spinster-driven New England project has specific political associations. As Kenneth W. Warren observes, Ophelia and Olive alike represent a 'New England idealism' that sometimes finds expression in sentimentalism. His analysis exposes affinities between attacks on sentimentalism's political projects and attacks (by realists) on sentimentalism as a kind of writing. Identifying Olive and others as iterations of the New England schoolmarm type, Warren notes that, 'enabled by Stowe's Miss Ophelia . . . male writers throughout this era sketched particularly unflattering portraits of those New England women driven by principle'.[28]

And indeed, the work of the Freedmen's Bureau prompts many accounts of angular women from New England who travel south to educate. Ronald E. Butchart describes the standard representation of this type (which, he shows, has little basis in fact): 'The teachers were young, single, white women from New England, of evangelical Protestant roots and abolitionist convictions' and 'they were endowed with particular regional character traits of New Englanders whose interpretation shifted depending on the standpoint of the viewer'. 'Southern historians', Butchart notes, 'portrayed them as fanatical meddlers at worst, foolish idealists at best.' They also made them definitively unattractive: as one such Southern writer puts it, these women were 'horsefaced, bespectacled, and spare of frame'.[29]

Others portray this type more reverently. In the *Atlantic* essays that later become part of *Souls of Black Folk*, Du Bois (a New Englander himself) refers to 'the gift of New England to the freed Negro' and describes in affectionate terms the 'saintly souls' of 'the crusade of the New England schoolma'am', or 'the crusade of the sixties, that finest thing in American history'. As Butchart observes, Du Bois portrays these women as 'selfless and noble'.[30] *The Bostonians*'s rendering of the New England schoolmarm type does not endow her with those qualities; Olive more consistently manifests the grim unattractiveness and wrongheaded, fanatical idealism imagined by Confederate apologists. As Warren notes, *The Bostonians* participates in a larger 'convergence of Northern realistic and Southern racist critiques of the female reformer, who as abolitionist, critic, author, New England school marm, or feminist suffragist endeavoured, sometimes hypocritically, to impose upon society a set of "impractical" moral values'.[31]

On the pages of *The Century* during *The Bostonians*'s serialisation, references to cultivation and educative democracy extend beyond the freedmen debate to articles that advocate Mugwump causes and liberal aims more broadly. An editorial declares that an election should be 'a time when the whole people shall receive, in candid and fair debate, some sound political education; a spectacle in which the reason and conscience of the people shall be . . . evidently exalted and honored'.[32] Charles William Eliot (then almost halfway through his forty-year term as President of Harvard) explains the nature and purposes of a 'liberal education'.[33] In an article titled 'The Education of the People', scholar Charles Waldstein (whom Norton would shortly recruit to be Director of the American School of Classical Studies in Athens), writes on the 'democratic spirit' in art and quotes George Washington: 'in proportion as the structure of government gives force to public opinion . . . it is essential that public opinion be enlightened'; 'popular government', Waldstein continues, must 'foster and cultivate . . . among the people' the 'democratic pleasures of art'.[34] An editorial comments approvingly on this piece, noting that 'the prime necessity is that we should go earnestly and systematically to work to inspire, to develop, to guide and clarify the taste of the people'.[35] These incidental local instances of liberal discourse should remind us of the larger and less immediately evident discursive context in which the novel was written and read in the 1880s. Reading *The Bostonians* in the pages of *The Century* reminds us that the novel stages a cultivation of a member of 'the people' at a moment when such cultivations are of pressing contemporary interest, and helps us to attend to the ways that James engages with liberal ideas and arguments present elsewhere in the magazine.

Most obviously, the *Century*'s recommendation that 'the people' be cultivated 'earnestly and systematically' finds an echo in Olive's all too earnest and systematic efforts to educate Verena. Early in *The Bostonians*, Olive is struck by the extent to which Verena remains 'untaught' (103). The girl's subsequent education and 'development' drive the novel's plot. Olive tells Basil that Verena 'has developed greatly', and Verena's father believes Olive will 'help her to develop'; Olive assures him that 'Verena's development was the thing in the world in which she took most interest; she should have every opportunity for a free expansion' (223, 146). But James questions exactly how free this expansion might be. The novel repeatedly figures Verena as an empty vessel ready to be filled. Of her speech about 'equality', Basil reflects 'she had been stuffed with this trash by her father', apparently understanding that her vacant mind can be 'stuffed' with whatever the most powerful person around her pleases. For Basil and Olive, this blank emptiness is enchanting, but James's narrator notes that such emptiness might also be seen as 'a singular hollowness of character' (55). This unusually receptive, exceptionally teachable hollowness serves as the basis for the novel's critique of certain liberal ideals. Each of the rivals for ownership of Verena – Olive, Basil Ransom and Henry Burrage – tries to be responsible for some sort of education for her. Their efforts evoke a contemporary conversation about the capacity of 'the people' for learning and thus for democratic citizenship. The novel's love plot thus stages the ongoing debate between, on the one hand, the liberalisms of Mill and Emerson and, on the other hand, the illiberalism of Carlyle.

The Schoolmarm and the Southerner

Readings of *The Bostonians* in the context of its serialisation have often worked with the standard negative twentieth-century account of 'the genteel', understanding *The Century*'s educational aims as a false front for a project that is actually disciplinary. Mark J. Noonan thus identifies Basil as the force for the 'genteel' in the text, noting that his magazine work 'may be usefully viewed as mimicking the project of "cultural containment" pursued by the leading genteel editors and realist writers of the day'.[36] But it seems odd that James would represent a group notoriously centred in Northern East-Coast cities in his Mississippian rather than his Bostonian. If we regard the work of the men associated with the genteel as an educative project of cultivation rather than a project of social control, we can locate the novel's mockery of those men more logically in its New Englander rather than its Southerner. James's representation of liberal education is indeed critical, but *The Bostonians* specifically resists an elision between Olive's controlling practices and Basil's. The novel's juxtaposition of these two suitors in fact works hard to differentiate between their respective oppressions of Verena, and thus points to a crucial moral distinction between the bodies of thought they represent. This reading may seem crudely allegorical, but James's portraits of these suitors define their political and intellectual affiliations quite overtly.

The novel links Olive with Boston liberalism's aims, vocabulary and institutions. In addition to embodying the New England schoolmarm type, she professes an eager optimism that echoes Emerson's calls for education that emancipates the individual; the centrality of education in her feminism matches Mill's similar emphasis in *Subjection of Women*.[37] The novel sets her amongst the institutions of a liberal, Unitarian Boston that embody its commitment to the ideals of cultivation, civic participation, and the triumph of democracy in Union victory: the Athenaeum, the Music Hall, Harvard and Harvard's Memorial Hall. In her deft account of the role of the 'Puritan', Unitarian, Bostonian type throughout James's œuvre, Laurel Bollinger notes of *The Bostonians*: 'that so much of the book describes Olive's individualized research and study – shared with Verena, but with Olive as a teacher – suggests a focus on self-improvement and scholarship typical of Unitarians'.[38]

Olive's stated aims for Verena resemble those of a liberal education that seeks to cultivate an independent thinker capable of using her voice in the public sphere and critically assessing a potentially demagogic popular press: when thinking to herself that the newspaper man Matthias Pardon 'wasn't half educated', Olive comforts herself with the reflection 'that an educative process was now going on for Verena (under her own direction), which would enable her to make such a discovery for herself' (111). Olive seeks to 'train and polish' the girl's remarkable 'qualities', and is 'constantly reminding Verena that this winter was to be purely educative' (103, 102, 156). When Verena announces brightly, 'I don't know German; I should like so to study it; I want to know everything,' Olive replies: 'We will work at it together – we will study everything' (77). And so they do: 'They threw themselves into study; they had innumerable big books from the Athenaeum, and consumed the midnight oil' (151–2).

The rejection of pleasure that characterises Bostonians throughout James's œuvre manifests explicitly in Olive's educational project, which is inseparable from her asceticism. What Verena learns in German is *Faust*, and Olive declaims for her, '*Entsagen sollst du, sollst entsagen!*', offering Bayard Taylor's translation: 'Thou shalt renounce, refrain, abstain!' As Daniel Karlin notes, Olive gets both quotations slightly wrong, and 'the effect of both misquotations is to give priority to "renounce"' (77, 432). Observing the 'culture' that packs Olive's parlour, Basil notes especially her 'German books', seeing in them evidence of 'the natural energy of Northerners'. Olive herself feels that reading Goethe of a winter evening is 'the highest indulgence she could offer herself' (17, 77).

Olive understands her task as a teacher to be awakening potential that lies dormant: she believes in the 'native refinement' of Verena and other American women, or 'their latent "adaptability"' and thrills at 'the way her companion rose with the level of the civilisation that surrounded her, the way she assimilated all delicacies and absorbed all traditions' (153–4). This mention of education as a path to 'civilisation' points to the larger liberal project manifest not just in the extension of the franchise but also in imperialism. Liberal imperialism is a useful reference point here, for Olive's liberal educative project oppresses even as it sees itself triumphantly emancipate.

Olive presumes to liberate and empower Verena through education, but her actual instruction is in fact a travesty of that liberal ideal: this education serves to shut down independent thought rather than foster it. In her 'strenuous parlour', reading is not about cultivating the capacity for open-minded reflection, but about 'facts and figures' and indoctrination (156, 128). The women read history with the aim of 'finding confirmation in it for this idea that their sex had suffered inexpressibly' (155). This is not autonomous self-development but a rigidly controlled force-feeding, a small-minded quest to confirm pre-existing belief. Art, like history, is bent gruesomely to serve Olive's narrow agenda: when the women go to concerts at the Music Hall, 'Bach and Beethoven only repeated, in myriad forms, the idea that was always with them. Symphonies and fugues only stimulated their convictions, excited their revolutionary passion, led their imagination further in the direction in which it was always pressing' (157). James presents a nightmarish perversion of the ideal of liberal cultivation: rather than fostering self-development, these great works of art only press the women further back into their crunched and benighted corner.

This 'educative process' in fact seeks merely to make Verena the mouthpiece for Olive's 'mission'. We can recall Basil's sense upon meeting Verena that she has been 'stuffed' with content when the girl says to him: 'She tells me what to say – the real things, the strong things. It's Miss Chancellor as much as me!' (55, 198). Olive, we read, 'poured forth these views to her listening and responsive friend; she presented them again and again . . . Verena was immensely wrought upon; a subtle fire passed into her; she was not so hungry for revenge as Olive, but at the last . . . she quite agreed with her companion . . . men must take *their* turn, men must pay!'

(161). Although Verena states that 'it was very different from the old system, where her father had worked her up', we may reflect that in fact the process by which Verena was 'stuffed' seems all too similar to the process by which 'a subtle fire passed into her' (343). Both the 'old system' and the new one depend upon Verena being a 'hollow' vessel which, once filled, will sing out the views of the person who happens to master her at the moment. As a subject for liberal cultivation, Verena is a miserable failure; and as the author of that failure, Olive is an accidental demagogue, or perhaps an accidental tyrant. She undertakes with Emersonian confidence the project imagined by Mill's *Subjection of Women*: using education to form an independent-minded liberal subject in female flesh. But her narrow perspective and domineering tendencies mean that her educative process controls rather than emancipates.

In representing the competition between Olive and Basil, the novel juxtaposes this accidental tyranny with a tyranny that is quite deliberate. While Olive attempts to be democratic and emancipatory and fails, Basil dismisses democracy and emancipation altogether: he believes Verena's capacities are naturally limited, and so seeks to master rather than to emancipate her. The battle of these suitors stages in the text a debate between two perspectives on human perfectibility and thus on democracy. While Olive espouses the ideas of liberal thinkers, Basil, we read, 'was an immense admirer of the late Thomas Carlyle, and was very suspicious of the encroachments of modern democracy' (169). More specifically, the antagonism between Olive the Northerner and Basil the Southerner reproduces in the pages of *The Bostonians* the argument between Mill and Carlyle about 'the negro question' and the American Civil War. Their 'sharp debate about black capacity', Butler notes, 'staked out two competing visions about difference and human potential that would continue to clash throughout the century'.[39] As Catherine Hall observes, 'Mill's imagined community was one of potential equality' in which 'a process of civilization' would allow blacks to gain membership, while 'Carlyle's imagined community was a hierarchically ordered one' in which whites ruled.[40]

When it is Basil's turn to 'educate' Verena, he does not do so by means of print; rather, he talks to her. This medium is consistent with the political stance that he thus communicates, which is not a stance that endorses any sort of literate citizenry: 'he thought the spread of education a gigantic farce . . . You had a right to an education only if you had an intelligence, and if you looked at the matter with any desire to see things as they are you soon perceived that an intelligence was a very rare luxury, the attribute of one person in a hundred' (286). After Basil holds forth, we read about his lesson's effect on Verena: 'these words, the most effective and penetrating he had uttered, had sunk into her soul and worked and fermented there. She had come at last to believe them' (336). Just as Olive's words earlier 'passed into her', Basil's words succeed at 'penetrating': Verena, we gather, has been 'stuffed' once again.

Basil's speech takes place in Central Park, and the unintelligent populace of his political imagination appears on the scene as if on cue: James's cityscape includes 'groups of the unemployed, the children of disappointment from beyond the seas' (296). Sara Blair's reading of this passage reminds us that Central Park, designed by Frederick Law Olmstead (a friend of Norton's) to foster taste and decorum, was 'an important site for testing claims about the character of the American mass public'; she shows that Basil sees only 'rabble' when he looks at a crowd.[41] This perception of the mass as a potentially dangerous throng totally unsuited for the responsibilities of citizenship is part of Basil's larger political perspective, which declares that persons like Verena need to be mastered and silenced, rather than cultivated and given the opportunity to speak.

The views starkly represented by Olive and Basil recall James's comparison of Emerson and Carlyle in his review for *The Century* of Norton's 1883 edition of the correspondence between these two friends. Noting the contrast between Emerson the 'optimist' and Carlyle the 'pessimist of pessimists', James observes that these differing perspectives translate into opposed political stances.[42] He notes Emerson's 'eminently gentle spirit, his almost touching tolerance, his deference toward every sort of human manifestation . . . his extreme consideration for that blundering human family whom he believed to be in want of light'.[43] James sees this hopeful, generous attitude towards humans as both a symptom of and a force for democracy, and contrasts it against the antidemocratic implications of Carlyle's pessimism. In its emphasis on this juxtaposition, James's review closely echoes Norton's own comments in his letters and journals of the 1870s and 1880s.[44]

Affirming the contrast that Norton sees in his two eminent friends, James illustrates it by describing their respective attitudes towards the speaking voice. Of Emerson, James writes: 'no one maintained a more hospitable attitude than his toward anything that any one might have to say. There was no presumption against even the humblest, and the ear of the universe was open to any articulate voice'; but Carlyle's pessimism tunes his ear differently. Having quoted

Carlyle's comment that 'Man, all men, seem radically dumb, jabbering mere jargons and noises,' James explains:

> The great Scotchman thought *all* talk a jabbering of apes; whereas Emerson, who was the perfection of a listener, stood always in a posture of hopeful expectancy and regarded each delivery of a personal view as a new fact, to be estimated on its merits. In a genuine democracy all things are democratic; and this spirit of general deference ... was the natural product of a society in which it was held that every one was equal to every one else. It was as natural on the other side that Carlyle's philosophy should have aristocratic premises, and that he should call aloud for that imperial master, of the necessity for whom the New England mind was so serenely unconscious.[45]

James thus portrays the contrast between Emerson and Carlyle, and between their attitudes towards democracy, by describing their attitudes towards the voices of speaking people. This attention to voice and speaking carries through into *The Bostonians*: the novel extends the review's commentary on the opposed perspectives of these two thinkers. Verena performs her capacity as a learner by bringing her voice into the public sphere, and the silencing of her voice in that realm ultimately marks the victory of Basil as her 'imperial master'. Olive's eagerness to hear Verena speak, in contrast, replicates Emerson's 'hopeful expectancy' before all human speakers.

But James's critical portrayal of Bostonian liberalism suggests that, in spite of her receptivity to Verena's voice, Olive in fact wants Verena to say quite specific things: this 'New England mind', intoxicated with Emersonian optimism about human possibility, is itself much more of an 'imperial master" than it means to be. In making Olive a figure that mocks the Bostonian liberalism that would later fall under the dread rubric 'genteel', *The Bostonians* offers a critical portrait of this movement that differs from the narrative associated with that term in much twentieth-century scholarship. The novel does not portray elite disciplinarians strategically deploying the ruse of culture in order to retain their grip on power. In *The Bostonians*, it is Basil the Carlylean who manifests that kind of disciplinary force in the text, and he does so without any ruses at all.

In Olive, James depicts something far more embattled and pathetic: a shy, unlikeable spinster who craves from 'the People' not obedience but 'a union of soul', and who – all too earnestly, and spectacularly ineffectively – uses education to work towards that aim (98, 71). James's language notably anticipates Du Bois's comment that what the 'saintly' teachers of Reconstruction offered their students 'was the contact of living souls'.[46] Du Bois praises that educational project; James represents Olive's as a failure. But Olive's failure, when it comes, is the failure of a spurned lover, not a deposed disciplinarian. A demagogue in spite of herself, she labours to offer an education that actually isn't one, and loses 'the people' when they succumb to the more potent charms of a master who prefers to keep them silent.

Rather than conflating Verena's oppression under Olive's accidental tyranny with her oppression under Basil's deliberate one, the novel's juxtaposition of these two suitors points to the difference between them. Basil's tyranny, it seems, will be a brutal one. Along with his forceful capture of Verena at the novel's conclusion, there is the troubling turn when he thinks to himself that 'if he should become her husband he should know a way to strike her dumb' (280). Paradoxically, *The Bostonians* both affirms that Verena is probably incapable of liberal cultivation and, at the same time, deplores the cruelty of denying her access to that cultivation. With notable acuity, James associates that denial both here and in *The Princess Casamassima* with physical violence: the denial of access to cultivation is the denial of liberal subjecthood, which is the denial of status as a citizen, which in turn gives licence to blows or bullets. In this plot about the Millian experiment of forming a liberal subject in female flesh, James suggests that flesh without the status of a liberal subject may be fundamentally unsafe. *The Bostonians* recoils at the moral obscenity of that danger even as it represents Verena's incompetence as a liberal subject.

That incompetence is a crucial element of the novel's political statement. Verena's pliant vapidity serves to criticise the democratic principles of 'a society in which it was held that every one was equal to every one else'.[47] The novel resists those principles by suggesting that the quality of one speaker's 'personal view' may be much greater than another, and that the speaking of the people may indeed be, as Basil believes, 'a jabbering of apes'.[48] But James's endorsement of Basil's views is not unqualified, nor is his response to Carlyle a simple affirmation of his ideas. *The Bostonians* affirms Carlyle's (and Basil's) sense that the people are jabbering apes, but it stops far short of affirming his view that they should therefore be mastered forcibly rather than offered a real chance at free expansion. The book endorses Carlyle's sense of the stupidity of the people, but it abhors the brutality implicit in his consequent recommendation of 'imperial mastery'.

This mixed statement speaks to a larger conversation in which other interlocutors express themselves with far less ambivalence. In making a member of 'the people' an unpromising student and thus an unpromising citizen, James makes moves characteristic of the antidemocratic realist critique of New England idealism that positions itself explicitly against Emerson's optimism and Unitarianism's faith in human perfectibility. He makes that sort of move again in an 1887 article that points to Emerson's 'ripe unconsciousness of evil'.[49] Such an unconsciousness figures prominently in the work of Wendell and Babbitt as they describe the fatal errors of Boston liberalism. Disparaging a Unitarian optimism about the capacity of the people to develop and be functional democratic citizens, Wendell admires instead the Calvinism that knows humans are generally depraved. James does not favour the sort of reactionary politics that Wendell does, but his writing about the capacity of the people shares key assumptions with Wendell's. As Bollinger observes, the 'positive view of human nature, quite unlike the Calvinist emphasis on innate human depravity, becomes the central point in [James's] treatment of Unitarianism, which . . . he tends to characterize as naïveté'.[50] James, like Wendell, attributes that naïveté to a New England idealism that worships education and democracy because it misperceives the people.

The Happier Few and the Miserable Many

Along with Unitarian naïveté, a key trait of James's New Englanders is their aversion to pleasure. They manifest the *'strictness of conscience'* that Arnold identifies as Hebraism; against their Bostonian asceticism, rigidity and obsession with moral duty, James pleads for something more like the *'spontaneity of conscience'* that belongs to Hellenism.[51] While Boston liberals like Norton and his cousin President Eliot find in Arnold's work the script for a rigorous practice of self-development and a lifelong effort to see things steadily and whole, James (like Wharton) tends to draw other lessons from Arnold: a posture of critical detachment, a practice of play, a sense that true culture depends on ease and leisure rather than narrowly dogged work. For Norton and Eliot, Arnold's ideas feed into a project of realising democratic ideals through education; for James and Wharton, those ideas have less democratic uses.

For Norton, Arnold's 'civilisation' refers usefully to an ongoing project of individual and national development; for James, however, 'civilisation' usually denotes a vast, corrupt, shadowy, gorgeous and vitally sustaining edifice fashioned over many centuries at an enormous cost of blood and suffering. In *The Bostonians*, and even more explicitly in *The Princess Casamassima*, James suggests – not without a cringe – that such a cost might be justified: the suffering of the many yields something worthwhile, which, regrettably, mostly just the few get to enjoy. Norton is preoccupied with the many, and his practice of culture is explicitly moral and political; James inclines towards a practice of culture that is more oblivious to explicitly political questions. His frameworks for thinking tend to emphasise not the public and the political but instead the private, personal or sensuously immediate. In this divergence between Norton and James, a thinker who offers the latter abundant resources is Walter Pater. Along with a Hellenic emphasis on the value of easy play, Pater's vocabulary of pleasure helps James express resistance to Norton's account of culture and civilisation.

The Bostonians suggests that Olive's politically motivated wish to forgo the enjoyment of art and pleasure is a sign of her inveterate wrongness. The Princess's analogous asceticism in *The Princess Casamassima* serves a similar function. Just as *The Bostonians* exposes the futility of Olive's belligerent suspicion of such pleasures, *The Princess Casamassima* ridicules the Princess's 'ascetic pretensions' (324). When we read the two novels together, we can see that the world of the New York Burrages in *The Bostonians* resembles the terrain on which Hyacinth takes in the rich experience that constitutes his cultivation in *The Princess Casamassima*. James describes both of these worlds in a Paterian idiom that emphasises variety and intensity of pleasure. The novels' play with Paterian ideas forms an important component of their engagement with Bostonian liberalism. That liberalism values self-development through the experience of art; so too do these novels – but they make such experience distinctly Paterian, thus departing from the accounts of self-development favoured by thinkers like Norton.

In both novels, it is this Paterian mode of cultivation that actually seems to achieve the aims of the liberal ideal. The liberal cultivation that the novel stages for Hyacinth is one that gives his acute sensibilities unprecedented access to the treasures of art and civilisation. At the Princess's rented country house, he is exposed to pleasures the like of which he has never met before: parks and gardens, Italian cuisine, a library full of old books, the music played by the Princess herself on the piano. This stay offers Hyacinth an 'exquisite experience', one in which 'novelty' and 'civilisation' work to change his views (245). Then he travels to the great cities of the Continent, where he lives 'intensely' and enjoys 'a rich experience', soaking up art, architecture and the vivid life on the streets of Paris and Venice

(296, 311). Like Verena's, Hyacinth's education includes reading; but while Verena, under Olive's direction, selectively mines histories for evidence of female suffering, Hyacinth chooses his own books and sinks deep into fiction, including the latest French novels. The ascetic Olive, in contrast, with her *Faust* and her 'German books', despises 'the writing of the French' (17, 77). Verena's reading is meant to educate by filling her with facts; Hyacinth's educates by giving him the experience of good literary art. Over the course of the novel, the experience through which he develops is described with a Paterian emphasis on maximised, varied sensation: in Paris, we read, 'he had seen so much, felt so much, learned so much, thrilled and throbbed and laughed and sighed so much' (292).

Hyacinth's cultivation helps us to see Verena's analogous learning more clearly. In the company of the Harvard law student Henry Burrage and his wealthy New York family, she has the opportunity to taste moments of self-development through the experience of culture; faintly, we see the spectre of a cultivated Verena that might have been. In the Burrages' New York, Verena feels, there is 'something in the air that carried one along, and a sense of vastness and variety, of the infinite possibilities of a great city, which . . . might in the end make up for the want of the Boston earnestness' (254–5). She tells Olive of 'the beauty of the park, the splendour and interest of the Museum, the wonder of the young man's acquaintance with everything it contained, the swiftness of his horses, the softness of his English cart, the pleasure of rolling at that pace over roads as firm as marble, the entertainment he promised them for the evening' – this entertainment including dinner at Delmonico's and a trip to see *Lohengrin*, about which Verena also raves, speaking 'of Wagner's music, of the singers, the orchestra, the immensity of the house, her tremendous pleasure'. Olive observes anxiously Verena's liking for New York, 'where that kind of pleasure was so much more in the air' (251, 261). The 'great city' full of pleasure stands in stark contrast to the Boston full of 'earnestness', and aligns itself with the Continental urban sites where Hyacinth practises cultivation.

Blair finds the aesthete Burrage 'an obviously insufficient figure, performing the rites of taste with the effect of narrowing, rather than enlarging, the boundaries of culture', and associates him with the toxic aestheticism of Gilbert Osmond in *Portrait of a Lady*.[52] But this reading of Burrage tends to take the paranoid and biased impressions of Olive as objective, disregarding the ways that the text distances itself from her perspective. It is Olive, not the narrator, who imagines the young man as 'this glittering, laughing Burrage youth, with his chains and rings and shining shoes' and places him in the category of 'young men in search of sensations' (107, 108). For Olive, that category is a terrifying one; but the novel does not share her views on this conspicuously Paterian group, nor does it endorse her rejection of the pleasures they would embrace. The aesthete in *Portrait* who anticipates Burrage is not Osmond, but Ned Rosier. Indeed, Burrage and Rosier both love their girls just as they love their fragile collectibles: Rosier sees Pansy as a 'consummate piece' and thinks of her as he would 'a Dresden-china shepherdess', savouring her 'hint of the rococo'; Burrage tells Verena 'that he liked her for the same reason that he liked old enamels and old embroideries . . . because she was so peculiar and so delicate' (131).[53] In the thwarted pairings of these benign aesthetes and their girls, James seems to suggest that pleasant, stupid people should marry each other.

Like his New York milieu, Burrage's Cambridge rooms are a site for cultivation. Burrage is, like the Princess, a collector of *bibelots* and a pianist; when Olive and Verena visit his carefully decorated rooms and hear him play, the text presents a Paterian sensuality that affirms pleasure as a legitimate source of moral, intellectual and aesthetic learning. Olive eases involuntarily into peace:

> There was a moment when she came near being happy . . . Olive was extremely susceptible to music, and it was impossible to her not to be soothed and beguiled by the young man's charming art [. . .] It was given to Olive, under these circumstances . . . to surrender herself, to enjoy the music, to admit that Mr. Burrage played with exquisite taste, to feel as if the situation were a kind of truce. Her nerves were calmed, her problems – for the time – subsided. Civilisation, under such an influence, in such a setting, appeared to have done its work; harmony ruled the scene; human life ceased to be a battle. She went so far as to ask herself why one should have a quarrel with it; the relations of men and women, in that picturesque grouping, had not the air of being internecine. In short, she had an interval of unexpected rest . . . (135–6)

Blair sees James presenting the 'harmony' of 'civilisation' available in Burrage's *bibelot*-strewn, music-filled rooms as an undesirable thing, 'from which the rough and tumble of contemporary social life, its contest over the forms of culture, are shut out'.[54] But the text in fact presents this 'harmony' as a very desirable thing indeed; and the novel has repeatedly suggested that the radicalism and asceticism from which Olive lapses here are both wrongheaded and selfishly motivated.

The pleasurable world of the Burrages is the only place where Verena ever shows any signs of competence as a liberal subject: there alone does she show a flash of reflective intelligence and dare to question the dogma of her teacher. Having spent some time with Burrage, Verena goes 'so far as to ask Olive whether taste and art were not something' (132). After the musical gathering in his rooms, she goes even farther:

> It would be very nice to do that always – just to take men as they are, and not to have to think about their badness. It would be very nice not to have so many questions, but to think they were all comfortably answered, so that one could sit there on an old Spanish leather chair, with the curtains drawn and keeping out the cold, the darkness, all the big, terrible, cruel world – sit there and listen for ever to Schubert and Mendelssohn. *They* didn't care anything about female suffrage! And I didn't feel the want of a vote to-day at all, did you? [. . .] Do you know, Olive, I sometimes wonder whether, if it wasn't for you, I should feel it so very much! (137)

Although Verena dismisses the reflective practice that drives liberal cultivation, her musing in fact constitutes exactly the kind of questioning that is central to the habits of liberal subjecthood: her expressed desire to avoid questioning is itself a question pointedly directed at the 'mission' of her mentor. When she considers what her beliefs would be 'if it wasn't for you', she thinks independently. In the course of her dalliance with independent thought, Verena describes a warm, well-furnished, curtained-off zone that, in accordance with Blair's account, excludes 'the rough and tumble of contemporary social life'; and in daring here to say she would like to reside within that pleasant realm 'for ever', she expresses views that the novel seems to endorse: 'badness' is not the first thing to note about every man, and 'taste and art' are indeed 'something'. In New York, the experience of pleasure once again prompts Verena to take an unusually critical perspective on her teacher: 'Olive's earnestness began to appear as inharmonious with the scheme of the universe as if it had been a broken saw' (260). When she has the chance to sense the 'harmony' of 'civilisation' in Burrage's Cambridge rooms and his luxurious New York world, Verena begins to perceive the ugly dissonance of Olive's 'Boston earnestness' (135, 255).

Whereas the easy culture in Burrage's rooms readily offers itself up for pleasure, the culture of Olive's home unconvincingly insists upon duty as the justification for any sensory gratification it may offer.

But it often seems not to offer any such gratification, and instead just dryly manifests a crusty sort of social prestige. Olive's Charles Street house gives the novel occasion to dwell critically on the word 'culture' and its variants. Olive feels that she and Verena 'owed it to themselves, owed it to the groaning sisterhood, to cultivate the best material conditions' because of their 'high intellectual and moral work' (153). Though she takes Verena's education as a justification for luxury, Olive's 'cultivate' here applies not to the girl's mind but to expensive domestic tangibles. For her, the sin of fine 'material conditions' becomes permissible only because education is happening; the novel itself, however, suggests that such materiality is the surest basis for any real education. Olive's unconvincing moral arithmetic is both hypocritical and mistaken.

The novel's account of Basil's visit to Charles Street exposes these contradictions. As Basil enters the room, we read that 'the artistic sense in Basil Ransom had not been highly cultivated'; he notes an abundance of 'upholstery' and 'accessories' along with those 'German books', and finds the space distinctly Bostonian. James's irony singes: Basil 'had always heard Boston was a city of culture, and now there was culture in Miss Chancellor's tables and sofas, in the books that were everywhere, on little shelves like brackets (as if a book were a statuette), in the photographs and water-colours that covered the walls, in the curtains that were festooned rather stiffly in the doorways' (16–17). The visiting Southerner, we read, is 'conscious at bottom of a bigger stomach than all the culture of Charles Street could fill' (18). James's text in the pages of *The Century* refers to 'the "culture" of Charles Street', while the text revised for book publication omits those quotation marks.[55] His edit registers a sensitivity to the charged instability of 'culture'. Basil's response suggests that, in addition to the false culture that inheres in domestic commodities, there is a another, truer sort of culture for which one simply feels a yearning in the gut. Even as James assails the Bostonian practice of culture in his portrayal of Olive, her parlour and her educative processes, he allows for a culture so real it elicits instinctive hunger. And indeed, Verena's rejection of Olive's masochistic asceticism, like Hyacinth's rejection of the Princess's, is a victory for the truer culture that consists in savouring the pleasures of art and civilisation – including the sensuous pleasures of the body and, quite specifically, eating. The urban educations of Verena and Hyacinth both feature delicious food.

The pleasures of food and art figure importantly in Hyacinth's rejection of the Princess's views. After he has savoured his experience abroad, he learns that the Princess has sold off her *bibelots*: 'When thousands and tens of thousands haven't bread to put in their mouths, I can dispense with tapestry and old china,' she announces, asserting that 'the world will be beautiful enough when it becomes good enough' (322–3). Hyacinth disagrees: 'I think there can't be too many pictures and statues and works of art . . . The more the better, whether people are hungry or not. In the way of ameliorating influences, are not those the most definite?' (323). This is not quite 'let them eat *bibelots*', but it is close. Expressing his regret that the Princess has sold off her 'beautiful things' in order to 'give to the poor', Hyacinth suggests that art matters more than bread for the hungry (326).

Burrage too collects 'beautiful things'; *The Bostonians* mocks his apparent need to possess 'a great many' of them, but also suggests that his philosophy of wanting to 'enjoy life', and his zealous practice of creating for himself 'a life . . . so crowded with beauty' are far more rewarding than Olive's conflicted policy of self-abnegation (130–1). In making a more articulate case for the value of 'beautiful things' than the cheerfully unintelligent Burrage possibly could, Hyacinth makes an argument that opposes the Bostonian's beliefs as well as those of his own radical mentor. Verena's rejection of Olive parallels his rejection of the Princess: in both cases, the easy, sensuous experience of art and culture prompts the young person to think independently.

Hyacinth announces his opposition to the Princess in a letter, writing that in his travels he has seen 'want and toil and suffering' of the people, and yet he has not 'minded them': instead, he has been struck by 'the splendid accumulations of the happier few, to which, doubtless, the miserable many have also in their degree contributed'. Hyacinth describes

> the monuments and treasures of art, the great palaces and properties, the conquests of learning and taste, the general fabric of civilisation as we know it, based, if you will, upon all the despotisms, the cruelties, the exclusions, the monopolies and the rapacities of the past, but thanks to which, all the same, the world is less impracticable and life more tolerable. (306–7)

As in Burrage's rooms, here in Hyacinth's epistolary manifesto the pleasures of 'civilisation' and its art surpass in importance the misery that is also part of it. Hyacinth tells the Princess that his rich experience has 'demoralised' him (307). After their visit to Burrage, Olive feels that 'they were both (Verena and she) quite demoralised' (136). Hyacinth discovers that, in Paris, 'he had grown more relaxed' and that this 'relaxation' discourages his pursuit of revolution (295). As she listens to Burrage, Olive grows 'calmed', finds 'rest' and questions her radical cause (135–6). This relaxed demoralisation, with its emphasis on pleasure, stands in stark contrast to the 'strenuous' and quite intensely moralising practices of the Bostonian educative process.[56] While the Princess and Olive stifle their sensibilities and reject aesthetic and sensory pleasures in favour of their revolutionary causes, Hyacinth rejects the revolutionary cause, accepts civilisation, and celebrates his throbbing sensibility as well as the art it savours.

In making a Paterian embrace of pleasure the criterion for successful liberal cultivation in the novels of 1886, James needles the Bostonian liberalism that Olive represents. When *The Bostonians* associates Burrage with 'young men in search of sensations' at Harvard, it subtly evokes friction between Norton's Ruskinian aestheticism and a newer Paterian aestheticism (108). Burrage attends the Law School, not the College, and his story takes place in the late 1870s – but it is worth noting that at the time of the novel's publication a Harvard student who was an aesthete would almost certainly have been attending Norton's enormously popular art history lectures, in spite of Norton's resistance to the Paterian ideas that those students found so thrilling.[57] That Burrage's Cambridge rooms are an important site of cultivation for Verena takes on new significance when we consider that Norton – who pursued his work as a scholar and teacher explicitly in the service of democratic liberal ideals – urged his students to make their rooms places of culture.[58] In Burrage's rooms, as in his family's New York world and at the sites of Hyacinth's steady growth, James represents productive self-development that depends upon Paterian pleasure – and also upon a certain inattentiveness to moral and political concerns. This is a vision of cultivation that would trouble Norton considerably. Jonathan Freedman identifies in James's expressed affinities with Paterian aestheticism a critique of Norton's moralistic Boston-based Ruskinian aestheticism.[59] But Norton's aestheticism is not really separable from his liberalism: art is central to his politics, and political morality is central to his views on art. In these novels, James's Paterian resistance to Norton's Bostonian aestheticism also functions as resistance to Norton's Bostonian liberalism. In this sense, Verena's and Hyacinth's successful learning through pleasure forms an extension to the more obvious critique of Bostonian liberalism that plays out in the representation of Olive's 'educative processes'.

Norton's liberalism understands civilisation and culture as processes of development not just compatible with but necessary for the realisation of democratic ideals; *The Princess Casamassima*, however, represents a fictional world in which democracy threatens both civilisation and culture. The novel resists liberal reform and liberal democracy partly by proceeding as if they did not exist, even in theoretical form. Instead of imagining reform and non-violent democratisation, it imagines anarchism and revolt. Within the novel, those who seek reform are anarchist revolutionaries, and those who actually live out some form of social change are not reformers: like Dr Prance in *The Bostonians*, Millicent Henning quietly manages to claim a certain power within the extant order, and eschews the grasping cohort who want to transform it. That cohort's anarchism, like Olive's feminism, is usually driven by selfishness. Olive seeks revenge rather than justice; similarly, these anarchists aim to invert the present hierarchy rather than to foster equality. Because *The Princess Casamassima* imagines the expansion of access to culture as self-serving theft and wanton destruction, it understands democracy as the destruction of civilisation and culture.

In unfolding its plot over the course of a series of Sundays, hailing 'public collections' by name and mentioning 'the question of opening the museums on Sunday', the novel alludes to the controversy about Sunday museum openings that spanned the last decades of the century, in which the Anti-Sabbatarian Sunday Society fought to give workers access to art and science museums (172, 438). Such access was meant to facilitate liberal cultivation; and indeed, Jordanna Bailkin identifies the controversy about museum openings as part of an ongoing debate through which 'Britons confronted the dilemmas facing both the Liberal Party and Liberalism itself'.[60] The novel evokes these dilemmas and gestures towards the role of museums in providing broad access to liberal cultivation – but it does so only to suggest that museums somehow fail in this function. Most of the many amusements that its characters enjoy on Sundays are not museums. And, oddly enough, Hyacinth's own political logic seems to deny not just the efficacy of museums but their very existence. His aesthetic revelations happen not at those thickly peopled public institutions but at a nearly empty private estate.

In spite of his own happy hours in the Louvre and the National Gallery, Hyacinth understands the democratisation of art as incompatible with its preservation. He writes that the revolutionary leader he has followed would wish to 'cut up the ceilings of the Veronese into strips, so that every one might have a little piece'. Hyacinth states resolutely: 'I don't want every one to have a little piece of anything' (308). This negative image of dissemination opposes the ideal of broad cultivation that drove American liberals. We can identify a contrasting analogue to Hyacinth's horrifying vision of the parcelled-out Veronese in the effort of American periodicals to give readers access to visual art.[61] In 1883, Gilder initiated the 'Old Masters Series', offering *Century* readers engraved reproductions of works of art from Europe, along with interpretive text.[62] Gilder's series aimed to provide readers with access to art otherwise unavailable to them, using print technology to reproduce and proliferate so that every reader might indeed 'have a little piece'. James's protagonist imagines such access and such distribution as incompatible with the preservation of the work of art itself.

Hyacinth's problems are problems that James takes personally. The young man, 'a youth on whom nothing was lost', has the novelist's own sensitivity (102). James makes this autobiographical element explicit in his preface to the novel. As he writes of his protagonist, 'To find his possible adventure interesting I had only to conceive his watching the same public show, the same innumerable appearances, I had watched myself, and of his watching very much as I had watched; save indeed for one little difference.' The difference is one of access: the story, he writes, will concern 'some small obscure intelligent creature ... capable of profiting by all the civilization ... yet condemned to see these things only from the outside'.[63] Thus the Princess exclaims to Hyacinth: 'Fancy the strange, the bitter fate: to be constituted as you are constituted, to feel the capacity that you must feel, and yet to look at the good things of life only through the glass of the pastry-cook's window!' (256). James carries out as a fictional experiment the presumption that he offers to his friend Perry in jest: 'I pretend to be one "of the people," moi.'[64]

That experiment ends with a suicide. *The Princess Casamassima* shows us a liberal subject who develops responsively into intellectual independence, only to arrive, independently, at the conclusion that lower-class persons like himself should not have the chance to become liberally cultivated, because such broad cultivation would result in the destruction of culture. As a cultivated member of 'the people', he now falls into a category he believes should not exist. Following the logic of his own political views, he eliminates himself: the revolver with which he had promised to assassinate a duke serves instead to blow a hole in his own chest. As in the case of Basil's ultimate rule over Verena, the novel's plot represents the defeat of liberal cultivation as a defeat that imperils the body of the young learner. Once again, flesh that fails to incarnate the ideal of the liberal subject is flesh that will suffer violence.

In *The Bostonians*, an incompetent liberal subject becomes a victim of demagoguery and tyranny; in *The Princess Casamassima*, a liberal subject's extreme competence perversely leads him to turn against democratisation and seek self-destruction. Both novels thus express significant doubt about the liberal democratic ideal of broadly diffused cultivation. But both express this doubt in a manner that is deeply ambivalent. James echoes Carlyle's antidemocratic assessment of the people's capacity for citizenship and, moreover, suggests that culture cannot survive democratisation – but he also represents the tragedy and the brutality that attend the denial of access to liberal cultivation.

Each plot concludes with sudden, muted violence: both books end with a silent gunshot and the obliteration of the young learner. As Basil prepares to kidnap Verena before her speech, he thinks of an assassin ready 'to discharge a pistol' (373). Then, we read, he, 'by muscular force, wrenched her away' and 'thrust the hood of Verena's long cloak over her head, to conceal her face and her identity' (391). Effaced and silenced by Basil's muscular thrust, Verena departs in tears under his control. In the other novel, we do not hear the pistol shot that kills Hyacinth, but we see its results: the Princess at first can only see 'something black, something ambiguous, something outstretched'. She slowly perceives Hyacinth with 'a horrible thing, a mess of blood, on the bed, in his side, in his heart' (483). Hyacinth's eyes and voice disappear as Verena's do, and like Verena, he becomes a sightless, silent thing rather than an autonomous human. The doubts that the novels express about democratised liberal cultivation, then, are expressed within texts that also vividly, even melodramatically, stage the human tragedy of thwarted cultivation and crushed liberal subjecthood. And the novels refuse to resolve this contradiction: they express doubt, and they also express enormous regret about that doubt.

The elusiveness of the democratic liberal ideal of a broadly cultivated 'people' would have significant consequences for James's ambitions as an artist. The public of potentially cultivated liberal subjects is also a market of readers. James's relations with that market were already vexed when he wrote to William Dean Howells in 1884: 'what is the use of trying to write anything decent or serious for a public so absolutely idiotic'.[65] *The Bostonians* and *The Princess Casamassima* arose from an urge to 'do something *great*!'[66] In the early 1880s, James wanted to write novels that would both find a wide audience and earn critical acclaim. The novels he actually wrote suggest that these two outcomes can only be mutually exclusive. In

December of 1886, after the resounding failure of both books, he writes to congratulate Norton on his edition of Carlyle's early letters. Having praised the edition, he adds: 'I doubt whether the general public will bite at it very eagerly. I don't know why I allude to this, though – for the general public has small sense and less taste, and its likes and dislikes, I think, must mostly make the judicious grieve.'[67]

Later, in a 1914 letter to his agent, James refers to 'that very minor and "cultivated" public to whom, alas, almost solely, my productions appear to address themselves'.[68] But during the same terrible year, James closes his 'The Long Wards' by surveying 'the crude and the waste, the ignored and neglected', and asking: 'what wouldn't it do for us tended and fostered and cultivated? That is my moral, for I believe in Culture – speaking strictly now of the honest and of our own congruous kind.'[69] A cultivated public was what Norton sought to make, but his 'kind' of culture was not identical to James's. After Norton's death in 1908, James remembered him as 'the representative of culture – always in the high and special sense in which he practiced that faith'.[70] Both Norton and James believed in culture, but they thought differently about the relationship between culture and democracy; on that matter, Norton's high and special faith was one James could not quite share.

Chapter 3

The Professor and the Mob in Wharton's *The Valley of Decision*

Edith Wharton's first novel, *The Valley of Decision* (1902), is a sprawling, conglomerate work of historical fiction, mixing genres as diverse as melodrama and scholarship. But the novel that Wharton published a few short years later, *The House of Mirth* (1905), is generally regarded as a formally elegant realist masterwork. How, then, does Wharton move so quickly from the messy experimentation of her first novel to the mature realism of her second? One story that has circulated to answer this question involves Henry James. James and Wharton were not yet good friends when he wrote to her about *The Valley of Decision* in 1902. In this well-known letter, James offers some advice to the new novelist, some twenty years younger than himself. Take up, he tells her, 'the *American Subject*. There it is round you. Don't pass it by – the immediate, the real, the ours, the yours, the novelist's that it waits for.' James famously adds: '<u>Do New York</u>!'[1] *The House of Mirth*, a realist novel of Wharton's own Manhattan world, would seem to follow this advice. So, as this story would have it, she reaches maturity as an artist at least partly because she prudently obeys the Master. This chapter proposes a different account of Wharton's emergence as a realist novelist: it shows her adopting towards an older male mentor a posture of bold rebellion rather than prudent obedience. The mentor in question is not James but their mutual friend, the elderly Professor Charles Eliot Norton. In this account, when James tells Wharton to write a realist novel, he is not magisterially instructing her to change course. Rather, he is reading her work perceptively, discerning correctly that she is already a realist, and urging her to go ahead and make the art that her own principles dictate.

By revising the story of Wharton's deferent obedience to James, this chapter performs one of the classic moves of feminist scholarship: it makes visible the agency of a female author who rebels against an older male mentor. This move would also typically involve positioning the author herself as a voice for feminist ideas; and indeed, over the years, much scholarship on Wharton has positioned her in precisely that way. In the rebellion exposed here, however, Wharton is the more conservative and at times misogynist voice, and the mentor against whom she rebels is the more democratic thinker. My argument is that, although *The Valley of Decision* is not itself a realist novel, it articulates fully for the first time the realist conservatism that will characterise Wharton's aesthetics and politics for the rest of her life; and that Wharton formulates this outlook in the first years of the twentieth century by engaging critically with the democratic liberal idealism that found so strident an advocate in Norton. Through friction with his ideas, she sharpens her own.

This local friction has broader significance because Wharton's realist response to Norton's idealism is, I want to suggest, an early iteration of what later becomes the narrative about the genteel or the genteel tradition. One of the reasons that this has not been noted is that *Valley*'s critique of idealism is overtly antidemocratic.[2] Later iterations of the narrative about the genteel are themselves progressive and democratic, and they assail something undemocratic or antidemocratic; in these later iterations, genteel idealism is the moribund opposite of a vital realism inseparable from democracy. In such later accounts, this idealism is an effeminate sterility, and this realism enacts a masculine vitality. Wharton's novel does the same gendering: it portrays a feminine idealism that is wrong and a masculine realism that is right, as well as an idealist woman who dies and a realist man who lives. But in *Valley*, the political orientations of idealism and realism are the exact inverse of those in later accounts: here, feminine idealism is fanatically democratic, and masculine realism understands more sagely that democracy is unfeasible and ill advised. When we read *Valley* as a critical response to Norton's idealism, we can see how Wharton contributes to the conservative body of thought that feeds into the narrative about the genteel as it forms. We also see that in its early iterations, that narrative does not necessarily attack an idealism that is antidemocratic, vapid, prudish and removed from the world; quite to the contrary, the target here is an idealism that is both intensely political and fervently democratic.

Wharton, like many others, embodies this democratic liberal idealism in an uptight, bookish woman: her scholar, Fulvia Vivaldi, is a costumed variant on the New England schoolmarm type we saw in James's Olive Chancellor. Olive presides over a failed attempt to cultivate an embodied liberal subject who is a member of 'the people'. Fulvia too wants to educate the people, but it is her own body that tests out the embodiment of the liberal subject, and her failure is fatal to herself: she is shot dead in the street by the mob she has tried to enfranchise. Like the novels by Adams and James discussed in the preceding chapters, then, *Valley* adds to a pile of corpses that imply the impossibility of embodying the liberal subject in flesh that is not white and male. But Wharton goes farther than either Adams or James: her attention to this impossibility produces a striking interrogation of the very notion of embodiment. While a thinker like Norton understands the embodiment of an abstract ideal as an empowering achievement, Wharton suggests that – in ways well known to those who live in female bodies – embodying an abstract ideal is not in fact empowering. In response to a bright vision of the ideal democratic liberal citizen made flesh, she offers an account of embodiment as a nightmare of paralysis and silence. That account participates in a larger portrayal of democracy as foolhardy and dangerous: rather than the articulate, capable citizens imagined in ideals like Norton's, Wharton shows us an illiterate mob. Her rebellion against the Professor is to represent theirs.

Wharton's friendship with the Norton household was developing during the years in which she wrote *The Valley of Decision*, with which Charles gave her particular assistance. 'Professor Norton', she recalled later, 'who had by this time become one of my great friends, followed the development of the tale with interest, and helped it on by one of the most graceful *gestes* ever made by a distinguished scholar to a beginner': he loaned her rare books from his private library.[3] Wharton began *Valley* in early 1900 and finished it in January 1902.[4] In 1899, she had become friendly with Sally Norton, with whom she would share the closest relationship and most frequent, sustained correspondence. But friendships with both Sally and Charles developed in the first years of the century.[5] This was due in part to the proximity of their summer residences in western Massachusetts. Wharton spent her first summer in the Berkshires in 1900 and purchased the farm that would become The Mount in early 1901; once her house there was complete, she recalled, 'a frequent excursion was to Ashfield, where Charles Eliot Norton spent the summer with his daughters in his little mountain farmhouse, and where there was always a friendly welcome, and the joy of long hours of invigorating talk'.[6] Although the elderly Charles did not return these visits, Sally was a 'beloved and frequent' visitor at The Mount. Wharton writes of her relationship with Charles: 'In the intervals between our meetings we wrote to each other, and, though our actual hours together were not many, I had to the end the warm enveloping sense of his friendship.'[7]

A mere glance at the summer homes over which Norton and Wharton preside makes plain immediately the differences that this chapter will labour at length to expose in text. One might observe first that both properties are neoclassical summer homes in the Berkshires, just as one might begin by noting that both Norton and Wharton are conservative elitists. But these houses, like these elitisms, differ from each other in important ways. With George William Curtis, Norton settled in Ashfield because he admired the plain, upstanding country living of the town's inhabitants; once there, they established a local school and an annual benefit to fund it. Wharton accurately calls the Norton place a farmhouse. Her own, much larger house incorporates certain vernacular forms, duly making graceful reference to its site; but in its architecture, as well as in the design of its interior and its formidable gardens, The Mount operates in a more formal mode that is significantly French.[8] While Norton's Ashfield follows the lines of the Federal period, Wharton's Mount spreads itself out more lavishly in the style of the colonial revival. His place appeals to an ideal of American democracy that involves articulate, bookish country folk in plain, comfortable farmstead homes; hers, by contrast, evokes models that are aristocratic or monarchical.

As we consider these two properties, Wharton's and Norton's differences would seem to be self-evident. And, indeed, their disagreements were multiple and overt. By the turn of the century, Norton advocated higher education for women but not female suffrage, while Wharton championed neither higher education nor suffrage for women. More significantly, as Frederick Wegener has shown, Wharton had an 'imperial sensibility that fundamentally shaped her social and political views', determining her support 'not only of a nascent American empire but of imperial Britain and France as well'.[9] Norton, however, took so strong a public stance against imperialism when the US declared war on Spain in 1898 that he received hate mail and was denounced violently in the national press. Wharton admired Theodore Roosevelt; the Norton household's disapproval of the President grew over time.

In the years around the publication of *Valley of Decision*, Wharton's letters to Sally manage their disagreements carefully, with light humour, jesting provocation and perhaps also obfuscation: in March 1901, she writes that she awaits a visit from the Norton's liberal friend, J. B. Harrison, 'with open arms, & perhaps when he discovers that I am a rabid Imperialist the shock may strike a few sparks out of him'.[10] Wharton wrote to Sally in August 1902: 'I had a very pleasant week at Newport. Dry, brilliant weather . . . magnificent tennis . . . & the sight & conversation of some old friends – if I mentioned the President among them, would Ashfield shudder at the name?' In the following week, she added, 'I think if you could have seen the President here the other day . . . you would have agreed that he is not all – or nearly all – bronco-buster.'[11] And then, in 1905, it would seem that Wharton actually lied to Sally about seeing Roosevelt, stating that rain had prevented her from attending the awarding of his honorary degree at Williams College, when in fact she had exchanged friendly remarks with the President at a reception there.[12]

So the differences in outlook that divide Norton and Wharton are neither subtle nor secret. Scholarship has left those differences mostly unaddressed, however: there is little work that focuses on these two thinkers, and the work that does exist tends to emphasise similarity, agreement and influence. The most insightful and comprehensive account of Wharton's political thought to date, Jennie Kassanoff's *Edith Wharton and the Politics of Race*, observes that Wharton and Norton share 'patrician anxieties' about a loss of power amongst the Anglo-Saxon elite.[13] More recently, William Blazek has pointed to Norton's substantial influence on Wharton's thinking about Italy and Italian art and culture.[14] I want to suggest that, in addition to that influence and that shared anxiety, there is disagreement and resistance arising from major divergences in political and aesthetic thought. Although both Wharton and Norton regard the trajectory of modern democracy with alarm, that shared alarm emerges from different perspectives. These perspectives are both aesthetic and political: for Norton and Wharton, the political and the aesthetic are not separable things.

Born Readers: Race and the Reading Citizenry

Partly because of their mutual sense of the inseparability of the political and the aesthetic, both Norton and Wharton understand reading, literacy and what Norton calls 'a taste for good reading' as political matters. In the years immediately after she writes her first novel with Norton's encouragement, Wharton publishes two magazine pieces about reading and the prospect of a vast reading public: 'The Vice of Reading' (1903) appears in the *North American Review*, while 'The Descent of Man' (1904) provides a witty tale for the more numerous readers of *Scribner's*. Norton too writes about reading in this period, as he launches his *Heart of Oak* books, starting work on the series in the early 1890s and releasing multiple editions after the turn of the century. Norton intends these books to be pursued sequentially over the course of a young person's development, from nursery rhymes and alphabet jingles, through fables and fairy tales, to narratives and poems in the later volumes: the series promises to offer 'masterpieces of poetry and prose for use at home and at school, chosen with special reference to the cultivation of the imagination and the development of a taste for good reading'. Norton explains in the Introduction to the first volume that the books are 'meant not only as manuals for learning to read, but as helps to the cultivation of the taste, and to the healthy development of the imagination of those who use them, and thus to the formation and invigoration of the best elements of character'. Such development, he writes, is the foundation for not just 'the sound exercise of the faculties of observation and judgment, but also the command of the reason, the control of the will, and the quickening and growth of the moral sympathies'.[15] This project was part of Norton's career as an educator. The books, his biographer notes, 'strove to reach a popular audience', and Norton and his publisher sought feedback on proofs from teachers.[16]

Norton's educational publishing project anticipated his cousin Charles William Eliot's fifty-volume Harvard Classics (1909), which promised a full liberal education in fifteen minutes of reading each day. Both of these projects participate in a liberal democratic endeavour to realise the ideal of the 'reading citizenry'.[17] Valorisations of education and literacy notoriously serve racist and exclusionary agendas during this period: literacy tests function as devices for restricting immigration and disenfranchising.[18] But advocacy of literacy and literacy tests does not always imply nativist opposition to immigration. Eliot favoured an education qualification for suffrage (for both white and Black men), but advocated *for* immigration. Although Norton is sometimes associated with a 'genteel' mode that is broadly nativist and antidemocratic in its conservatism, his advocacy of reading expresses a rather different understanding of the relationship between race, democracy and education. As Butler points out, liberal thinkers of the Civil War generation (like Norton) are easily misunderstood when their ideas are read in the context of the later decades of the century. Noting that their arguments about literacy tests in particular have been simplified, she argues that 'liberals saw literacy as an indispensable (and fundamentally empowering) path to meaningful political participation rather than as a tool of disempowerment'.[19]

Norton and Eliot both occasionally express sentiments consistent with nativism, but nativism is not the foundation of their elitism and racism. Rather, their elitism and racism are grounded in the liberal logic of development that posits progression from barbarism to civilisation, and observes development at different stages and paces amongst different races. That virulent nativists also sometimes refer to this logic does not mean that thinkers like Eliot and Norton draw from it the same conclusions. In a 1901 letter, Norton recalls explaining to his students 'that civilization was a purely relative term, meaning the sum of the acquisitions of the race at any given time, and not as white people are apt to assume a possession exclusively theirs'.[20]

But, especially as he recoils in horror at the Venezuela crisis in 1896, Norton is much less sanguine than Eliot about civilisation and culture in the US: surveying 'the ignorant, whether of foreign or native birth', he worries that 'the character ingrained by a long inheritance of ignorance and semi-barbarism is seldom to be essentially modified in the course of a single generation'. In letters, he bemoans 'the rise of the uncivilized whom no school education can suffice to provide with intelligence and reason', and says he is not sure after all that 'Democracy insures a teachable people.'[21] But even as Norton despairs over the prospect of civilising the masses, he is also working, like his cousin, to accomplish just that, not least in the *Heart of Oak* project.

That project itself might seem to be an educational endeavour significantly committed to exclusionary principles, however, for Norton's Introduction notes that its selections are 'chosen from the masterpieces of the literature of the English-speaking race', and announces that the child who reads them 'will share in the common stock of the intellectual life of the race to which he belongs; and will have the door opened to him of all the vast and noble resources of that life'.[22] This comment draws from the ideas that inform the work of Norton's academic colleagues in English departments across the nation, who frequently understood their work as a racial and national project. Woodrow Wilson remarks on that project in the same year: it is, he says, only 'out of our own English books that we can get and appropriate and forever recreate the temper of our own race . . . We shall lose our sense of identity and all advantage of being hard-headed Saxons if we become ignorant of our literature, which is so full of action and of thoughts fit for action.'[23]

To equate Norton's comments about the English-speaking race with those of Wilson is, however, to efface other relevant interlocutors. We will later see Norton's friend, George William Curtis, similarly evoke 'the English-speaking race' when urging the expansion of culture and democracy; in Curtis's case, that evocation features in an argument for a racially inclusive democracy in which African–Americans have equal political rights. Curtis and Norton, liberals of the Civil War generation, use the language of Anglo-Saxonism and the Teutonic origins theory to make democratic arguments. These arguments thus participate in a racial essentialism that understands liberty and democracy as the natural property and special capacity of the Anglo-Saxon or English-speaking race. What stands out about these arguments now is their reliance on that racist theory. But during the later nineteenth and early twentieth centuries, the fixed association of Anglo-Saxon whiteness with democracy was not especially controversial. This makes reading difficult: in ways that are no longer self-evident, statements about Anglo-Saxon whiteness can evoke democracy, and statements about democracy can evoke Anglo-Saxon whiteness. The racist ideas that Norton deploys in his Introduction are, in fact, a part of what makes it an argument for democracy. Indeed, the Teutonic origins theory itself makes the prestige and superiority of democracy central to its white supremacist narrative of history. To the extent that Norton's Introduction draws from that theory, it is more emphatic in its advocacy for democracy, not less so.

Norton begins his Introduction by stating that a taste for good reading, 'like most others, is usually not so much a gift of nature as a product of cultivation. A wide difference exists, indeed, in children in respect to their natural inclination for reading, but there are few in whom it cannot be more or less developed by careful and judicious training.'[24] The instability and vagueness of racial language leaves open the possibility that Norton understands 'the English-speaking race' to be a permeable or, indeed, a forcefully assimilative category. Elsewhere, he advocates the study of poetry as a means of cultivating 'the Imagination which unites us with our race, which lifts us out of mere narrow provincialism into our share in the eternal brotherhood of man'.[25] In this comment, the English-speaking race becomes the human race. We could read this as a white supremacist denial of humanity to those who do not speak English; I would suggest that it is more accurately characterised as an inclusive exhortation that draws from Anglo-Saxonism's ideas about assimilation. Given Norton's emphasis on the possibilities of education, we could read his Introduction to the *Heart of Oak* books as a text that contradicts itself by working within the racist framework of the Teutonic origins theory even as it argues that all children can and should practise cultivation. Alternatively, we might read it as a text that promotes the cultivation of all the Anglo-Saxon children in an Anglo-Saxon democracy. Whichever of these readings we find more persuasive, we see in Norton's Introduction a text that exerts itself both to describe and to realise a democratic ideal of widespread cultivation.

Like Norton and Eliot, Wharton refers to a logic of development that draws from evolutionary science; like them, she holds a perspective that is biologically materialist and understands biological material to be fundamentally pliant over time. But while Norton and Eliot emphasise the possibilities implied by that pliancy, and actively work for education, Wharton does not. Instead, she expresses an anti-democratic opposition to systematic education. Her magazine pieces directly attack the democratic ideal that defines education, reading and thoughtful debate as the basis for competent citizenship, as well as the ideal that imagines a crucial function for college professors as educators of the broader public in this ongoing practice of learning and discussion. 'The Vice of Reading' specifically assaults the Victorian liberal certainties that inform Norton's *Heart of Oak* project. Wharton's arch, provocative speaker proclaims that the times have brought about 'the production of a new vice – the vice of reading'. While Norton's Introduction urges the deliberate adoption of reading as an improving practice, Wharton assails 'reading deliberately undertaken – what may be called volitional reading'. This sort of reading, she argues, is both vicious and false. 'Real reading', Wharton continues, 'is a reflex action; the born reader reads as unconsciously as he breathes; and, to carry the analogy a degree farther, reading is no more a virtue than breathing.' Thus, for the 'born reader', reading happens 'instinctively' or 'intuitively', while the bad reader is a 'mechanical reader' whose sin is that she tries. For the 'born reader', reading happens by accident, naturally; for the 'mechanical reader', it is an effort, a duty and a source of pride. Wharton clarifies that those persons not born to read need not necessarily bemoan that fact: 'To be a poor reader may . . . be considered a misfortune; but it is certainly not a fault. Why should we all be readers?'[26]

But those born to be poor readers should abstain entirely, lest they fall into reading that is merely 'mechanical'. Wharton's imagery over the course of the article links mechanical reading with low cultural production, commerce, domestic labour, speed and democratic modernity. Her opening lines make the link between democratic modernity and mechanical reading explicit, stating that the rise of the 'vice of reading' has been caused by 'that "diffusion of knowledge" commonly classed with steam-heat and universal suffrage in the category of modern improvements'.[27] 'The Vice of Reading' objects to a modernity in which technology changes daily domestic experience, citizenship belongs to the poor as well as the rich, and the poor and middling, as well as the leisured rich, may learn to read and participate in culture. The article manifests this objection by rejecting entirely the concept and practice of wilful learning. Those who are born readers will read naturally; those who have to try never will. Education that happens by accident yields competence and wisdom; education 'undertaken deliberately' only fosters tediousness and cheap false smarts.

Wilful learning, of course, is the cherished virtue and central practice of Victorian liberalism. Wharton attacks that liberalism, noting with derision that, amongst some mistaken persons, the 'zeal for self-improvement is supposed to confer brains'. Brains, Wharton suggests, cannot, in fact, be conferred. She clarifies that, of course, 'the gift of reading is no exception to the rule that all natural gifts need to be cultivated by practice and discipline; but unless the innate aptitude exist the training will be wasted. It is the delusion of the mechanical reader to think that intentions may take the place of aptitude.' In short: 'to read well is an art, and an art that only the born reader can acquire'.[28] Wharton's article is flip in tone, but this rejection of education and this appeal to 'innate aptitude' are significant, not least because they chime with what we find elsewhere in her work. Against the fluid social organisation of democratic modernity and the liberal idea that eventually, through education, the broader population can rise to responsible, reflective citizenship, she posits a static model: those not already practising the habit of cultivation should not strive to adopt it. Some are born into the mental habits that justify full citizenship, and others are not; this is fine. As Wharton puts it: 'Why should we all be readers?'

While 'Vice of Reading' attacks the liberal ideal of self-improvement through education and literature, the short story 'Descent of Man' attacks the liberal ideal of elite intellectual leadership. Professor Linyard of Hillbridge University, referred to throughout simply as 'the Professor', is a scientist frustrated by the degradation of science in popular culture. He writes 'The Vital Thing', a satire of popular science writing. To his surprise, the book is an enormously lucrative success: readers are too idiotic to perceive that it is satire, so they adore what they take to be its sunny, affirming message. Caught in the trap of needing money to fuel his vapid wife's consumption habits, the Professor becomes a writer of optimistic trash rather than a scientist in pursuit of unremunerative truth. So 'Descent', like 'Vice', is a text about reading and the capacity of the broader public to read well: its plot turns on the absence of that capacity.

More specifically, its plot turns on the inability of the public to read what a professor has written. Wharton emphasises the complete separation of his academic world from the public world in which his book finds unexpected success. There is no meeting point between these two realms: the Professor finds that 'even in this reverberating age the opinions of the laboratory do not easily reach the street'. Rather than leading a broader practice of learning, Wharton's professors are marginal, isolated and dedicated to obscure specialisations (Linyard's is beetles). The eager publisher of the Professor's book, Harviss, was his college friend when they were both students at Hillbridge. As a college-educated publisher, Harviss has a key role to play in Norton's ideal. But he has become as insensitive a reader as the masses to whom he caters: he too fails to pick up on the satire. When the Professor enlightens him, he huffs, 'of course you address yourself to a very small class of readers.' 'Oh,' replies the Professor, 'infinitely small.' The masses, the Professor comes to feel, will miss his joke; but 'as for the initiated, they would know at once'. But his resolution that 'the elect would understand; the crowd would not' leaves us wondering whom that 'elect' might include, if not college-educated men like Harviss.[29] In this instance, higher education led by scholars has failed; instead of going out into the world and disseminating broadly the means of cultivation, Harviss disseminates mind-numbing trash, and makes a tidy profit in doing so.

The proper nouns of the story would seem to aim its critique rather specifically. Harviss's and Linyard's names divide between them the syllables of Harvard; and Linyard works at Hillbridge University, which neatly mixes Shady Hill and Cambridge. Hillbridge, it should be noted, also features in Wharton's 'The Pelican' (1898), where it resembles Williams College, and Harvard appears under its own name. Like 'Angel at the Grave' (1901) and 'The Pretext' (1908), 'Pelican' and 'Descent' are tales of academic New England. Like those stories, they are deeply interested in female intellectual capacity and the relationships between scholarship, commerce and the vulgarisations of mass culture. 'Angel' is widely understood to portray a Milton-like Norton stifling his daughter Sally's sexual and romantic life. That reading flattens the complexities of both 'Angel' and Sally's biography; but there is no question that the Norton family and its Massachusetts haunts feed Wharton's imagination as she writes these tales.

Although the protagonist of 'Descent' is a scientist, the stupidity at the centre of the tale is a literary stupidity; the issue that drives the plot is not bad science but bad reading. And, indeed, Harviss says of 'The Vital Thing': 'It will sell like a popular novel if you'll let me handle it in the right way.'[30] Like the art and literature that are the stuff of Norton's scholarly work, this Professor's field has undergone a transformation as access to it has broadened:

> When Professor Linyard first plied his microscope, the audience of the man of science had been composed of a few fellow-students . . . In the intervening quarter of a century, however, this little group had been swallowed up in a larger public. Every one now read scientific books and expressed an opinion on them. [. . .] The mob had broken down the walls of tradition to batten in the orchard of forbidden knowledge. The inaccessible goddess whom the Professor had served in his youth now offered her charms in the market-place. And yet it was not the same goddess, after all, but a pseudo-science masquerading in the garb of the real divinity.[31]

The shift that Wharton evokes in this description of a Professor and a mob is similar to the transformation that Norton describes in 'The Intellectual Life of America' (1888) as he argues for 'the wider diffusion of the higher education': he asks whether the works of civilisation 'hitherto confined to a select and comparatively small body, can be preserved, diffused, and made the foundation of a social order in which all advantages shall be more equally shared'.[32] 'Descent' offers a negative reply to this question: in this story, what used to belong to 'a few' has suffered a fatal vulgarisation as access to it has widened.

'Descent' indicates that this vulgarisation happens because, in reality (as opposed to the realm of the ideal), the broad diffusion of science (or culture) necessarily takes commercial form. Rather than disseminating the means of cultivation, Harviss sells consumer goods to consumers. The Professor notes that Harviss 'looked as if he had been fattened on popular fiction; and his fat was full of optimistic creases'. As the publisher's fiction-fed fatness suggests, text is a consumable commodity here, rather like grocery goods or sticky sweets: what the Professor observes the 'mob' do, after all, is 'batten' upon fruits previously forbidden. Reading a positive popular review of his work that is 'full of extracts', the Professor notes 'how well they would look in a volume of "Selections"'; later, Harviss says to him, 'Write another book – write two, and we'll sell them in sets in a box: The Vital Thing Series. That will take tremendously in the holidays.'[33] These comments suggest that book is not an integral, crafted whole, but a commodity that can be broken up into smaller commodities, ready to sell, or repackaged and reproduced indefinitely for continuing profit. Its material form – whether broken down into particulate 'Selections' or boxed up for Christmas – matters much more than the ideas it bears. This commodification of the text is also a commodification of the author, who is similarly broken down, packaged and distributed: 'his head', we learn, 'began to figure in the advertising pages of the magazines' and then duly progresses 'from the magazine and the newspaper to the biscuit-tin and the chocolate-box'.[34]

'The Vice of Reading' and 'The Descent of Man' thus assail the key elements of Norton's ideal of American democracy. The broader public is not a body of potentially literate and capable citizens ready to be educated (by professors, among others) into habits of reflection and debate: it is a 'mob' notably unreceptive to opportunities for development. A crowd of stupid, pleasure-hungry consumers, its inability to read well is central to both its fundamental intellectual incompetence and its relationship with the Professor, whom it can only misunderstand. Just as reading and publishing are at the core of Norton's vision for democratic citizenship, they are at the core of Wharton's critique of that vision.

Idealism and Realism

It would seem that the disagreement that Wharton and Norton most openly discussed, as the years went by, was about her commitment to realism. Wharton recalls in her memoir:

> He never ceased to interest himself in my work, or to encourage me to go forward, although the more I developed the more, in literary matters, our points of view diverged. He was obviously disturbed by my increasing 'realism', my exclusive interest, as a novelist, in the life about me, which seemed to him so devoid of the stuff of romance; he would have been happier if I had never come any nearer to the nineteenth century than I did in 'The Valley of Decision'. But no friendly pressure, even from the critics I most esteemed, could turn me from the way I seemed meant to follow; and with a magnanimity unusual in a man of his age Charles Norton accepted this, and kept me in his heart.[35]

So as James urges Wharton to write about 'the immediate, the real, the ours, the yours' and the modern New York that is part of what she herself calls 'the life about me', Norton urges her away from this 'increasing "realism"', preferring the 'romance' and the more remote eighteenth-century Italian setting of *Valley of Decision*. Although Wharton did consider writing a sequel to *Valley* in the years after its publication, she ultimately rejected Norton's counsel.[36] We have her to thank for recording one of his most notorious remarks about the sort of 'realism' for which she eventually became known. She recalls: 'hearing (after the appearance of "The House of Mirth") that I was preparing another "society" novel, [he] wrote in alarm imploring me to remember that "no great work of the imagination has ever been based on illicit passion"!'[37] Wharton quite properly plays this prudish admonition for laughs. But Norton's comment is, in fact, richly loaded with meaning, as is his remark to her in a letter of July 1901, when she was writing *Valley*: 'You are an artist, and with such gifts that your task is plain and sacred, – to make your work the perfect expression, so far as perfection is possible, of your own ideal.'[38]

Norton's advice to Wharton arises from his fervent belief that great works of the imagination must express the highest ideals. Thus he announces in an 1895 letter commenting on the proper subject of art: 'I hold with the poets and the idealists; not the idealizers, but those who have ideals, and, knowing that they are never to be realized, still strive to reach them and to persuade others to take up the same quest.'[39] Norton holds that art expresses the morality of the society that makes it, and also teaches that morality to those who subsequently open themselves up to learn from it. For him, then, as for his friend Ruskin, there is no separating art and society, nor any severing of aesthetics from politics. Norton refers repeatedly in his writings and letters to 'the ideals of our American democracy', or 'the old American ideals' and also to 'ideals' more closely associated with art and leisure, and most powerfully expressed in poetry.[40] He understands these categories of ideals as synonymous. For him, it is only when people engage in the cultivation of the imagination that great art offers, and only when they thus put themselves in contact with the ideals communicated by masterworks, that they can come to embody the thoughtful, morally serious citizen demanded by 'the ideals of our American democracy'. The study of good art and literature thus figures centrally within Norton's vision of democracy: by cultivating their imaginations through the study of such art, men and women make themselves better citizens. Reading forms a core practice of citizenship, and educators, including college professors, have a key role to play: their teaching crucially helps citizens gain access to cultivation. The work of a professor of art or literature is both fundamentally democratic and fundamental to functioning democracy.

While 'Vice' and 'Descent' attack specific ideals advocated within Norton's democratic liberal idealism, *Valley* criticises not just those ideals, but also idealism itself. The novel tells the story of one Odo Valsecca, a nobleman of Pianura, who leans towards liberal ideals but ultimately defends the old aristocratic regime of which he is part. His sometime lover, the beautiful scholar Fulvia Vivaldi, embodies the liberalism with which he dallies before coming to his senses, which he does most fully after the plot exterminates her.[41] Fulvia meets her death while wearing academic regalia, just after she gives the first address of her scholarly career. Speaking in Latin, she offers a 'panegyric of constitutional liberty' – indoors, to a select audience of university and state elite – as the crowd outside generates a 'growing murmur' that rises to a 'roar'.[42] Having spoken, she goes out to the street and is promptly shot through the heart by that roaring crowd. While 'Descent' asserts that the Professor's academic ideas 'do not easily reach the street', *Valley* suggests that such attempts to reach the street may, in fact, be fatal. Rather than merely misreading the scholar's work, this mob assassinates the scholar.

The themes that play out in Wharton's fictional encounters of professors and mobs were also apparently at play in conversations about *The Valley of Decision* as it was written and after it was published. Wharton herself took on the role of scholar when she wrote the novel, as her need for Norton's books suggests. And she seems to have seen scholarship as central to the novel's achievements: her descriptions of the book emphasise its intensely researched descriptive function as a 'picture' rather than the dynamic drama of its plot. She wrote to Sally Norton, 'I meant the book to be a picture of a social phase,' and described it to her publisher as 'an attempt to picture Italy at the time of the breaking up of the small principalities at the end of the 18th century'.[43] Norton echoes this understanding the novel as a static 'picture' rather than a dramatic fiction when he writes to his friend Samuel Ward in 1902 that it offers 'a wonderfully complete and vivid picture of the Italy of the period'. In this letter to Ward, Norton calls Wharton a 'woman of genius' and, like the author herself, emphasises its descriptive, researched qualities: 'She calls it "a novel," but it is rather a study of Italian thought and life during the latter part of the eighteenth century, in the form of a story . . . The intellectual element in the book is stronger than the emotional and passionate . . . Her knowledge of Italy is that of a scholar.'[44]

As a 'study' by a 'scholar' thus recognised by a professor who was a leading authority in the field, *Valley* itself ventures into precisely the terrain that 'Descent' imagines: once published, it offers up scholarly production in the modern literary marketplace. The issue of how the book might fare in that marketplace seems to have figured in Wharton's exchanges with Norton, which prefigure the themes of her short story. In the same 1901 letter that he names her 'plain and sacred' duty as an artist, Norton observes approvingly:

> You have no reason for permitting the publishers to trade on you for their own selfish ends, to make money out of you in ways disagreeable to you, & most inappropriate to you [. . .] No matter whether your work be popular; if it be, as it will be, worthy of you, sunrise is not more certain than that there will be in time worthy appreciation of it.[45]

In his letter to Ward the following year, Norton explicitly states that the book's high quality will prevent it from selling well: 'It is too thoughtful and too fine a book to be popular', he writes, 'but it places Mrs. Wharton among the few foremost of the writers in English to-day.'[46]

In the context of Norton's many letters to Ward, this comment takes its place in a long series of remarks about the larger public's lack of appetite for good reading and intellectual substance. The correspondence between these two old men seems to have been a site for both to speak in a sad, retrospective mode about the lost hopes of their younger days in a bright Emersonian New England. Rather repetitively, they write to each other about disappointed aspirations for the US, pursuing an ongoing conversation about the emerging limitations of American democracy. So it makes sense that Norton would choose to write to Ward about Wharton's book, for *The Valley of Decision* is a novel about the limitations of democracy. For Norton, the idea that this excellent book would not find a broad readership powerfully indicated the extent of those limitations. And the novel's plot, like the plot of 'Descent', affirms his sense of an opposition between the scholarly and the popular.

That affirmation may be one reason that Norton so enjoys a book that criticises both his cherished ideals and the idealism that governs his political and aesthetic thought. Norton indicates that he admires the book because of its scholarly merits as a study of eighteenth-century Italy; but it is also true that he and Wharton agree about a great deal. The violent, illiterate peasantry of *Valley of Decision* figures forth the stuff of nightmares that they share: they are both elitists worried by the actual state of American democracy and the American people. Wharton, however, objects not just to actual democracy but to the ideal of democracy, and also idealism at large. For Norton the idealist, the apparent failures of actual democracy do not preclude fidelity to 'the ideals of American democracy'. Even so, Norton may have welcomed Wharton's critique of idealism in *Valley of Decision* because his idealism – and his liberalism more broadly – have a persistently mournful, self-flagellatory quality, as the Conclusion to this book will discuss.

It may also be the case that Norton did not feel the novel's barbs directed at himself because his stand-in in the text had been rendered unrecognisable: in *Valley*, the murdered body in the street wears academic regalia, but it is the body of a woman. The most subtle element of Wharton's critique of liberal idealism depends on the sex of this body, which she uses to interrogate the process of embodiment central to that idealism's agenda. The novel's attack on democratic liberal thought is synonymous with its attack on idealism: it declares that democratic liberalism is wrong because it is predicated upon unrealistic ideals. And the novel suggests that idealism is a distinctly feminine cognitive and intellectual tendency: Wharton's critique is essentially misogynist in that she assails idealism by feminising it.

Considering Fulvia and himself, Odo observes that there is a 'difference in their mental operations', and notes that, 'like most women possessed of an abstract idea she had unconsciously personified the idea and made a religion of it' (2:222, 2:96). Later, he thinks to himself that 'Fulvia's enthusiasms were too unreal, too abstract. She lived in a region of ideals, whence ugly facts were swept out by some process of mental housewifery which kept her world perpetually smiling and immaculate' (2:258). Odo thinks, 'Only a woman's convictions, nourished on sentiment and self-sacrifice, could burn with that clear unwavering flame' (2:182). A visiting Englishman observes that, 'like some of the most accomplished of her sex, she was impatient of *minutiae*, and preferred general ideals to particular instances' (2:213). In Fulvia's intellectual universe, even the ostensibly 'particular' is not actually so: during the latter part of her final address, Odo observes, 'she had left the abstract and dropped to the concrete issues'; but these issues are 'the constitution, the benefits and obligations it implied, the new relations it established between ruler and subject and between man and man' (2:279). This list of 'concrete issues' is, in fact, quite specifically a list of abstractions, prescriptive descriptions of a more perfect system that does not currently exist.

Because of Fulvia's disproportionate influence, her personal errors become systemic in Pianura. The visiting Englishman – whose commentary enters the novel via an embedded 'unpublished fragment' from his 1789 travel diary – gives her practical political advice ('Plant turnips, madam!'), but senses that it will not be heeded: 'I fear', he states, 'all the heads here are too full of fine theories to condescend to such simple improvements' (2:200, 214). He observes of Odo, 'happy indeed is the prince who surrounds himself with scholars instead of courtiers!' (2:209). But these scholars do not seem to serve well. The Englishman is 'disappointed to find among [Odo's] chosen associates not one practical farmer or economist, but only the usual closet-theorists that are too busy planning Utopias to think of planting turnips' (2:210). Fulvia, whom the Englishman admires for being 'learned in the closet', seems to be the central force among these scholarly theorists (2:212).

Odo worries over 'Fulvia's unquestioning faith not only in the abstract beauty of the new ideals but in their immediate adaptability to the complex conditions of life' and is 'struck with her undiminished faith in the sufficiency of such generalizations. Did she really think that to solve a problem it was only necessary to define it?' (2:182, 224). He feels 'keenly . . . the difference between theoretical visions of liberty and their practical application' (2:228) His male mind maintains a 'perpetual accessibility to new impressions', and this is 'a quality she could not understand, or could conceive of only as weakness' (2:222–3). The novel imagines Fulvia's limitations in a distinctly Whartonian way: 'Her own mind was like a garden in which nothing is ever transplanted.' The signal feature of Fulvia's idealism is rigidity: 'She allowed for no intermediate stages between error and dogma, for no shifting of the bounds of conviction' (2:223).

In holding resolutely to her high ideals rather than maintaining an 'accessibility to new impressions', Fulvia fails to see the actual people of Pianura. But Odo comes to realise that this population is not at all ready for 'the benefits of free speech, a free press, a secular education': 'the people were hungry, were fever-stricken, were crushed with tithes and taxes. It was hopeless to try to reach them by the diffusion of popular knowledge. They must first be fed and clothed; and before they could be fed and clothed the chains of feudalism must be broken' (2.180). The breaking of those chains is, apparently, a lengthy process; in the mean time, the people need turnips, not education. This futile 'diffusion of popular knowledge' anticipates the 'diffusion of knowledge' derided in 'Vice of Reading' and dramatised as a farce in 'Descent'.

The novel does not merely suggest that these people are incapable of becoming cultivated liberal subjects; it also suggests that they have no desire for such development. Wharton represents the masses who prefer the solace of a strong church to the rights and responsibilities conferred by a secular, liberal constitution. In the climactic moment of Fulvia's murder, the mob is actually rioting against its own liberation. Odo's wife, the Duchess, warns him of 'forcing on [his] subjects liberties which they do not desire!' She asserts: 'in striking at the Church you wound the poor . . . It is their faith you insult . . . they will hate you for it in the end!' (2:234–5). And they do. But not as much as they hate Fulvia, the woman who has pushed Odo to this point. Instead of the rational illumination her ideals propose, they prefer the sensuous ritual and comforting continuity offered by their Catholicism. Though they are dressed in eighteenth-century Italian garb, their preference for sensuous satisfaction and easy comfort makes them closely resemble the unintelligent modern consumers who misread the Professor's book in 'Descent'.

In its representation of a broader public unreceptive to education, *The Valley of Decision* takes up the questions that 'Vice of Reading' handles more archly. The novel betrays its interest in 'innate aptitudes' by calling upon a rich vocabulary of racial tropes. In his diary fragment of 1789, the visiting Englishman spews generic liberal rhetoric, expressing his approval of 'the just protests of the poor against the unlawful tyranny of the privileged classes' and his 'joy' at 'the dawn of that light of freedom which hath already shed so sublime an effulgence on the wilds of the New World'. The Italian *abate* with whom he converses disagrees. The Englishman reports: 'he declared that in his opinion different races needed different laws, and that the sturdy and temperate American colonists were fitted to enjoy a greater measure of political freedom than the more volatile French and Italians – as though liberty were not destined by the Creator to be equally shared by all mankind!' (2:201–2). An asterisk marks this exclamation, pointing the reader to a note at the bottom of the page which reads, 'I let this passage stand, though the late unhappy events in France have, alas! proved that my friend the abate was nearer right than myself. June, 1794' (2:202). Later in the fragment, another asterisk qualifies the English gentleman's observation that Fulvia is 'as agreeable in discourse as learned in the closet' with a catty, competitive rejoinder 'by a Female Friend of the Author' (2:212).

Wharton's multilayered narration calls upon the reader to interpret these annotated archival materials embedded in the text of the novel. Just we are invited to imagine the amending Female Friend and infer her jealousy, we are invited to observe the youthful, exuberant idealism of the Englishman, to regard it as wrong – and then, if we have done so, nod in satisfaction at his subsequent retraction. The novel delivers this parable of humiliated idealism gently, working by implication and pairing this instance of truth via asterisk with another that is conspicuously light and humorous. The idea that the Englishman wrongly dismisses is precisely the idea evoked by Norton's engagement with the Teutonic origins theory: some races are more suited for liberty than others.

The novel also works to discredit the view that reading and discussion can form the foundation of a functioning democracy. Odo specifically dismisses a political outlook that emphasises the importance of words. He thinks to himself: 'Sentimental verbiage: he saw it clearly now. He had been the dupe of the old word-jugglery which was forever confounding fact and fancy in men's minds. For it was essentially an age of words: the world was drunk with them, as it had once been drunk with action; and the former was the deadlier drug of the two' (2:289). Odo's belated recognition of the toxicity of a politics based on 'verbiage' or 'words' notably disparages that politics not just by associating it with drunkenness, but by (again) feminising it ('sentimental') and placing it in opposition to 'fact'.

A political discourse based on mere 'words', he senses, can ground itself in the deluded misperceptions of the idealists. After Fulvia's death, Odo begins articulate more fully the importance of 'fact' and that which is 'real' over the 'ideal':

> Certainly in the ideal state the rights and obligations of the different classes would be more evenly adjusted. But the ideal state was a figment of the brain. The real one ... was the gradual and heterogeneous product of remote social conditions, wherein every seeming inconsistency had its roots in some bygone need, and the character of each class, with its special passions, ignorances and prejudices, was the sum total of influences so ingrown and inveterate that they had become a law of thought. (2:292)

As it disparages the 'ideal' in favour of the 'real', this statement evokes complex, gradual, organic forms of growth and change, and Odo's meditation on deep, complex 'roots' deploys organic imagery that reappears throughout Wharton's œuvre as she describes social and political phenomena. More specifically, Odo's realisation here has a close analogue in Wharton's only other overtly political novel, *The Fruit of the Tree* (1907). Like Odo's epiphany, this one comes late in the novel after a character has suffered, lost and learned: Wharton's protagonist Justine realises that 'human relations' are 'a tangled and deep-rooted growth, a dark forest through which the idealist cannot cut his straight path without hearing at each stroke the cry of the severed branch: "*Why woundest thou me?*"'[47] As James Tuttleton has persuasively argued, the whole of *The Fruit of the Tree* works to criticise 'abstract idealism'.[48] Justine's sense of a 'deep-rooted growth' echoes Odo's perception of the 'roots' of apparent contradictions and the 'ingrown and inveterate' nature of influences. Both of these late, hard-won realisations emphasise densely accumulative organic complexity and the importance of perpetually alert attention to local particulars, and both dismiss idealisms that omit such attention, fail to see that complexity, and thus too rashly seek sudden change without awareness of what that change might destroy. In these fictional epiphanies about idealism's failures, Wharton articulates the realist organic conservatism that will shape her responses to art and politics for the rest of her life.

The Learned Lady

Wharton's articulation of this outlook during the early years of the twentieth century involves fierce grappling with questions about the intellectual capacity of women. As the nod to Darwin in the title of 'Descent' reminds us, 'innate aptitudes' for learning and citizenship were seen to vary across sex as well as race. All of the texts by Wharton discussed in this chapter manifest an interest in the problem of the female intellectual and her agency or lack thereof. In these texts, her representations of female intellect and female intellectuals present a striking pattern of thwarted or disembodied agency, and of female bodies in which agency cannot easily reside. In these texts' treatment of women's claims on intellectual agency and political power, Wharton engages with controversies within the discourse of liberalism, where female education and female suffrage are central questions during the nineteenth century and into the twentieth. In focusing her treatment of these questions on the issue of embodiment, she extends her critique of democratic idealisms like Norton's. Like Henry Adams's

Esther and Madeleine and James's Verena and Hyacinth, Wharton's Fulvia offers a narrative of troubled embodiment; as in the case of Adams's characters, her sex life suffers; and, as in the cases of James's characters, her story ends in a gunshot and a silencing. But Wharton goes farther than Adams and James do. She questions not just the feasibility of cultivating the embodied liberal subject, but the premise of embodiment itself.

Over the course of his career, Norton envisions two different forms of embodiment for women, each of which serves liberal democracy in some crucial way. In the aftermath of the Civil War, he advocates both education and suffrage for women, suggesting that woman might indeed come to embody the ideal liberal subject. In an 1867 article for *The Nation*, he notably anticipates some of Mill's ideas in *Subjection of Women* (1869) as he argues, 'by the possession of the right to vote, and by the exercise of it, the mass of women will be made as fit to vote as the mass of men are'.[49] Norton proposes here a mode of embodiment that empowers by conferring agency: female flesh embodies the ideal liberal subject and thus gains the rights of democratic citizenship. Evidence suggests that Norton may not have held these views comfortably: though he advocates Mill's ideas about education and democracy, his letters repeatedly make sour personal remarks about Mill, and specifically disparage his feminism.[50] As time passes, Norton becomes wore worried about the effects of an expanding franchise, and his public stance falls into line with these private remarks. In commencement addresses at Bryn Mawr in 1896 and at Radcliffe in 1901, Norton speaks out against female suffrage. In the Bryn Mawr address, he quotes an article by John Morley that mentions 'Mill's memorable little book on the "Subjection of Women"', but misquotes Morley by misremembering the book's name, calling it 'The Subjugation of Women'.[51]

And indeed, Norton seems to have forgotten his Mill: departing from earlier affinities with Mill's liberal feminism, he instead distinctly echoes Ruskin's advice to women in *Sesame and Lilies* (1865) and goes so far as to quote approvingly an anti-New Woman poem from *Punch*. A woman's education, Norton tells the Bryn Mawr graduates, should be dedicated 'not to learning in itself that she may become a scholar, not to the acquisition of the arts and sciences in the practice of which she may compete in the open world with man'; rather, her duties as a woman are distinct and separate from those of men, and they lie in the home. In educating her children there, Norton reminds his listeners, woman 'is shaping the progress of civilization and determining the fate of the nation to which she belongs. It is for this great, if inconspicuous duty, that her own education should be consciously directed.' He concludes by saying:

> I have urged you to maintain perpetually strong and fresh your own youthful ideals, and the chief reason why you should do so is that you yourselves may be worthy of being the ideal objects of the love of others. You are, you will become the embodiments in life of the ideals which men cherish and reverence. And it is the noblest service which you can render to make yourself to the living representatives of the highest ideals of beauty in character and conduct.[52]

Norton's Radcliffe address five years later repeats this material almost verbatim, and then adds: 'Be faithful . . . to your own ideals, so that you may exhibit in the world the fair image of true womanhood.'[53] This is an argument for an embodiment that produces not a female liberal subject, but an Angel in the House who complements the male liberal subjects to whom she is wife and mother. As an ideal, she is an object, acted upon (loved, cherished, reverenced) by others, and the chief action she performs is exhibiting an image of true womanhood, the abstract ideal that she makes flesh.

'Vice', 'Descent' and *Valley* interrogate both the argument that women should embody the ideal liberal subject and the argument that women should embody ideals as Angels in Houses. This interrogation finds expression in these texts' pattern of reference to female intellectual agency and its absence. In 'Descent', female intellect exists, but only in disembodied form. The Professor dallies adulterously with his idea for 'The Vital Thing', who is his 'companion'. The story participates in Wharton's critique of liberalism, but it deploys the liberal tactic of using the non-Western exotic as a sign for asymmetrical, oppressive power relations between men and women. Wharton describes an intellectual 'empire' represented with sexualised orientalist imagery: 'This unseen universe was thronged with the most seductive shapes: the Professor moved Sultan-like through a seraglio of ideas.'[54] In this 'idea', the story offers a portrait of a feminine entity whose 'sparkle' and sexiness derive from her engagement in 'the central depths of thought'; but this thinking female exists only figuratively and bodilessly, and only as a passive object acted upon by the male thinker who conceives and then owns her. For that male thinker, this female idea is far more congenial than an actual woman: 'The most fascinating female is apt to be encumbered with luggage and scruples: to take up a good deal of room in the present and overlap inconveniently into the future;

whereas an idea can accommodate itself into a single molecule of the brain or expand to the circumference of the horizon.'[55]

'The Vice of Reading' too offers a female intellect that is not housed in human flesh. The article does not explicitly gender its 'mechanical reader', but elsewhere in Wharton's œuvre the mechanical mind is a distinctly female one. 'The Pelican' too ridicules a woman presuming to intellectual work who eventually reduces herself to a 'lecturing-machine'; the male narrator describes her with a slew of mechanistic images, noting that she is always becoming 'more successful and more automatic'.[56] To portray the intellectual woman as 'mechanical', moreover, is not unusual. Wharton scholars have pointed to Paul Bourget's description of the intellectual girl in his taxonomy of types of the *jeune fille américaine* in his account of his 1893 visit to the US, and several have suggested that his account may refer to Wharton, the conversation-starved young autodidact he met in Newport. Bourget disparages the intellectual girl by noting that she has packed herself like an iron stomach full of Darwin, Huxley, Spencer, Renan and Taine, has swallowed up all ideas, theories and facts, but *tasted* none of them. She reads voluminously, both the *Revue des deux mondes* and avant-garde journals from the *Quartier Latin*, but cannot distinguish between them. She is never wrong; she never makes an error, and one never catches her not knowing something. For Bourget, this is all to her discredit: '*Un esprit se trompe. Un esprit ignore. – Jamais une machine à penser.*'[57] Bourget's *machine à penser*, like Wharton's 'mechanical reader', is too much of a striver. Both Bourget and Wharton object to the intellectual who insists upon her intellect, or who becomes an intellectual through effort, rather than being 'born' into it. And for both of these thinkers, intellectual women are part of an unappealing democratic modernity: in their mechanical imagery, technology, feminism and social mobility merge in a welter of unwelcome newness.

Wharton dedicates *Valley* to Bourget and his wife Minnie, 'in remembrance of Italian days together'; William Vance identifies him, along with Norton, as one of the Italophile readers whom Wharton has in mind as she writes the novel.[58] Later, in her memoir, Wharton would portray her own scholarship in writing *Valley* as anything but 'mechanical'. *Au contraire*, she suggests, the book emerges almost by accident:

> I have often been asked whether the writing of 'The Valley of Decision' was not preceded by months of hard study. I had never studied hard in my life, and it was far too late to learn how when I began to write 'The

> Valley of Decision' ... The truth is that I have always found it hard to explain that gradual absorption into my pores of a myriad details – details of landscape, architecture, old furniture and eighteenth century portraits, the gossip of contemporary diarists and travellers, all vivified by repeated spring wanderings guided by Goethe and the Chevalier de Brosses, by Goldoni and Gozzi, Arthur Young, Dr. Burney and Ippolito Nievo, out of which the tale grew. I did not travel and look and read with the writing of the book in mind; but my years of intimacy with the Italian eighteenth century gradually and imperceptibly fashioned the tale and compelled me to write it.[59]

Wharton's process is mystical ('difficult to explain') and wholly organic. Her written scholarship is not something she does, but something that more or less happens to her: details absorb into her pores, Goethe and others vivify those details, the tale grows, intimacy fashions the tale, and then, at last, Wharton is 'compelled' to write it. At no point in this account does Wharton exert herself; at no point, in fact, does she make herself the active subject of any clause: she is either the direct object or, more often, absent entirely.

This account adopts the 'natural' posture of prestige evoked by Bourget and by 'Vice', but it also exposes a problematic similarity between lowly 'mechanical' intellectual production and high-prestige 'natural' intellectual production. To be intellectual in an 'automatic' or 'mechanical' fashion is to lack autonomy and thus agency. Wharton presents herself as the very opposite of the feminised mechanical mind: her scholarly work is effortless, surely the product of a 'born' intellect rather than a wilfully built one. But in presenting her scholarship as elegantly involuntary, she performs an abandonment of agency that threatens to align her with the *machine à penser*. Mechanised action is action without agency; but so is the involuntary action that Wharton describes. Her account of her own scholarship is thus infected by the problem that appears elsewhere in her œuvre: intellectual agency resides uneasily in the female body.

Within the novel produced by the mystical process that Wharton describes, women who claim agency as intellectuals are ridiculous. Odo encounters 'learned ladies' in liberal circles:

> [they] aspired to all the honors of scholarship, and would order about their servant-girls in Tuscan, and scold their babies in Ciceronian Latin. Among these fair grammarians, however, he met none that wore her learning lightly. They were forever tripping in the folds of their doctors' gowns, and delivering their most trivial views ex cathedrâ;

and too often the poor philosophers, their lords and fathers, cowered under their harangues like frightened boys under the tongue of a schoolmaster. (1:151)

The 'fair grammarians' recall Bourget's *machine à penser* and Wharton's mechanical reader: they insist too much and try too hard. Fulvia is of these women's class but not like them: as the novel repeatedly emphasises, she avoids the presumptuous behaviours associated with performing learning too boldly – and Odo admires her for this. He feels 'a distinct satisfaction in learning that Fulvia Vivaldi had thus far made no public display of her learning. How much pleasanter to picture her as her father's aid, perhaps a sharer in his dreams' (1:149).

Problems arise in Pianura partly because Fulvia ceases to be passive and subservient; instead of serving in the home as her father's helpmate, she aims to involve herself in the public world and impose her idealism on the government. The novel describes this inversion of gendered power structures in scholastic terms. Near the end of the story, as Odo encourages Fulvia the day before she is to give her first academic address in public, he says, 'when we meet tomorrow . . . it will be as teacher and pupil, you in your doctor's gown and I a learner at your feet' (2:274). In spite of her earlier passive modesty, Fulvia has come to resemble the ridiculous 'fair grammarians': she takes the role of schoolmaster, and Odo, the cowering boy. When the young Englishman visits the court, he hears that 'the Duke is the devoted slave of a learned lady'; observing Fulvia's role, he thinks to himself (and records in dramatic italics): '*Here is the hand that rules the state*' (2:205, 213). Odo later comes to see the same, realising with dismay that 'he was no longer the sovereign: the rule had passed out of his hands' (2:237).

Fulvia's hold on power is fraught, however. Paradoxically, she seems to be carrying out simultaneously each of the forms of embodiment that Norton imagines for women over the course of his career, both the earlier form that confers agency and the later form that denies it. For her, to claim agency is also to lose it. She has engaged in the learning and cultivation that makes her an embodiment in female flesh of an ideal citizen – or even, as a scholar, a teacher of citizens. But in doing so, she also seems to be living out the programme prescribed by Norton for the graduates of Bryn Mawr when he urges them to become 'the ideal objects of the love of others' and 'the embodiments in life of the ideals which men cherish and reverence'.[60] The novel states bluntly: 'the girl stood for the embodiment of the purifying emotions that were to renew the world' (2:121). Fulvia herself feels she has become to Odo 'the embodiment of a single thought' (2:222). A glance at the alluring female 'idea' of 'Descent' is instructive: adulterous, sexy and intellectually sparkling, Fulvia resembles that idea. In the short story, the consciousness (if, indeed, there is one) of the idea is sealed off from the Professor's mastering perspective. But *The Valley of Decision* gives us access to that consciousness. In Fulvia, it psychologises that objectified entity, and asks what it feels like to be an idea: to have no luggage, no scruples, nor any flesh at all; to take up space neither in the present nor in the future; to shrink or expand according to the convenience of one's master.

For Fulvia, the experience is painful, limiting and lonely. She feels, with 'a pang of unreasoning regret', that in becoming an 'embodiment' for Odo she has become 'a formula, rather than a woman' to him (2:222). The novel reports: 'She had chosen to be regarded as a symbol rather than a woman, and there were moments when she felt as isolated from life as some marble allegory in its niche above the market-place' (2:218). Fulvia finds that to be a 'thought', 'formula' or 'symbol' is to enter into a coldness of personal and sexual relations. For her, to embody an ideal is to become inhuman, desexualised, marmoreal and static. Not merely the novel's idealist, she is also its embodied ideal; and just as the novel shows her idealism to be fatally wrong, it shows her embodiment to be a deadly prison.

Even as she speaks boldly in public just before her death, apparently exercising political agency in its most typical and potent liberal form, that agency is eerily compromised. Fulvia starts slowly, but then, we read, 'her theme possessed her. One by one she evoked the familiar formulas.' She orates in front of a fresco representing scholars of the past, and Odo sees in those figures 'forbears of the long line of theorists of whom Fulvia was the last inconscient mouthpiece'. During Fulvia's peroration, he observes, 'her old convictions repossessed her and she soared above human fears' (2:277–9). This language suggests that the soaring Fulvia does not own her ideas; rather, they own her. A mere mouthpiece for them, she is both not conscious and not human. In this ostensibly triumphant moment, then, there are shades of the strange agency of the mechanical reader or the female intellectual who is really a *machine à penser*. There are also shades of Wharton's own oddly involuntary intellectual work.

The solution to Fulvia's problems of embodiment and agency is her murder. After she is shot, Odo kneels and holds her, and we read: 'No wound showed through her black gown. She lay as though smitten by some invisible hand. So deep was the hush that her least whisper must have reached him; but though he bent close no whisper came. The invisible hand had struck the very source of life' (2.286).

Fulvia's failure even to whisper last words contrasts with her address in Latin some moments before: the intellectual woman speaking in the public sphere has been securely silenced. Later, gazing at Fulvia's corpse, Odo observes:

> she had grown, beneath the simplifying hand of death, strangely yet most humanly beautiful. Life had fallen from her like the husk from the flower, and she wore the face of her first hopes. The transition had been too swift for any backward look, any anguished rending of the fibres, and he felt himself, not detached by the stroke, but caught up with her into some great calm within the heart of change. (2:287–8)

This assassination is oddly peaceful, quiet and bloodless. At the moment of her death, both Fulvia's 'wound' and the striking 'hand' are 'invisible'; and the 'invisible hand' that strikes her dead then reappears as the 'simplifying hand of death'. This recalls the Englishman's thought on observing Fulvia ('*Here is the hand that rules the state*') and Odo's subsequent realisation that 'he was no longer the sovereign: the rule had passed out of his hands' (2:213, 2:237). There is, then, a reassertion of male dominance exerted through the bullet from the crowd and the force of death itself. As an inversion of the unnaturally inverted power structure that has been troubling Pianura, this murder is simply a correction.

Having felt the pain of being a 'thought', 'formula' or 'symbol, rather than a woman' to Odo, and having risen 'above human fears' as she exercised political agency in public, Fulvia here in death becomes 'strangely yet most humanly beautiful'. Strange indeed: paradoxically, she becomes human flesh again once her body is killed. She acquires a human body when she ceases to be an embodiment of an ideal, but the body she acquires is a dead one. Wharton's odd floral simile emphasises this paradox: in the phrase, 'life had fallen from her like the husk from the flower', life itself is a dead husk, and the living flower beneath that husk is a corpse. This is all backwards. But what it represents is backwards too: Fulvia can be either a living cold marmoreal ideal or a dead human body. Bodiless ideals do not have agency, and dead human bodies do not either.

In Fulvia, Wharton offers an nightmarish account of a distinctly female experience of embodying an ideal: she portrays that experience as one of voiceless paralysis. This portrayal would serve powerfully in a feminist riposte to the sort of antisuffrage argument that Norton makes in his commencement addresses. But *Valley of Decision* does not seem to want to use it for that purpose. Instead, this interrogation of embodiment serves importantly in Wharton's critique of an idealism that defines the embodiment of ideals as a supreme goal. Rather than making a feminist argument by pointing to the specific horror of female experience, the novel portrays that specific horror in order to imply that, under a truly idealist regime, Fulvia's nightmarish experience would be universal. Putting the stuff of a feminist argument to work in her conservative critique, Wharton suggests that democratic liberal idealism is wrong partly because the process of embodying an ideal cannot ever be a process of empowerment. Rather than empowering, it silences and denies agency: the rigidity that makes idealism a limiting outlook also makes embodiment a living death.

A little over two decades after Wharton describes Fulvia lying dead on the street in her academic robes, she herself becomes a woman in full regalia: we have a photograph of her grinning wide on the day she receives an honorary doctorate at Yale in 1923. She was proud to be the first woman recipient. That photograph, along with a 1915 essay in which she expresses a change of heart about female suffrage, might tempt us to observe Wharton growing, over the course of her career, into a feminism more consistent with later, more progressive feminisms. But Wharton's feminism, such as it is, remains mostly local, self-interested and consistent with the perpetuation of racial, economic and social hierarchies. Its sexually emancipatory elements, too frequently misrecognised as revolutionary, in fact often adapt the patterns of good old-fashioned aristocratic libertinage, or express attitudes that Wharton herself identifies as conventional amongst the French bourgeoisie.

She points frankly to the limitations of her own political perspective as she recounts in that 1915 essay how a man enlightened her on the question of women's suffrage: Jean du Breuil patiently explained to her that it was not women like herself who needed the vote, but the poorer women who did not have power. In recounting this anecdote, Wharton emphasises the profound ignorance of those women: in their 'animal fatalism', they know neither what the vote is nor why others seek it on their behalf.[61] During same year that she wears regalia at Yale, Wharton writes in a letter, 'I'm not much interested in traveling scholarships for women – or in fact in scholarships, tout court! – they'd much better stay at home and mind the baby. Still less am I interested in scholarships for female Yids, and young ladies who address a total stranger as "Chère Madame" and sign "meilleurs sentiments".'[62] Social upstarts, Jews and women who do not keep to their place all merge together here as unwelcome elements of democratic modernity; and education, specifically the provision of education for those otherwise without the means to afford it, is the signal feature of that modernity, the topic that sets her off. This is where Norton and Wharton diverge: he saw the expansion of education as a means of making a cultivated citizenry, while she associated it with presumption and insubordination.

In spite of their disagreements, Norton and Wharton were friends who agreed about a great deal. They were both elitists who venerated and lived by culture; their mutual fondness fed on shared adoration of Italian art and literature in particular. Wharton's expressed attitude towards Norton tended to be affectionate above all. We see this not just in her recollections of him in her memoir, but in the sonnet she wrote to honour him on the occasion of his eightieth birthday, which imagines him as a figure exhorting others towards light. Titled 'High Pasture' and dated 'Ashfield, November 1907', the poem draws from experience that Wharton also describes in *A Backward Glance*, where she writes of 'memories radiant with the beauty of the long mountain drive from Lenox to Ashfield, with sunsets watched from the summit of "High Pasture"'. Recalling Norton's conversation on these occasions, she notes, 'Every word he spoke, every question he asked, was like a signal pointing to the next height.'[63] Wharton's sonnet – appropriately Petrarchan, given the honouree – contains two voices. The Norton-like speaker of the quatrains urges listeners to 'come up' above the mist and darkness, declaring defiantly, against plain fact, that 'night is not, autumn is not'; the speaker of the sestet leaves behind 'the sodden tracks of life [. . .] Befogged in failure, chilled with love's decay' in order to honour the first speaker's call and its affirmation that on the 'height illumined of the mind' there is 'day and still more day'.[64] Wharton's imagery of the Ashfield sunset is fairly generic, but it is worth noting that Norton, in his public speaking, drew from the same generic tropes of darkness, light and ongoing day as he spread his message of culture.[65] Wharton's evocation of 'day and still more day' in her poem for Norton seems significant too, given that *The New Day* was the title of the sequel to *Valley of Decision*, which she abandoned as she became a realist novelist against Norton's wishes.[66]

The Valley of Decision articulates Wharton's realism before she manifests it in her novels. The aesthetic and political views that she formulates in the novel would characterise her thinking for the rest of her life. She expressed these views especially sharply in her statements against literary modernism, which she associated with democratic modernity, and which she deplored for what she saw as its formal looseness and its thematic focus on the pathological. As Wegener observes, Wharton's critical writing in the era of modernism manifests 'a wider antiliberal, indeed antidemocratic critique'.[67] Most centrally, Wharton objected to the way that (as she saw it) modernist writing proceeded from theory. She writes in 1923 to Bernard Berenson: 'I *know* it's not because I'm getting old that I'm unresponsive. The trouble with all this new stuff is that it's à thèse: the theory comes first, & dominates it. And it will go the way of "unanimisme" & all the other isms. – Grau ist alle Theorie.'[68] Wegener points out that Wharton repeats this quotation from *Faust* in her *Writing of Fiction* (1925), where she writes, 'Goethe declared that only the Tree of Life was green, and that all theories were gray.'[69] This disparaging of 'theories' in her commentary about writing extends a long pattern of organic imagery about plants and soil and roots, and also closely echoes her description of *The Valley of Decision* some twenty years earlier: she told her publisher in a letter of 1901 that Odo 'tries to apply the theories of the French encyclopaedists to his small principality'.[70] In the novel itself, she writes that, unlike Fulvia, Odo feels 'keenly . . . the difference between theoretical visions of liberty and their practical application'; the visiting English gentleman observes of Odo's court that 'all the heads here are too full of fine theories' (2:228, 2:214). For Wharton, the aesthetic error of the modernists is the same as the political error committed in Pianura: working from an abstract ideal or a theory, imposing those abstractions without regard for actual complexity and empirically gathered local detail.

During the first years of the twentieth century, Wharton formulates this realist conservatism in conversation with Norton's liberal idealism. What begins then as an anti-Victorianism stays mostly the same as the world changes around it, and thus becomes within decades an antimodernism, confidently expressed by a mature novelist in opposition to the experimenters of her time. Wharton herself comments on this irony, drawing explicitly the link between her relationship with Norton and her relation to modernism: recalling Norton's opposition to her realism, she notes, 'we who fought the good fight are now jeered at as the prigs and prudes who barred the way to complete expression – as perhaps we should have tried to do, had we known it was to cause creative art to be abandoned for pathology!'[71] The status of prude, as Wharton observes, is mobile. What remains remarkably constant over the years, however, is her political thought, which does not alter substantially in response to the local particulars of the early twentieth century. In this fixedness, as in her affinity for scholarly pursuit, Wharton resembles the heroine that she kills off.

Part II

The Remnant at Harvard: Whiteness, Higher Education and Democracy

Chapter 4

Universal White: Discrimination and Selection in James's American Scene

When Henry James returned to the US in 1904 for the first time in many years, one of the new things he noticed was the majestic walls and gates around Harvard Yard. Several years before, President Charles William Eliot had issued an appeal to alumni, and they had offered up their dollars. McKim, Mead and White had gone to work; rustic wooden fences had gone down, and neoclassical barriers of brick and iron had gone up.[1] Barrett Wendell wrote to Henry's brother William, who was away from Cambridge: 'they are building fences and things [. . .] One doesn't quite know the place, which suddenly seems ever so much more monumental than it used to be.'[2] Charles Eliot Norton, always hard to please in matters architectural, disapproved: while 'perhaps appropriate enough . . . for the inclosure of ornamental grounds', he wrote, the new fencing failed to 'suggest the seclusion becoming to a place of study' and 'the character which should distinguish the wall of a scholastic institution'. He added: 'not one of the gates is of conspicuous merit as a work of art'.[3] Henry liked the walling-in of the Yard. 'In the land of the "open door,"' he would write, these walls and gates show 'the way in which the formal enclosure of objects at all interesting immediately refines upon their interest, immediately establishes values.' Within Harvard's new walls, James finds space for what Americans, to his dismay, otherwise overwhelmingly eschew: 'the art of discrimination'.[4]

This chapter takes James's reaction to these walls and gates as the starting place for a wide-ranging reassessment of his thinking about race, nativism and democracy in the early twentieth century. Scholarship interested in these issues has lavished attention on the passages of *The American Scene* (1907) that discuss people who are not white, moneyed and Protestant. Some find in these passages evidence of an edgier, more progressive James; others use the same passages to assail James as conservative, anti-Semitic or racist.[5] Here, I turn from these much-read passages to focus instead on James's treatment of places like Harvard. James's notebook indicates that he planned a chapter titled 'The Universities and Colleges: An Impression', containing material 'not elsewhere workable-in'.[6] In his writing about universities and colleges, James articulates an aesthetic that prizes discrimination, differentiation, delimitation and exclusion. The articulation of this aesthetic unmistakably carries some political meaning; the way you read that meaning, however, will depend significantly on how you – as an intellectual, a scholar, a teacher, a critic or a writer – understand your own political obligations and powers.

Walls and gates figure saliently in political discourse at the time of James's US visit. He contemplates the new enclosure at Harvard not too long after Thomas Bailey Aldrich warns: 'Wide open and unguarded stand our gates'; Aldrich revises Emma Lazarus's 'sea-washed, sunset gates' and the 'golden door' that beckons, open wide, at the end of her sonnet.[7] James is not the only one to observe a contrast between the wide-open US and the gated enclosure of Harvard. In 1893, Wendell hails Harvard men as 'native Yankees of the old stock' who come from an 'old New England, still pure/ Of foreign taint', and in the same publication anticipates Aldrich's unguarded gates as he protests: 'the floodgates are opened. Europe is emptying itself into our Eastern Seaports; Asia overflowing the barriers we have tried to erect on the Western coast.'[8] Some two decades earlier, Wendell's colleague, friend and teacher, Norton, had also mentioned Harvard as he discussed 'barriers'. In an 1871 letter to Edwin Lawrence Godkin, Norton wrote: 'The Nation & Harvard & Yale Colleges seem to me almost the only solid barriers against the invasion of modern barbarism & vulgarity'.[9]

This sentence accompanies Norton with eerie reliability when he appears in twentieth-century scholarship, often serving to affirm that he is part of an antidemocratic Anglo-Saxon gentry alarmed at its loss of power in an era of immigration.[10] The quoted fragment serves well as evidence for this account of Norton: elite institutions of higher education, it seems to say, serve as a bulwark against the coming flood of democratic vulgarity. And, especially since Norton was quite capable of making remarks about the 'invasion' of the Irish in Boston and earlier being only mildly critical of Know-Nothingism, his 'barriers' may appear identical to the walls and gates of later anti-immigrant fantasy.[11] Norton has thus been associated with the younger Harvard men who found the Immigration Restriction League, or positioned, along with Wendell and Henry Adams, as one of the teachers who helps to shape their nativism. These representations of Norton affirm the narrative about 'the genteel tradition', which holds that men like him and Godkin retreat into bitter, impotent passivity as the US changes around them.

This passivity serves an important function in Ross Posnock's *Trial of Curiosity* (1991), which remains the most sustained examination of James's relation with the thinkers of 'the genteel tradition.'[12] In that influential book and in essays of 1995, 1998 and 2009 that reiterate its arguments, the passive, closed-off retreat of genteel thinkers helps to define by contrast James's active, open engagement with democratic modernity.[13] *Trial of Curiosity* brilliantly exposed the James recognised by Jamesians today, one who savours immersive surrender to experience and lives by radical curiosity. But its argumentation, and that of those subsequent essays, occasionally leans on accounts of the 'genteel' and the 'Victorian' that are at odds with evidence.

Posnock emphasises James's differences from the affluent, white, 'genteel' thinkers who were his long-time friends, and highlights his affinities with a younger set of writers whom he did not know, including Randolph Bourne, Walter Benjamin, W. E. B. Du Bois, John Dewey, Alain Locke and Ralph Ellison. Reading *American Scene* as 'a calculated act of affiliation with the new century and its possibilities', Posnock observes it register ambivalently a 'transition from a Victorian culture of hierarchy and homogeneity to an urban modernity' that is heterogeneous and democratic. This urban modernity is the site for a pragmatist receptivity to complexity and indeterminacy, which rebels against an older order that prefers detachment, mastery, judgement and incurious remove. Du Bois, he notes, sees that William James's pragmatism, along with Boasian anthropology, can work against 'the theory and practice of white supremacy'.[14] *The American Scene*'s 'pragmatist commitment to immersion, hazard, contingency' thus participates in a 'trajectory' that 'displays political power and even courage'. Contributing to the development of 'pragmatist pluralism', the text formulates ideas before their time: its 'message', Posnock writes, 'was too radical to have an immediate impact in a political landscape hollowed out by nativism and Jim Crow'.[15]

Along with subsequent books by Sara Blair and Barbara Haviland, *Trial of Curiosity* pushed back against an earlier generation of scholarship that classed James among genteel authors retreating from life into art. These studies overturn what Pierre Walker calls, in an essay committed to the same recuperative project, 'the cliché that James was not publicly engaged'.[16] As Kenneth W. Warren observes, 'Both Blair and Posnock appear to want to turn their readings of James to political account.'[17] More specifically, both portray a James whose receptive, fluid, flexible or open-ended ways of thinking constitute an oppositional stance towards more racist or more conservative patterns of thought. Observing James's '"mixed"' performances of gender and whiteness, Blair sees him work 'to create a more open-endedly, fluidly "Anglo-Saxon" or Anglo-American cultural subject'; she extends that analysis in a 2012 essay that notices his 'strikingly indeterminate idiom of race'.[18] Indeterminacy carries specific political implications for Posnock too: James's 'flexibility', he writes, 'marks his distinction in the largely nativist patrician world in which he lived. Lacking deeply felt class loyalties, James in his own genteel way was an outlaw.'[19]

As Gert Buelens observes, both Blair and Posnock participate in 'an attempt to invest the Jamesian aesthetic with combative rhetorical force', emphasising the 'contestatory' elements in James's prose.[20] They describe a James whose texts resist, oppose or contest ways of thinking that are more hegemonic and fixed. In these accounts, James's inveterate habit of analysing persons, places, manners, forms and experiences – his astonishingly fruitful practice of exercising what he calls 'an imagination to which literally everything obligingly signified' – exercises political agency, often in a more or less subversive manner.[21] Warren questions this account; he writes, 'I would want to . . . warn the project of cultural studies critique of the incipient conservatism endemic to the political drama of the intellect,' and cautions against the 'overestimation' of 'intellectual victories', 'a distortion that contributes to a species of political quietism'.[22] Posnock counters that James himself rejects such warnings: 'James's aesthetic practice is simultaneously political practice'. This is 'explicit in *The American Scene* where he adroitly deploys ambiguity to disrupt the ideological containments of "American simplicity"' (for which, as Posnock notes, James expresses his hatred).[23] The book enacts 'a pragmatism that turns aesthetics from contemplation to action that cuts against the grain of capitalist efficiency and utility'.[24] 'Rather than remaining aloof in static contemplation,' Posnock later explains, 'James actively solicits and corporeally experiences shock as the imprint of the material pressure of change': he 'engages viscerally' with the heterogeneous modern US.[25]

Calling his own argument 'analogical', Posnock observes a 'stark, obdurate literalism' in Warren's remark that *American Scene*'s 'handling of the race problem falls dreadfully short of the clear denunciations of lynching and mob violence that prevailing conditions called for'.[26] Posnock makes concessions to this sort of literalism when he writes that 'James was rarely active politically (his response to World War I being an exception)' and takes the role of public intellectual only in his 1898 essays for *Literature* magazine and in *The American Scene*.[27] William James, as Posnock notes, inhabits that role: he advocated against both lynching and imperialism. Taking another counterexample close to home, we might also recall that Wilky James's side was ripped open by a shell just before a canister ball hit his foot; as stretcher bearers tried to help him, one's head was blown off.[28] Though Henry James lived through the Civil War and the age of lynching, his corporeal shocks were *frissons*, and his viscera were always safe. He generally declined to participate in activism or in discourse understood to be political; and he lived comfortably amongst the very wealthy, watching them avidly. If he offers a model of radical, antiracist, anticapitalist political agency, that model is one that notably asks almost nothing of the elite white person who adopts it.

So how should we describe the political agency James exercises? More broadly, how should we talk about the relation between the political agency of writers and the political agency of their texts, which might cause 'impact' only later, in the hands of others, as part of a 'trajectory'? These are troublesome questions because we ourselves (as writers, critics, restless analysts) are implicated by whatever answers we offer. If we say that James failed to exercise political agency because he did not volunteer to fight for the Union with a Black regiment like Wilky, or because he was not a public intellectual like William, we implicitly adopt specific definitions of political writing, political agency and the political. But that specificity matters: the models of political agency that Wilky and William exercise (and that James eschews) are exactly those celebrated by the Harvard-based liberal thinkers associated with the genteel. William, himself a Harvard-based liberal thinker, does not merely take on the role of public intellectual; he also argues explicitly for the role of an educated elite in US democracy.

William's arguments on that subject participate in a long, vast conversation about the political duties and powers of intellectuals. The testy mid-1990s exchange between Posnock and Warren itself forms an episode in that conversation, which is always self-reflexive, and which extends into current debates about impact, public humanities, formalisms, presentist approaches to teaching and scholarship, and the politics of critique and postcritique.[29] Caroline Levine's recent work on 'forms' notably advocates an omnivorous habit of analysis that resembles James's, and Anna Kornbluh identifies in James's interest in architecture (including walls, doors and gates) an expression of a potent realism that 'drafts and constructs worlds' rather than simply representing them.[30] Both Levine and Kornbluh find in practices of analysis similar to James's a model for intellectual work that exercises political agency.

But embracing that model need not mean casting James himself as a presentist formalist *avant la lettre*. 'Forms' notably does not mean in James's work what it does in Levine's. While her definition of the term is commodious, his is more restrictive; what bothers him in the US is not an abundance of bad forms but (as he puts it) 'the so complete abolition of *forms*'.[31] James, like Edith Wharton, objects to formlessness. For both, forms are what flourish in Europe, where they are inextricable from a context of social hierarchy – as opposed to the social democracy of the US, which dissolves form, washing it out into flat white blankness. And although James lives for and by the practice of analysing social and aesthetic forms, he resists arguments for the political utility of that practice. As teachers, we can and should work to make James's intensely generative practice of reading a broadly accessible one; but we should also notice that James himself describes the pleasures of limited access, privacy and exclusivity.

He does so in his responses to precisely the thinkers that Posnock dismisses as Victorian and genteel. Taking a less dismissive approach to those thinkers, we can see more clearly what James says in response to their ideas. For Victorian liberals like Arnold, Mill, Godkin and Norton, the political agency of intellectuals and artists is a primary concern: in their writing and in their own careers, they are committed to the idea that the cultivated elite has a duty to serve and guide the larger community. They subscribe to the characteristically Victorian view that art and politics are not separable, and that culture has crucial functions in democracy. Unlike James, they are all directly engaged in government roles, political activism, education, political writing and editing, or some mix of those things. If, as Posnock suggests, the genteel thinkers seem more committed to practices of conclusion and judgement than James, that is perhaps because their writing frequently seeks to intervene in overtly political discourse, while James's does not. But in fact, far from privileging practices of conclusion and judgement, their liberalism often explicitly valorises openness to new evidence and new ideas. They presume to seek progress through the clash of diverse ideas in contest, and the practice of self-development that they advocate is always unfinished.

Famously, when Arnold describes culture as 'a study of perfection', he specifies: 'Not a having and a resting, but a growing and a becoming, is the character of perfection as culture conceives it.'[32]

Fluid and flexible ways of thinking can serve a range of political agendas; for the Civil War generation, the most notable practice of inflexible certainty was John Brown's. As Louis Menand observes in his study of the shift from Victorian to modern in the US, some in this generation come to valorise forms of uncertainty under the rubric of pragmatism partly because they see first-hand that certainty leads to the bloodshed of the battlefield.[33] But enslaved people had been shedding blood for many years before that because of flexible thinking amongst enfranchised whites about when and if slavery should be opposed: certainties lead to killing, but so too do open-ended refusals to decide.

The splendid density of James's prose makes it possible to draw from his entangled sentences a range of political ideas. *American Scene* does not really argue for any of them; as Buelens shows, James's text often asks to be read in ways that are not primarily political, and often eagerly confesses its aim to be not politics but pleasure and a kind of intellectual and aesthetic play.[34] That kind of play can, of course, signify politically, but (as sociologists of class have observed) its political signification is often conservative or exclusionary. The argument to the contrary – the argument that aesthetic engagement can and should be inclusive and democratic – is an argument we find in Victorian claims about the practice of culture.

To see those claims more clearly, we can start by reconsidering Norton's comment about Harvard and Yale as 'barriers'. Turning to the 1871 letter from which this fragment is drawn, we see that Norton's words do not, in fact, support the narrative about him that they have served. The one scholar who gives this letter a sustained reading actually notes an unusually 'radical' or 'revolutionary turn of mind' here, as Norton expresses approval of the recent Paris Commune and observes capital's '"unfair advantage over labour"'.[35] Norton's biographer notes that 'barriers' were a particular fixation for him in the early 1870s, when he also describes Harvard as a 'breakwater'.[36] In both private correspondence and published writing, what Norton repeatedly imagines barriers shutting out is not democratic or immigrant hordes, but a barbarism that inheres in wealth or plutocracy. Norton refers to 'barriers' in his 'Intellectual Life of America' (1888), where he declares that modern democracy depends on institutions of higher education, which 'are the chief barriers against the ever-rising tide of ignorance and materialism'.

Here, once again, Norton's 'barriers' are not elite fortresses against the flood of democracy: in this argument, the university is a barrier that wards off a rising tide of barbarism, ignorance and materialism that would destroy democracy. Norton does not say here that universities should protectively wall in the well-bred few: rather, he argues that the 'most direct remedy' for American democracy's dysfunction 'lies in the wider diffusion of the higher education'. 'The conception of a liberal education', he writes, 'needs revival and reinvigoration, not in the interest of the few, a select and eminent class, but in the interest of the many, of the whole community.'[37]

Along with his cousin, President Eliot, Norton sees a crucial public role for institutions of higher education and their graduates. Such institutions, Norton writes in 1890, 'are the head-waters of the stream of education by which the general intellectual and moral life of the community is in large measure supplied and sustained'.[38] Decades earlier, he had declared, 'Culture is like a river which flows downward from the heights, still widening as it flows, – till . . . it spreads its fertilizing waters over a continent, and the whole nation drinks of its refreshing stream.'[39] Norton's images of head-waters and widening flows present an alternative to the misread 'barriers' that have been associated with him, and stand in contrast to Wendell's nativist 'floodgates'. Norton and Eliot alike evoke a flow that moves outward from universities, rather than an incoming tide that threatens them. As Eliot steps down from his presidency in 1909, he affirms that one of the purposes of a university is 'to send forth into the American community an annual flood of young men who mean to serve their country and their race, who have enough of the keen sense of public duty'.[40] These ideas about service are literally carved into the walls and gates that go up around the College Yard under Eliot's leadership; in 1901, he helps to write the inscription for Dexter Gate, which (still) tells those entering from the street, 'ENTER/TO GROW IN WISDOM', and reminds those exiting, 'DEPART/TO BETTER SERVE THY COUNTRY AND THY KIND'.[41]

Both Eliot and Norton exhort the educated elite to pursue this duty of service. Surveying 'the lack of intellectual elevation and of moral discrimination' that regrettably prevails in the US, Norton asserts in 'Intellectual Life' that 'the American people are not to be blamed or condemned . . . Those only among us are to be blamed who, having better opportunities for self-culture . . . receiving better education, understanding better the meaning of things, accept with indifference the conditions of inferiority, and make no effort to raise the general standards of character and conduct.' Norton bemoans the 'mediocrity' and 'vulgarity' that dominate in the US, pointing to 'a predominance of the taste and standards of judgment of the uneducated and unrefined masses, over those of the more-enlightened and better-instructed few'.[42] This last phrase echoes the text that Norton quotes elsewhere in the same essay: Mill's *On Liberty*, which discusses leadership by a 'more highly gifted and instructed One or Few'.[43]

Both Mill's comment and Norton's speak to the larger conversation about the political role of the cultivated minority, or what Arnold calls 'the remnant'. James would be familiar with the conversation not just because of his general attentiveness to Arnold, but also because, in the years leading up to his US visit, exchanges about the remnant became especially heated in the liberal Boston–Cambridge milieu that remained, in spite of his expatriation, familiar terrain for him. Questions central to the conversation about the remnant had figured previously in exchanges between Norton and James, notably flaring up around the Arnoldian term 'criticism': in 1873, James had insisted to Norton, 'I *do* ... believe in criticism.' He worried, however, that it was 'vastly overdone'. Disparaging 'so much preaching, advising, rebuking & reviling, & so little *doing*', James adds: 'A single positive attempt, even with great faults, is worth, generally most of the comments & amendments on it. You'll agree to that.' But James goes on to say: 'I regard the march of history very much as a man placed astride of a locomotive, without knowledge or help, would regard the progress of that vehicle. To stick on, somehow, & even to enjoy the scenery as we pass, is the sum of my aspirations.'[44] The relationship between enjoyment and criticism would remain a source of disagreement between James and Norton for decades to come; and efforts to define 'criticism' and '*doing*' would drive the Harvard-centred conversation about the role of the educated elite in a democracy.

That conversation plays out in scattered addresses and essays, often published in *The Atlantic Monthly* or *The Forum* and then subsequently in books.[45] More broadly defined, of course, this conversation is not contained within these publications, this moment or Anglo-American liberalism at large: it carries on in our own time, and also extends backward as far as classical and biblical texts. Its long history shows in the fact that Arnold's interventions refer not just to contemporary interlocutors, but also to Plato and Isaiah. Even considering just the British nineteenth century, we find along with Arnold's 'remnant' Coleridge's 'clerisy' and Carlyle's 'Hero as a Man of Letters' and 'Aristocracy of Talent', as well as

Mill's discussion of that 'One or Few'.[46] On the other side of the Atlantic, Ralph Waldo Emerson makes multiple arguments about an aristocracy of especially capable men, perhaps most notably in his Harvard Phi Beta Kappa addresses of 1837 and 1867. For thinkers linked to Harvard, the most important nineteenth-century interlocutors are often Arnold and Emerson, whose ideas and terms weave through later arguments.

We can see this conversation play out across a wide body of texts, including George William Curtis's 'The Duty of the American Scholar to Politics and the Times' (1856), 'The Public Duty of Educated Men' (1877) and 'The Leadership of Educated Men' (1882), as well as Wendell Phillips's 1881 Harvard Phi Beta Kappa address, 'The Scholar in a Republic', Arnold's writings on America from the early 1880s, and responses and reformulations by President Eliot, Norton and others around the turn of the century. Godkin publishes 'The Duty of Educated Men in a Democracy' in 1894; shortly thereafter, his antagonist Theodore Roosevelt lets loose 'The College Graduate and Public Life', one of a number of repetitive statements on that theme. In 1897, President Eliot lectures on 'The Function of Education in Democratic Society'; and in fact, many of the works in his sprawling œuvre might reasonably bear that title. William James engages with these questions in a 1902 address that discusses the role of Dreyfusard-style *intellectuels*; he further develops these ideas in a 1907 address on 'The Social Value of the College-Bred'. His student, W. E. B. Du Bois, had by then been writing on the subject for years, making perhaps the most famous intervention in this conversation with 'The Talented Tenth' (1903). Du Bois's arguments about the function of the educated minority extend into his Atlanta University studies, especially *The College-Bred Negro* (1900), as well as the *Atlantic* articles that become part of *Souls of Black Folk* (1903). Du Bois's call for a Black remnant echoes the call issued by Emerson, Arnold and others: generally, the remnant they hail is also racially specific, and it is white.

This long chapter shows how James's writings about US democracy respond to this conversation. Its first section surveys arguments about 'numbers' in the conversation about the remnant from Arnold, Emerson and Norton before examining James's engagement with their ideas in his 1898 essays on American letters, which consider opposed visions of a remnant from Godkin and Roosevelt. With conspicuous reference to Arnold, James responds to those visions by offering one of his own. James's own remnant, however, seeks pleasure, not service; his essays model the sort of 'reading into' that such a remnant might practise, transmuting the stuff of politics into the stuff of art.

The next section of the chapter juxtaposes James's articulation of an aesthetic of 'discrimination and selection' in *American Scene* and 'Question of our Speech' (1905) with political writing about 'distinction and separation' by Norton and Eliot. While they value the nation's institutions of higher education as training grounds for a hard-working remnant, James finds in the same institutions precious cloisters and refuges. Their universities serve the public and democracy; James's offer private pleasure. Comparing their valorisations of heterogeneity with James's, I show that his praise for difference and differentiation serves nostalgic conservatism as readily as it does democratic pluralism; and, moreover, that his negative account of white homogeneity disparages egalitarian democracy as readily as it does racism or nativism. The political trajectory to which James most obviously contributes, I suggest, is the elitist one that also includes Wharton, who shares his aesthetic of discrimination. But James fits uneasily in any political trajectory: while thinkers like Eliot and Norton are interested in heterogeneity and homogeneity as political phenomena, James is interested in them as aesthetic qualities and aesthetic experience, and his texts are not especially interested in the political functions of the aesthetic.

The final section of the chapter shows that James's 1909 essay on Norton portrays him as the type of the serene Puritan New Englander. That type figures importantly in influential later twentieth-century iterations of the narrative about the genteel, where it manifests a prudish conservatism opposed by insurgent democratic energy. But in James's essay, I argue, the serene Puritan type carries nineteenth-century connotations that make it the proponent of democracy rather than democracy's enemy. James's essay describes explicitly his difference from Norton the New Englander: while the Professor abjures pleasure and insists on the moral, public and democratic functions of art, culture and criticism, James does not.

Numbers and the Remnant

When James contributes to a series of essays on American letters in *Literature* during the spring and summer of 1898, he tells William Dean Howells (also a contributor) that they are 'drivel', and explains: 'I simply couldn't afford not to accept. But I am too out of it all, & too ignorant.'[47] Drivel or not, these essays begin to formulate the response to the conversation about the remnant that James would develop further during his 1904–5 tour. For James, as for many others, the primary point of departure for any discussion of literature, culture and cultivation in US democracy is Matthew Arnold's writing on the subject.[48] It is no surprise, then, that one of his 1898 essays silently quotes Arnold as it takes up 'the question of numbers'; for Arnold, as for Emerson and Norton, numbers and numerosity are key issues in the discussion about the role of the cultivated elite in a democracy. The 1898 series engages with that discussion in its reviews of Roosevelt's *American Ideals* (1897) and of Godkin's *Unforeseen Tendencies of Democracy* (1898). In taking up books by these two authors, James effectively stages their interlinked disagreements about imperialism and the proper work of the remnant. His reviews take the tone of his relations their authors: he is prickly towards Roosevelt and amicable towards Godkin. But James does not respond to any of these thinkers by taking up their political arguments as such. Faced with questions about imperialism and democracy, he appropriates the suggestive raw stuff of which those questions are formed and fashions it into something new.

For James in these essays, encountering political ideas is, like the rest of experience, a process of analysis that is also a process of aesthetic engagement that is, above all, a process of art-making. Godkin, Arnold, Emerson, Norton and (differently) Roosevelt all imagine a cultivated elite that saves democracy; what James's cultivated elite does is read – in the richest, most generative sense possible. His 1898 essays model that practice, which finds even fuller expression in *The American Scene*, where his restless analyst sees in American numbers and numerosity superlatively interesting matter to 'read into'. We may see important political functions for that sort of reading, but James himself does not argue for those functions.

Literature had already oriented itself towards questions about the vast reading public and the fate of culture in democracy, noticing Norton and Eliot as well as Arnold in treating those topics ('Professor Norton', one item states, 'has long been one of the most public-spirited of the citizens of Cambridge, Mass., taking an active part in local politics').[49] When James reviews Godkin's book alongside Nicholas Murray Butler's *Meaning of Education* (1898), the pairing of these books locates them within the liberal discourse that understands democracy and education as crucially interconnected matters. James approvingly quotes Butler: '"The difficulties of democracy," he excellently says, "are the opportunities of education."'[50] But while the review goes so far as evoke this conversation about democracy and education, it stops short of participating in it. James does not address Butler's policy ideas; as the review draws to a close, he quotes without comment an extremely long passage about college entrance examinations, and one has the sense that he is running out the clock. *Unforeseen Tendencies* speaks to the difficulties of democracy and opportunities of education when it describes the decline of 'persuasion' in public discourse, expressing the liberal perspective that understands the practices of thoughtful reading, writing and discussion as central to citizenship and crucial to democracy. Godkin writes, 'nothing is more striking in the reading public to-day, in our democracy, than the increasing incapacity for continuous attention', and also points to the perils of having a 'governing class' that is not a 'reading class'.[51]

James himself takes up the topic of reading and readers in the essay of this series titled 'The Question of the Opportunities'. For Godkin, this topic is part of an analysis of democracy's functioning; for James, it is part a discussion of the literary marketplace. He presciently imagines a fragmentation of that marketplace that also happens to be a shattering of the public sphere Godkin desires. James pictures a 'breaking up into pieces' that shows 'the public we somewhat loosely talk of as for literature or for anything else is really as subdivided as a chess-board, with each little square confessing only to its own *kind* of accessibility'. He adds: 'Then, for all we know, we may get individual publics positively more sifted and evolved than anywhere else, shoals of fish rising to more delicate bait.'[52]

Such a shoal did not rise to meet the essays in which James offered this vision. This is perhaps not surprising; *Literature*'s negative 1897 review of *What Maisie Knew* declares that James 'has had his special public, and has been content to appeal only to educated people'. *Maisie*, the review concludes, 'is a serious study, and the reader who does not mean to study it had better leave it alone'.[53] Unlike other contributions to the same series, James's essays are printed with glosses in the margin that compress his complexities into an easy tag for each paragraph. These aids were, apparently, insufficient. Telling Howells that he has 'had to stop' this series, James explains: 'The people wrote to me practically, that they found they were, largely through my voluminosity, intensity, &c., &c., overdoing that department, and that unrest was visible among their clientèle.'[54] The discontent, he implies, was mutual. James's writing about the marketplace for literature in *Literature* is itself subject to the pressure of that marketplace: in keeping with Godkin's worries, these readers cannot or will not bring continuous attention to prose that is voluminous and intense.

Godkin treats incapacities like these as a public, political problem; James treats them as a personal, financial and aesthetic one.

In the essay that imagines that elite shoal hungry for delicate bait, James calls American literature 'literature for the million, or rather for the fast-arriving billion', noting the 'mere numbers of the huge, homogenous and fast-growing population'. (James clarifies: 'homogenous I call the huge American public, with a due sense of the variety of races and idioms that are more and more under contribution to build it up, for it is precisely in the great mill of the language, our predominant and triumphant English . . . that the elements are ground into unity.') He writes: 'This question of numbers is brought home to us again and again with force by the amazing fortune apparently open now, any year, to the individual book – usually the lucky novel – that happens to please.'[55] When James refers here to 'the question of numbers', he silently quotes Arnold, who declares in his own essay about culture in American democracy, 'A Word about America' (1882), that 'the question of numbers is of capital importance'.[56] The numerosity of the US population and its rapidly growing 'millions' is an ongoing theme within the conversation about the role of the cultivated elite in democracy. Arnold's discussion of numerosity extends to the US questions already salient in Britain: the 1867 Reform Act had prompted John Morley to declare, 'the contest will lie between brains and numbers on the one side, and wealth, rank, vested interest, possession in short, on the other'.[57] Arnold takes up this topic most conspicuously in one of the lectures he delivers on his American tour of 1883–4, 'Numbers; or, the Majority and the Remnant', which repeats material from his 'Word About America'.

In that essay, Arnold observes that both Britain and the US can boast 'individuals . . . lovers of the humane life, lovers of perfection, who emerge in all classes'; he specifies, however, that 'the important question is: In what numbers are they to be found?' Taking up the subject again in 'Numbers', he clarifies, 'the important thing . . . is not that the remnant bears but a small proportion to the majority': what matters is its 'positive bulk'. The great scale of 'modern States', he suggests, means that, for the first time, 'the remnant might be so increased as to become an actual power'. And the population of the US is the largest of all. Arnold exhorts his American audience: 'you are fifty millions and growing apace. What a remnant yours may be, surely! A remnant of how great numbers, how mighty strength, how irresistible efficacy!' Arnold's American remnant is auspicious not just because of its unprecedented scale, but because of its racial composition, made, like the English, of 'German stock'.[58]

When Emerson discusses the function of the educated elite in the US, he too refers repeatedly to numbers, numerosity and millions. What distinguishes Emerson's numbers is how readily and benevolently they grow. Speaking at Harvard's 1867 Phi Beta Kappa proceedings, Emerson hails his audience as a remnant whose numbers are infinitely expansive. 'When I say the educated class,' he states, 'I know what a benignant breadth that word has, – new in the world, – reaching millions instead of hundreds.' Pointing to the function of the 'exceptional men', 'the educated class' or 'the cultivated class', he asserts that 'the truth, the hope of any time, must always be sought in the minorities'. Emerson suggests that the proportion of this class within the larger whole is important: 'The question . . . is', he affirms, 'whether the high qualities which distinguished them can be imparted?' This 'whether' question will preoccupy Emerson's interlocutors as the century advances and turns. Emerson himself answers it with a resounding affirmation: 'The poet Wordsworth asked, "What one is, why may not millions be?" Why not? Knowledge exists to be imparted.'[59]

Norton speaks directly to these arguments about the bulk and proportion of the remnant in 'Intellectual Life'. When that essay appears in November 1888, Arnold and his views on culture in the US are at the forefront of public conversation: the issue of the *New Princeton Review* that includes Norton's article also contains one of the many articles on Arnold published that year, which saw both his death and the publication of his *Civilization in the United States* (in which he refers to 'an American friend of mine, Professor Norton').[60] Norton's article engages conspicuously with Arnold's ideas, as well as Emerson's and Mill's; like Arnold and Emerson, Norton points to the unprecedented American 'millions', noting the 'magnificent spectacle' of so many living with civil liberty and material comfort.[61] 'Intellectual Life' contradicts Arnold's assertion that it is the 'positive bulk' of the remnant that matters, as well as Arnold's recommendation of reform for secondary rather than higher education; following instead Emerson's emphasis on proportion over bulk, Norton argues for the 'wider diffusion of the higher education'. But he handles this question with less optimism (and less verbal grace) than his late friend. Taking up Emerson's 'whether' question directly, he asks 'whether the highest results attained by the civilization of the past, and hitherto confined to a select and comparatively small body, can be preserved, diffused, and made the foundation of a social order in which all advantages shall be more equally shared'. Norton differs from Emerson not just in his more awkwardly wordy formulation of this question, but also in the tenor of his answer to it: 'The indications at present', he writes, 'are doubtful, and admit of widely differing interpretations.'[62] In an alarmed essay of 1896, troubled by the Venezuelan boundary dispute, Norton again takes up the 'whether' question. 'The signs', he says this time around, 'are dubious': 'the century closes not only with a numerically greater, but also a proportionately larger part of our community in a state of ignorance than that with which it began.' Attributing these 'increasing proportions of popular ignorance' to immigration, he also points to the ignorance 'of the native-born who are on the outskirts or outside the pale of civilization'. Norton suggests that neither Arnold's nor Emerson's scheme for a functioning remnant is playing out: even as the bulk of the total population grows, the proportion of the remnant within it decreases. His conclusion quotes Arnold's words about seeing steadily and whole, and exhorts readers to do their duty, affirming that 'it is on the minority of the people and on the individual effort of each member of it that the issue depends'.[63]

Two years after Norton makes this appeal, James's essay transforms 'the question of numbers' into a 'question of opportunities'. Arnold, Emerson and Norton are interested in the American millions as a political phenomenon. For James, those millions provoke questions that are about the English language and the literary marketplace. He too notes that the US alone will 'meet fate on such a scale', making up 'the biggest public' of all; but his image of 'shoals of fish rising to more delicate bait' reimagines the visions of the remnant offered by their earlier considerations of American numerosity.[64] James's cultivated elite differs from theirs in that it does not serve a public function. Rather than playing a crucial role in democracy, this remnant indulges its exceptionally delicate taste. Its signature activity is neither influencing nor leading; it buys, reads and ascends upward, away from the duller majority swimming below.

James's reviews of Godkin and Roosevelt speak obliquely to the conversation about the remnant, not least by bringing on to the pages of *Literature* two voices so conspicuously in disagreement on that subject. That disagreement had played out in periodicals during the spring and summer of 1894. In March, Godkin made an argument about the role of educated men in a democracy in *The Forum*, notably presenting President Eliot as an exemplar. Several months later, in the July number of the same publication, Roosevelt took up Godkin's terms and contested his argument. Then, in August, Roosevelt published in *The Atlantic* an essay that repeated material from his *Forum* piece under a title that more directly pointed to the topic of Godkin's article.[65] Both of these essays by Roosevelt appear in the book that James reviews for *Literature* in 1898. There is much for James to dislike in that volume: it includes 'True Americanism', with its rallying cry for assimilation, its reference to 'that flaccid habit of mind which its possessors style cosmopolitanism', and, worse still, its rather specific dig at 'the undersized man of letters, who flees the county because he, with his delicate, effeminate sensitiveness, finds the conditions of life on this side of the water crude and raw'.[66] James's review huffs that Roosevelt's 'value is impaired for intelligible precept by the puerility of his simplifications'.[67]

Roosevelt's remarks about effeminacy and cosmopolitanism are part of the argument he makes about the remnant (which is, like most arguments on that subject, also an argument about masculinity). He rejects the claims of Godkin's *Forum* article, which declares that educated men are not currently performing their duty, which is 'talk', or 'criticism'. 'In "talk,"' Godkin notes self-referentially, 'I include contributions to periodical literature.' He defines 'criticism' forcefully: 'the word means *judging*'. Such judgements, he suggests, advance civilisation. Expressing a nostalgic affinity for forms of representative government that consolidate power in the hands of the educated, Godkin observes: 'There is probably nothing from which the public service of the country suffers more to-day, than the silence of its educated class; that is, the small amount of criticism which comes from disinterested and competent sources. It is a very rare thing for an educated man to say anything publicly about the questions of the day.'[68]

Roosevelt protests that 'talk' counts for little. He affirms that the educated man who wishes to be effective politically must possess the 'rougher, manlier virtues, and above all the virtue of personal courage, physical as well as moral', and must be willing to move from his elite circles into the 'hurly-burly'. Taking up the terms used by Godkin, Roosevelt repeatedly praises action or 'doing', and disparages 'talking' or 'criticism': 'the man with a university education', he declares, 'is in honor bound to take an active part in our political life . . . He is bound to rank action far above criticism, and to understand that the man deserving of credit is the man who actually does the things, even though imperfectly, and not the man who confines himself to talking about how they ought to be done.' Roosevelt specifically recommends seeking public office. But even those who work in the professions 'are bound to act intelligently and effectively in support of the principles which they deem to be right and for the best interests of the country'. What exactly it would mean to act in this way, Roosevelt does not say. But he specifies: 'It is not the man who sits by his fireside reading his evening paper, and saying how bad our politics and politicians are, who will ever do anything to save us.'[69]

The sole passage that James's review quotes from Roosevelt's book is a comment about the remnant. Roosevelt discusses the 'heavy moral obligation' that rests 'upon the men with a collegiate education, the men who are graduates of our universities'; what James quotes is his remark that 'an educated man must not go into politics as such; he must go in simply as an American . . . or he will be upset by some other American, with no education at all, but with much natural capacity'.[70] James retorts: 'A better way perhaps than to barbarize the upset . . . would be to civilize the upsetter.'[71] In this rebuttal, James invokes the project of civilisation pursued by thinkers like Norton, whose 'civilizing mission' plays out in the classroom and the library rather than the battlefield of imperial war.

James hails that mission in his 1909 commemorative essay on Norton, but refers only in passing there to 'scandal' in Norton's professional life; the scandal left undiscussed is one in which Norton earns hate mail and vilification in the national press for publicly opposing the Spanish–American War.[72] That war forms a quiet backdrop to James's essays in *Literature*, which appear during the spring and summer of 1898 as conflict explodes into violence. As James reviews books by key voices in the debate about US imperialism, he does not take up the subject, though he opens the essay published just days after the Battle of Manila Bay by mentioning 'the sudden state of war'.[73] When James reviews Godkin's book in late June, he does not discuss that war, though the book under review takes up issues directly related to it, including virulent expansionism and the role of newspapers in rousing antiforeign sentiment and thirst for blood.

It is not necessarily surprising that James avoids these topics: his publication venue is a British magazine dedicated to literature, and (as John Carlos Rowe has observed) James was never a rigorous critic of American imperialism.[74] James in his letters speaks repeatedly and passionately about his loathing for the war, its violence, and the jingoistic politics that drive it. Alongside those remarks we also find comments like: 'Thank God, however, I've no *opinions*' and 'I won't attempt to go into it – it's all beyond me.'[75] Here, as elsewhere, James's response to the pain of others is swift, empathetic and not especially concerned with the political frame in which that pain plays out.

James's mentions of imperialism in letters tend to treat political questions aesthetically. In May, after the destruction of the Spanish fleet, he writes to Howells: 'I hate & loathe the war & have an ineradicable pity & tenderness for poor old proud, plucky, ruined Spain – so harmless & decorous, so convenient & romantic in Europe, with all her ruin & her interest, & her charming little boy king & lovely, gallant, admirable Queen-Regent, so continentally appealing & irresistible.'[76] This is a pacifist recoil at violence that evolves over the course of a long sentence into a kind of eager imaginative play with tropes. Later, in August, James again writes to Howells, and explains apologetically that his own letters' 'silence' about the war 'isn't in the least indifference; it is deep embarrassment of thought – of imagination'. He continues:

> I have hated, I have almost loathed it; and yet I can't help plucking some food for fancy out of its results – some vision of how the much bigger complexity we are landed in, the bigger world-contacts, may help to educate us and force us to produce people of capacity greater than a less pressure demands. Capacity for *what*? you will naturally ask – whereupon I scramble out of our colloquy by saying that I should perhaps tell you beautifully if you were here and sitting with me on the darkening lawn of my quaint old garden at the end of this barely endurable August day. I will make more things than that clear to you if you will only turn up there.[77]

As he plucks 'food for fancy' here, James evades the question, dipping into open-ended questioning briefly before swerving over to an affectionate invitation and the potent idea of an English summer evening. But he entertains the notion of empire as education again in his letter to Henry James III in the following year:

> To live in England is, inevitably, to feel the 'imperial' question in a different way . . . Expansion has so made the English what they are – for good or for ill, but on the whole for good – that one doesn't quite feel one's way to say for one's country 'No – I'll have *none* of it!' It has educated the English. Will it only demoralize *us*?[78]

In these responses to imperialism, James not only responds aesthetically to political phenomena; he also lingers in open-ended questioning, refusing to judge or conclude. For Posnock, that kind of refusal indicates James's modernity and his fundamental difference from thinkers like Godkin, whom he locates within 'the genteel tradition' and associates with 'antidemocratic elitism'.[79] Godkin does indeed valorise '*judging*' as the duty of an educated elite, but James's review does not register that. The receptive embrace of open-endedness that Posnock attributes to James is a mode that James himself locates in

Godkin's way of thinking. James points to Godkin's 'fundamental reservation of judgment', saying that the book is appealing in large part because its inquiry is not 'conducted on the assumption of any early arrival at the last word'. James adds: 'The time required for development and correction, for further exposure of dangers and further betrayal of signs, is the very moral of his pages.'[80]

Though James appreciates Godkin's open-ended analyses, he seems to find the book otherwise rather dull. As Posnock rightly observes, *American Scene* 'should be read as a response to Godkin, repairing his deficiencies'. What James finds lacking in *Unforeseen Tendencies*, Posnock argues, is attention to the 'messy fact' of class conflict and agitation for equality in modern democracy.[81] But Godkin's book, and his career as editor of *The Nation*, are significantly preoccupied with exactly that messy fact. What James says he finds missing from *Unforeseen Tendencies* is 'manners' and the 'social': Godkin's 'picture', he writes, 'becomes suggestive in proportion as we read into it some adequate vision of the manners . . . with which the different political phenomena he lays bare . . . are intermixed'. Godkin, he suggests, neglects 'social conditions', which are really 'at so many points . . . whether for contradiction, confirmation, attenuation, or aggravation – but another aspect of the political'. *American Scene* attends carefully to 'social conditions' and 'manners', the aspects of the political that Godkin fails to treat; his book, James suggests, is interesting only 'in proportion as we read into it' those missing elements. James uses the same phrase elsewhere in same series with reference to William Archibald Dunning's *Essays on the Civil War and Reconstruction*, about which he says: 'I have found it irresistible to read into them, page by page, some nearer vision of the immense social revolution of which they trace the complicated legal steps.'[82]

James's review performs this practice of 'reading into', which is at once interpretive and creative. Faced with Godkin's and Butler's rather dry books on systems and policies, James refrains from engaging with questions about those subjects, and instead submits his sensibility to the experience of these books' words, images and characters, experimenting to see how each 'beguiles and evokes'. He has, he writes, 'surrendered myself almost romantically' to those impressions and suggestions, and his review documents that beguiling. His review embroiders the content of the texts discussed with imagery (a lighted lamp in darkness; a vast prison; a mysterious faceless boss). Among the stimulations to the imagination that *Unforeseen Tendencies* offers is the case of the author himself, the old man's profound engagement with politics: 'the impression he is able to give us, on that score, of extreme, of intense saturation'.[83]

In its self-referential practice of 'reading into', the review anticipates *American Scene*: reading is the defining practice of James's 'restless analyst', whose relentless habit of alert observation generates that text. This analyst notably finds a supreme object for analysis in American numerosity. Here, as in 1898, James takes up Arnold's 'question of numbers' and turns it in new directions. He encounters in the US a 'too-defiant scale of numerosity and quantity – the effect of which is so to multiply the possibilities, so to open, by the million, contingent doors and windows'. The US presses upon the observer 'extent and reduplication, the multiplication of cognate items.' Such 'scale' and 'numerosity' strike James's analyst especially when it comes to the phenomena of immigration and assimilation. The children of immigrants become 'millions of little transformed strangers', helping to prompt 'the great "ethnic" question ... on a corresponding scale and with a corresponding majesty'. 'The cauldron, for the great stew, has such circumference and such depth that we can only deal here with ultimate syntheses, ultimate combinations and possibilities.' The unprecedented scale of American numerosity elicits the practice of open-ended curiosity, the 'liberty of waiting to see' – 'that blest general drop of the immediate need of conclusions, or rather ... that blest general feeling for the impossibility of them'. Dwelling in such indeterminacy, James's analyst 'feels himself justified of the inward, the philosophic, escape into the immensity'. Confronting the unparalleled numerosity and scale of the US, he 'rests in it at last as an absolute luxury'.[84]

If, in this luxurious escape into immensity, this eager watching and waiting, we see resistance or opposition to a more conservative political stance, we may be doing just what James himself does to Godkin's book on modern democracy: reading into it what we ourselves find interesting. The practice of reading into things is a practice that James celebrates; he does not, however, dwell on the efficacy of such reading as a form of political agency. The one who argues repeatedly for the political force of analysis in the public sphere is Godkin, who holds that the intellectuals of the remnant can indeed exercise such agency if they would only express judgements publicly. James does not embrace that vision for a cultivated elite. In his own practice of reading, which is also a practice of dwelling pleasurably in indeterminacy and curiosity, he performs the work that his own remnant would do. Like the discerning fish of his rising shoal, James seeks food for fancy, rises to delicate bait and reads.

Diversity, Distinction and the Note of the Exclusive

Delimitation, enclosure, borders and exclusion are central political topics as James writes in the early years of the twentieth century. So too are homogeneity, assimilation, uniformity and standardisation – and their contraries: heterogeneity, diversity, difference and unassimilated purity of type.[85] These concepts and terms operate throughout James's writing about the US. They also operate in statements by Eliot and Norton about the composition of Harvard and the US as a whole. Norton and Eliot treat inclusion, exclusion, diversity and homogeneity as questions of politics and policy in the university and the nation. James, however, is interested in these things as aspects of aesthetic experience. This is not to say he considers them trivial. *The American Scene* and 'The Question of Our Speech' develop a portrait of the US as a flat, colourless, bland, uniform, bright-white, wide-open, all-access, commercialised expanse – in comparison to the Old World, where there is form, difference, differentiation, texture, colour, hierarchy, tone, manners, exclusion, darkness and mystery. These texts thus offer a magisterial articulation of an aesthetic of discrimination and delimitation that James develops elsewhere in his œuvre as well.

How does James's writing about discrimination, delimitation, homogeneity and heterogeneity relate to overtly political writing on those subjects? How does his valorisation of 'discrimination' relate to forms of discrimination that disenfranchise or draw blood? How does his praise for walled-off privacy relate to exclusionary policies and practices regarding immigration or access to higher education? Warren and Walter Benn Michaels have each observed a relationship between James's practice of making aesthetic distinctions and the logic of segregation in the era of Jim Crow.[86] This section of the chapter approaches these questions by considering James's aesthetic of discrimination alongside Norton and Eliot's writing about inclusion, exclusion, 'diversity' and 'homogeneity'.

As James writes, these concepts bear an ample range of political significations. He declines to take up specific political questions about inclusion and exclusion, or homogeneity and heterogeneity, and instead dives into the sensuous aesthetic experience of these properties, hailing the rich pleasures of exclusion, enclosure and privacy. We may find in his text a powerful model of analytical practice that might be democratically and inclusively accessible. But James himself specifically praises the pleasure of what is walled off, enclosed and not available to everyone. Similarly, we may find in James's critical portrait of white, bland, flattened homogeneity a pleasing condemnation of Anglo-Saxonist assimilationism or capitalist mass consumer culture. As James writes, however, flattened white homogeneity is often associated with egalitarian democracy. So when James derides uniform whiteness, the political implications of that derision are not at all self-evident. And, moreover, political implications are not what preoccupy James: for him, this flat whiteness and this undifferentiated uniformity, like these enclosures and differentiations, signify and matter mostly in so far as they feed into his practice of making art, which is synonymous with his practice of watching, reading, perceiving, experiencing and living.

'And, then, oh golly!, the question of the Gate and the enclosure', James writes in his notebook as he dwells on the overwhelming surplus of stimulation that Cambridge offers him. James ponders: 'The Gates – questions of the Gates of the fact of *enclosure* and of disclosure in general – the so importunate American question (of *Dis*closure – call it so!) above all.' Harvard's gates give James an occasion to talk about making art. Finding an analogue for these gates in his own England, he refers to 'my vision of the old high Cambridge and Oxford *grilles* and their admirable office of making things look *interesting* – MAKE so – by their intervention'; he thinks about how to write about the fact that '*within* the College Yard, its elements and items gain presence by what has been done . . . the less "good" thing enclosed, approached, *defined*, often looks better than the less good thing *not* enclosed, not defined, not approached'.[87] Cambridge gives James a surfeit of material: 'God help me! It gives and gives; everything seems to give and give as I artfully press it. And what pressure of mine *isn't* artful? – by the divine diabolical law under which I labour!!'[88] In *American Scene*, the finished text that comes after these musings, James praises 'the definite, the palpable affirmation and belated delimitation of College Yard'. He writes:

> The high, decorated, recurrent gates and the still insufficiently high iron palings – representing a vast ring and even now incomplete – may appear, in spots, extemporized and thin; but that signifies little in presence of the precious idea on the side of which, in the land of the 'open door,' the all-abstract outline, the timid term and the general concession, they bravely range themselves. The open door – as it figures here in respect to everything but trade – may make a magnificent place, but it makes poor places.[89]

The Open Door policy, formulated by James's friend, John Hay, concerned trade between China and other countries; James does not address it here.[90] Instead, characteristically, he lights upon a vivid, suggestive idea – the US as the land of the open door – and turns it to his own uses: he compares the new borders around Harvard Yard to the absence of such borders in and around the United States. For James, the Yard's delimitation shows the value of delimitations generally: 'This especial drawing of the belt at Harvard is an admirably interesting example of the way in which the formal enclosure of objects at all interesting immediately refines upon their interest, immediately establishes values.'[91]

James's comments on the power of delimitation to make things *'interesting'* recall the title essay of Arnold's *Civilization in the United States* (1888), which observes repeatedly that the absence of 'beauty' and 'distinction' in the US means that it cannot fully achieve one of the key features of civilization, which is to be *'interesting'*.[92] In 'A Word More about America', Arnold had pointed approvingly to the 'homogenous' character of the US, caused by the absence of the 'distinction of classes', and exhorted his countrymen: 'Our very classes make us dim-seeing [...] inequality is our bane.' 'Our society should be homogeneous,' he declares, and recommends restrictions on the transmission of wealth and titles as a means of achieving that end.[93] Arnold recites this material at the beginning of 'Civilization in the United States', and goes on to discuss 'distinction' more broadly. Immediately before mentioning 'Professor Norton', Arnold writes: 'Do not tell me only, says human nature, of the magnitude of your industry and commerce; of the beneficence of your institutions, your freedom, your equality; of the great and growing number of your churches and schools, libraries and newspapers; tell me also if your civilization . . . is *interesting*.' Offering an extended comparison of the US and Britain that echoes James's own famous litany of what the US lacks, Arnold declares 'the great sources of the *interesting* are distinction and beauty: that which is elevated, and that which is beautiful', and observes: 'in truth, everything is against distinction in America, and against the sense of elevation to be gained though admiring and respecting it'.[94] Arnold defines the *interesting*, the quality of achieved civilisation, as something that arises from the sort of 'distinction' that is absent in the US.

Although Arnold does not say that 'distinction' is equivalent to 'distinction of class', William Dean Howells takes that as implicit. He hails 'the abolition of that "distinction" which Mr. Arnold found wanting in our life' as a great American achievement; pointing to 'the snobbishness . . . which alone makes distinction possible', he states, 'distinction of the sort that shows itself in manner and bearing towards one's fellow-men is something that can exist only through their abeyance, not to say their abasement. Our whole civilization . . . is founded upon the conviction that any such distinction is unjust and deleterious, and our whole political being is a protest against it.'[95] Howells offers this response to Arnold in 1888; James offers another response in his writings of the early twentieth century. As T. J. Lustig shows, James's affinity with Arnold wanes over time.[96] But James shares Arnold's sense that the civilisation in the US too often fails to be '*interesting*'; as he pleads for 'interest', 'discrimination' and 'civilization', he echoes Arnold's observations about distinction in America.

James finds elements of the *interesting* at Harvard: the values established by its delimitation provide welcome respite. James writes: 'As the usual, in our vast crude democracy of trade, is the new, the simple, the cheap, the common, the commercial, the immediate, and, all too often, the ugly,' any exception, any thing or person 'not turned out to pattern, any form of suggested rarity, subtlety, ancientry, or other pleasant perversity, prepares for us a recognition akin to rapture'. What Harvard offers within its walls is this recognition – or, as James puts it elsewhere, reassurance. And, James notes, 'reassurance is required, before the spectacle of American manners at large, whenever one most acutely perceives how little honour they tend to heap on the art of discrimination'. Later he points to 'the sense, constantly fed, and from a hundred sources, that . . . it is of the genius of the American land and the American people to abhor, whenever may be, a discrimination. They are reduced, together, under stress, to making discriminations, but they make them, I think, as lightly and scantily as possible.'[97]

In 'The Question of Our Speech', James details what it means to make discriminations. He tells his audience,

> to discriminate, to learn to find our way among noted sounds . . . to begin to prefer form to the absence of form, to distinguish color from the absence of color – all this amounts to substituting manner for the absence of manner: whereby it is *manners themselves* . . . that we shall (delicious thought!) begin to work round to the notion of.

Here the site for practising discrimination is language. James explains:

> By the forms and shades of our language I mean the innumerable differentiated, discriminated units of sound and sense that lend themselves to audible production, to enunciation, to intonation: those innumerable units that have, each, an identity, a quality, an outline, a shape, a clearness, a fineness, a sweetness, a richness, that have, in a word, a value, which it is open to us . . . to preserve or to destroy.

This value matches the value generated by delimitation at Harvard. The 'vocal habits' of Americans generally fail to preserve such value: they make for 'vast, monotonous flatness and crudity'. James tells his audience that American common schools and newspapers, while 'excellent for diffusion, for vulgarization, for simplification', are 'quite below the mark for discrimination and selection, for those finer offices of vigilance and criticism in the absence of which the forms of civility, with the forms of speech most setting the example, drift out to sea'.[98]

James later refers to 'discrimination and selection' and 'forms' again, when he defines art itself in his preface for *Spoils of Poynton*. 'Life being all inclusion and confusion, and art being all discrimination and selection,' he writes, the latter seeks and finds 'the hard latent *value* with which it alone is concerned.'[99] This would seem to be the kind of 'value' that Americans destroy when they speak; and the kind of 'value' that the 'formal enclosure' at Harvard creates when it 'establishes values' in so exemplary a way. James's 'hard latent *value*' and the fact that he praises French 'vowel-cutting, an art as delicate in its way as gem-cutting', link the value he invokes with Walter Pater's 'hard, gem-like flame'.[100] As in *The Bostonians*, we see James express a more Paterian aestheticism that pushes back against the more Ruskinian aestheticism that Norton preaches at Harvard. That earnest Ruskinian aestheticism is profoundly and explicitly engaged with political and moral questions. James's Paterian mode resists that Ruskinian mode partly by avoiding its moralistic insistence on service, unselfishness and duty.

Such an insistence is salient when Norton and Eliot talk about Harvard, which they see as a training ground for the remnant. Norton writes that for an institution to offer a true liberal education, 'its life must be recognized as an integral part of the life of the state, and it must have proved the worth and power of its discipline by the character of those whom it has nurtured, and by the services which they have rendered to the community'.[101] Eliot expresses this same idea throughout his career, especially in addresses to incoming freshmen and to alumni, in which the call to public service forms one of his frequent themes, along with appeals for money and exhortations to sexual purity, self-control and hard work. 'American universities', he declares in a typical remark, 'are schools of public spirit for the communities in which they are situated. They promote thought and labor for the public.'[102]

As they describe Harvard and other institutions of higher education, then, Eliot and Norton offer celebratory invocations of exactly the qualities that James's aesthetic of discrimination deplores: openness and lack of differentiation. Both identify democracy as the source of these qualities. Like Arnold, they discuss absence of 'distinctions' as characteristic of egalitarian democracy. Norton writes, 'There is no community in which artificial distinctions have less influence ... Student life at Harvard is essentially and healthily democratic ... there are no marked distinctions except the natural ones of character and capacity.'[103] Eliot affirms: 'the whole organization of college life is intensely democratic, and there is a complete fusion of the whole body of students'. In no other 'portion of American society', he says, are there 'so few distinctions and separations based on social inequalities as in the American colleges'; such 'distinctions', he reiterates, are 'less conspicuous in American colleges and universities than in any other large congregations of Americans coming from families which are strange to one another'.[104]

Both educators point to the diversities of the student body and see Harvard making unity from difference. Norton declares that an institution of liberal education 'must be open upon equal terms to all students of whatever race or social position. It must afford such assistance to poor students of good character and capacity as may enable them to secure a full proportionate share of the opportunities it offers'. He proudly says of Harvard's students: 'They come from forty States and Territories of the Union, and a few from foreign countries. They represent every grade of society, every variety of creed – Orthodox, Liberal, Roman Catholic, Agnostic, Jew; every shade of political opinion; and they meet and mingle on terms of even more complete equality than those which commonly exist in society.'[105] Pointing to Harvard's 'diversity' in a 1911 address, Eliot resists the idea that democracy produces a regrettable flattening: 'Free schools, public conveyances, and public entertainments resorted to in common by all classes', he notes, 'level up much more than they level down.' Eliot's understanding of 'diversity' is grounded in the interlocking assumptions of classical liberalism and evolutionary science. The diversity that he celebrates at Harvard is the range of aptitudes and types allowed to develop and compete freely in his elective system. He asks:

> Can you imagine a greater diversity of human capacity, disposition, taste, and personal ambition than exists in Harvard College? I cannot. The diversity is wide; and it is not superficial, but deep. Think of the variety of races brought together in Harvard College; of the variety of religions represented here; and of the variety of households, – every

kind of household from the poorest to the most luxurious, with every sort between. The diversity of mental capacity is immense, and so is the variety of personal ambition.[106]

Eliot explains that Harvard makes a unity from this diversity through shared ideals; the College, he proposes, thus forms a model for the nation.

As Marcia Graham Synnott notes, Eliot 'frequently rejected anti-democratic and racist attitudes in his correspondence and maintained that considerable ethnic diversity was compatible with democratic government and the advancement of civilization'. Under his leadership, Harvard's 'student composition began to diversify significantly' – in comparison, that is, with institutions like Princeton and Yale.[107] Eliot welcomed immigration and spoke of the ample capacities of immigrants for learning. These stances fit, however, within a perspective that is elitist, eugenicist and segregationist. Eliot and Norton alike reject 'distinctions' that are 'artificial' and 'based on social inequalities'; but they recognise without hesitation 'the natural ones of character and capacity', which they understand to be shaped partly by the historical experience of one's race over many generations.[108]

Eliot endorses the democratic freedom that allows the most talented to rise, and he expects those winners to be white because he believes their races have been in more advanced states of development for longer. He supports higher education for Black men specifically and explicitly because such education is, in his opinion, crucial for racial segregation; his chiselled admonition to 'serve Thy Kind' addresses multiple racially specific remnants among the Harvard men passing beneath it. As he celebrates such service, he suggests that it comes more naturally to white people, along with an aptitude for democracy more broadly: having hailed universities as 'schools of public spirit', he adds, 'the Teutonic virtue called "public spirit" is the salvation of a democracy'.[109]

For James, as for Eliot, thinking about Harvard's student body ramifies outward to the US as a whole. The College makes James think about diversity, difference, assimilation, sameness – and, more concretely, about immigration and race. As he contemplates the newly enclosed Yard and the young men within it, James's narrating imagination leaps momentarily to something he would see in the future: at 'Ellis Island, the seat of the Commissioner of Immigration, in the bay of New York', he will observe 'the ceaseless process of the recruiting of our race, of the plenishing of our huge national *pot au feu*, of the introduction of fresh – perpetually fresh so far it isn't perpetually stale – foreign matter into our heterogeneous system'. James wonders 'what might be becoming of us all, "typically," ethnically, and thereby physiognomically, linguistically, *personally*'. Harvard's student body offers yet another site for contemplating 'the great "ethnic" question' that New York also poses. There, James dwells with pleasure on the irresolvability of the question: 'What meaning . . . can continue to attach to such a term as the "American" character? – what type, as the result of such a prodigious amalgam, such a hotch-potch of racial ingredients, is to be conceived as shaping itself?'[110]

Like the inhabitants of the Lower East Side, Harvard's young men provide an occasion to dwell pleasurably on this indeterminacy. So too, apparently, does the university's cosmopolitan faculty. James's notebook entry on Cambridge and Harvard ponders his brother William's colleague, Hugo Munsterberg, who suggests to James the interesting idea of 'the "foreigner" coming in and taking possession'. James ponders '*this* particular light on it – this Harvard professor-of-the-future light, this determined high Harvard absence-of-prejudice light'. Such light illumines an especially 'interesting' aspect 'of the question that hangs so forever before one here, and *more and more the more one sees*: that of what the effect of the great Infusion (call it that) is going to be'.[111]

Although Harvard calls up questions about the heterogeneity of the US for James, he does not find in its student body the diversity that Norton and Eliot celebrate. *American Scene* points immediately to one form of diversity that Eliot conspicuously opposed. James finds that Harvard's students are, like so much in the US, too uniform, for they are all men, and all men in the US are creatures of commerce. Comparing this uniformity to the variety in English, French and German contexts, James notes: 'in the collegiate cloisters and academic shades of other countries this absence of a possible *range* of origin and breeding in a young type had not been so felt. The question of origin, the question of breeding, had been large – never settled in advance; there had been fifty *sorts* of persons, fifty representatives of careers.' Although the College provides a welcome respite from the general American tone, it cannot match its European counterparts: like the nation at large, it manifests 'the continuity of the fusion, the dimness of the distinctions'. The 'human show' in the US, especially amongst the prosperous, thus 'registers itself on the plate with an incision too vague and, above all, too uniform'. Aside from the exaggerated distinction of the sexes, here are 'no other signs of differentiation'.[112]

Precisely the qualities that Norton and Eliot praise in Harvard – 'fusion' and absence of 'distinctions' – strike James as deeply regrettable. Norton and Eliot see those qualities arising from democracy and shared ideals; and they view those qualities as consistent with a 'diversity' of naturally unequal capacities, types and affinities. When Eliot admires the absent 'distinctions and separations' at Harvard, he valorises qualities that James derogates in his advocacy of 'discrimination and selection'. Both Norton and James are less confident than Eliot that democracy levels up more often than it levels down. Norton points to the 'levelling tendency of democratic institutions' as one of the things that threatens the success of 'modern democracy'.[113] James too invokes the conventional idea that democracy fosters flattening and sameness. His comments about differentiation do not, as Norton's and Eliot's do, directly address political questions about inclusion and exclusion in the student body or the population of the US. For James, the issue is that 'uniformity' starves the artist: he calls it 'the scant diversity of type that left me short, as a story-seeker or picture-maker'.[114]

James seeks and celebrates differentiation and difference. As he ponders Harvard's relative insufficiencies, the places he recalls as finding such differentiation in satisfying measure are Oxford and the Sorbonne: Old-World, soaked in imperial wealth, superlatively exclusionary. So James's valorisation of diversity, difference and heterogeneity does not imply a democratic, antiracist rejection of something more conservative that valorises sameness. There is nothing that neat going on here. The old Bostonians value diversity as a feature of a liberal public sphere and as a biological phenomenon that can flourish in democratic conditions; they celebrate the power of shared democratic ideals to foster unity (not uniformity) in a diverse student body or a diverse national population. James, fondly remembering the relentlessly rich differentiations of Europe, values diversity as the condition of artistic fecundity.

Norton and Eliot celebrate Harvard as an open, diverse institution training a remnant committed to public service; James celebrates Harvard and other institutions of higher education as closed-off sites for the practice of discrimination. Precious exceptions to the bland homogeneity of the US, they contain the value that delimitation generates, and they keep out the ugliness and commerce that prevail everywhere else. Like Norton, James values universities as an exception to what Norton calls 'materialism' and James calls 'money-passion'. But while Norton's universities are a force for combatting that passion, James's offer a refuge from it; while Norton's look outward toward public service, James's are oriented inward, towards the private pleasure of the restless analyst. James observes:

> almost any institution pretending to university form [is] stamped here with the character and function of the life-saving monasteries of the dark ages. They glow, the humblest of them, to the imagination – the imagination that fixes the surrounding scene as a huge Rappaccini-garden, rank with each variety of the poison-plant of the money-passion – they glow with all the vividness of the defined alternative, the possible antidote, and seem to call upon us to blow upon the flame till it is made inextinguishable.[115]

Once again, the value that resides in Harvard's enclosure resembles Pater's flame. That value reappears when James visits the Libraries of Congress, which, like Harvard, recall for him walled-off sites for religious contemplation: 'The Universities and the greater Libraries . . . repeat, in their manner, to the imagination . . . the note of the old thick-walled convents and quiet cloisters . . . they have the incalculable value that they represent the only intermission to inordinate rapacious traffic that the scene offers to view.'[116] James refers to such value again as he describes the refuge offered by 'the Public Libraries in the United States', which, he writes, 'like the Universities . . . may often affect the strained pilgrim as a blessedly restful perch'. Comparing them to 'the mast-heads on which spent birds sometimes alight in the expanses of ocean', he states: 'It is to the inordinate value, in the picture, of the non-commercial, non-industrial, non-financial note that they owe their rich relief.'[117]

James's accounts of universities, colleges and libraries emphasise solitary, private pleasure; he notably visits both Harvard and Johns Hopkins when he can stroll their empty campuses mostly alone. Harvard is 'hushed to vacation stillness'; at Hopkins, James's 'impression' is 'the more charming . . . for the fact of halls and courts brooding in vacation stillness'. Harvard suggests a 'cloister . . . the place inaccessible . . . to the shout of the newspaper, the place to perambulate, the place to think, apart from the crowd', and the 'rapture' available there consists in 'lonely ecstasies'. At Hopkins, James delights specifically in the unpeopled quality of the university, enjoying 'the late afternoon light in deserted haunts of study'.[118] In this emphasis on private resources for aesthetic experience, *American Scene* echoes *Princess Casamassima,* where Hyacinth finds Medley Manor a more effective site for cultivation than public museums, and says about the prospect of a democratically distributed Veronese: 'I don't want every one to have a little piece of anything.'[119]

This kind of private pleasure is typically expensive, and the exception proves the rule. Visiting a café in the Bowery, James appreciates 'its almost touching suggestion of discriminations made and preserved in the face of no small difficulty':

> These are the real triumphs of art – the discriminations in favour of taste produced not by the gilded and guarded 'private room', but by making publicity itself delicate, making your barrier against vulgarity consist but in a few tables and chairs, a few coffee-cups and boxes of dominoes. Money in quantities enough can always create tone, but it had been created here by mere unbuyable instinct. The charm of the place in short was that its note of the exclusive had been arrived at with such a beautifully fine economy.[120]

What James admires here is not a democratisation of access to culture, but a canny, resourceful democratisation of the processes of exclusion that make sites for discrimination. He admires the instinct that, without money, can create the 'note of the exclusive', the effects that usually belong to the 'gilded and guarded "private room"'. James's 'barrier against vulgarity', like Norton's, inheres in the practice of culture; but, unlike Norton's, this barrier features in a vision of enclosure and exclusion, rather than an argument for 'wider diffusion' of that culture.

James again emphasises the value of exclusive, secluded contemplation over open, public democracy-saving functionality in his ambivalently critical account of the Boston Public Library (like many of Harvard's gates, also the work of McKim, Mead and White). For James, this library is notable for openness to the world, the manner in which it fails to be a delimited, walled-in, protecting cloister. He views this accessibility as a characteristically American feature: 'here, once more . . . every one is "in" everything, whereas in Europe so comparatively few persons are in anything'. James notes that the library is 'practically without *penetralia*', and compares 'a library without *penetralia*' to 'a temple without altars'. This altarless temple speaks directly of democratic social organisation: it suggests 'the personal port of a democracy that, unlike the English, is social as well as political'. James writes: 'social democracies are unfriendly to the preservation of *penetralia*; so that when *penetralia* are of the essence, as in a place of study and meditation, they inevitably go to the wall'. In Europe, by contrast, 'the British Museum, the Louvre, the Bibliothèque Nationale, the treasures of South Kensington, are assuredly, under forms, at the disposal of the people; but it is to be observed, I think, that the people walk there more or less under the shadow of the right waited for and conceded'.[121] Here, under neither forms nor shadows, the people walk right in. James describes:

> the multitudinous bustle, the coming and going, as in a railway-station, of persons with carpet-bags and other luggage, the simplicity of plan, the open doors and immediate accesses, admirable *for* a railway station, the ubiquitous children, *most* irrepressible little democrats of the democracy, the vain quest, above all, of the deeper depths aforesaid, some part that should be sufficiently *within* some other part, sufficiently withdrawn and consecrated, not to constitute a thoroughfare.[122]

These observations about the library's lack of depth, absence of penetralia and excessive flat openness refer back to the architectural observations occasioned by visits to the clubs of New York. James notes that in the US he encounters 'the universal custom of the house with almost no one of its indoor parts distinguishable from any other'. He explains: 'This diffused vagueness of separation between apartments, between hall and room, between one room and another, between the one you are in and the one you are not in, between place of passage and place of privacy, is a provocation to despair which the public institution shares impartially with the luxurious "home."' These architectural habits, he contends, manifest 'the inveterate suppression of almost every outward exclusory arrangement'. This 'effacement of difference' between interior and exterior, works so that 'every part of every house shall be, as nearly as may be, visible, visitable, penetrable, not only from every other part, but from as many parts of as many other houses as possible, if only they be near enough'.[123]

Neither contemplation nor conversation is possible in such open, undelimited spaces, which, like the library, are expressive of social democracy: this architectural tendency is 'positively serving you up for convenient inspection, under a clear glass cover, the social tone that has dictated it'.[124] James sees the effects of such a tone in rural New England too, observing 'the difference made . . . by the suppression of the two great factors of the familiar English landscape, the squire and the parson', not to mention 'the pervasive Patron, whose absence made such a hole'. Comparing 'a simplified social order with a social order in which feudalism had once struck deep' helps James's restored absentee to begin to develop an 'explanation of so much of the ugliness'. 'The ugliness', he writes, 'was the so complete abolition of *forms*.'[125] The absence of forms, the absence of penetralia, the lack of delimitation and of any 'exclusory arrangement' are all produced by and expressive of the absence of certain social hierarchies. James savours the delimitations, enclosures, privacies, forms and shadows that he finds in places where such hierarchies still make themselves felt. In this respect, his aesthetic of discrimination has a distinct relationship with discrimination that is social and political rather than aesthetic. *The American Scene* is not the first text in which James suggests such a relationship: as Warren notes in passing, in *The Bostonians*, 'feminism and abolitionism are conveyed in terms of liquid metaphors washing away all solid form and distinction', and these dissolutions correlate with aesthetic failures and incompetences among those movements' proponents.[126]

James's articulation of an aesthetic of discrimination and delimitation in *American Scene* and 'Question of Our Speech' closely resembles certain remarks by Edith Wharton, who repeatedly advocates a similar aesthetic. Her *Decoration of Houses* (1897) anticipates James's comments about *penetralia* and delimitation in its interest in 'privacy', as well as 'privacy and distinction'. In 1901, she publishes a letter about American English that pleads for the preservation of 'shades of speech': 'hundreds of useful distinctions', she writes, 'have been lost'.[127] Like James, Wharton worries about language as a site where differentiation, enunciation and difference are not being properly kept up in the modern US. The speech of immigrants draws the attention of both novelists. James writes that those who have acquired English treat it as they would 'so many yards of freely figured oilcloth, from the shop, that they are preparing to lay down, for convenience, on kitchen floor or kitchen staircase'.[128] Wharton echoes these comments in 1919 when she bemoans the state of English in the US, noting 'what that rich language has shrunk to on the lips, and in the literature, of the heterogeneous hundred millions of American citizens who, without uniformity of tradition or recognized guidance, are being suffered to work their many wills upon it'.[129] She later extends this commentary in her 1934 memoir, with reference to James's image: her parents, she recalls, taught her that 'you could do what you liked with the language if you did it consciously, and for a given purpose – but if you went shuffling along, trailing it after you like a rag in the dust, tramping over it, as Henry James said, like the emigrant tramping over his kitchen oil-cloth – that was unpardonable, there deterioration and corruption lurked'.[130]

Noting that 'form' and 'selection' are important concepts for Wharton, Frederick Wegener observes that her 'formalism (and thus her aesthetic) [is] fundamentally ideological in concept and effect'; as he shows, Wharton explicitly links this aesthetic to preferences for undemocratic social and political forms.[131] In a 1927 essay she argues that novels feed on the 'weight of a long past', as well as 'the concentrated flavor which comes of long isolation' or 'the comparative isolation of each social group'; older modes of living serve to 'differentiate the dull people, and to give a special color to each of their humdrum backgrounds'. The life of the modern US, by contrast, is 'safe and uniform', 'flat and monotonous'; it is a place of 'mediocrity', 'universal diffusion' and, above all, 'standardization'. Disparaging that flat uniformity, she praises diversity that comes from hierarchy. 'Traditional society', she asserts, 'with its old-established distinctions of class, its pass-words, exclusions, delicate shades of language and behaviour, is one of man's oldest works of art.' She observes the US 'inheriting an old social organization which provided for nicely shaded degrees of culture and conduct', and sacrificing that inheritance to the 'impoverishment' of simplification and uniformity. She points to the 'dense old European order, all compounded of differences and *nuances*, all interwoven with intensities and reticences, with passions and privacies, inconceivable to the millions brought up in a safe, shallow, and shadowless world'.[132]

Like her late friend, Wharton bemoans the effects upon art of that blank, bright flatness and prefers that dense, intricate old order, with its textures, shades, differentiations, concentrated flavours, exclusionary privacies and established distinctions. These Old-World distinctions enclose private spaces of discrimination for the elite, and ensure that when 'the people' gain access to such spaces, they do so, as James puts it, 'more or less under the shadow of the right waited for and conceded'. Unlike the 'social democracy' of the US, this is a realm where delimitations and barriers stand firm, and thus create excellent conditions for making art.

Wharton's derisive invocation of American uniformity is not alone: during the early twentieth century, 'uniformity' figures frequently in critical accounts of standardised mass consumer culture. Another salient sort of sameness at this moment is the anglophone homogeneity imagined by Roosevelt's assimilationist Americanism. Both of these sorts of sameness earn the criticism of Randolph Bourne, whose visionary 1916 argument for a 'trans-national America' valorises heterogeneity instead. As Posnock points out, Bourne's vision carries echoes of *American Scene*. But Bourne's echoes of *American Scene* do not indicate that *American Scene* makes an argument like Bourne's. When James is writing that text, Bourne's essay does not yet exist, and prominent reference points on the matters of 'homogeneity' and 'uniformity' are Arnold and Mill, respectively. To this list we might add Tocqueville, whose arguments about 'uniformity' Mill discusses at length, quoting his remark that 'the general character of old society was diversity; unity and uniformity were nowhere to be met with. In modern society, all things threaten to become so much alike.'[133] When we observe James's critical portrayals of homogeneity and uniformity anticipate twentieth-century accounts of those qualities as the effects of assimilation, exclusion and racism, *American Scene* can look antiracist or democratic. But we might instead see these critical portrayals refer to a discourse in which uniformity is the effect of modernity and of an empowered democratic majority; or one in which homogeneity is the effect of (or condition for) egalitarian democracy. Through this lens, *American Scene* looks rather different: we observe not a complaint about the effects of racism or nativism, but a complaint about certain effects of the idea that all men are created equal.

Norton points to Mill's arguments about 'assimilation' and the rise of 'a general similarity among mankind' in his 'Intellectual Life'.[134] Worrying over the 'similarity of condition and uniformity of custom' in the US, Norton quotes *On Liberty*: 'the circumstances which surround different classes and individuals, and shape their characters, are daily becoming more assimilated'. 'This assimilation', Norton declares, 'has gone on more rapidly than ever during the generation that has passed since Mill wrote, and nowhere with more rapidity than in America.'[135] In Norton's alarmed account, common schools and newspapers, which are supposed to be the means of building a capable citizenry and a functioning public sphere, instead serve simply to foster vulgarity and sameness. Geography, technology, party politics, 'mechanical methods of instruction' in common schools and 'the absence of class distinctions' further conspire to eliminate 'strongly marked distinctions of national type'. But 'The main source of uniformity', Norton explains, 'is to be found in the predominance of one race and of a single language over the whole area of the country.' 'Widespread uniformity of mental conditions tends to stagnation of mind,' Norton warns; 'where uniformity is the rule, life becomes less diversified, rich, and interesting'. Still leaning heavily on Mill, Norton warns that the uniform society is one that risks tyranny of the majority, the 'despotism of custom' and a dangerously unaware 'servile habit of mind'.[136]

Like Eliot, Norton leans on the classical liberal argument that progress arises from the free expression and the open competition of a rich variety of ideas. And, though far less engaged with scientific thought than Eliot, he too expresses this argument with reference to evolutionary science, observing that 'a struggle for existence is as essential for the distinction and vigor of ideas' as it is for that of 'plants and animals'. He writes: 'The prevailing conditions tend to diminish that variety of experience and thought, that difference in tradition and conviction, that collision of ideas of varied origin, which are requisite to progress in high civilization. The advance of truth is largely dependent upon the diversity of opinion among men, – upon contradiction and discussion.'[137] Norton appreciates 'diversity' and despairs at 'uniformity' because he wants a flourishing liberal public sphere so that democracy will thrive and civilisation advance.

Distinct from that dulling 'uniformity' is the 'homogeneity' that Arnold (and others) associate with egalitarian democracy. That homogeneity comes from an absence of class distinctions, but it also tends to imply an absence of racial distinctions, or, more specifically, whiteness. As Arnold discusses the relative inattention to 'distinctions of rank and class' in the US, he writes: 'When the immigrant from Europe strikes root in his new home, he becomes as the American.'[138] Because there is a tendency to (as Bourne puts it) 'think of ideals like democracy as magical qualities inherent in certain peoples', evocations of homogeneity serve both argumentation for democracy and argumentation for white supremacy, and sometimes both at once.[139]

These perceived associations between homogeneity, egalitarian democracy and whiteness demand our attention as we read *The American Scene* – because that text repeatedly represents American sameness as white. James develops an extraordinary pattern of images of domestic cleaning that portray a blank, flat, washed-clean, rinsed-out US. He notes with regret that Italians in the US lose their distinctive and salient 'colour'. Using imagery that Bourne later echoes, James observes an effect 'like that of the tub of hot water that reduces a piece of bright-hued stuff, on immersion, to the proved state of not "washing"': the 'ambient air' of the US, he suggests, is like a tub or a 'terrible tank' that rinses Italians of their interesting 'colour', yet fails to retain in its waters the colours thus washed out.[140]

James imagines distinctive national characteristics not just rinsed out to colourlessness but also painted over by whitewash. He describes immigrants 'glazed ... over as with some mixture, of indescribable hue and consistency, the wholesale varnish of consecration, that might have been applied, out of a bottomless receptacle, by a huge white-washing brush'.[141] This brush shows up repeatedly. When the ease of travelling across the 'continuity' of 'grand territorial unity' in the US evokes for James the American aversion to 'making discriminations', he muses:

> It was only another case of the painting with a big brush, a brush steeped in crude universal white, and of the colossal size this implement was capable of assuming. Gradations, transitions, differences of any sort, temporal, material, social, whether in man or in his environment, shrank somehow, under its sweep, to negligible items; and one had perhaps never yet seemed so to move through a vast simplified scheme.[142]

Such a brush appears again as James notices 'uniformity' and the 'scant diversity of type' amongst the monotone bourgeois, among whom only the distinction of sex stands out; James remarks that their 'neutrality of respectability might have been figured by a great grey wash of some charged moist brush causing colour and outline, on the pictured paper, effectively to run together'.[143] In 1913, James uses this imagery again in an especially sharp articulation of his aesthetic of discrimination:

> The fatal fusions and uniformities inflicted on our newer generations, the running together of all the differences of form and tone, the ruinous liquefying wash of the great industrial brush over the old conditions of contrast and colour, doubtless still have left the painter of manners much to do, but have ground him down to the sad fact that his ideals of differentiation, those inherent oppositions from type to type, in which drama most naturally resides, have well-nigh perished.[144]

Like Wharton, James regrets the absence of differentiation that modernity brings, and specifically deplores the implications of that loss for literature, which thrives in conditions that preserve types, differences and delimitations.

Along with the images of the whitewashing brush, the big brush and the terrible tank or tub, James refers to 'the huge democratic broom that has made the clearance and that one seems to see brandished in the empty sky'.[145] In the sky above Boston, James sees another cleaning implement: 'a huge applied sponge', one that washes out the colour of a distinctive American milieu. This 'sponge saturated with the foreign mixture and passed over almost everything' replaces the 'Puritan "whip"' that earlier loomed there; James registers the loss of the 'small homogeneous Boston of the more interesting time', replaced by a 'bigger, braver, louder Boston' in which the labourers strolling on the Common of a Sunday are not speaking English.[146]

In associating homogeneity with a lost Boston, James evokes a common idea. During the later nineteenth century and well into the twentieth, Old New England frequently serves to represent homogenous egalitarian society, epitomising at once democracy and Anglo-Saxon whiteness. Norton too evokes a lost Boston. During the early nineteenth century, he notes, 'the community was more homogeneous'; for him, this lost Boston figures nostalgically in a bygone Emersonian moment of 'exhilarating hope, of large promise, of legitimate confidence', a time when 'the blessings of the novel American experiment in democratic institutions were widely diffused, and generally acknowledged, while the perils and evils accompanying them were, as yet, little felt, and hardly recognized'.[147] James, in contrast, values the old Boston as something that is 'interesting' in its intensely saturated colour.[148] He finds that the effect of the US is to wash out the distinctive character of such homogeneous linguistic and racial communities, which would otherwise, in their rich diversities of type, keep an artist well fed.

One of the things James appreciates about Norton is that he is not thus washed out: the sponge that passes over Boston misses the Professor. Like Godkin, with his 'intense saturation' in politics, Norton offers a distinctive impression: James notes 'how interesting a *case*, above all, my distinguished friend was ever to remain to me'.[149] This friend displays the traits of a well-preserved type: the Massachusetts Puritan. James finds his 'case' so interesting partly because it offers such saturated colour, and partly because this type is so different from his own. James's account of this difference in his 1909 essay about Norton feeds into a narrative about 'the genteel tradition', which then evolves over time and, paradoxically, makes that essay less readily legible. The final section of this chapter works to explain how that happens.

Serene Puritan *Crânerie*: James and the Genteel Tradition

The earliest comment on James's relationship with the 'genteel tradition' comes from the 1911 speech in which George Santayana coins that phrase. Santayana says that both Henry and William 'were as tightly swaddled in the genteel tradition as any infant geniuses could be . . . Yet they burst those bands almost entirely.' Henry James, he continues, has accomplished this bursting 'by adopting the point of view of the outer world, and by turning the genteel American tradition, as he turns everything else, into a subject-matter for analysis'.[150] As Posnock shows in *Trial of Curiosity*, James's analytical practice is receptive, generous and open-ended. When James 'reads into' the object of his analysis, he transmutes it into the stuff of art – with warmth, intense interest and eager fascination. But Posnock sees James's analytical practice take on a quietly biting quality when it encounters this tradition and those associated with it. In observing a James who strategically mutes criticism of the men associated with the genteel, he joins an august tradition, one that might be said to begin with Henry Adams.

Adams in 1903 reads James's biography of the expatriate sculptor William Wetmore Story as a coded indictment of the 'type bourgeois-bostonien'. He tells James that he can see in the text 'what is beneath, implied, intelligible only to me, and half a dozen other people still living', and declares: 'You strip us, gently and kindly, like a surgeon, and I feel your knife in my ribs.' Adams concludes: 'No one else will ever know it. You have been extremely tactful. The essential superficiality of Story and all the rest, you have made painfully clear to us, but not, I think, to the family or the public.'[151] The 1903 letters between James and Adams prefigure the 1914 exchange in which Adams reacts to James's memoir; when Adams once again reads suspiciously and sees grim darkness, James calls it 'charming'. He uses the same word to respond to his brother William's similarly suspicious reading of his 1909 commemorative essay about Norton.[152] Echoing Adams, William had written: 'the way in which you subtly killed him was inimitable. But only the few will understand the neatness.'[153] T. S. Eliot extends this pattern when he comments on the same essay: 'Even in handling men whom he could, one supposes, have carved joint from joint – Emerson or Norton – his touch is uncertain; there is a desire to be generous, a political motive.'[154] In quiet escalation of violence, Eliot takes up Adams's knife but makes it the implement of a butcher rather than a surgeon. Academic readers have carried on this tradition. Richard Poirier sees James wielding sharp steel in his essay on Norton: 'James is dissecting his specimen with particular delicacy of touch'; 'the critical bent of the piece', he writes, operates via 'innuendo' rather than 'assertion'.[155] Posnock too sees a delicacy: he writes that James finds Godkin's *Unforeseen Tendencies* 'impoverished and bitter. But since Godkin was an old friend, James's judgment is delicately rendered': 'under the apparent blandness' of James's words, Posnock detects 'his acute implication'.[156]

When we see James respond delicately to these old friends, what are we seeing? This final section of the chapter approaches this question by reading James's 1909 commemorative essay on the recently deceased Norton. There as elsewhere, I would suggest, James's politeness is no false front: it signifies just as much as any sharpness.[157] In this essay, James quite overtly describes the difference between Norton and himself, but the political implications of that overt description are not as straightforward as they may seem. He explicitly identifies Norton as a New England type and explicitly notes his own difference from that type; but misrecognition of that type can distort our understanding of what this text says. Such misrecognition comes easily because of differences between earlier and later iterations of the narrative about the genteel, differences signalled by the shifting connotations of the words 'Puritan' and 'serene'.

Later in the twentieth century, these words figure prominently in iterations of the narrative about the genteel that describe a prudish, elitist, vapid idealism, in which 'Puritan' means moralistic squeamishness about sex, and 'serene' describes the cloistered realm in which the idealising proponents of the genteel sequester themselves, complacently secure in their remove from the rough, real democracy of the US. New England is often named as the site or the origin of this genteel mode. James's essay clearly anticipates – and, I would suggest, serves as a source for – this later account of the 'genteel'. He refers to Norton's Massachusetts lineage and describes him as a 'son of the Puritans', obsessed with morality and given to absolutely inflexible certainty. James observes in Norton an 'unqualified confidence in one's errand, the serenest acceptance of a responsibility and the exercise of a critical authority never too apt to return critically upon itself'. The Professor's approach to art manifests a 'large and nourished serenity', a serenity that, James suggests, is rather at odds with the 'bewilderment' and 'mystification' and 'terribly fine and complicated issues' that art actually presents.[158]

Because the most influential iterations of the narrative about the genteel are democratic and progressive (or, as in the case of Santayana's, too often miscategorised as such), we might see James's essay as an early formulation of such democratic thinking. But the narrative about the genteel becomes so saliently democratic and progressive only around the second decade of the twentieth century and after, as it is developed by thinkers like Van Wyck Brooks, Malcolm Cowley and Vernon Louis Parrington, among others. When James writes in 1909, realist critiques that assail the New England idealism of serene Puritan types are not as likely to be democratic and progressive. And the connotations of 'Puritan' and 'serene' are in flux. While keeping in mind the later meanings of those words that consolidate more fully after he writes, we should also recall their older meanings, which James himself had been invoking for decades.

'Serenity' and 'barricades' or 'barriers' feature saliently in Parrington's account of the 'genteel' in *Main Currents in American Thought* (1927–30). Parrington's 'genteel tradition' is a moribund, conservative force opposed by a more democratic realism. It belongs to 'Brahmins' who seek 'a barricade against the intrusion of the unpleasant' or 'barriers against the intrusion of the unpleasant'; such barriers seek to preserve 'the serenity of the Brahmin mind'. Using the same phrase, Parrington describes James participating in this genteel retreat from the rough, vital realities of the modern US: he writes that the novelist found 'it was impossible to barricade himself securely against the intrusion of the unpleasant', so he 'fled from it all'. James, he writes, is 'the completest embodiment' of the genteel tradition's 'vague cultural aspirations'. Parrington suggests that James's affinity for discriminations is part of what makes him genteel: 'aloof from the homely realities of life', his James inhabits 'a world of fine gradations and imperceptible shades'.[159]

This portrait of James contributes to the consensus that Posnock productively contests some fifty years later. As his argument severs James from the genteel cohort and points to alternate affiliations, the negative characteristics of the genteel remain, and serve to flatter James by contrast. Quoting that promiscuous fragment in which Norton refers to Harvard, Yale, and *The Nation* as 'barriers against the invasion of modern barbarism and vulgarity', Posnock portrays a Norton who seeks 'serenity' behind 'barriers' in the manner of Parrington's Brahmins: his 'consummately serene' Norton 'conceives of the aesthetic as serene contemplation, a view that functions as part of a larger cultural strategy implemented by a Victorian, Protestant leisure class.'[160] James is a contented member of exactly that class, but Posnock suggests that the novelist excepts himself from it by adopting a different, more active conception of the aesthetic: James, he argues, rejects 'Norton's lofty style of discrimination' and instead practices 'an inclusive, not an exclusionary, form of discrimination.'[161]

Norton and James do indeed think about 'discrimination' differently, just as they think differently about barriers, inclusion and exclusion; these differences reflect the fact that, although they share profound commitments to culture, criticism and civilisation, they sometimes understand those terms differently, or with different emphases. The kind of discrimination that Norton calls for in 'Intellectual Life' is 'moral discrimination'.[162] James notices Norton's attention to morality, and identifies it as the trait of a type: he writes in his 1909 essay that Norton has visited Italy and England with 'relish' but 'never, as a good New Englander, without certain firm and, where they had to be, invidious discriminations'.[163]

For James, Norton's practice of discrimination has a crude quality: as the Professor lectures his students at Harvard, vulgar inferiority is 'tracked' into 'strongholds' and then 'branded'.[164] James had associated this verb with a New Englander before: 'Brand' is the name of the Unitarian minister of *The Europeans* (1878), the stiffly moralistic foil to his rival, who is Continental and fun. Their rivalry anticipates that of the Bostonian Olive Chancellor and the New Yorker Henry Burrage in *The Bostonians* (1886). As Laurel Bollinger shows, Brand figures in a larger pattern of representation of anhedonic Unitarian Bostonians and New Englanders in James's œuvre, which also notably includes Babcock of *The American* (1877). Bollinger helpfully draws attention to the critical reception of such representations, noting that Constance Fenimore Woolson pleads: 'During the war, the Brands had a chance: they marched to war with tremendous earnestness ... Their strong convictions fired the assault; they headed the colored regiments; they made, by their motives and beliefs, even small actions grand.'[165] Woolson's comment offers a useful counterpoint to James's gentle mockery of these New Englanders, and reminds us to ask: what exactly is he mocking?

Most obviously, part of what he mocks in the Puritan–Unitarian Bostonian type – to great comic effect – is a deadly earnest, dourly moralistic rejection of pleasure. Babcock announces to Christopher Newman, 'I have a high sense of responsibility. You appear to care only for the pleasure of the hour'. He adds: 'Art and life seem to me intensely serious things, and in our travels in Europe we should especially remember the immense seriousness of Art.'[166] This response to art and Europe recalls James's report of visiting the Louvre with Norton. In an 1872 letter to William, he writes:

> The Nortons are excellent, but I feel less & less at home with them, owing to a high moral *je ne sais quoi* which passes quite above my head ... Charles ... takes art altogether too hard for me to follow him ... I daily pray *not* to grow in discrimination & to be suffered to aim at superficial pleasure.[167]

Memories of Norton in Paris may inform James's 1909 description of his old mentor's persistent fidelity to conscience over pleasure, which he attributes to Norton's 'Puritan' heritage and finds exceptionally 'interesting':

> Nothing in fact *can* be more interesting to a haunter of other intellectual climes and a worshipper at the aesthetic shrine *quand même* than to note once more how race and implanted quality and association always in the end come by their own; how, for example, a son of the Puritans the most intellectually transmuted, the most liberally emancipated and initiated possible, could still plead most for substance when proposing to plead for style, could still try to lose himself in the labyrinth of delight while keeping tight hold of the clue of duty, tangled even a little in his feet; could still address himself all consistently to the moral conscience while speaking as by his office for our imagination and our free curiosity.[168]

Norton's Puritanism ensures that he never speaks for 'style', 'delight', 'imagination' and 'free curiosity' alone. Rather, in the mixture that Norton offers, these things are always mingled with 'substance', 'duty' and 'moral conscience'. This interests James because he himself is less mixed, as 'a worshipper at the aesthetic shrine *quand même*'. While James can dispense with that high moral *je ne sais quoi*, Norton cannot. He lives in the tradition of his antecedents, New England ministers of whom James observes: 'their accomplishments and their earnestness had been almost wholly in the moral order'.[169] As a New Englander who holds tight to duty, Norton does not surrender fully to aesthetic delight – unlike James, who does. James's repeated recourse to French in describing this difference affirms his distance from the Puritan Anglo-Saxon tradition that Norton perpetuates (we will see Wharton draw out this contrast too).

Later twentieth-century invocations of New England's moralistic Puritanism share with James's this emphasis on rejection of sensuous pleasure and commitment to morality; in those later invocations, these are tendencies that manifest prudishness and petty snobbery. Parrington, for instance, describes a 'genteel tradition' that belongs to Brahmins for whom 'the idea of morality . . . and the idea of excellence' had alike 'become empty conventions, cut off from reality'; as such, they are 'little more than a refuge for respectability'.[170] When James refers to Norton's Puritan dedication to moral conscience, however, he is not necessarily making reference to this same empty respectability.

James attributes to Norton's lineage in the 'aristocracy of Massachusetts' the 'heritage of character and conscience' to which he owes his 'strong and special strain of confidence'. He notes the 'incontestable *crânerie* of [Norton's] attitude – a thing that one felt to be a high form of sincerity'.[171] *Crânerie* – a word of complex, multivalent meaning – implies here something like stubborn confidence with an edge of showy vanity. James observes this sort of confidence in Norton's labours at Harvard, in which he sees 'an exhilarated invocation of close responsibility, an absolute ease of mind about one's point of view, a thorough and never-failing intellectual wholeness'.[172] Posnock quotes this sentence in order to contrast 'James's enthusiasm for the indeterminate, open-ended quality of the present moment' and his '"restless" curiosity' against the 'smug aesthetic serenity' of the 'genteel intellectual', which manifests 'the patrician orthodoxy's disgust with modern cosmopolitan democratic culture'.[173]

But in evoking Norton's inflexibility, James may not be evoking a conservatism of the sort Posnock suggests. John Jay Chapman describes this inflexibility too in his own essay about Norton. Like James, he attributes this tendency to Norton's elite Massachusetts heritage. Pointing to Norton's 'mulishness', he writes: 'Norton's sense that he had a mission probably arose out of his clerical caste, and from the strong aristocratic feeling of those old Puritan first-families, who felt that they must be leaders in Israel.' In discussing Norton's stubbornness, both James and Chapman are working with an old trope: the inflexibly certain New England Puritan. Chapman writes that Norton 'belonged to the Puritan race and was first cousin to President Eliot . . . In fact, he was very like Eliot'.[174] Eliot, as Chapter 6 will detail, was associated with 'Puritan' heritage and tendencies.

We should be cautious in discerning the political connotations of any given usage of 'Puritan' in the early twentieth century. For much of the nineteenth century, the inflexibility of New England Puritan types – a broadly recognised trait – implies not conservatism but radicalism. During the antebellum and wartime periods, 'Puritan' connotes radical abolitionism – as when Julia Ward Howe hails John Brown as 'Puritan of the Puritans'.[175] In the decades after the war, it can also refer to a less radical antislavery tradition, one that belongs to Unitarian New England and understands itself as a transatlantic liberalism committed to liberty. (Chapter 6 will discuss these usages at length.) In both the radical and the less radical versions of this Puritan type, stubborn inflexibility is a key feature. George William Curtis, a strident voice for 'Puritan' liberalism in the later decades of the century, identifies Charles Sumner and William Lloyd Garrison as representative Puritans and quotes to show specific examples of such inflexibility.[176] This New England 'Puritan' tradition – even in its more moderate strain - is associated with the Union cause, antislavery sentiment, idealism, and sternly fanatical faith in education and democracy. So when James distances himself from Norton's moralistic New England habit of inflexible certainty, the political implications of his distancing are not necessarily democratic or emancipatory.

The serenity that James attributes to Norton is part of his inflexible certainty; like that certainty, this serenity may seem to place the old Professor amongst the conservative opponents of democracy, but does not necessarily do so. While in the later twentieth century 'serene' tends to refer derisively to retreat from and distaste for democracy, earlier, the term seems to carry specific associations with hopefulness about democratic possibility. Early and late, 'serene' is used with remarkable frequency to describe Emerson and Emersonian optimism; but perceptions of Emersonian optimism differ and also change over time. As Randall Fuller notes, 'the image of Emerson in the early twentieth century had become . . . conflated with genteel identity'; his name 'was increasingly associated with a waning gentility that, in hindsight, appeared homogenous and stultifying'. Fuller locates Brooks's attack on the 'genteel' in a 'countertradition of Emerson criticism' that also includes Thomas Carlyle – and Henry James.[177]

As Chapter 2 discussed, James stages in *The Bostonians* (1886) an encounter between the arguments of Carlyle and Emerson about democracy and education, attending to Norton's edition of that pair's correspondence as he does so. The novel expresses a sort of wishful affinity for Emerson's sense of human possibility, but suggests that Carlyle's perception of human stupidity and evil is, alas, right. This mixed and occasionally anguished stance in fact closely resembles Norton's own. In 1873, having visited Emerson to collect Carlyle's letters to him, Norton writes to Carlyle about Emerson's 'serene confidence', and distances himself from it. In the same year, Norton and James notably insist to each other in letters that their respective patriotisms are not 'serene'.[178] But, as the Conclusion to this book will observe, Norton holds on to Emersonian ideals even as he abjures Emersonian optimism.

Howells notably makes serenity the posture of the egalitarian democrat as he responds to Arnold in 1888, announcing: 'So far from feeling cast down by Mr Arnold's failure to detect distinction [in the US], we are disposed to a serene complacency by it.'[179] Here as elsewhere, 'serene' serves to refer to an Emersonian confidence in democracy. In his 1883 review of Norton's edition of the Carlyle–Emerson correspondence, James, like Norton, uses 'serene' to characterise the optimistic, democratic perspective that belongs to Emerson and New England. Having mentioned Emerson's 'serene good faith', he suggests that 'Emerson's serenity' and his optimism about mankind are the products of his 'democratic' milieu; Carlyle's opposed 'aristocratic premises', he writes, inform his call 'for that imperial master, of the necessity for whom the New England mind was so serenely unconscious'.[180]

Here and in an 1887 review, James compares the serene Puritan Emerson with Carlyle and Hawthorne, other Puritan thinkers more alert to depravity. While Emerson manifests a 'ripe unconsciousness of evil', James observes, 'Hawthorne's vision was all for the evil and sin of the world; a side of life as to which Emerson's eyes were thickly bandaged'. Emerson, he writes, 'was as deeply rooted a Puritan as Carlyle, but he was a Puritan refined and sublimated, and a certain delicacy, a certain good taste would have prevented him from desiring (for the amelioration of mankind) so crude an occurrence as a return of the regiments of Oliver.[181] James evokes the softer New England 'Puritanism' that is distanced from certain Puritan tendencies to violent agitation. But that distance from radical violence does not render this more refined, more tasteful Puritanism equivalent to the sort of antidemocratic sentiment expressed by Carlyle; indeed, here this Emersonian variety of Puritanism stands as the opponent or opposite of that kind of antidemocratic thinking. It seeks 'the amelioration of mankind' and believes that amelioration is possible.

James's account of Emerson's 'ripe unconsciousness of evil' anticipates elements of the realist conservative critique that finds sharp articulation in the work of Barrett Wendell and, more famously, Irving Babbitt. Wendell too uses 'serene' to refer to New England thinking that is Emersonian, optimistic, idealistic and democratic in its high estimate of human nature. In 1893, expressing doubt about 'our tremendous national faith in democracy', which rests precariously on 'the assumption that human nature is perfectible', he disparages 'the serenely optimistic dogmas of the last century or more', which falsely assume that perfectibility and thus (wrongly) preserve that faith.[182] Later Wendell observes 'serene insolence' in both Emerson and his prose. Noting Emerson's disobedient individualism, he concedes that the writer is, nevertheless, 'brave, honest, serene, and essentially pure with all that purity which is the deepest grace of ancestral New England'.[183] That ancestral New England purity notably reappears in Wendell's own 1909 commemorative essay on Norton, where the dead man shows that 'spiritual purity ... is what our ancestral spirit means to us of New England'.[184]

Both Wendell and Babbitt are affectionate mentees and self-professed acolytes of Norton, and their status as heirs of his humanism obscures differences between their thinking and his. A reactionary, an imperialist and an especially enthusiastic racist, Wendell suggests that the New England idealism that believes in human perfectibility is both wrong and dangerous in its support for democracy. Norton remains committed to that idealism throughout his life: his biographer James Turner takes care to emphasise that, even in his last years, Norton persisted in 'the long hope that had infused his life' and 'never believed "the old ideals" dead'.[185] It is not surprising, then, that Wendell's own commemorative essay on Norton also includes a recollection of what it is like to disagree with him. Like James and Chapman, Wendell points to Norton's stubbornness:

> there was something occasionally and momentarily repellent about the calm certainty of his conviction. In controversy, he would sometimes appear so sure of himself that you were prone to fancy his vision infirm ... he would now and then prove so far from sympathetic that you might well have supposed him to have left out of consideration any view of the question but his own.[186]

Given what Norton and Wendell actually disagree about, this passage of Wendell's essay should caution us against too quickly deciding that James's own account of Norton's inflexibility is a critical portrayal of vapid conservatism.

The 'calm certainty' that Wendell finds in Norton recalls the moribund 'calm' of the rigid Unitarian orthodoxy that *The Education of Henry Adams* locates at Harvard. James's Norton manifests a Puritan certainty that matches the dogmatic inflexibility of his Olive Chancellor and also of Wharton's Fulvia Vivaldi, both rigid females who advocate the principles of Bostonian liberalism. This Puritan certainty also finds representation in the fanaticism of the Puritans whom Wharton portrays for the French. In different ways, Adams, James and Wharton all position themselves apart from this New England mode of moralistic certainty and dogged sincerity. James will gesture towards it once again in his 1915 essays in *The Atlantic* and *The Nation*, in which Norton and Godkin feature prominently. As this book's Introduction notes, those essays describe this certainty repeatedly as a serene complacency. We should avoid easy assumptions about what kind of questioning and doubt this serene complacency dispels.

Adams's and James's critical accounts of serene certainty are recognised as key articulations of early twentieth-century thought. As we encounter them, these interrogations of complacency look like celebrations of doubt, uncertainty, open-mindedness, and unabashed pleasure in sensuous and aesthetic experience. And, indeed, they are that. As such, their political flavour feels subversive and emancipatory. Against a dourly rigid establishment whose racism and classism are well documented, they advocate a pliant, complex mode that is aesthetically aware, receptive to irony and difference. That is all true; but it is also true that part of what these authors distance themselves from when they interrogate the absolute certainty of New England liberalism is a certainty that education and democracy are worthy ideals; that the duty of elite educated men in a democracy is service to the community; that such service must consist in action and have effects; and that the most glorious achievement of such service is the victory of the Union.

James quite explicitly describes his own difference from the serene Puritan type to whom this sort of certainty belongs; while it suffers compulsions toward conscience, duty and political action, he is a 'worshipper at the aesthetic shrine *quand même*'; the 'high moral *je ne sais quoi*' belongs to others. His remnant worships at the unmixed shrine of the aesthetic, seeking pleasure; its practice of curiosity and discrimination is neither duty nor service: it is, as he puts it, a luxury. The thinker whose life in culture does have explicitly, deliberately political functions is Norton, who understands reading, writing and teaching as crucial forms of political agency. If we as intellectuals understand our work to exercise political agency in service of democracy, we carry on in new forms his Victorian project.

Chapter 5

The Tenth Mind: Adams and the Action of the Remnant

Henry Adams joked about his own damnation to his friend, President Theodore Roosevelt, in a letter of 1907, following the private circulation of his *Education* to a select set of readers. Roosevelt was among them, as was Harvard President Charles William Eliot. 'Having passed your censorship' and that of several others, Adams writes to Roosevelt,

> I have a greater than you all to face, – Charles Eliot's! I am still trembling before him as though I were always an undergraduate, while the thunders and lightnings of my own family are as gentle cooing of doves. If they scold or sneer, I can happily suppress the whole thing, as is my wont; but Charles Eliot's sentence will be damnation forever.[1]

Adams was right to anticipate disapproval. President Eliot was one of just three of readers out of one hundred who took Adams's instructions literally and returned the book to its author.[2] Whatever marks he may have made are lost, but the gossip that survives is consistent with a sentence of damnation. Bliss Perry, Professor of English at Harvard and former editor of *The Atlantic*, later recalled: 'Once, when [*The Education*] was under discussion by a group that admired Henry Adams, President Eliot, whose unsubtle nature was incapable of appreciating sustained literary irony, dropped his voice and remarked to the man next to him: "An overrated man and a much overrated book".'[3] This sotto voce comment was not, apparently, anomalous. In a 1920 letter, Eliot wrote to his cousin Grace Norton: 'I should like to be saved from loss of faith in democracy as I grow old and foolish. I should be very sorry to wind up as the three Adamses did. I shall not, unless I lose my mind.'⁴

In his grimly literal practice as a reader, as well as his moralistic readiness to issue a sentence of damnation for a lapse of faith in democracy, Eliot manifested qualities associated with the 'Puritan', Unitarian, New England liberalism for which he was a self-professed and widely acknowledged representative. *The Education* aims squarely at this Bostonian, Harvard-based orthodoxy and fires without mercy. Its primary weapon in doing so is precisely the irony that Eliot fails to appreciate (which is logical, since he is one of its targets). Because the liberalism that *The Education* attacks is elitist and conservative, many readers have been inclined to notice and admire the book's rebellious qualities, seeing in its ironies and subtleties irreverent disruptions of a staid old power. But rebelliousness and irreverence can exercise power rather than disrupting it. Like the open-ended uncertainty discussed in the preceding chapter, irony has no fixed political orientation; and yet, as Lee Konstantinou notes, it is 'inescapably connected to political life because it forms, dissolves, and governs communities and informs action'.⁵ Matthew Stratton's study of irony in the early twentieth-century US notes that 'politics of every stripe requires action at some point', and that irony can, in its commitments to complexity and detachment, work against action.⁶ Along with other histories of irony, Stratton's emphasises that its political effects and significations tend to be site-specific, dependent on context and speaker.

Professor Perry would not be the last literary scholar to point to *The Education*'s irony. Irony, complexity and detachment are qualities that professors of English have valued highly; sincerity and unsubtlety tend to rank lower in twentieth-century hierarchies of literary taste. In those hierarchies, President Eliot's literal way of reading ranks low: trained as a chemist, and called an 'antihumanist' by George Santayana, Eliot reads the way Perry trains his students not to.⁷ Shamoon Zamir implicitly acknowledges this hierarchy of taste when (writing in 1995) he points to *The Education*'s 'complexity and subtlety' in order to show, via comparison, that these qualities also pervade W. E. B. Du Bois's *Souls of Black Folk* (1903); those qualities might be missed, he notes, because of the 'forcefulness of Du Bois's primary intention', which is 'the exposure to a predominantly white audience of the conditions of black life in America'.⁸

Zamir's 'forcefulness of ... primary intention' resembles the 'instrumentality' that Kenneth W. Warren later describes as a defining feature of African–American literature during the era of Jim Crow. Warren writes:

> black writers knew that their work would in all likelihood be evaluated instrumentally, in terms of whether or not it could be added to the arsenal of arguments, achievements, and propositions needed to attack the justifications for, and counteract the effects of, Jim Crow . . . Writers also knew that their work would likely be viewed as constituting an index of racial progress, integrity, or ability.

He adds: 'The pressure exerted by these instrumental or indexical expectations shows up not only in the way that writers and critics regard African American literary texts but also within the works themselves.'[9] Du Bois himself takes up these issues in 'Criteria of Negro Art' (1926), where he declares 'all Art is propaganda . . . whatever art I have for writing had been used always for propaganda for gaining the right of black folk to love and enjoy'.[10] Du Bois's argument, like Warren's, recognises that the perceived race of the author affects the meanings his text might bear. The way a statement signifies depends partly on who says it; what functions as irony in one mouth might not function that way in another.

It is not a coincidence that both Du Bois's forceful instrumentality and Eliot's unsubtle literalism should end up juxtaposed with *The Education*'s complexity and subtlety. This force, instrumentality, unsubtlety and literalism belong to the New England liberalism that Du Bois and Eliot both express, and that liberalism is one of the things *The Education* attacks. When *Souls* manifests a righteous sincerity about its demands, when it argues for the practice of culture and when it calls the missionaries of culture to their work, it makes moves characteristic of that liberalism. This is not surprising, because the author of *Souls* is, among other things, a Harvard man from Massachusetts. At Eliot's university, Du Bois meets racism and feels himself 'in Harvard but not of it'; Du Bois would later publicly criticise Eliot, and there is some evidence that Eliot publicly criticised Du Bois.[11] But in the early years of the twentieth century, these two thinkers agree about a great deal. Elitist, eugenicist and passionately committed to education and democracy, both men argue for the duties and powers of the cultivated minority, or what Matthew Arnold calls 'the remnant'. Both are major figures in the Harvard-centred conversation about that minority described in the preceding chapter, and both engage with Emerson's thinking about that minority. The sincere arguments that thinkers like Du Bois and Eliot make within the conversation about the remnant are crucially constitutive of *The Education*'s celebrated ironies: without them, it would have far less to ironise. This chapter reads the young Du Bois as a New England liberal and considers *The Education* alongside his writing in order to think through the political meanings of those ironies.

Although *The Education*'s engagement with the conversation about the remnant is salient, it has not received much attention, perhaps because the book so assertively declares itself something exceptional and apart. Having pointed to Rousseau's writings on education, Adams's 1907 Preface declares: 'The student must go back, beyond Jean Jacques, to Benjamin Franklin, to find a model even of self-teaching. Except in the abandoned sphere of the dead languages, no one has discussed what part of education has, in his personal experience, turned out to be useful, and what not. This volume attempts to discuss it.'[12] Even with its specifications about 'self-teaching' and utility, this aggressive claim on novelty erases peers and antecedents that are actually very obvious. One might start, for instance, with the *Forum*'s 'How I Was Educated' series. Running from 1886 to 1887 and then appearing as a book in 1888 and 1896, the series included contributions from the nation's most eminent educators, a number of them Bostonians like Adams.

But Adams's disavowed antecedents and interlocutors are in fact far more numerous. In recent articles, Jessica Wells Cantiello and William Decker read *The Education* in the traditions of teacher memoirs and the education-as-life autobiographical narrative, respectively. Cantiello observes that Adams's attitude 'contrasts markedly with that of the bulk of the teacher-memoirists, who hailed from humbler backgrounds, taught in primary and secondary schools, and viewed the future of education with hope and optimism'. These teachers, especially those who taught poor immigrant and African–American students, 'use their stories to advocate for systemic change', documenting that 'all students can and will learn'. In this context, she concludes, *The Education* 'stands as a kind of ironic counternarrative'.[13] Decker's parallel discussion of *The Education* in the context of the life-as-education genre points both to unrecognised antecedents and to unclaimed heirs; he urges us to think about Adams's text 'not only in conjunction with the works he cites . . . but also in relation to the titles he does not'. This means reading *The Education* not merely alongside 'Jean-Jacques' and Franklin, but also Frederick Douglass, Booker T. Washington, Du Bois and Mary Antin. *The Education*'s 'thematic legacy', Decker argues, 'belongs as much to those for whom the acquisition of literacy and professional skills exists as a path to empowerment as to those for whom education supports the retention of privilege'. *The Education*, he suggests, fits within an American tradition of life-as-education in which Adams's most salient heirs are African–American male autobiographers. Decker adds in a footnote: 'Perhaps the life narrative that most clearly figures in *The Education*'s line of descent is *The Autobiography of W.E.B. Du Bois*.'[14]

That life narrative was published in 1968, but in the early years of the twentieth century, Du Bois and Adams were already linked socially, professionally and intellectually through their mutual connections at Eliot's Harvard.[15] When we force *The Education* back into that context and view it as just another intervention in the Harvard-centred conversation about the duties and powers of the educated elite around the turn of the century, Du Bois emerges as an especially relevant interlocutor. This Harvard world is a small world: the Bliss Perry who puts into print President Eliot's derisive remark about Adams is also the editor of *The Atlantic* who publishes several of the articles by Du Bois that become part of *The Souls of Black Folk* (1903).[16] As Cantiello notes in passing, those articles are part of the body of sincere utterance to which *The Education* forms an 'ironic counternarrative'.[17]

Both Adams and Du Bois are preoccupied with education, and both are inconstant liberals. Each embraces liberalism early in his career and then moves away from it as he ages: Du Bois towards a more democratic radicalism, Adams towards a less democratic illiberalism. In the early years of the twentieth century, they sit at different places on these trajectories: Du Bois still advocating his youthful liberalism, Adams past his own dramatic apostasy from that faith. *The Education* takes up topics that figure importantly in Du Bois's works from this period, including the periodical articles that become part of *Souls*, the essay 'The Talented Tenth' (1903), and sociological studies about education from Atlanta University, especially *The College-Bred Negro* (1900). 'Talented Tenth', like *Education*, is a now-canonical text with important but only occasionally remembered origins in this conversation about the remnant. These texts stand as two interventions in this conversation that are still widely read, even as many others have been forgotten.

Zamir and Emily Donaldson Field are among the few scholars who have considered the relationship between *Souls* and *Education*. Field points to Adams's and Du Bois's substantially overlapping intellectual and social worlds at Harvard. Though she finds no definitive evidence that Adams read *Souls*, she sees him engage with the idea of 'double-consciousness' and deploy 'tropes similar to those in *The Souls of Black Folk* in order to mock and trivialize complaints against racial injustice, to claim his own marginality, and to recoup the power he alleges he has lost'.[18] I want to suggest that *The Education*'s engagement with the ideas in *Souls* goes even farther. Adams may or may not have read Du Bois's work; but the resonances between their texts suggest that, at the very least, both Adams and Du Bois are responding to some of the same interlocutors and provocations. Adams's representations of school, Harvard and Boston take up concepts and words that are prominent in Du Bois's work, and this engagement with these concepts and words forms a key part of his larger attack on Bostonian liberalism and its ideas about education.

The first section of this chapter surveys the Harvard conversation about the remnant to show that there is irresolution about the nature of the remnant's work and action, with the threat of ineffectual impotence ever present; within this irresolution, Eliot and Du Bois make some of the most forceful arguments, both proposing a remnant that works in the professions. They both advocate and perform a specific mode of action for the educated elite: one marked by a tendency to forcefulness of intention, certainty, sincerity, directness and commitment to effective action. The chapter's next section shows how Adams identifies that mode of action as Bostonian, disparages it and argues (with reference to the figure of Hamlet) for a different mode of action: one that inheres in indirection, irony, doubt, retreat, passivity and hesitation. In contrast to the conformity and consensus that Adams sees in Boston orthodoxy, this mode of action is disruptive and individual. Noting that such forms of action are especially easy and safe for the powerful, the following section looks at the passages of *Education* that take up concepts and scenes also treated in Du Bois's work. In these passages in particular, *The Education* performs the mode of action that it describes, and this makes for a striking performance of privilege.

The chapter's conclusion notes that Adams's account of Bostonian inaction is picked up by twentieth-century thinkers like Van Wyck Brooks and built into the narrative about the genteel, which is then sometimes deployed to disparage Adams himself, making him representative of a cohort of intellectuals impotent in their inaction, alienation and remove. In Adams's own text, however, these practices of passivity do not actually produce impotence. Quite to the contrary, they manifest and consolidate power. *The Education* and its ironies are a performance of that power, and the book's immediate and enduring success shows that Adams's argument is right: passivity, retreat, detachment, complexity and subtlety can indeed exercise power, especially when they are enacted by someone who already has plenty of it.

Better Men: The Talented Tenth and the Remnant at Harvard

The question of the political agency of the intellectual elite poses itself with a specific urgency for Black writers in a violently white supremacist society.[19] Du Bois points to this violence in *Dusk of Dawn* (1940). Looking back on an 1899 lynching, he recalls: 'one could not be a calm, cool, and detached scientist while Negroes were lynched, murdered and starved'.[20] But, as Du Bois knew, one could, many had and many would. Writing in *The Crisis* in 1914, he names Eliot, along with Woodrow Wilson 'and millions of others [who] have given no encouragement to lynching, except by silence!/ *Except by silence!*/ EXCEPT BY SILENCE!' He adds:

> Humanity is progressing toward an ideal; but not, please God, solely by help of men who sit in cloistered ease, hesitate from action and seek sweetness and light; rather we progress today, as in the past, by the soul-torn strength of those who can never sit still and silent while the disinherited and the damned clog our gutters and gasp their lives out on our front porches.[21]

In criticising Eliot for silence, passivity and retreat, Du Bois admonishes him to cease shirking a duty they had both written about extensively. Eliot was in fact a frequent commentator on public questions. But not about lynching: about the urgency of that issue, he and Du Bois apparently disagreed. On the imperative of elite, learned men to speak, however, they were in broad agreement.

Du Bois's reference to Arnold's 'sweetness and light' expresses a commonplace twentieth-century reading of Arnold's culture as both exclusionary and sequestered away from life and politics. But Arnold himself, writing about 'the remnant' in the early 1880s, had offered one of the most vivid accounts of an ineffectual cultivated elite, and argued for that elite to claim and exercise its powers in the US. Eliot, like Du Bois, engages with Arnold and also with Emerson as he intervenes in the conversation about the remnant. Within this conversation, interlocutors agree that the educated elite should be a political force, but there is irresolution and discord about how exactly they should do so.

We find consensus only in the consistent characterisation of effectual action as male; otherwise, questions about the nature of this cohort's action remain unresolved. If the college-bred are to have a social function, how precisely does that function operate? What should a member of the remnant *do*? For self-conscious members of the educated elite, this is not merely a theoretical quandary, but an immediate personal problem, one that overlaps with the equally immediate problems of vocation and of manhood. Adams grapples with these questions as a young man under the influence of Mill and Tocqueville: he seeks to be part of leading cadre of public moralists, variously writing, publishing, editing and teaching. In a letter of 1862, he famously writes to his brother: 'what we want, my dear boy, is a *school*. We want a national set of young men like ourselves or better, to start new influences not only in politics, but in literature, in law, in society, and throughout the whole social organism of the country.'[22]

The Harvard Phi Beta Kappa proceedings serve as a forum for arguments about whether and how the educated elite might exercise power. In that forum, Emerson's 'American Scholar' (1837) sets out ideas and terms to which subsequent arguments repeatedly return. Praising education that comes from action and nature, as well as books, Emerson defines a scholar in whom masculinity, enfranchisement and action are interlinked. When he returns to the same forum after an eventful interlude of thirty years, he offers an optimistic vision of an expanding cohort of 'exceptional men'. Hailing his audience as an 'educated class', 'cultivated class' and a 'knighthood of virtue', he closes with bright augury: 'I read the promise of better times and of greater men.'[23] Several years earlier, George William Curtis's wartime Phi Beta Kappa address had reiterated arguments from his widely circulated 'The Duty of the American Scholar to Politics and the Times' (1856), which exhorts scholars to use their voices and their votes in the 'great fight of Freedom', and also urges them to be ready to die 'a martyr of Liberty'.[24] Conspicuously engaging with these earlier addresses in the same forum, Wendell Phillips's 'The Scholar in a Republic' (1881) assails college-bred men who fail to participate fully in the social movements or 'agitations' that educate the masses. His ideal college-bred man is an 'agitator' whose object is 'to tear a question open and riddle it with light': this scholarly light does the work of bullets.[25] Phillips advocates less figurative violence as he criticises scholars' continuing failure to ally themselves with John Brown, and as he praises the Russian Nihilists who had recently assassinated the Czar. His address apparently offended many in the assembled audience, and President Eliot offered a brief rebuttal in his after-dinner speech.[26] This dissensus at the 1881 Phi Beta Kappa proceedings points to a broader irresolution on the question of the remnant's action.

Arnold takes up this unresolved question two years later during his 1883–4 tour of the US. Quoting Plato, he offers an especially vivid image of a powerless and ineffective cultivated elite: the remnant, he writes, 'may be compared . . . to a man who has fallen among wild beasts; he will not be one of them, but he is too unaided to make head against them'. Knowing that he cannot fight the beasts, 'he will resolve to keep still, and to mind his own business; as it were standing aside under a wall in a storm of dust and hurricane of driving wind; and he will endure to behold the rest filled with iniquity, if only he himself may live his life clear of injustice and impiety, and depart . . . in mild and gracious mood, with fair hope'. In these conditions, Arnold notes, 'the remnant were impotent'.[27] The spectre of such impotence persistently haunts the discussion about the public role of college-bred men. Adams invokes it even as he tells his brother that the US needs a *school*: such a school, he complains, 'is what America has no power to create'.[28]

During the year in which Adams first circulates *The Education*, questions about the action of the remnant come up repeatedly in writing by and about the Harvard community. In November, William James delivers an address at Radcliffe on 'The Social Value of the College-Bred' (1907). Echoing a speech he had given some five years earlier, as well as his student Du Bois's argument in 'Talented Tenth', James hails 'the better kind of man', or 'the best of us', affirming that 'our better men *shall* show the way and we *shall* follow them'. Pointing to the role of such men in the Dreyfus affair, he proclaims: '"Les intellectuels"! What a prouder club-name could there be than this one . . . !' 'Social Value' may, in fact, respond to an argument about the educated elite in *The Education*: James notably comments that a college-bred ability to judge character 'might well atone for . . . our ignorance of dynamos'. But even as he celebrates the college-bred, James refrains from specifying the mechanism by which their leadership operates. When he comes to this question, he resorts to metaphor and seems to lose control of language. Picturing a 'human ship' beset by the winds of 'affections, passions, and interests', James imagines the college-bred as 'the judicious pilot's hand upon the tiller'; this 'bird's-eye view of the general steering function of the college-bred amid the driftings of democracy', he says, 'ought to help us to a wider vision of what our colleges themselves should aim at. If we are to be the yeast-cake for democracy's dough, if we are to make it rise with culture's preferences, we must see to it that culture spreads broad sails.'[29] With considerably more coherence, Du Bois had compared his 'Talented Tenth' to 'yeast' several years before.[30] Here, in James's remarkable sea-storm of baking and sailing, the college-bred man is at once up by the mast, down on the deck and fermenting mindlessly like a single-celled fungus. Though William's brother might raise an eyebrow at this disarrayed metaphor, it points to a truth: among those who make arguments about the role of the educated elite in democracy, the mechanism and form of that elite's agency remain a matter of dispute.

Earlier that year, in February 1907, Roosevelt had made a strident intervention in that dispute when he gave an address at Harvard titled 'The College Man'. Delivered around the time when he would have received Adams's book, the address reprises (verbatim) the arguments that Roosevelt had made in his 1894 articles countering Edwin Lawrence Godkin's call for educated men to engage in 'talk' and 'criticism'. Godkin writes that the US suffers from 'the silence of its educated class', calling for that class to break its silence and engage in 'talk' and 'criticism'; Roosevelt disparages 'talk' and 'criticism', praises 'doing', and calls for elite leadership that is ready to hold public office and ride into battle.[31] This vision of leadership figures implicitly in a dust-up in the press in March of 1907, when Roosevelt was misunderstood to say that he would assume the presidency of Harvard upon ceasing to be President of the US. Roosevelt himself, 'almost exploding with laughter', offered a comical picture of that outcome: 'me riding up to the President's office on a cayuse with a couple of forty-ones strapped to my waist, Bat Masterson following me with a knife between his teeth ready to be made Dean of the Faculty'. Eliot too made light of the mix-up, though his humour was, characteristically, much dryer. He remarked in an after-dinner speech: 'Pres. Roosevelt is said to want my job when I get through. Let me say that I don't want his when he gets through.'[32] The *Harvard Graduate's Magazine* reported all this with much amusement in September. That amusement depends on an appreciation of the stark difference between the models of leadership and masculinity that each of these men advocates and performs: it is as absurd to think of the dusty gunslinger at Harvard as it is to think of Eliot on the back of that cayuse.

Several months later, in November 1907 – the same month that William James delivers 'Social Value' – a hagiographic feature on Eliot appeared in the *North American Review*, making him the paragon of a model of elite leadership that involved no forty-ones and no knives: President Eliot, the profile affirms, argues for a cultivated elite that leads through its work in the professions. Setting aside many other topics it might have taken up, the profile focuses specifically on the question of what kind of work the educated elite ought to do. Presenting Eliot himself as an exemplar, it recites his argument that influence resides in the work of the professions rather than in public office, quoting heavily from a piece Eliot had published in *The Atlantic* in 1896. 'President Eliot', the profile states, 'is one of those great citizens whose influence is of larger value to us than the authority exercised by public officers – presidents, governors, or lawmakers'; he 'naturally sets a smaller value upon the deeds of the man of action than upon the plans, the theories, the discrimination, the sense of proportion, the prescience, the beliefs and the achievements of the scholar and man of reflection'.[33] This is not an especially accurate summary of Eliot's views, but the profile is using Eliot to make a point. Like the amused report in the *Harvard Graduate's Magazine*, it positions the Harvard President as the opposite of the Roosevelt type. Roosevelt argues for doing and deeds that include holding office and riding off to battle; perhaps unexpectedly, his college man has distinct similarities with Phillips's scholar–agitator, in that he is ready for violence and also for close contact with those outside his own class. Eliot's remnant does fight in wars, sometimes – but in peacetime, instead of participating in 'agitation', it usefully suffuses the professions.

'It is often assumed', Eliot writes in his 1896 essay, 'that the educated classes become impotent in a democracy, because the representatives of those classes are not exclusively chosen to public office.' This is incorrect, Eliot explains: 'In a democracy, it is important to discriminate influence from authority. Rulers and magistrates may or may not be persons of influence; but many persons of influence never become rulers, magistrates, or representatives in parliaments or legislatures.'[34] And, in fact, public office may not be the most effective role:

> legislation and public administration necessarily have a very second-hand quality; and more and more legislators and administrators become dependent on the researches of scholars, men of science, and historians, and follow in the footsteps of inventors, economists, and political philosophers. Political leaders are very seldom leaders of thought; they are generally trying to induce masses of men to act on principles thought out long before.

'The real leaders of American thought in this century', he sums up, 'have been preachers, teachers, jurists, seers, and poets.'[35]

Eliot echoes this list in a letter that states that 'colored people. . . should have access to all trades and all professions . . . they should be in due proportion not only laborers, farmers and mechanics, but builders, bankers, lawyers, physicians, preachers, and teachers'. This list of vocations notably leaves out the seers and poets he names among his white remnant. Eliot specifies in this letter, as elsewhere, that the training of a Black remnant is necessary because it is essential to racial segregation, which he supports: 'The provision of a higher education for negroes', he explains, 'is the logical consequence of the proposition that the black and white races should be kept pure.' Eliot affirms that 'Northern opinion and Southern opinion are identical' on this matter, and later alludes unmistakably to racial impurity caused by sexual incontinence amongst Southern white men: 'the Northern white's race feeling seems to be really much more robust than that of the Southern white's. The Northerner's is simply impregnable, like the self-respect of a gentleman.'[36]

Du Bois works against exactly this sort of racism, but he too advocates the formation of a Black remnant, and he too envisions a remnant doing its work in the professions. Atlanta University's 1909 brochure quotes Eliot: 'the colored race in our land must have its own representation in all departments of professional life'.[37] Across multiple genres, his writing investigates and reports on the careers and professions of college-educated Black men. Recognising that the saving remnant imagined by thinkers like Emerson, Arnold and Eliot has always been a white one, he argues that his race too needs one of its own:

> In the professions, college men are slowly but surely leavening the Negro church, are healing and preventing the devastations of disease, and beginning to furnish legal protection for the liberty and property of the toiling masses. All this is needful work. Who would do it if Negroes did not? How could Negroes do it if they were not trained carefully for it? If white people need colleges to furnish teachers, ministers, lawyers, and doctors, do black people need nothing of the sort?[38]

The vocation for the remnant that Du Bois most forcefully recommends is teaching. 'The Talented Tenth' argues that it is 'in the furnishing of teachers that the Negro college has found its peculiar function'. 'College-bred Negroes', he continues, 'were first teachers, and then teachers of teachers. And here it is that the broad culture of college work has been of particular value.' Du Bois writes: 'the Negro race in the South needs teachers to-day above all else'. He continues: 'It is getting increasingly difficult to get funds for training teachers in the best modern methods, and yet all over the South ... comes the wail, "We need TEACHERS!" and teachers must be trained.'[39] This ventriloquised shout speaks of specific circumstances: as James D. Anderson documents, the 'nineteenth-century momentum' of institutions of higher education for Blacks in the South 'declined sharply after 1900'; funding grew scarce, and the 'campaign to develop black higher education was rapidly diminishing in scope and activity'.[40] Du Bois advocates for his remnant and its central vocation in a time of contested rights, economic deprivation and pervasive violence.

Both Du Bois and Eliot subscribe to the logic of differentiated development over time that structures liberal thinking about race, civilisation and education. Both make arguments that are broadly liberal, emancipatory and democratic; and both are elitist, eugenicist thinkers who use a Darwinian frame of reference to describe a natural hierarchy of ability. They both insist repeatedly on 'inequality' and 'aristocracy': affirming that capacities are naturally unequal, they value systems that allow those of naturally higher capacities to flourish and lead. Both believe in empowering the especially capable to exercise their power productively and benevolently.[41] And each recommends to broad audiences specific programmes of reading for a self-guided 'liberal education'.[42]

Both Eliot and Du Bois (along with William James) self-consciously interpret Emerson's ideas about liberal culture for a new century, and each refers to Emerson and Arnold as he makes his argument about the role of the educated elite.[43] In his 'New Definition of a Cultivated Man' (1903), Eliot specifies that he means '"cultivated man" in only its good sense – in Emerson's sense' and echoes Arnold when he says this man is 'not finished, but perfecting'. He then names Arnold and quotes *Culture and Anarchy* approvingly: 'In Arnold's phrases the first step for every aspirant to culture is to endeavor to see things as they are or, "to learn, in short, the will of God."'[44] In 'Talented Tenth', Du Bois gestures towards the same interlocutors when he uses Arnold's phrase to call his tenth a 'saving remnant', and Emerson's by hailing its members as 'exceptional men'.[45]

As he discusses the value of learning, teaching and culture in 'The Talented Tenth' and elsewhere, Du Bois often sounds like Charles Eliot Norton (whom he names as a personal correspondent and as one of Harvard's great teachers) addressing the subscribers of the *New Princeton Review* or writing in *The Forum*.[46] Especially in 'Sons of Master and Man' and 'Of the Wings of Atalanta', *Souls*, like 'Talented Tenth', expresses ideas that Norton (much more engaged with art and literature than his cousin Eliot) also repeatedly advocates, calling for 'missionaries of culture', and pointing to the university as a force for ideals and idealism against crude materialism. Interestingly, Du Bois shares tendencies with a fictional Boston liberal too. *Souls* quotes the lines from *Faust* that Henry James puts in the mouth of Olive Chancellor, who is, like Du Bois, committed to a project of educating the untaught.[47] In James's *Bostonians* and in *Souls*, '*Entbehren sollst du, sollst entbehren*' invokes a self-denying bookishness. But while James gently mocks that bookishness and actually gets the quotation slightly wrong, Du Bois is gravely serious about these words.

Both Du Bois and Eliot exclude women from their remnants. These exclusions prevent these thinkers from accessing compelling arguments about how the remnant might exercise its public function. In her study of Black women intellectuals of the period, Brittney Cooper notes:

> Black women thinkers have always been public intellectuals, both because they cared about producing accessible forms of knowledge for and with communities involved in the Black freedom struggle, and because the confluence of racism and patriarchy exempted them from access to academic institutions and from the protections of the private sphere. Black women have never had the luxury of being private thinkers.[48]

Cooper's analysis helpfully identifies private thinking as a luxury. That classification has implications for Adams's publication practices, which, over time, increasingly eschew publicity. 'Luxury' is also one of the (many) words that Henry James uses to describe his practice of open-ended observation and analysis; and luxury, as we shall see, is what Wharton identifies as a criterion for the full flowering of 'real culture'. Adams, James and Wharton embrace such conditions of privacy and abundance. Those conditions are what Du Bois (like James's fictional spinster before him) aspires to renounce when he recites Goethe's '*Entbehren sollst du*'. For Du Bois, as for other New England liberals in the early years of the twentieth century, the most pressing duty of the cultivated elite is not to play, nor to savour, but to serve. How exactly one should do so is a question about which they do not always agree. This is an issue that *The Education* takes up: as in his novels of the early 1880s, Adams hits at a vulnerable spot, an area of discord and irresolution in liberal discourse. Early and late, his attacks on liberal thought have the precision of an inside job.

Bostonian Calm and the Action of the Scholar

One of the ways that Adams signals his participation in the long conversation about the action of the remnant is by making a place in *The Education* for Hamlet, who also figures in 'American Scholar'. Adams uses Hamlet as Emerson does: the greatest failure to act in all of English literature serves him as a device for redefining action. Emerson casts Hamlet as an emblem of the present: 'We, it seems, are critical; we are embarrassed with second thoughts; we cannot enjoy any thing for hankering to know whereof the pleasure consists; we are lined with eyes; we see with our feet; the time is infected with Hamlet's unhappiness, – / "Sicklied o'er with the pale cast of thought".' Emerson asks: 'Is this so bad then? Sight is the last thing to be pitied.'[49] Similarly, Adams revises the (literal, unsubtle) reading that would see Hamlet's habit of doubt and hesitation as a pattern of impotent failures to act. *The Education* suggests that what we think of as action may, in fact, be passive, and what we might call passivity is, in fact, the only real form of action. In this account, that real action inheres exclusively in individual, disruptive moves that depend on irony, detachment, complexity, uncertainty and indirection. False action, by contrast, is based in collective, consensus-based moves that depend on sincerity, commitment, certainty and directness. In *The Education*, this latter mode of action belongs to Boston, Harvard, and the Unitarian orthodoxy that governs these places; 'liberal' is one of the words Adams uses to describe this orthodoxy disparagingly, along with 'mild' and, above all, 'calm'.

'Calm' is what Du Bois in 1940 calls the detachment of the scientist who can gaze upon the displayed knuckles of a lynched man and keep right on coolly researching.[50] The calm that characterises *The Education*'s Bostonians in 1907 carries a different charge: it is sincere rather than detached. It resembles the stubborn certainty that Henry James, two years later, describes in his commemorative essay about Charles Eliot Norton. Adams, James and Wharton will all distance themselves from this Bostonian mode of certainty, which they associate variously with the 'Puritan' or the 'Unitarian'. President Eliot, like his cousin Norton, is repeatedly cast as a paragon of this Bostonian mode, and proudly claims both of those labels.

The Education mounts a sustained attack on Bostonian calm and makes Harvard its epicentre. 'If Harvard College gave nothing else,' Adams writes, 'it gave calm', just as 'nothing quieted doubt so completely as the mental calm of the Unitarian clergy' (68, 36). Adams's account of the beliefs that constitute the Boston–Harvard–Unitarian consensus governing this conformity is one of the most quoted passages of *The Education*; absolute certainty, moralistic smugness, confidence in human perfectibility and dogmatic rejection of dogma characterise his Bostonian orthodoxy:

> Viewed from Mount Vernon Street, the problem of life was as simple as it was classic. Politics offered no difficulties, for there the moral law was a sure guide. Social perfection was also sure, because human nature worked for Good, and three instruments were all she asked: Suffrage, Common Schools, and Press. On these points doubt was forbidden. Education was divine, and man needed only a correct knowledge of facts to reach perfection [. . .] In uniform excellence of life and character, moral and intellectual, the score of Unitarian clergymen about Boston, who controlled society and Harvard College, were never excelled. They proclaimed as their merit that they insisted on no doctrine, but taught, or tried to teach, the means of leading a virtuous, useful, unselfish life, which they held to be sufficient for salvation. For them, difficulties might be ignored; doubts were waste of thought; nothing exacted solution. Boston had solved the universe; or had offered and realized the best solution yet tried. The problem was worked out. (36–7)

When Adams imagines himself a trembling undergraduate about to receive a sentence of 'damnation' from President Eliot, it is presumably this path to 'salvation' from which Eliot would have seen Adams err. And indeed, Eliot's stern addresses to incoming undergraduates repeatedly emphasise the duty of Harvard men to be virtuous, useful and unselfish. When he gives these addresses, he admonishes those men in a relentlessly literal and sincere mode to be the potent, effectual remnant that will serve the public and make democracy flourish.

For Adams, the 'calm' of Boston consensus means a conformity. Across multiple texts, he describes Harvard men, Boston children, his own siblings and himself as uniform iterations of the same type. 'Type bourgeois-bostonien! A type quite as good as another, but more uniform,' Adams writes to Henry James in 1903: 'all of my New England generation . . . were in actual fact only one mind and nature; the individual was a facet of Boston'.[51] *The Education* develops this account of conglomerate uniformity. Harvard is a 'mild and liberal' factory of conformity, overseen by Eliot of the 'bland smile', who speaks 'mildly' and gives the institution his 'steady, generous, liberal support' (55, 274, 283). As a student there, Adams is struck by the 'bewildering impersonality' of all his classmates: 'all were identical'; they are 'like so many mirrors of himself, an infinite reflection of his own shortcomings' (67). When he becomes a professor, little has changed: he sees his students as pleasantly malleable, but all 'cast more or less in the same mould' (285).

All these identical Bostonians operate without independent agency. Adams's account of Bostonian consensus suggests that collective action based on shared certainties is, in fact, a kind of automation or passivity: uniformity and conformity make calm, not action. Harvard is what happens if one does nothing: 'Any other education would have required a serious effort, but no one took Harvard College seriously.' Young men arrive at the university just as their fathers before them did, 'generation after generation', as if by conveyer belt: 'custom, social ties, convenience, and, above all, economy, kept each generation in the track' (55). 'Generation after generation' (again), Bostonians send their boys to Harvard 'for the sake of its social advantages' (65). Those advantages seem to consist in the enforcement of conformity and of membership in local orthodoxy. Rather than making 'leaders of men', Harvard produces 'respectable citizens' (55). Its process of production erases individual agency: 'In effect, the school created a type but not a will. Four years of Harvard College, if successful, resulted in an autobiographical blank, a mind on which only a water-mark had been stamped' (56). The implication of this self-referential remark is clear: Henry Adams's mind and the pages of his autobiography bear more than a watermark. This particular boy from Boston did not stay 'in the track'.

The ideas Adam attacks in *The Education* had been his own. The 1862 letter to his brother in which he bemoans the impossibility of making a '*school*' presents individual action as ineffective and collective action as effective. The US falls behind other nations, Adams notes, because other nations have ways of organising collective work: geniuses in France and Britain have structures that steer them away from 'random, insulated work, for special and temporary and personal purposes', but in the US, no such structures exist. Adams sees 'no means, power or hope of combined action for any unselfish end'.[52] Here, in 1862, Adams presents 'combined action' as the only effectual kind. In *The Education*, however, the 'combined' nature of Bostonian action is what makes it impotently passive: from this later perspective, the only kind of action that counts is individual. Who achieves this sort of action in the book? Roosevelt, for one, whom Adams famously characterises in its pages as 'pure act'. His 'restless and combative energy' is 'more than abnormal': his force inheres partly in his anomalousness (387). In manifesting 'the singular primitive quality that belongs to ultimate matter', this Roosevelt resembles the type that Adams observes in Grant: 'men whose energies were the greater, the less they wasted on thought', 'forces of nature, energies of the prime', men 'for whom action was the highest stimulant', who 'made short work of scholars' (387, 248). Here as elsewhere, Adams locates value and power in a primitive irrationality, thumbing his nose at the local god Education, not to mention its attendants Suffrage, Common Schools and the Press.

Adams had already started developing an individualist account of action in *Democracy* (1880), and done so while deriding Boston and its obsession with 'culture'. Adams's character Madeleine makes sallies into reading and art on the advice of 'her Boston friends, who suggested that higher education was precisely what she wanted'. Noting that, in Boston, boys are 'all properly taught Greek and Latin, English literature, ethics, and German philosophy', she expresses an anti-Boston sentiment that Adams would seem to share: 'What then? . . . Now tell me honestly what comes of it. I suppose you have there a brilliant society; numbers of poets, scholars, philosophers, statesmen, all up and down Beacon Street. Your evenings must be sparkling. Your press must scintillate. How is it that we New Yorkers never hear of it?' Madeleine in the novel and Adams in a letter both respond to this Bostonian dogma with an Emersonian demand for independent manly action. Madeleine continues her diatribe: 'You are just like the rest of us. You grow six inches high, and then you stop. Why will not somebody grow to be a tree and cast a shadow?'[53] As Chapter 1 notes, this attack echoes an 1875 letter in which Adams himself poses Madeleine's question, albeit without the image of the giant tree-phallus standing alone in the glaring sun. Adams writes to his correspondent: 'Are we never to produce one man who will do something himself, is the question I am helplessly asking.'[54]

In his 1862 letter about the need for a *school*, Adams comments on his tendency to dwell in doubt and shy from action. These comments are part of a pattern: Adams repeatedly casts himself as Hamlet. Here, in the letter to his brother, he complains that he has a mind not given to certainties: to him, 'what is evil never seems unmixed with good, and what is good always streaked with evil; an object never seems important enough to call out strong energies till they are exhausted, nor necessary enough not to allow of its failure being possible to retrieve'. This sort of mind, 'which is not strongly positive and absolute, cannot be steadily successful in action, which requires quickness and perseverance'. Thus, Adams writes, 'I have steadily lost faith in myself ever since I left college, and my aim is now so indefinite that all my time may prove to have been wasted, and then nothing left but a truncated life.'[55] The sort of mind that Adams the young liberal regrets not having here is precisely the sort of mind that the older Adams assails in his negative portrayal of Boston liberals: full of faith in itself, certain of what is good and what is evil, sure of what is important, and definite in its aims.

Pointing to the series of allusions to Shakespeare's play in the *Education*, Charles Vandersee declares, 'what is perfectly clear is that Adams intended to portray himself as a Hamlet figure'. As Vandersee notes, Adams pledges 'to circumvent the temperamental Hamlet in himself and to adopt, with proper seriousness, the dogmas and attitudes of his time', which means falling in line with '"the followers of Tocqueville, and of John Stuart Mill"'.[56] *The Education* portrays that temperamental Hamlet, noting that the boy Henry Adams suffers a pathological intensification of 'qualities of New England character in no way peculiar to individuals', such that 'his brothers were the type; he was the variation'. The young Henry thus possesses qualities including 'the habit of doubt; of distrusting his own judgment and of totally rejecting the judgment of the world; the tendency to regard every question as open; the hesitation to act except as a choice of evils; the shirking of responsibility' (12). The allusions to *Hamlet* in the *Education* align Victorian Britain's Darwinism with Boston's Unitarianism as local forms of unreflective orthodoxy. Historically speaking, we can observe that both that Boston Unitarianism and London Darwinism belong in the broad tent of nineteenth-century liberalism; and, indeed, *The Education*'s parallel representations affirm this, as do the repeated references to evolutionary science in the arguments from Eliot, Norton and Du Bois alike about the crucial duties of the educated elite.

The young Adams of *The Education* conforms to Darwinian orthodoxy: he 'had no need to learn from Hamlet the fatal effect of the pale cast of thought on enterprises great or small. He had no notion of letting the currents of his action be turned awry by this form of conscience. To him, the current of his time was to be his current, lead where it might.' This young Adams imagines action as a great flow, as of water or wind: action consists in suppressing his own thought and yielding to this flow. Like the Bostonians who stay 'in track' as they file into Harvard, Adams will stay in the 'current' that guides his generation, and 'force himself to follow wherever it led', because to do otherwise – to leap off the track, out of the current, into doubt and questioning and pathless terrain – would be to make himself a Hamlet (218). This young Adams makes the classic Bostonian error. He mistakes complacency for action, and congratulates himself at the resulting calm: 'Figuring himself as already a man of action, and rather far up towards the front, he had no idea of making a new effort or catching up with a new world. He saw nothing ahead of him. The world was never more calm' (266).

Yet even as the young Adams seeks to stay on track, the older Adams's text itself does otherwise. The passage that names Hamlet and quotes his soliloquy continues: 'The mania for handling all the sides of every question, looking into every window, and opening every door, was, as Bluebeard judiciously pointed out to his wives, fatal to their practical usefulness in society. One could not stop to chase doubts as though they were rabbits' (218). Bluebeard's wives die when they pursue doubt; Hamlet, in the quoted soliloquy, avoids death by doing the same. In the former case, doubt delivers them to the homicidal husband; in the latter, it pulls him back from suicide. What are we to make of this? And why the image of rabbits? Like the odd implication that Bluebeard's wives would ever care for the rather Bostonian imperative of having 'practical usefulness in society', those scattering rabbits form part of an incongruous, increasingly nonsensical proliferation of images and references, one that notably seems to veer off track, even as it affirms young Adams's project of staying with the current. Adams would later remark in a letter: 'My views on education are radically revolutionary, but no one cares . . . So I have always found my American audience . . . Nothing diverts the American mind from its ruts.'[57] Whether tracks, currents or ruts, worn pathways for thought earn Adams's suspicion and disdain.

The young Adams of *The Education* is very pleased with himself for taking from Hamlet the lesson that doubt has a 'fatal effect' on action. In his home town, after all, doubt is 'forbidden' (36). But the narrating older Adams knows better. The action Hamlet fails to achieve as the currents of his action are turned awry is, of course, killing himself. Instead of the 'fatal effect' that young Adams recalls, doubt in fact keeps the Prince alive in the passage that he remembers. Hamlet's action arises from and consists in doubt. *The Education* thus uses Shakespeare's Prince to say: doubting is the very breath of life; succumbing to complacency is as good as self-annihilation. Adams's play with *Hamlet* aligns such self-annihilation with the unreflective certainty of the Unitarian or Darwinian liberal. The younger Henry Adams misreads Hamlet's soliloquy, but the older Henry Adams draws this lesson from it: let your resolution sicken and take on the pale cast of thought. Only the current that turns awry will claim the name of action. This later, wiser reading is implicit in the ironic staging of his younger liberal self reading wrongly.

In staging that bad reading, *The Education* makes Hamlet a figure for action. This might seem to be the sort of disruptive, individual, unexpected move that the text is defining as the only kind of action at all. But *The Education* uses Hamlet not so differently from the way Emerson had used him in 'American Scholar' seven decades earlier. And during those seven decades, as Unitarianism itself changed, Emerson had transformed from a local heretic to a local deity. Laurel Bollinger notes that, even by the early 1880s, 'Unitarianism had become far more Emersonian than literary scholars have generally acknowledged': 'while still committed to reason rather than inspiration as its primary source of authority', she writes, 'it no longer resembled the faith Emerson critiqued'. When Arnold visits Boston in 1883, his mildly critical lecture on Emerson provokes scandal: 'It was', said a local reporter, 'like spitting in the prophet's beard.'[58] So the mild calm of Harvard is a milieu in which Emerson's ideas are themselves part of the orthodoxy, not a rebellious departure from it. Eliot's own writing about Emerson makes this evident.

In its Emersonian individualism, then, *The Education* is, in fact, in the track of Bostonian thinking. Bostonian liberalism might be seen as collectivist in that it emphasises civic engagement, but it is, like most liberalisms, deeply committed to individualism. One form of collectivism that Eliot and other liberals sometimes criticise is labour unionism. That movement recognises that collective or 'combined' action is a mode of political agency especially useful to those who do not already have power. The Bostonian liberals that Adams smears as effectively collectivist were not, in fact, collectivists; but his portrait of them implies that collective action, a kind of action that is particularly useful to the disempowered, is actually ineffective passivity. The action that counts, by contrast, is the sort of surprising, individual disruption that princes can undertake without risk or cost. Vandersee observes: 'Both Hamlet and Henry Adams were royal personages.'[59] As the following section will show, *The Education* performs this princely mode of action especially extravagantly in its discussions of teaching, learning and school.

Education and Power: Schools, Schoolmasters, Truants

The Education smashes the local idol of Education and thus performs irreverence towards authority; its representations of school, schooling and education celebrate independence and disobedience, and thus present themselves as insubordinate. But this irreverence is itself a performance of power; and, rather than subordinating power, these celebrations of disobedience consolidate it. The power that they consolidate is one that depends partly on money and family name, but mostly on maleness and whiteness. Adams portrays teaching and teachers in several contexts: his time as a schoolboy, as a student at Harvard College, and then as a Professor of History at the same institution, having been hired by President Eliot. As we saw in Chapter 1, Adams is preoccupied with the power dynamics of the classroom. *The Education* portrays school as a site of the student's domination and coercion. A schoolmaster is 'a man employed to tell lies to little boys' (15). Little boys, therefore, hate school. Adams writes: 'In any and all its forms, the boy detested school, and the prejudice became deeper with years'; 'The dislike of school was so strong as to be a positive gain. The passionate hatred of school methods was almost a method in itself' (40). Adams's views do not change as he leaves boyhood. Looking back, he feels much the same: 'the man of sixty can generally see what he needed in life, and in Henry Adams's opinion it was not school' (41).

Real learning exists outside of school, in leisurely, sprawling, unstructured pleasure: 'summer and country were always sensual living, while winter was always compulsory learning. Summer was the multiplicity of nature; winter was school' (14). Learning happens not in cold coerced school, but in warm summer freedom: 'the happiest hours of the boy's education were passed in summer lying on a musty heap of Congressional Documents in the old farm-house at Quincy, reading Quentin Durward, Ivanhoe and The Talisman, and raiding the garden at intervals for peaches and pears. On the whole he learned most then' (41). When Adams leaves school for the last time, he feels 'no sensation but one of unqualified joy that this experience was ended ... school was what in after life he commonly heard his friends denounce as an intolerable bore' (55). This is the personal record of a curious, intelligent child's encounter with the delights of autonomous learning. It is also a fundamentally elitist account of education that makes learning a rich white boy's game. School is boring, coercive and devoid of real learning, which is only available elsewhere: available to a child whose summers include no work, and whose family happens to have a library and an orchard and old Congressional Documents lying around. The structure of institutional learning offers no learning; only free leisure educates. That free leisure is expensive, but this account obscures that expensiveness and the power it implies. Instead, *The Education* positions itself as bravely and cleverly rebellious in its opposition to power, which it locates falsely in the schoolmaster, rather than in the wealth (dependent on whiteness) that inheres silently in the orchard, the library, the Congressional documents and the certainty of school in winter.

Adams's account of the schoolmaster and the school reformulates the elements of Du Bois's 'Negro Schoolmaster in the New South', published in *The Atlantic* in 1899, which became the fourth chapter of *Souls*.[60] Also a first-person narrative, this text speaks from the perspective of the teacher rather than the student. Du Bois writes: 'I loved my school, and the fine faith the children had in the wisdom of their teacher was truly marvellous. We read and spelled together, wrote a little, picked flowers, sang, and listened to stories of the world beyond the hill.' This school is not winter: here, the sensuous, emancipatory learning of pleasure and nature is not the province of summer, but part of the work that the schoolmaster assigns. This is a schoolmaster, moreover, who works 'together' with his students rather than lying to them, lording it over them and denying their freedom. Du Bois reports that truancy is a particular problem at his school: 'At times the school would dwindle away, and I would start out.' The young teacher goes 'toiling up the hill' and covers ground in order to visit the homes of his students (little Lugene, Mack and Ed, the Lawrences) to try to persuade their parents, whom, like their children, Du Bois presents as individuals. Poverty is pervasive, and the reason for the students' absence is the work that needs to be done: 'the crops needed the boys'; 'Lugene must mind the baby'; in the case of the Lawrences, 'the doubts of the old folks about book-learning had to be conquered again'. The uphill toil of coaxing attendance is part of this schoolmaster's work: if he does not fight for it continuously, this school will 'dwindle away'.[61]

The Education's account of schooling also handles the issue of truancy. Adams reports that, one summer morning at Quincy, at the age of six or seven, he perpetrates 'a passionate outburst of rebellion against going to school' (17). Then, far above, at the top of the staircase, the door of the President's library opens and the elderly man himself emerges. He takes young Henry's hand 'without a word' and walks him each step of the way, 'near a mile on a hot summer morning over a shadeless road to take a boy to school'. The anecdote is amusing: the power of the Presidency turned to the project of getting a resistant child into the classroom; the image of an old man and a small boy hand in hand on a long summer road. Adams narrates with mock-heroic irony: he makes the boy's forced attendance at school a matter of political liberty, describing the old man's coercion as 'contrary to the inalienable rights of boys, and nullifying the social compact'; the President is 'a tool of tyranny' (18). The mock-heroic mode functions effectively here because this little boy's rights, like his access to the orchard and the library and the musty Congressional Records, are in fact totally secure. Field does not discuss content from 'Negro Schoolmaster' or this scene from *The Education*, but these two scenes of truancy support her argument that Adams's text repeats elements of Du Bois's in a way that functions to mock or to parody. In Adams's text, 'inalienable rights' are the stuff of a joke; in Du Bois's text, they are not.

There is a particular and meaningful logic to the humour here. As Cantiello observes, Adams can disparage schoolmasters and school because his access to education is and has always been certain. His anecdote about truancy dramatises precisely that truth: even if this little boy screams and stamps and tries his utmost to avoid school, school remains for him a total inevitability – one enforced by the structures of power embodied in his own flesh and blood. That is what his long walk is about, in contrast to Du Bois's, which is about continuously, laboriously working to reconstitute a school so far from inevitable, so precarious, that it is always on the verge of disappearing.

Du Bois's account of teaching in 'Negro Schoolmaster' notably individualises the students he teaches, describing their varied physical appearances (with attention to skin tone) and calling each by name. This individualisation corresponds with an affirmation that education humanises. Du Bois writes: 'It is the trained, living human soul, cultivated and strengthened by long study and thought, that breathes the real breath of life into boys and girls and makes them human, whether they are black or white, Greek, Russian or American.'[62] By contrast, when Adams describes his experience learning and teaching at Harvard, he emphasises the extent to which all Harvard students are not especially human: they are uniform automatons, young men filling the same chairs 'generation after generation', 'cast more or less in the same mould' as they arrive (55, 65, 285).

A lack of human individuality also characterises the 'young men, in Universities or elsewhere' hailed in *The Education*'s 1907 Preface, as it implies that the book forms a sort of extension to Adams's work as a professor (8). Elsewhere, Adams wrote that the book was 'meant as my closing lectures to undergraduates in the instruction abandoned and broken off in 1877'.[63] Even as the Prefaces point to this function, they transform these young men into inhuman, abstract entities without any evident power of independent action. Adams uses specialised language to operate this abstraction: 'man as a force must be measured by motion from a fixed point. Psychology helped here by suggesting a unit – the point of history when man held the highest idea of himself as a unit in a unified universe' (5). 'The young man himself,' Adams writes, 'the subject of education, is a certain form of energy; the object to be gained is the economy of his force', and then adds: 'The manikin, therefore, has the same value as any other geometrical figure of three or more dimensions, which is used for the study of relation . . . it is the only measure of motion, of proportion, of human condition' (8). The matter of being considered human or not is, here, a really interesting issue with which to play; and Adams borrows words freely from specialised discourses to do that playing.

Adams's account of being a student and a teacher at Harvard discusses ratios, percentages and numbers, specifically multiples of ten. 'Harvard College', Adams writes,

> was a good school, but at bottom what the boy disliked most was any school at all. He did not want to be one in a hundred, – one per cent. of an education. He regarded himself as the only person for whom his education had value, and he wanted the whole of it. He got barely half of an average.

Adams goes on to explain that nobody in his cohort learned mathematics: 'In the one branch he most needed – mathematics . . . failure was so nearly universal that no attempt at grading could have had value.' 'Here', Adams observes, 'his education failed lamentably . . . he needed to read mathematics, like any other universal language, and he never reached the alphabet' (60). But readers will have seen that this failure does not, in fact, prevent Adams from using this 'universal language'. One need only look several lines above these words to see that he readily turns it to his own purposes, making one hundredth of a student body become suddenly one per cent of an education, and then making half of an average education into what one student gets – just as he plays freely with terms like 'force', 'energy', 'unit', 'geometrical', 'dimension' and 'measure' in the Prefaces (5, 8). Adams talks about not knowing mathematics even as he uses the terms of mathematics to say unmathematical things. His narrator appropriates specialised language this way, makes explicit professions of ignorant incomprehension, and yet (rightly) expects to retain readers' respect and attention. In this narrator's voice, these usages are not nonsensical or wrong; they are edgy, innovative, interesting.[64]

Multiples of ten show up not just when Adams is a student, but also when he is a teacher. He writes that 'barely one in ten' students have 'minds ... of an order above the average': 'nine minds in ten take polish passively, like a hard surface; only the tenth sensibly reacts'. So Adams the teacher decides he will 'try to cultivate this tenth mind, though necessarily at the expense of the other nine' (281–2). The education of Adam's 'tenth' operates in a manner precisely the opposite of Du Bois's. Rather than serving to lift up the other nine-tenths, the education of this tenth mind happens at their expense. In Adams's Harvard classroom, we see a dizzying shift in scale. Instead of the sweep and reach of a whole race, all those called 'Negro' in the United States, we find a group of Harvard men gathered at a seminar table; instead of a nationwide cohort of trained minds ready to work for justice and power, we find just one mind. That mind stands out because it alone avoids the uniform passivity of the rest. Singular and white, this gentleman becomes the sole true object of education, the tree that casts a shadow.

Adams's account of his own teaching emphasises the autonomy of his students. Unlike the schoolmaster of his youth, he treats these boys like equals: 'He frankly acted on the rule that a teacher, who knew nothing of his subject, should not pretend to teach his scholars what he did not know, but should join them in trying to find the best way of learning it' (282). In opposition to the 'system' of the institution, 'which could lead only to inertia', Adams's teaching encourages independent thought, conflict and competition: he makes 'pretty efforts to create conflicts of thought among his students' (283). This pedagogy is consistent with his account of action: if there is no friction, no disruption, nothing is accomplished. Consensus means stasis; progress and development lie in conflict. Adams is explicit about this: 'his mind required conflict, competition, contradiction even more than that of the student. He too wanted a rank-list to set his name upon.' If permitted his own reforms, Adams asserts, 'he would have seated a rival Assistant Professor opposite him, whose business should be strictly limited to expressing opposite views'. But the Harvard system, characteristically committed to conformity and consensus, specifically prevents 'contradiction or competition between teachers' (283).

Adams takes an anti-establishment stance towards the 'system' of Harvard, proposes equality between teacher and student, and adopts a collaborative, self-consciously innovative pedagogy. So his approach (which, as Chapter 1 explains, he draws from John Stuart Mill) superficially resembles emancipatory, democratic pedagogies that value the independence and autonomy of the student. And his valorisation of ideas in contest makes his classroom a liberal public sphere in miniature. But this pedagogical model applies in *The Education* to a small group of white men at a seminar table in Cambridge. Like the orchard and the library, Adams's seminar room is a place of radical freedom. And like the orchard and the library, it is a place to which only a select set has access.

Adams exercises the freedom of that select set when he misuses with impunity the specialised language of mathematics and physics; he also exercises it in his habit of criticism via self-deprecation, which we can observe in his response to Eliot's initial invitation to teach at Harvard. Adams writes to Gaskell in September of 1870: 'I am to teach mediæval history, of which, as you are aware, I am utterly and grossly ignorant [. . .] I gave the college fair warning of my ignorance, and the answer was that I knew just as much as anyone else in America knew on the subject, and I could teach better than anyone that could be had.'[65] Adams later recounts in *The Education* that, upon receiving Eliot's invitation, he is 'pleased and grateful for a compliment which implied that the new President of Harvard College wanted his help', but affirms that he knows 'nothing about history, and much less about teaching' (271). He adds: 'He knew no history; he knew only a few historians; his ignorance was mischievous because it was literary, accidental, indifferent' (273). He unspools as dialogue the exchange he had described in his earlier letter to Gaskell: '"But, Mr. President," urged Adams, "I know nothing about Mediaeval History." With the courteous manner and bland smile so familiar for the next generation of Americans, Mr. Eliot mildly but firmly replied, – "If you will point out to me any one who knows more, Mr. Adams, I will appoint him."' 'The answer', Adams writes, 'was neither logical nor convincing' (274).

In 1892, Eliot invited Adams back to Harvard to receive an honorary degree, and persisted when Adams declined. As Samuels observes, Adams's self-deprecation in refusing the honour actually serves to criticise the institution over which Eliot presides.[66] Adams protests that he has 'no claim to such distinction, either as instructor or author, on any French or German standard', neatly implying that Harvard's standards for distinction fall below those. Harvard should, Adams suggests, instead honour Hay and Nicolay's *Life of Lincoln*, a work which offers, among other things, 'the chance for once to escape from the circle of University limitations, and to take a lead in guiding popular impressions'.[67] This comment points directly to the failure of Eliot's remnant: confined within its narrow circle, hampered by its limitations, it neither leads nor guides the broader public.

Adams's deployment of the tactic of criticism via self-deprecation operates not just to assail Harvard, but more specifically to attack Eliot's great reforms of the institution. *The Education* foregrounds this effort by Eliot: 'The fault he had found with Harvard College as an undergraduate must have been more or less just, for the College was making a great effort to meet these self-criticisms, and had elected President Eliot in 1869 to carry out its reforms' (279–80). As Adams reports to Gaskell, his own hiring is part of that great reform. But, of course, Adams fails: 'On the whole, he was content neither with what he had taught nor with the way he had taught it' (284). Adams's failure is also the failure of Eliot's reforms. The 'system' does not permit the changes that Adams attempts: 'In spite of President Eliot's reforms and his steady, generous, liberal support, the system remained costly, clumsy and futile. The University, – as far as it was represented by Henry Adams – produced at great waste of time and money results not worth reaching' (283). In a subsequent articulation, Adams even more explicitly folds into one his own failure and the failure of Eliot's reforms: 'The College had pleaded guilty, and tried to reform. He had pleaded guilty from the start, and his reforms had failed before those of the College' (286).

Adams's attack on universities both precedes and extends beyond *The Education*, which is merely one episode in a longer critique, one that includes his 1892 remark to Eliot about the 'narrow circle of University limitations', as well as the provocations of his *Letter to Teachers of American History*, disseminated selectively in 1910. Writing of that text to Gaskell, Adams recounts, 'I flung my little volume in professorial faces last winter, and – so to speak – kicked my American Universities in the stomach as violently and insultingly as I could.'[68] *The Education* affirms in passing that 'Henry Adams never professed the smallest faith in Universities of any kind, either as boy or man, nor had he the faintest admiration for the University graduate, either in Europe or in America' (67). At the end of his undergraduate education at Harvard, he reports: 'As yet he knew nothing. Education had not yet begun' (69). Later, even after Eliot's reforms, the institution remains useless: 'The lecture-room was futile enough, but the faculty-room was worse. American society feared total wreck in the maelstrom of political and corporate administration but it could not look for help to college dons' (286). Adams writes of his time as an Assistant Professor at Harvard: 'The seven years he passed in teaching seemed to him lost' (284).

This comment, as well as his earlier reference to the 'great waste of time' that university work involves, fits into a conspicuous pattern: in addition to describing Adams's own educational work as a failure, *The Education* describes time spent at institutions of formal education as time wasted (283). Spans of years eerily collapse when spent at school, which somehow eats time. This is true of early schooling, study in college and teaching too. Adams recalls that, as a boy, his mind was not 'given time to act' at school: 'Schoolmasters never gave time.' Thus, 'He always reckoned his school-days, from ten to sixteen years old, as time thrown away' (40). Ancient languages, Adams reports, 'he could . . . learn more completely by the intelligent work of six weeks than in the six years he spent on them at school [. . .] Indeed, had his father kept the boy at home, and given him half an hour's direction every day, he would have done more for him than school ever could do for them' (40–1). He later affirms, 'these first six years of a possible education were wasted in doing imperfectly what might have been done perfectly in one, and in any case would have had small value' (55). Harvard is no better: 'The four years passed at College, were for his purposes, wasted'; and 'the entire work of the four years could have been easily put into the work of any four months in after life' (60–1). When he goes out into the world after his formal education has concluded, Adams feels has 'thrown away ten years of early life in acquiring what he might have acquired in one' (64).

These archly dismissive statements have an important relationship with a body of sincere utterance about formal education, one that includes most of President Eliot's œuvre; it also, as Cantiello points out, includes a vast swathe of teacher-memoirs; and it includes Du Bois's writing about teaching and education. The *Education*'s ironies depend on this body of sincere utterance. In order to see how those ironies operate, we need to juxtapose *The Education* awkwardly with texts that belong to different genres and undertake different projects. That these juxtapositions seem jarring, inappropriate or irrelevant is part of what signifies here.

Consider, for example, the sincere voices that Du Bois includes in *The College-Bred Negro*. The study records answers from a survey question about early education, offering short quotations from seventy-nine respondents. One man writes: 'Twelve years of my life was spent as a slave. I worked at driving cows, carrying dinner to the field-hands and running rabbits . . . When I was freed I did not know a letter, but I worked my way through Webster's "blue back" speller.' Another testifies: 'I was born in a stable; my father died when I was two years old. I blacked boots and sold sulphur water to educate myself until I was 18.' And another: 'About the close of the war rebel soldiers stole me from my parents in South Carolina and took me to Georgia. I ran away to Tennessee, where I worked as a janitor in a white school and studied at night by the aid of the principal who was very friendly. He afterward sent me to Howard University.' A woman reports: 'At a very early age I assumed the responsibility of housekeeper, as my mother died and I was the oldest of a family of five; hence I labored under many disadvantages in attending school, but nevertheless I performed my household duties, persevered with my studies, and now I feel that I have been rewarded.'[69]

Adams's unrelenting attacks on formal education are, of course, a rigorous critique of antiquated pedagogy and a protest against a powerful 'system'. Juxtaposed against these statements, however, they look a bit less like that and a bit more like a lighted match tossed blithely into a pile of hundred-dollar bills, a showy display from one richly empowered by the system itself. Along with these voices recorded by Du Bois, we might also consider certain facts. 'Of all barriers to education, violence was especially prevalent,' notes Stephanie Evans as she discusses African–Americans' access to education after Emancipation. Pointing to Black women's lack of access to education in particular, she adds 'statistically, for every five black women who had graduated with a college degree by the turn of the twentieth century, one black woman had been lynched'.[70] To read *The Education* with this in mind, and to listen to Adams's voice alongside the voices recorded in *The College-Bred Negro*, is to violate the decorum that divides genres, and it is also to read in an extremely literal and unsubtle way. A reader more appreciative of irony, subtlety and complexity might say that this juxtaposition manifests humourless moralising or aggressive politicisation; that reader might helpfully explain to the bluntly literal reader that *The Education* actually celebrates *real* education, that its ironies express that gist, and that the real education it celebrates can belong, in principle, to everyone.

But what the book defines as *real* education are forms of learning available primarily to rich white children, just as it defines as *real* action modes of action that especially suit those who already have power. Literally, what *The Education* says about school is that it is not worthwhile, and that it accomplishes nothing. In the early twentieth century, who can say that? Whom does such a statement affect, and how? Adams offers his critique with the ease of one for whom access to education has always been secure. As Cantiello notes, he can point to the worthlessness of school and college because his own education is so available as to be mandatory; he can complain that school and Harvard are an intolerable bore because they are an inevitability for him. He can remark that 'the degree of Harvard College had been rather a drawback to a young man in Boston and Washington' precisely because it is not (285).

It is not just education that is secure for Adams, but intelligence. The signature move of *The Education* is its repeated emphasis not just on the futility of education, but also on the sheer incompetence and ignorance of Henry Adams. Adams repeats that his education was a failure, that he knows nothing, that, in spite of trying, he has learned nothing. As David Ball's sensitive reading shows, Adams stages 'intellectual work that resolutely confronts its own impossibility': *The Education* operates a 'transvaluation of the meaning of failure throughout its extended meditations'.[71] Such meditations carry wildly varying levels of risk for different speakers. In making extravagantly sustained statements of incomprehension and bewilderment, Adams risks little; others (to this day) risk a great deal. Anyone is welcome to confess failure to learn; but the way that statement signifies depends on who says it. In the early twentieth-century US, a text about a Black person or a white woman that repeatedly affirms its subject's intellectual incompetence and incomprehension is probably not a brave proto-modernist work of genius; it might look more like a scientific study or a minstrel-show script. In those kinds of texts, the futility of education is not ironic, nor is it provocative: it entirely real, utterly mundane and viciously consequential.

By organising itself around ironic, self-deprecating statements most readily feasible for people like himself, Adams's book makes itself a remarkably lavish spectacle of performed privilege. *The Education* thus enacts the logic that also drives an oft-repeated joke from Edith Wharton's husband, Teddy. Teddy, the story goes, was late for a lunch in Newport, so 'he hailed a passing butcher's cart and rode up Bellevue Avenue in it'. Later, a parvenu friend said to him: 'Wharton, I hear that you rode up the Avenue in a butcher's cart. I wouldn't do that if I were you.' Teddy replied: 'No, if I were you I wouldn't do that either.'[72] Like the story of little Adams the would-be truant, this is an amusing tale; and like that story, it is a razor-sharp fable about power. Teddy's joke refers to the same rule that makes *The Education*'s irony work: the meaning of an action or an utterance, and its effects, depend on the power of the person speaking or acting. A remark that exposes one speaker to debasement, ridicule or violence can, in the mouth of someone else, serve to demonstrate perfect imperviousness to those risks. Like Teddy's butcher-cart ride and his joke about it, *The Education* makes use of that imperviousness. And, as in the case of Teddy's joke, this performance of power has been widely hailed for its deft wit.

The Type of Passivity: Adams and the Genteel Tradition

During the year when *The Education* first circulates, Roosevelt speaks at the Harvard Union about 'The College Man', and William James speaks at Radcliffe about 'The Social Function of the College-Bred', Van Wyck Brooks is attending the College and writing for *The Harvard Monthly*. The young Brooks takes up the unresolved questions about the action of the remnant, and (as this book's Conclusion will observe) his angry account of its impotence becomes an influential iteration of the narrative about 'the genteel tradition'. Adams is at once a source for that narrative and an object of its critique. Brooks, like others, quotes Adams's texts in order to develop the narrative about the genteel. In 'Literary Life' (1922), which also quotes William James's 'Social Value', Brooks points to Adams's 1862 letter about the need for a *school* of better men. Assailing Adams's increasingly contemptuous and evasive publication practices, he observes: 'if Henry Adams had merely signed his work and accepted the consequences of it, he might by that very fact have become the founder, the centre, of the school that he desired'. Quoting (and italicising) Adams's comment about having '*no power to create*' such a school, Brooks writes: 'Here we have the perfect illustration of that mass fatalism of which I have spoken, and Henry Adams himself, in his passivity, is the type of it.'[73]

Twentieth-century applications of 'genteel' to Adams vary, partly because of the messy overlap between what (mostly) historical scholars call 'genteel reformers' and what (mostly) literary scholars call 'the genteel tradition'. Vernon Louis Parrington and then Robert Dawidoff, among others, position Adams (with Henry James) as an opponent of or exception to the genteel tradition; Ross Posnock, however, makes Adams (with Edwin Lawrence Godkin) one of the 'mainstays of the genteel tradition'.[74] Posnock works from, among other sources, John G. Sproat's *The Best Men: Liberal Reformers in the Gilded Age* (1968). That book, as Andrew Slap observes, 'codified' Richard Hofstadter's interpretation of liberal reformers as a 'displaced elite class trying to regain power'.[75]

Hofstadter's *Anti-Intellectualism in American Life* (1962) calls *The Education* the 'towering literary monument' of the 'genteel reformers'.[76] Although Hofstadter calls the book a 'masterpiece in the artistry of self-pity', he also treats it as a more or less reliable document: his account of ineffectuality, like Brooks's, draws evidence from the story Adams tells about himself. Hofstadter uses *The Education* to pursue an argument about the action and power of a cultivated elite: 'Politically and morally, as Henry Adams so poignantly demonstrated, the genteel reformers were homeless. They had few friends and no allies.' Quoting *The Education*, Hofstadter states that 'coarse and ruthless' types take control from these ineffectual men, and explains: 'The genteel reformers were as much alienated from the general public as they were from the main centers of power in the business corporations and the political machines'; they 'were barred from useful political alliances and condemned to political ineffectuality'.[77]

Both Brooks and Hofstadter draw from Adams's writing about the remnant as they help to develop the narrative about the genteel, which fashions for the twentieth century a new image of the passivity, retreat and inaction that Arnold describes amongst the impotent Athenian remnant. Twentieth-century thinkers often use the narrative about the genteel for progressive purposes, but the contours of that narrative are significantly reactionary. In its evocations of dispossession and bewilderment in the context of modernity, this story reissues the perennial plot of loss that figures centrally in the mythology of racial pessimism. In reciting this story, the narrative about the genteel offers a muted, metamorphosed, well-meaning iteration of that lethally evergreen white supremacist narrative, the tale of decline and replacement.

To regard Henry Adams, son of a dynasty, published historian, Harvard professor, intimate of Hay and Roosevelt, inhabitant of a splendid H. H. Richardson mansion and habitué of superb Parisian salons, as a spokesman for a cohort in any way *disempowered* is to refer to an extraordinary potency exercised before that loss. 'No allies'? 'Homeless'? 'Barred from useful political alliances'? Compared to whom? Adams himself is perceptively self-aware about this. Just after the amusing story about the President forcing him to go to school, he tells another amusing story from his boyhood: 'The Irish gardener once said to the child: – You'll be thinkin' you'll be President too!' The child is taken aback because 'to him, that there should be a doubt of his being President was a new idea. What had been would continue to be' (20). The grandson, living in the age of the Dynamo, will not have all the power his grandfather had. What a bewildering surprise: to discover that one is not entitled to hold

Federal office, preside over a military, and wield the power of life and death over many other humans. In *The Education*, this white boy's feeling of thwarted entitlement is something interesting and sometimes comedic. But the role this feeling plays in US history and politics is a profoundly sinister one.

We might indeed call Adams the type of passivity: he practised retreat, indirection and irony; he deprecated himself; he refused to publish; he sent *The Education* to just a hundred friends; some years later, he died. As he lay inert, that book went to press, critics heaped praise on it and the public rushed to buy it. In 1919, it won the Pulitzer. Since then, readers have continued to hail its audacity and cleverness. With such passivity, who needs action? As Adams recognised, the efficacy and power of action depend on the actor. The forms of action that *The Education* endorses and performs are forms of power that work well for the privileged. The book's bravura performance of these forms of action in the age of the Dynamo, and that age's eagerness to celebrate it, show that the dispossessions of modernity leave plenty of the old power intact.

Chapter 6

Pure English: Wharton and the Elect

At the height of 1919's Red Summer, named for the blood spilled in a season of especially intense and widespread white supremacist violence, Edith Wharton writes from Paris to her friend, Harvard Professor of English Barrett Wendell. Before describing the recent victory parade on the Champs Élysées, Wharton tells Wendell that she has instructed her publisher to send him a copy of her new book, *French Ways and Their Meaning* (1919). She also asks if he has seen *The America of Today* (1919), a collection of essays edited by their mutual friend, Gaillard Lapsley. Pointing in particular to the contribution from Henry Seidel Canby, Professor of English at Yale, she writes, 'Prof. Canby has some good things – or nearly good – to say on modern American literature.' But she objects to 'his tiresome distinction between aristocratic & democratic forms'. Bemoaning a 'patriotism' that, as she sees it, refers to the US's failures rather than its achievements, she asks: 'How much longer are we going to think it necessary to be "American" before (or in contradistinction to) being cultivated, being enlightened, being humane, & having the same intellectual discipline as other civilized countries?'[1]

Wharton's remark expresses casually a logic that structures her thinking profoundly: 'How much longer?' implies a development over time into cultivation and civilisation. This chapter examines the differing applications of this logic in the competing theories of inequality that belong to Wharton, her friend Professor Wendell, and Wendell's longstanding opponent, Harvard President Charles William Eliot. I consider *French Ways*, *Backward Glance* (1934) and several of Wharton's essays against the backdrop of the perennial antagonism between Wendell and Eliot. Wendell's opposition to Boston liberalism is uniquely durable, intimate and explicit. Wharton is neither as politically reactionary nor as zealously white supremacist as he is, but the consonances in their thinking show how she, like him, dissents from core claims in liberalisms like Eliot's. The juxtaposition of Wharton's writing and the conversation between these eminent Harvard men allows us to locate her ideas within a larger contest of different theories about what makes some people better than others.

Wendell's *France of Today* (1907) is commonly named as one of Wharton's influences as she writes *French Ways*, which, as Jennie Kassanoff's authoritative reading affirms, offers Wharton's 'most sustained treatment of race and nation'.[2] And indeed, *French Ways* shares with *France of Today* several themes and emphases. But the relationship between these texts is in fact more substantial and more complicated. *France of Today* is one of a linked pair of books that result from Wendell's year as the inaugural Hyde Professor at the Sorbonne in 1904–5. James Hazen Hyde (Harvard '98, Francophile, moneyed, beset by scandal) had endowed the professorship in order to foster mutual understanding: each year, a professor from Harvard was to explain American history and culture to the French, and then go back to the US and explain the French to the Americans. In *France of Today*, Wendell undertakes one part of his work as Hyde Professor; he undertakes the other part in *Liberty, Union, and Democracy* (1906). In addition to the material in that book, Wendell also apparently offered to his French audiences material from his *Literary History of America* (1900), a foundational text in the genre. His work as Hyde Professor thus forms a direct extension of his work as one of the US's first literary historians.

The Hyde Professorship falls within Wharton's social orbit in Paris after she settles there in 1907, and she knows several of the men who hold the post during the first decade of the twentieth century.[3] *French Ways*, I want to suggest, results from an involuntary, impromptu Hyde Professorship of sorts, one into which Wharton finds herself pressed by exigencies of the World War I, as she takes on what Julie Olin-Ammentorp identifies as 'ambassadorial' work.[4] She not only explains the French to the Americans in the addresses that become *French Ways*; she also explains the Americans to the French in the address 'L'Amérique en Guerre' (1918).[5] Wharton seems to have undertaken the work of a Hyde Professor somewhat uneasily. We should recall that her first novel violently exterminates its female academic just after she dares to take the podium. To her American audience, Wharton pleads:

> I have been asked to come and talk to you about France . . . I never expected to speak in public. I consider it a man's job and not a woman's; and I never *did* speak in public till last February, when I was asked to try to explain to a French audience some of the reasons why America has come into this war.[6]

But if she is thrust unwillingly into this role, Wharton operates deftly within it, presenting a slightly different self to each audience.

The fact that Wharton's wartime addresses informally replicate the project of Wendell's Hyde Professorship is not the only reason to read those addresses alongside his work. Because language, race and nation are understood during the period as closely interconnected, Wharton's writing about race and nation is deeply concerned with the stuff of Wendell's academic field. As Kassanoff argues, Wharton makes language and literature central to her argument about race and nation: she endorses a 'Pure English' that prevails in a 'Land of Letters' or a 'Republic of Letters', which Kassanoff describes as 'a linguistic sanctuary for the educated few'. 'In formulating a theory of language and literature,' Kassanoff observes, 'Wharton fashioned a deeply conservative model of citizenship and writing.'[7]

The centrality of language and literature within Wharton's thinking about race and nation manifests assumptions that pervade nineteenth-century philology and racial science. Those assumptions shape the work undertaken in early twentieth-century English departments by both German-trained philologists and gentleman generalists like Wendell: the teaching and study of English in the US was, from the outset, driven substantially by narratives of Anglo-Saxon belonging, inheritance and conquest.[8] So Wharton's thinking about language, race and nation has an important relationship to the history of English as a field of academic study. And we should note that Wendell was not Wharton's only link to the literary professoriate. She had particular admirers at Yale in William Lyon Phelps and Canby; among Harvard's literary men, Charles Eliot Norton and Bliss Perry were also friendly acquaintances.

Perry was Hyde Professor in 1909–10. One of his duties in that role was to help select a lecture hall at the Sorbonne suitable for the visit of Theodore Roosevelt.[9] When Roosevelt spoke there on 23 April 1910, Wharton attended. The now-famous speech he gave, 'The Man in the Arena', offers one of the many expressions of Roosevelt's argument about manhood and the duties of 'the college man'. At the Sorbonne, Roosevelt repeats what he says elsewhere about the proper work and duties of the educated minority in a democracy: his calls for action, citizenship and manhood respond to the contested question about what that minority should be and do. A decade later, Wharton's *The Age of Innocence* (1920) would invoke the recently deceased Roosevelt and point to his ideas about the duties of the educated minority. When Newland Archer and Ned Winsett discuss gentlemen going into politics (or, rather, not doing so), Winsett remarks, 'you're in a pitiful little minority', and advises: 'You'll never amount to anything, any of you, till you roll up your sleeves and get right down into the muck.'[10] This appeal for a descent into the muck recalls Roosevelt's appeal for a plunge into the hurly-burly. Noting the link between 'Man in the Arena' and Winsett's appeal, Geoffrey R. Kirsch shows that Wharton embraces Roosevelt's exhortation to active, engaged citizenship for both the individual and the nation – most overtly, in her remarkable service during World War I (that service includes publishing *The Book of the Homeless*, to which both Wendell and Roosevelt contribute).[11]

Age of Innocence's attention to Roosevelt's ideas about the duty and action of the educated elite is part of Wharton's broader response to what this book has called the conversation about the remnant. This response extends into *A Backward Glance*. Recalling the period of her youth in that text, Wharton notes that not one of her cultivated gentlemen friends 'rendered the public services that a more enlightened social system would have exacted of them. In every society there is the room, and the need, for a cultivated leisure class; but from the first the spirit of our institutions has caused us to waste this class instead of using it'.[12] Wharton inverts the typical form of arguments about the remnant, which usually describe the duty of the cultivated minority to act. Instead, she locates agency in society as a whole, which either wastes or uses that minority. And the value of that minority itself inheres not in duty or action but in 'leisure'. This is in stark contrast to Eliot's remnant, which eschews leisure in favour of duty, work and service.

As the preceding chapters have shown, Eliot is a key voice in the conversation about the duties and powers of the 'college man' or the 'college-bred', in which Roosevelt too participates, along with other Harvard thinkers around the turn of the century. In that conversation, Eliot argues for political equality, education and democracy. His vision for the remnant is a meritocratic elite significantly dedicated to civic duty. He sees social mobility and open competition as the means of making that elite; or rather, those elites, each administering to its own part of a nation segregated by race. But Wendell and Wharton, in contrast, valorise order and hierarchy rather than social mobility. We might be tempted to observe here a simple dichotomy between the views of nostalgic conservatives like Wendell and Wharton and future-minded liberals like President Eliot. Such a dichotomy would pit a conservative hereditarian claim for blood and stasis against liberal arguments for pliancy, perfectibility, development, change and potential. But, in fact, there is no clean separation of blood and education in this particular conversation about the superiority of some persons over others.

In Wendell's, Wharton's and Eliot's views about what makes an elite, we see a unanimous certainty about the relevance of both biological materiality and the experience of culture and civilisation. All three of these thinkers can be described as hereditarian; and development over time is central to the way all three understand superiority. Darwinian evolutionary science informs, in different ways, each of their theories of inequality. This is consistent with what Kyla Schuller and other scholars of nineteenth-century thinking about race have recently emphasised: hereditarianism and biological materialism do not imply the impossibility of change.[13] Rather than simply imagining fixed capacities, these systems of thought can posit considerable mutability both in individuals and in races, and they can serve a range of ideological agendas. Looking at the ways that Wendell, Eliot and Wharton define America's elect helps to make this clear. All three thinkers posit a cultivated elite deserving of power. Eliot envisions a remnant, trained at institutions like his own, working within the professions in order to guide and serve the broader public. But Wendell and Wharton are less confident of the plausibility of this scenario for the remnant's leadership. Modern democracy, in their view, presents a less auspicious site for the exercise of civic duty by a cultivated elite. While Eliot hails development enabled by a system that values change, Wharton envisions a development that depends instead on preventing change and preserving stasis.

Wendell's, Wharton's and Eliot's differences on questions about the relative force of heredity and culture are differences of emphasis and detail – most specifically, details related to the question of time, or pace of acquisition: 'how much longer?' They think differently about how the differentiated development of persons, families and races happens over time. Given that the differential development of races over time is perhaps the single most important structuring idea of Wharton's ambassadorial wartime writing about race and nation, the conversation in which these differences play out is an apt lens through which to view those texts. The varied theories of inequality articulated by these thinkers deploy the logic of development over time in divergent ways: Eliot looks to the future and emphasises speed of acquisition as well as differentiation across races; Wendell and Wharton have no such confidence in that speed. They attend more assiduously to the threat of degeneration that lies latent in the logic of development; and they let their gazes linger longer on the past. Eliot's progressive, eugenic optimism emphasises that blood and education can, in a democracy, shatter old castes: free competition fosters the consolidation of truer aristocracy. Wharton, however, emphasises that education can only act upon what blood and race dictate. And she proposes a model of education that can consolidate and perpetuate caste as effectively as any system of aristocratic bloodlines might.

The first section of this chapter explains how these divergent ideas about development over time shape the theories of inequality and definitions of aristocracy expressed by Wharton, Eliot and Wendell. The following sections explain the importance of the concept of the 'Puritan' in the long disagreement between Wendell and Eliot, and examine Wharton's own use of that term. While Eliot hails a 'Puritan' tradition doggedly committed to democracy, education and public service, Wharton and Wendell disaffiliate themselves from the 'Puritan' strain of Anglo-Saxonry, locating themselves in an alternate white tradition that is neither liberal nor democratic: moving southward from icy New England towards the stable hierarchies of warmer locales, this alternate tradition seeks leisure and pleasure, not democracy and service. Finally, the last section of the chapter looks ahead to the conclusion that follows, noting that these uses of 'Puritan' are adapted by the thinkers who develop the narrative about 'the genteel tradition', which describes an educated elite that fails because it retreats, powerless. That narrative of failure, this chapter shows, has important sources in the thought of writers like Wendell and Wharton, where it is never cleanly separable from a narrative of white dispossession and racial replacement.

Aristocracies: The Value of Duration

When Wharton complains in her 1919 letter to Wendell about the 'tiresome distinction between aristocratic & democratic forms', what she does not mention is that Canby names her, along with Henry James, among the authors writing 'aristocratic literature'.[14] The term 'aristocratic' falls readily on Wharton in subsequent years, and generally not as a compliment. Given the tendency to call Wharton 'aristocratic', it is worth noting how carefully she herself explains that she is not an aristocrat. Surveying her antecedents in *Backward Glance*, Wharton writes that her family comes from a 'prosperous class of merchants, bankers and lawyers', and adds: 'My own ancestry, as far as I know, was purely middle-class.' She notes that her mother 'always said that old New York was composed of Dutch and British middle-class families, and that only four or five could show a pedigree leading back to the aristocracy of their ancestral country.' Listing those families by name, she adds, 'though my family belonged to the same group as this little aristocratic nucleus I do not think there was any blood-relationship with it'.[15]

This meticulous explanation of how blood is not noble implies some measure of respect for the notion that noble blood exists. Wendell, in *France of Today*, makes this deferential logic explicit. He praises the easy frankness with which a member of the French bourgeoisie will announce himself as such; unlike Americans, who consider 'bourgeois' an insult because of their 'dogmatic denial of social superiority', the French bourgeois acknowledges readily that there is a class superior to his own.[16] Wharton's own account of her descent from respectable merchants, like Wendell's, locates a personal line of descent in a hierarchy of blood. But for both of these friends, and also for Wendell's antagonist Eliot, it is not merely blood but time that produces an aristocracy. Each of these thinkers has a distinct way of understanding how development over time, along with the heritable stuff of blood, dictates that one person will be better than another.

The opening paragraph of Werner Sollors's book about tensions between 'consent' and 'descent' as 'the central drama in American culture' gives Wendell a starring role. Placing the Professor in a line of scholars of New England Puritanism that extends to his own peers in the later twentieth century, Sollors quotes from *Liberty, Union, and Democracy* to show that Wendell 'saw at the core of "the American national character" a denial of legitimacy and privilege based exclusively on descent'. Sollors rightly declines to say that Wendell is always pleased by such denials; he classes him among 'descent-oriented believers in hereditary election' who 'view American identity as something they have safely and easily received by birth and descent, but something that foreign-born workers would have to strive long and hard to achieve'.[17] In spite of his orientation towards descent, Wendell not only recognises the possibility of immigrants' assimilation over multiple generations; he also marvels over his own Harvard classroom as a place where young men of various European races (including Jewish students) become 'Yankees like their native Yankee teacher'. Wendell notoriously registers irritation that Mary Antin calls herself and her family 'American', thus disregarding families like those of Wendell and his wife, which, he notes, 'have been here for three hundred years'. Earlier, he had written that immigrants might become fully American only when the traditions of their former countries 'have faded into dim knowledge of whence a family came – without any definite personal memories . . . Generally this takes at least a hundred years.'[18]

Wendell here notably imagines assimilation as a negative process of forgetting rather than a positive process of acquisition. This is consistent with the tone and thrust of much of his historical writing. He departs from liberal accounts of civilisation and development in that he does not as readily assume that forward movement is good progress: stagnation and stasis, he suggests, can also have their benefits. His *Literary History* repeatedly evokes temporal maroonings and isolated realms of delay, in which one place moves more slowly into the future or stops moving altogether, even as modernity advances (for better or worse) elsewhere. These discontinuities of space and time play out not just transatlantically, but also across the regions of the United States. Race is one of the differentiating categories over which these discontinuities play out. Wendell writes: 'However human, native Africans are still savage'; thus, he says, 'the spectre of darkest Africa loomed behind' formerly enslaved people, though 'civilised conditions' had caused them to lose their 'superficial savagery'. Elsewhere, he observes, 'though native Africans are not literally Neolithic, they certainly linger far behind the social stage which has been reached by modern Europe or America'.[19]

Eliot calls *Literary History* 'highly interesting and meritorious' when he mentions it in a letter. But he goes on to criticise two elements of it, and these criticisms neatly pinpoint his abiding disagreements with Wendell. First, he objects to *Literary History*'s suggestion that humans fall into corruption when exposed to the full range of experience. In response to this idea, Eliot invokes the classically liberal axiom that free exposure to a wide range of experience and ideas yields not corruption but progress.[20] Wendell's humans are, as we shall see, mostly depraved and thus not especially susceptible to improvement. Eliot's humans are perfectible: not merely at the level of the individual, but also at the level of the race. He observes development over time not just in one man's schooling, but also in the transmission of heritable traits over generations. The mutability and pliancy implied by Eliot's commitment to perfectibility are thus consistent with, rather than opposed to, the biological materialism that understands capacity to be innate. Eliot's thinking, in keeping with the times, becomes more overtly eugenicist in the early twentieth century; but already, in his 1869 inaugural address, he portrays pliant educability and heritability as not just compatible but interdependent. He declares: 'Thanks to the beneficent mysteries of hereditary transmission, no capital earns such interest as personal culture.'[21]

Eliot's second criticism of *Literary History* more explicitly concerns Wendell's treatment of blood and development. Wendell's preoccupation with 'birth and family', or 'birth and descent', Eliot writes, 'seems snobbish in an American, and will cause many people to underestimate his judgment and good sense'. Wendell does not see, Eliot notes,

> how quickly American men and women acquire not only the manners and customs but the modes of thought and speech, and the sentiments which prevail among "ladies and gentlemen." The sons and daughters of mechanics, farmers, and shopkeepers have not only the bodily characteristics of persons of "gentle birth" but their best mental and spiritual qualities.[22]

This criticism forms an extension of an exchange in the preceding year. Eliot had objected to Wendell's use of the word 'gentry' to describe Boston's elite: instead, Eliot proposed, he ought to use 'the real New England word "quality"'.[23] This semantic dispute is indicative. Wendell's 'gentry' emits the odour of the Old World; Eliot's 'quality' suggests status founded in demonstrated superiority. Eliot's elect define themselves by merit: he hails the 'aristocracy' of Harvard men who demonstrate talent as scholars, professionals and soldiers. This aristocracy of merit, he emphasises, is drawn from both the poor and the rich, and it inhabits a college that is 'intensely democratic in temper'.[24]

Although Eliot's aristocracy rises through freedom and competition rather than birth, it is emphatically an aristocracy of blood. Meritocratic and eugenicist, Eliot attends closely to history and time: he understands capacity to be the product of antecedents' experience and behaviour. Noting the disadvantages that certain 'stocks' have faced in the past, he points to the deleterious effects of those past disadvantages on present capacities. Superior 'family stocks', he suggests, are found amongst the hard-working New England villagers and the families whose sons have gone to Harvard and Yale for hundreds of years. This white aristocracy of talent and virtue, he suggests, is justified partly *because* these families were not enslaved.[25] For African–Americans, the case is different. Eliot affirms that it is 'very unreasonable to expect that people who had so recently been savages and slaves should all acquire in forty years the primary virtues of civilization'; he points the necessity of 'four or five generations more to teach the mass of the negro population'.[26] These generations form an exception to the 'American men and women' whom he sees acquire the traits of ladies and gentlemen in the course of just one generation. For the mass of African–Americans, as for the mass of immigrants, Eliot recommends education; he also suggests that both Black and white men should pass education tests to qualify for suffrage.[27] Faced with the question 'how much longer?', Eliot emphasises 'how quickly' development actually happens. But he observes both the speed of acquisition and the starting point differ across races.

Eliot's appreciation for rapid acquisition marks his divergence from perspectives like Wharton's and Wendell's. Wendell too points to the flux of social mobility that brings families of good stock in and out of money over the years (both he and Eliot notably echo Oliver Wendell Holmes's original account of the Brahmin class in this respect). But Wendell does not share Eliot's optimism about potential development; and Wharton, for her part, specifically disparages rapidity in education. For persons and for races, she recommends education that takes time. Like Eliot's, her moment of adequate education recedes perpetually into an unattainable future. But while Eliot endorses and works to expand access to education in the present, she does not. And while he seeks development that depends on change and pliant mutability in intellectual capacity, as well as in social status, she seeks development that depends on the stable rigidity of preserved order, which she describes as 'continuity'.

'Continuity' is one of the four qualities that *French Ways* defines as 'typically "French"'. 'French culture', she affirms, 'is the most homogeneous and uninterrupted culture the world has known,' whereas the US has regrettable tendencies towards rupture and heterogeneity. She repeatedly evokes a France that is 'mature' and a US that is 'childish'. France, she tells the Americans, is 'a civilisation so profoundly unlike ours – so much older, richer, more elaborate and firmly crystallised'; thus 'French customs necessarily differ from ours more than do those of more primitive races.' She affirms:

> The French are the most human of the human race, the most completely detached from the lingering spell of the ancient shadowy world in which trees and animals talked to each other, and began the education of the fumbling beast that was to deviate into Man. They have used their longer experience and their keener senses for the joy and enlightenment of the races still agrope for self-expression.[28]

This comment about the difference between French and American people alludes to an idea that Wendell makes more explicit: those who develop into civilisation become more human, but those who linger in savagery remain less so.

Wharton's interests focus more narrowly than Eliot's or Wendell's on differentiated development amongst the white races. She defends in her Preface her 'use of the labels "Anglo-Saxon" and "Latin," for purposes of easy antithesis': these categories help her to mark out distinctions between 'those whose social polity dates from the Forum, and those who still feel and legislate in terms of the primæval forest'. Like both Eliot's and Wendell's, her account of who a person is depends on that person's blood, the experiences of the ancestors who define that bloodline, and the pace at which their race has, collectively, advanced into civilisation from savagery. 'Most things in a man's view of life', she observes, 'depend on how many thousand years ago his land was deforested.' 'Our forbears', she tells her American readers, were 'men whose blood is still full of murmurs of the Saxon Urwald and the forests of Britain', who were then 'plunged afresh into the wilderness of a new continent', whereas the French are 'children of the Roman forum and the Greek amphitheatre'.[29] In her addresses to both the French and the Americans, Wharton offers contrasting patterns of imagery to represent civilisation and its contrary, primitive savagery: easy warmth represents the former, while the latter finds figuration in cold and vastly forested wilderness. This imagery is, to some extent, generic, but (as we shall see) Wharton puts it to particular uses, especially in her portrait of the US for the French.

Wharton's discussion of differentiated development across the Latin and the Anglo-Saxon races recasts the terms of the liberal conversation about the remnant. While thinkers like Eliot spend a great deal of time discussing the proper function of the cultivated minority, Wharton implies that they take up the wrong question. She suggests that focusing on the proportional size or the responsibilities of this elite class is beside the point. 'What matters', she says, 'is the esteem in which *the whole race* hold ideas and their noble expression.' She explains: 'In each of the great nations',

> there is a small minority which is at about the same level of intellectual culture; but it is not between these minorities (though even here the level is perhaps higher in France) that comparisons may profitably be made. A cross-section of average life must be taken, and compared with the same average in a country like ours, to understand why France leads in the world of ideas.[30]

Wharton compares the 'Anglo-Saxon imagination' to the French, and observes that 'it was the Puritan races – every one of them non-creative in the plastic arts – who decided that "Art" (that is, plastic art) was something apart from life'. The French, however, are 'a race of creative artists', and thus, in France, 'people who pack the music-halls and "movie-shows"' also go to 'national theatres [and enjoy] with keen discrimination a tragedy by Racine or a drama of Victor Hugo's'. In the US, this is not the case. The sense of 'volupté' that is natural to the French race is 'found only exceptionally in the Anglo-Saxon imagination'.[31] Race, in this account, sets expectations about and perhaps limits on what education might accomplish. When Wharton reads in a book by George Santayana the comment that 'in some nations everybody is by nature so astute, versatile, and sympathetic that education hardly makes any difference in manners or mind', she writes in the margin: 'France'.[32] As we saw in Chapter 3, Wharton's 'Vice of Reading' speaks of 'born readers' in an arch tone; but ideas about fixed capacities extend into the more sincere sectors of her œuvre.

While Eliot notes with frustration that Wendell fails to see 'how quickly' white people can learn and acquire the habits of the elite, taking that speed as evidence of capacity and success, Wharton argues that quick learning is not learning at all. She sees pretence and speed as characteristic of American attempts at education: Americans, she observes, seek immediate gain, believing that money and learning can both stack up fast. Possibly thinking of Tocqueville's commentary on Americans' preference for the shortest possible path, she repeatedly deplores the American fondness for 'short-cuts'.[33] To her French audience, she explains, 'we take shortcuts and byways, while, more wisely, you take the paths traced by a long and glorious tradition'. To the Americans, she makes a nearly identical statement: 'America, because of her origin, tends to irreverence, impatience, to all sorts of rash and contemptuous short-cuts; France, for the same reason, to routine, precedent, tradition, the beaten path.' Disparaging 'Anglo-Saxon training', she warns: 'As long as America believes in short-cuts to knowledge, in any possibility of buying taste in tabloids, she will never come into her real inheritance of English culture.' Wharton observes with dismay that, in recent years,

> Every sham and substitute for education and literature and art had steadily crowded out the real thing. "Get-rich-quick" is a much less dangerous device than "get-educated-quick," but the popularity of the first has led to the attempt to realise the second. It is possible to get rich quickly in a country full of money-earning chances; but there is no short-cut to education.[34]

Neatly eliding a disdain for *nouveaux riches* with one for the newly educated, Wharton's comments directly assail initiatives like Eliot's

Harvard Classics (1909), which promised to offer readers the equivalent of a liberal education in fifteen minutes a day. Eliot sought the efficient expansion of access to liberal education; for Wharton, such efficiency and dissemination necessarily commercialise and degrade the culture they purport to offer, which cannot be encountered in any limited increment of minutes, nor any deliberate, purchased programme of learning at all. The democratisation of culture is, for Wharton, the trashy commercialisation of culture. The problem is not that there is no education in the US, nor that there is no interest in culture, but that 'culture' there has 'come to stand for the pretence rather than the reality'. Wharton notes: 'Education in its elementary sense is much more general in America than in France. There are more people who can read in the United States; but what do they read? The whole point, as far as any real standard goes, is there.' Wharton elides education or culture for which one pays with the promiscuously advertised detritus of consumer society: Americans fall for claims about education just as they fall for claims about beauty creams and medical quackery. Recalling the literature sold like dry goods or confectionery in 'Descent of Man', she declares: 'It is the pernicious habit of regarding the arts as something that can be bottled, pickled and absorbed in twelve months (thanks to "courses," summaries and abridgements) that prevents the development of a real artistic sensibility in our eager and richly endowed race.'[35]

The French, again, present a perfect contrast: Wharton explains that they 'are too incredulous of short-cuts and nostrums to turn to such promises with much hope . . . [They] distrust any way but the strait and narrow one when a difficulty is to be mastered or an art acquired.' They understand that 'Real civilisation means an education that extends to the whole of life, in contradistinction to that of school or college: it means an education that forms speech, forms manners, forms taste, forms ideals, and above all forms judgment. This is the kind of civilisation of which France has always been the foremost model.' As she describes this mode of acquisition, Wharton refers not just to 'real civilisation', but also to 'real education and real culture'. She assures us that the French 'are above all democratic in their steady conviction that there is no "royal road" to the worth-while things'.[36] But this denies the practical effect of a theory of education that classifies all attempts at efficiency as 'sham' or 'pretence', that sees all attempts at broader dissemination as fatally contaminated by commerce, and that discredits formal education as inadequate, favouring instead forms of education that happen informally or in the home.

The canonical sociological argument about forms of education that happen so automatically, so early and so informally that the aptitudes and tastes they produce seem to be innate, instinctive, 'the gift of nature', comes from Pierre Bourdieu. Bourdieu describes modes of engagement with 'legitimate culture' that serve to consolidate and perpetuate social hierarchies, and identifies an 'aesthetic disposition' that depends on distance from 'economic necessity'.[37] As Bourdieu suggests, the effect of ideas like Wharton's is exclusion: these views make education and culture inaccessible to anyone without a great deal of leisure, anyone who pays for access to culture in ways that are effortful, incremental or scrimped – rather than pre-emptive, total and imperceptible. Bourdieu contends that these leisured modes of cultural consumption perform and consolidate power that comes from wealth: tastes and habits that seem to be natural, he suggests, are actually a product of class. In the system he describes, social mobility is limited because legitimate culture is not readily available to anyone who does not already have it.

For Bourdieu, this exclusion is a covert function of ideology that requires exposing: his late twentieth-century sociological work labours to reveal the economic capital behind cultural capital. But Wharton actually describes a system like this quite explicitly – not, like Bourdieu, in order to critique it, but in order to endorse it. She writes in 1927: 'Leisure, itself the creation of wealth, is incessantly engaged in transmuting wealth into beauty by secreting the surplus energy which flowers in great architecture, great painting, and great literature. Only in the atmosphere thus engendered floats that impalpable dust of ideas which is the real culture.'[38] Race predicts what the effects of education might be, but real education, like real culture, is, by definition, unavailable to most. If you have to enquire crassly what it costs, you will never take a breath of the air in which it floats; if you find yourself asking anxiously 'how much longer?', the answer is likely: very long indeed. Bourdieu's work has been substantially revised by subsequent sociologists, who have argued, among other things, that his theories apply only in the Parisian–French milieu he studies. But in her portrait of France, Wharton is arguably writing about precisely that milieu, which she chooses to inhabit partly because she likes the rigidity of its class structure.

Wendell makes a remark that is characteristic of the structures observed by Bourdieu when he declares in an essay on education that 'English style, like happiness, may finally turn out to be most nearly attainable only by those who never directly seek it.'[39] For Wharton too, language and literature form important sites for performing the aesthetic disposition. In her childhood home, she notes, 'we spoke naturally, instinctively good English'. The language and literature of her childhood home correspond with Bourdieu's account especially strikingly, not just in this ostensibly inborn quality but in their effortless playfulness. 'Excessive respect for the language', Wharton assures us, 'never led to priggishness, or precluded the enjoyment of racy innovations.' Not just 'slovenliness', but also 'pomposity' is forbidden; 'better' English means English that is 'easier, more flexible and idiomatic'. Her family values 'an easy idiomatic English, neither pedantic nor "literary"'. Hence their delight in 'the humorous and expressive side of American slang'. The formative texts that Wharton mentions are not *Hamlet* or *Paradise Lost*, but nonsense books by Edward Lear and Lewis Carroll.[40] These easy affinities also belong to Henry James and Theodore Roosevelt, whose wordplay and fun storytelling Wharton describes fondly. James's letters offer a 'nonsense-world, as four-dimensional as that of the Looking Glass, or the Land where the Jumblies live' and 'his best nonsense flowered out of unremembered trifles'. Roosevelt and Wharton bond enthusiastically over allusions to 'The Hunting of the Snark'.[41] The marker of belonging for these speakers of English is exactly the marker identified by Bourdieu: a readiness to romp, a childish lightness that comes from a confident sense that one's gifts are natural. Petit-bourgeois strivers may grimly stake out their terrain by alluding to serious works; readers with nothing to prove can play. But, as Bourdieu's work argues, that sort of play in fact proves a great deal. Secure in their culture, they risk nothing by looking silly; their easy, impervious silliness (like Adams's self-deprecation and like Teddy Wharton's ride on that butcher cart) thus performs and consolidates power.

Bourdieu's theory forms a useful reference point here partly because it describes a relationship between education and qualities that are perceived to reside in blood. For Wharton, such gifts are a specifically racial inheritance, however dependent upon leisure and wealth their expression may be. The easy play with English that she admires in James and Roosevelt is what she elsewhere refers to affectionately in passing as 'the boyish love of pure nonsense only to be found in Anglo-Saxons'.[42] Interestingly, the mode Bourdieu identifies as a crucial force for exclusion is one that Wharton names as definitively and uniquely Anglo-Saxon. Formal education of the sort Eliot recommends for the masses and elite alike 'hardly makes any difference' (to borrow Santayana's phrase) not just because it is not 'real', but also because race predicts what education might accomplish. And yet, over long stretches of time, '*the whole race*' can develop. Even in America. In the same passage of

Backward Glance that she explains that her blood is not aristocratic, Wharton expresses cautious optimism about the state of society and culture in the US: 'the idea that time could transform a group of *bourgeois* colonials and their republican descendants into a sort of social aristocracy' used to seem ridiculous, she observes. But now she cannot deny 'the formative value of nearly three hundred years of social observance: the concerted living up to long-established standards of honour and conduct, of education and manners. The value of duration is slowly asserting itself against the welter of change.'[43] Wendell and Eliot were both dead by the time Wharton wrote this, but in these remarks about 'the value of duration', we see her participating in the conversation to which they too had contributed, a conversation about the differentiated development over time of persons, families and races.

Doctrines of Election: The Puritan Liberal and the Last Calvinist

As Wharton tells her French audience about the history of the US, there is a certain group for whom she expresses frank dislike, even as she acknowledges that they are the primary source of the American spirit. 'They were – let's admit – fanatics: tedious, ghastly, unbearable people,' she says, and soon thereafter reiterates: 'They were, as I've said, fanatics: hard, cruel, jealous people.' (*'C'étaient – osons le dire – des fanatiques, gens ennuyeux, odieux, insupportables'*; *'C'étaient, je l'ai dit, des fanatiques: gens durs, cruels, jaloux'*).[44] The unbearable people to whom Wharton refers here are the Puritans. During the late nineteenth and early twentieth centuries, 'Puritan' and, more broadly, 'New England' are loaded, unstable concepts that carry force in debates about Americans and American history. Scholarship by Joseph Conforti, Kenyon Gradert, Michael Kammen, David S. Reynolds and John Seelye (among others) shows that writers during this period tend to adapt and use 'Puritan' freely as they express their own views.[45] In order to see more fully and clearly how 'Puritan' operates in Wharton's writing, it is helpful to recall that this is perhaps the single most hotly contested concept in the long dispute between Eliot and Wendell.[46] This section of this chapter surveys the usage of 'Puritan' and explains how Eliot and Wendell used it; the next section builds on this foundation in order to show what Wharton does with the concept.

In the antebellum period, Northerners and Southerners alike associate 'Puritanism' with New England reform movements and abolitionism, or, more broadly, with 'radical individualism and subversive social agitation'.[47] Gradert documents the centrality of 'Puritanism' in abolitionist thinking and rhetoric, where it tends to be associated with militant subversion and a 'revolutionary Protestant print heritage': in William Lloyd Garrison's *Liberator*, for example, 'the Puritans appeared every other issue, on average', and 'more frequently as tensions rose around slavery'.[48] The idea of Puritanism, Gradert notes, can serve specific functions for women writers; Seelye too points to a sentimental 'feminized' strain of antislavery 'Puritanism', represented by Harriet Beecher Stowe and her New England affiliations.[49]

These meanings and associations feed into the ubiquitous analogy that compares sectional conflict in the US to the English Civil War, seeing Puritans and Cavaliers opposed in each case. Southern writers in particular develop this analogy, but they are not alone in doing so. Comparing the type of the Northern Puritan with the type of the Southern Cavalier, the historian George Bancroft attributes to the former a dedication to 'duty', 'liberty', 'justice', 'universal education' and, above all, 'the underlying principle of democratic liberty'.[50] Gradert points to the 'heroic myths of the Reformation and the Puritans that found their most influential expression in Bancroft's histories'.[51]

Bancroft's account is carried forward conspicuously by George William Curtis, whose addresses, both during and after the Civil War, associate 'Puritan' with antislavery sentiment, the Union cause and egalitarian democracy. Curtis affirms in 1885 that Garrison sounds 'the key-note' of Puritanism as he argues for abolition; 'the Puritan spirit' in his account drives not just Garrison and Charles Sumner but also John Bright in Britain. This transatlantic 'Puritan spirit' belongs to the 'English-speaking race': it is 'the unconquerable spirit which swept the Stuarts out of England, liberalized the British Constitution, planted the Republic in America, freed the slaves upon this soil, and made the Union a national bond of equal liberty.' While affirming that Anglo-Saxons like himself demand their rights instinctually, Curtis also argues that all humans ought to have those rights. He appeals to 'the equality of human rights based upon our common humanity'. Though 'we are not ... equal in capacity, in circumstance, or condition', he states, 'equality of right' does not exclude those men who are 'weaker', 'duller' or 'darker'.[52] Curtis's 'Puritanism' is an Anglo-American liberalism that is democratic and specifically emphasises inclusive political rights across racial lines.

In Curtis's writing and elsewhere, 'Puritan' can still invoke the Union cause long after the war; so too can representations and appeals to 'Old New England' and other regional expressions of colonial revivalism. Conforti notes that 'Colonial revival commemorations of the 1870s not only encouraged patriotic and nativist nostalgia for earlier times that led to the imaginative birth of Old New England. They also provided a vehicle for New England leaders to pursue what Reconstruction had failed to accomplish: the cultural consolidation of the military victory over the South.'[53] These pursuits continued well into the twentieth century. Kammen notes the role of Puritans and other representations of regional history in a 'second American civil war' that is 'fought and refought' between the two World Wars.[54]

During the later nineteenth century, narratives about Puritans and New England depart from antebellum narratives by emphasising decline. Conforti notes that although mid-nineteenth-century narratives about New England tend to find in the region's past 'a Whiggish historical script that envisioned continual cultural and material improvement', later nineteenth-century engagement with the idea of New England tends to offer narratives of decline and degeneration rather than progress.[55] The demographic realities of mass immigration and rural depopulation readily feed into narratives of wholesome white villages abandoned and left to decay as insalubrious cities teem with illiterate Catholics subject to the Boss. Conforti notes, however, that there are different varieties of enthusiasm for Old New England during this period, some more despondently nativist than others. Kammen affirms: 'For several decades following the 1870s the reputation of American Puritanism was really in a state of disputed disarray.'[56] Within this disarray, and well into the twentieth century, writers freely adopt the unstable term 'Puritan' for their own purposes.[57]

Eliot strives to rebuilt Harvard's relationship with the South, but his pride in the Puritan heritage of his region, his institution and his own family is overt. The Puritan affiliation to which he lays claim is not that of radical or sentimental abolitionism, though it is linked to both. Antebellum 'Puritanism', variously violent or evangelical, contrasts specifically against the politer abolitionism associated with William Ellery Channing and Unitarianism; but Eliot's later 'Puritanism' is often explicitly Unitarian. Stripped of associations with violence and sentimental femininity alike, this Puritanism stands for liberty and democracy above all. Eliot thus carries forward into the twentieth century key elements of Curtis's account of the Puritans, which he sometimes expands to include the Pilgrims more broadly.[58]

Eliot repeatedly hails the Puritans and their values, identifying himself proudly as their descendant. Both his admirers and his opponents associate him explicitly with Puritanism; an adulatory 1927 study of his Unitarianism, for example, bears the title *Charles W. Eliot, Puritan Liberal*.[59] In his own writing, Eliot contributes to the narrative that links together Puritanism, idealism, liberty, democracy and education; he understands his own work as an educator to live out the ideals of the Puritan spirit. Even as narratives about Puritans and Old New England shift to emphasise decline instead of progress, Eliot claims the idea of Puritans for his own outlook, which is emphatically oriented to progressive development.[60]

Like many writers who treat subjects regarding Old New England, Eliot describes his own ideal and then projects it on to the early English settlers of Massachusetts. The Pilgrims, he declares in a 1910 address, showed 'unreserved recognition of the great law of progress in human society'; they practised 'principles of equality and political justice', and 'there existed among them to an extraordinary degree equality of conditions'. They were (like Eliot himself) elitist, meritocratic eugenicists committed to an ethic of hard work: 'they had no theory of social structure which was not perfectly consistent with the facts concerning the extreme diversity of human capacities and powers. No community ever recognized its leaders more frankly, or followed them better.' These leaders were committed to service; the community was 'tied together by strong bonds of sympathy and helpfulness. It was the duty of the strong among them to help the weak. To give mutual aid and comfort was a fundamental principle of their lives . . . They preferred the interest of the whole community to the interest of any individual or section in it.' 'Their minds and hearts', he writes, 'were filled with that burning love of freedom which later inspired Cromwell's soldiers and the Independents and Nonconformists of the English Commonwealth.'[61] Like Curtis, Eliot finds in Puritanism a transatlantic heritage committed to democracy, education and political equality – with social equality and equality of capacity carefully excepted.

Wendell has different uses for Puritans. Disparaging the Unitarian outgrowth of Puritanism as a regrettable mistake, he attends to the insights of the Calvinism that prevails before that error.[62] This Calvinism helps Wendell to describe inequality that is natural, fixed and righteous. He aggressively revises the narrative that makes New England Puritans part of a glorious liberal tradition that is both abolitionist and democratic. Instead, he discusses the Calvinism of early New England as the beginning of a robust American tradition of conservatism committed to inequality and order. He writes: 'The saving faith in order so deeply ingrained in American character may be traced in no small degree to the neglected doctrine of election. Throughout the Puritan generations our ancestors never swerved from the conviction that most of us must always have our betters.' Like Wendell's deferent French bourgeoisie, these Calvinists are admirable for their recognition 'that in every human region there are a few men who are essentially better than the mass of their fellows'; 'among the deepest phases of Puritan conviction', he adds, is the understanding that upon encountering one of these superior persons, 'it is our constant duty ... reverently to thank God that here is something nobler than such as we'. Wendell writes that this Calvinist system 'was not only supremely ideal, it was supremely orderly; and orderly with such hierarchical precision as should hold in deepest horror the vagaries of anarchy'. This is a horror Wendell himself knows well. He declares: 'Literal faith in the doctrine of election has long languished in America. Yet the traces of that doctrine ... are not far to seek in the national character of the country.'[63] They are certainly not far to seek in Wendell's own pages.

In the passages of *Literary History* that provoke Eliot's criticism, Wendell describes Unitarianism as a hothouse misgrowth of Puritans' idealism, one that can thrive only in their uniquely uncrowded and homogenous milieu. Back in wicked, complex, overpopulated England, conditions produce a closer acquaintance with humankind that affirms the Calvinist understanding of depravity. Without that check and that awareness of reality, New Englanders develop a grossly mistaken sense that human nature is perfectible, based on the limited sample of themselves in their little white villages. Thus develops a Unitarianism characterised by 'respect for what is good in human nature as contrasted with the Calvinistic insistence on what is bad'.[64] Wendell elsewhere explicitly identifies Eliot as an exemplar of this regrettable Unitarian misgrowth, with its mistaken faith in perfectibility and thus in democracy. Referring in a letter to 'the honest bigotry of [Eliot's] Yankee Unitarianism', he notes: 'His whole conception of life seemed to me based on dogmatic assumption of human perfectibility.' Pointing to what he calls 'my own constant dissent from his principles', Wendell acknowledges: 'My personal relations with Eliot had been by no means cordial.'[65] This disagreement between Eliot and Wendell has profound political implications. As Wendell puts it: 'What is good merits freedom; what is bad demands control.'[66]

Wendell is not the most famous Harvard Professor of Literature to assail Eliot's faith in progress: Irving Babbitt's attack in 'President Eliot and American Education' (1929) is better known. As a voice for the New Humanists and one of the teachers who helps to develop a conservative tradition that extends to T. S. Eliot, Babbitt makes a bigger name for himself in the longer term. But when Babbitt attacks President Eliot, he echoes Wendell closely: he describes Eliot as a thinker in the 'Puritan' tradition who fails to retain the old (and correct) Puritan perception of evil, and instead naively expects progress because he projects his own nature onto all of humanity.[67] Both of these literary scholars offer versions of a standard realist critique of democratic liberalism.

The standard account of Wendell as a genteel idealist tends to obscure his vehement, repeated denigrations of a specific idealism that belongs to New England. Casting himself explicitly as a realist opposed to Eliot's idealism, Wendell suggests that science is on his side. He writes: 'What Calvinism regarded as evidence of the total depravity of man, indeed, is very like what modern science calls the struggle for existence. What it regarded as evidence for the doctrine of election is very like what people have in mind nowadays when they talk about the survival of the fittest.' He later reiterates:

> Earthly life, the modern evolutionists hold, consists in a struggle for existence wherein only the fittest can survive; for every organism which persists, myriads must irretrievably perish [. . .] Total depravity is only a theological name for that phase of life which in less imaginative times they name the struggle for existence; and likewise election is only a theological name for what our newer fashion calls survival of the fittest.[68]

For Wendell, evolutionary science and Calvinism alike offer ways of describing preordained hierarchies. For Eliot, in contrast, evolutionary science offers a framework for discussing relative inequalities that change and develop over time; it informs his eugenic thinking and his advocacy of education alike.

Purement Anglo-Saxonne: Puritans and Patroons

In opposing idealism and appealing to realism and science, Wendell's comments align with Wharton's argument in *Valley of Decision* (and elsewhere) against inflexible liberal idealism. As Carol Singley notes, Wharton has her own 'Calvinist impulses' that intermingle with Darwinian theory.[69] With such theory in mind, both Wendell and Wharton position themselves as conservative realists who understand the actual incompetence (or the depravity) of the people and thus the unfeasibility and danger of democracy. And, like Wendell, Wharton identifies 'Puritans' as idealists and distances herself from them. Acknowledging that the Puritan tendency to self-sacrificing idealism is a foundational element of American culture and is also what has brought the US rightly into the war, Wharton nevertheless affirms her longstanding distaste for idealism at large. Having mentioned the *'raisons soi-disant idéales'* for which the US has entered the conflict, she comments on the term 'ideal': 'I confess this word scares me a bit: I'm still not sure I understand it.'[70] In this tendency to idealism, as in other respects, 'Puritan' serves as the opposite of 'French' in both *French Ways* and 'Amérique en Guerre'. The French value an 'intellectual frankness' that prescribes confrontation with reality; but the Puritans, in their inflexible idealism, resemble the modernist writers and advocates of liberal democracy whom we saw Wharton criticise in Chapter 3. Like those troublemakers, these are disruptive fanatics who proceed *'à thèse'* instead of attending, like good realists, to local particulars.

Wharton's treatment of Puritans draws from the American conversation described in the preceding section, and also from thinkers like Matthew Arnold and Alexis de Tocqueville – both of whom, like Wharton, write with acute awareness of the French counterexample. Wharton and Eliot alike draw from Arnold's thinking: Eliot hails an Arnold who says educated men are driven by 'the passion for pure knowledge' and 'the passion for being of service or doing good'; Wharton prefers an Arnold who describes a 'sweetness and light', or a 'real culture' that thrives in the calm leisure that rebellious, dissenting people like Puritans too often disrupt.[71]

From Tocqueville (among others) Wharton draws the idea that Americans manifest a notable tendency towards *'inquiétude'*, a restlessness, a motivating dissatisfaction that keeps them moving.[72] Broadly understood to be an Anglo-Saxon trait, this sort of perpetually conquesting agitatedness elicits both admiration and ire. In his discussion of the functions of 'Puritan', Gradert points to Jefferson Davis's 1862 remark that 'our enemies are a traditionless and a homeless race; from the time of Cromwell to the present moment they have been disturbers of the peace of the world'.[73] Working with such ideas, Wharton develops an account of the Puritans as an unpleasant people whose unpleasantness derives from their affinity for disruption and mobility. Like Davis, Wharton expresses distaste for ruptures from tradition and unwillingness to put down roots. She views with alarm the severing of the US from 'the old European races whose art reaches back through an unbroken inheritance of thousands of years of luxury and culture'. As

Kassanoff notes, Wharton contrasts that severing against the unbroken line of French tradition, the 'continuity' that makes them supremely civilised. Unlike the Anglo-Saxons, the French stay at home: Wharton points to their 'clinging to the same valley and the same river-cliff, that have made the French, literally as well as figuratively, the most conservative of western races'.[74]

If the French prefer stasis, the Anglo-Saxons prefer movement, conquest and adventure; the Puritans are a subset of Anglo-Saxons in whom these tendencies seem to be especially concentrated. Wharton tells her French audience that the Puritans were the sort of people 'that nature seems to produce every once in a while, when it's a matter of setting in motion a great popular movement, or clearing a new continent: because likeable, reasonable people will never change a thing about the order of the universe'.[75] She finds the French reasonable and likeable precisely because they do not try to change the order of the universe. Wharton recognises, however, that disturbers of the peace have their purpose. She grudgingly acknowledges the achievements of these conquesting people in her addresses to both the Americans and the French; but she gives an especially negative account of them to her French audience, offering what she calls a *'triste tableau'* of Puritan life in the early colonial period.

Wharton's tableau is not, however, merely sad: it is a dramatic, almost pornographic, account of ascetic zealots. These Puritans subject their bodies to freezing and lashes; perched on a rock by the stormy Atlantic, they live in perpetual fear and snow, swallowed incessantly by the icy dark of the uncleared forests, through which they piously hack their way to unheated houses of worship, which are not even built of stone. There they sit for hours (up to six, even when the weather is *'sibérien'*) as the pastor declaims that unbaptised infants will burn eternally in hell, that men gathering wood on Sunday will be hung, and that the same fate awaits those who dare to attribute the slightest sin to the elect. The sermon and prayers go on so long that these bone-chilled worshippers often return home through the perilous forest well after nightfall. And then, of course, there are the punishments of whipping and worse inflicted on those who blaspheme and those deemed witches.[76] This account is exceptionally vivid but actually rather conventional in its account of the cold grimness of Puritan life; in fact, it closely echoes a passage in Eliot's address 'Why We Honor the Puritans'. Both Wharton and Eliot are drawing from conventional tropes about New England and Puritans; in Eliot's address, those tropes pile up to a climactic moment and a dramatic turn when he hails these icy people as 'heroes of democracy'.[77] In Wharton's address, that turn never comes.

Wharton's fanatical snowbound New England colonies belong to a larger pattern of imagery. In 'Amérique en Guerre' and *French Ways* alike, she associates harsh, cold weather with the savage North, and mild warmth with civilisation: savagery and cold merge together as adversarial forces, and both the invaders of ancient France and the indigenous peoples of North America take on these qualities. Wharton describes the earliest French peoples withstanding 'waves of cold, invasions of savage hordes' in order to take sustenance from Phoenicia, Greece and Rome, so that traces of their 'great tradition [are] kept alive, in the hidden nooks which cold and savages spared, little hearths of artistic vitality'. Similarly, the colonists on American ground find themselves 'grappling with cold, hunger, Indians'; they face 'the long winters of New England, the fear of Redskins, the perpetual fear of a violent death and eternal punishment'.[78]

Wharton's frigidly intolerable Northern colonies and colonists have a balmy, congenial counterpart in the early colonies of the South, which she represents as, like the French, the Puritans' opposite: 'While New England thus developed, laboriously and with much anguish', she tells the French, things proceeded very differently in Virginia, which was, she notes, 'directly attached to the English crown, and divided into large estates granted to certain nobles and gentlemen'. In this royalist, aristocratic settlement, 'the climate was mild, the land fertile'; in the Southern colonies, 'under the merciful reign of the Anglican Church there developed a civilized society in comparison with which the colonists of New England were like the savages of the stone age'.[79]

In *French Ways*, it is France rather than the American South that stands as the temperate civilised place: 'France . . . is a country singularly privileged in her formation, and in the latitude she occupies,' with 'rich soil', and mountains 'creating almost tropic corners under a temperate latitude' – 'a land of temperate beauty and temperate wealth'.[80] The South and France align in these texts as the better places of fertile earth, fine weather and secure hierarchy. Wharton explicitly suggests that such pleasant conditions and climates actually foster conservatism: the French are static people partly because their home territory is so comfortable. On the other hand, the Puritans, cold and uncomfortable wherever they go, are forever performing the Anglo-Saxon tendency to be on the move, seeking something better, leaving home, disrupting fixed order and dominating whatever they find.

Wendell too sees the South as a site of peculiar and laudable conservatism. In his temporally disjointed vision of American history, all of the colonies form an unmodern spur that breaks off Elizabethan England and thus stays stagnant as England modernises; for Wendell, the South is a spur off this spur, a super-stagnated part of a stagnant realm. This preservation involves an abstention from democratic modernity that is, for Wendell, deeply desirable: the system of government by 'men of the socially better sort . . . persisted at the South long after . . . the North', whereas, regrettably, 'the old conception of social status in the North had altered far more radically than in the South'. Noting these different temporal paces, Wendell takes up the idea 'that Southerners descend from Cavaliers, and Yankees from the socially inferior Roundheads'. 'Though this fact is more than debatable,' he continues, 'the Southerner belief in it indicates a truth; at least up to the Civil War the personal temper of the better classes in the South remained more like that of the better classes in seventeenth-century England than anything else in the modern world'.[81] Wendell insists not upon any actual historical link between Cavaliers and the South, but on the truth evident in the elective affiliation of the Southerners with that label.

Though Wendell calls himself (in a letter to William James) 'the last of the Calvinists' and identifies as a Yankee of pure blood, he has no admiration for the dour, insurgent Roundheads of the North: his sympathies lie with those in silks and plumes. Describing his own heritage, he emphasises that the Puritans of Massachusetts are not his people. 'My family was of Dutch origin,' he writes, pointing to a New York antecedent of the late seventeenth century, 'a merchant and a magistrate, of genially convivial habit and frequent carelessness of obligation', who bears a son who is 'convivial, like his father'.[82] Disaffiliating from the democratic, liberal, Unitarian, Roundhead version of Puritan New England, Wendell locates his bloodline instead in a Dutch tradition of commerce and conviviality.[83]

Wendell is not alone in laying claim to a white heritage that is Dutch rather than Puritan. Wharton does this too, and so does Roosevelt. But Wharton and Wendell use stories of these bloodlines in ways that differ revealingly from Roosevelt's. Like everyone else, Roosevelt bends the pliant 'Puritan' to suit his own purposes: speaking at the construction of the Pilgrim Monument in 1907, he acknowledges that he is not 'of Puritan blood' before going on to use the Puritans as evidence in an argument for regulating corporations. As Eliot does, Roosevelt hails the Puritans' dedication to work and their disdain for leisure.[84] Although Wendell and Wharton both admire

Roosevelt, their uses of 'Dutch' and 'Puritan' differ dramatically from his: while he appeals specifically to the value of hard work, they appeal specifically to the value of leisure. Especially for Wharton, the Dutch stand as ancestors who are given to pleasure, commerce and order. These traits contrast specifically against the ascetic idealism and habit of revolution that belong to the Puritans. As Seelye notes, there is a 'conventional Knickerbocker image of the Netherlander as a fat burgher in kneebreeches with pipe and floppy Flemish hat, conceived as a drowsy counterpart to the ambitious, restless Yankee': this is the 'Dutch as the Puritan's antithesis and antagonist'.[85]

Wharton invokes this idea of the Dutch as she describes her lineage. The Dutch, in her account, stand with the South and France against the freezing, fanatical masochists of New England. She opens her address to the French by gesturing to her own racial makeup, mentioning her 'purely Anglo-Saxon origins'. (She refers to herself as *'la personne d'origine purement anglo-saxonne qui a l'honneur de vous parler'*.)[86] Later, she becomes more specific: 'I myself, the descendant of Dutch merchants and their English successors, I confess I don't mind not having been raised in the shadow of the sad theocracy of Massachusetts.'[87] The Knickerbocker set from whom Wharton claims descent are neither sad nor theocratic. Their New York is a place of 'love of profit, respect for rank and fortune, a taste for lavish meals and for sleep under the duvet': in short, the 'wholesome enjoyment of earthly possessions'. Contrasting the cold, hungry idealist Puritan against the sensuous, well-fed Dutch merchants – 'opulent bourgeois, shrewd people of business' – Wharton offers an extended comparison between 'dark and fanatical Massachusetts, founded in 1620 to establish "the reign of the spirit," and the state of New York, founded seven years earlier to establish the reign of the dollar':

> On the one hand, democratic equality, scorn for wealth, horror at any hint of the titles and privileges of old Europe; on the other hand, a society at once commercial and patrician, descended from the oligarchy founded by the West India Company, which divided up immense tracts of land between certain early colonists, who became 'patroons' – which is to say, lords – with feudal privileges, judicial power, and the right to name a representative to the colonial assemblies.

While democratic, egalitarian Massachusetts stands for 'desire to sacrifice all to moral and intellectual convictions', oligarchic New York stands for 'desire to grow rich' and *'jouir de l'existence'*.[88] Wharton's

New York, in its frank, relaxed enjoyment of sensuous life and its more *ancien-régime* style of governance, resembles her portraits of the South and of France. Unlike the anhedonic theocrats perched self-righteously on sea-battered rocks immediately north, these New Yorkers, like the Southerners and the French, recognise the legitimacy of the power that belongs to lords, *seigneurs* and patroons. And in Wharton's account, these elites share an unabashed commitment to the voluptuous pleasures found both at the table and under the duvet.

Her juxtaposition of a convivial New York and a dour New England continues, years later, in *Backward Glance*, where she repeatedly mentions Boston's narrow-minded insularity and false sense of its own importance, and once again contrasts her own antecedents against New England types. Wharton opens her memoir with pages of information about her predecessors who emigrated from Europe. She notes, 'On both sides our colonial ancestry goes back for nearly three hundred years, and on both sides the colonists in question seem to have been identified since early days with New York, though my earliest Stevens forbears went first to Massachusetts.' Wharton speculates that her antecedents were 'probably not . . . of the stripe of religious fanatic or political reformer' and thus could not 'breathe easily in that passionate province', so they went to 'the easier-going New York, where people seem from the outset to have been more interested in making money and acquiring property than in Predestination and witch-burning'. This is an environment of 'greater suavity and tolerance'. She summarises: 'Milder manners, a greater love of ease, and a franker interest in money-making and good food, certainly distinguished the colonial New Yorkers from the conscience-searching children of the "Mayflower."' Wharton's emphasis on pleasure and leisure extends into the traits she hails in her English ancestor Ebenezer Stevens, which include 'his love of luxury, his tireless commercial activities . . . the abounding energy, the swift adaptability and the *joie de vivre*'. As this last phrase suggests, in spite of his English blood, this cosmopolitan war hero and man of business has a certain Continental receptivity to aesthetic and sensory enjoyment. Wharton notes 'the exquisite polychrome mantels that he found the time to bring all the way from Italy, to keep company with the orange-trees on his terrace'.[89]

Wharton offers in *Backward Glance* a picture of her Dutch-descended New York home that implicitly affirms racial and social hierarchy, and also leads into a crisp articulation of political ideology. In this passage, Dutch conviviality and 'gastronomic enthusiasm' are part of an old structure that includes 'our two famous negro cooks,

Mary Johnson and Susan Minneman. These great artists stand out, brilliantly turbaned and ear-ringed, from a Snyders-like background of game, fish and vegetables transformed into a succession of succulent repasts by their indefatigable blue-nailed hands.'[90] Elizabeth Ammons has argued that in this passage 'Wharton's Africanism grounds the concept of whiteness, specifically Anglo-Saxonness'.[91] In fact, the whiteness here is even more specific than that. Wharton's 'background' locates these women within a Dutch still life, fixing them within that tradition.

In this passage, Dutch background and Dutch habits of eating and entertaining merge with a stable hierarchical order in which Black women are in the kitchen cooking as the white guests gather upstairs. After a lyrically sensuous account of the art that these women make, Wharton muses nostalgically: 'the *gourmet* of that long-lost day, when cream was cream and butter butter and coffee coffee, and meat fresh every day, and game hung just for the proper number of hours, might lean back in his chair and murmur "Fate cannot harm me."' Wharton cites this gourmet quoting a humorous poem; once again, it is light literature that signals secure status.[92] The stability of this unharmable gourmet matches the stability of signifiers and routines in his lost world, which is now gone. Wharton explains:

> I have lingered over these details because they formed a part . . . of that ancient curriculum of house-keeping which, at least in Anglo-Saxon countries, was so soon to be swept aside by the 'monstrous regiment' of the emancipated: young women taught by their elders to despise the kitchen and the linen room, and to substitute the acquiring of University degrees for the more complex art of civilized living. The movement began when I was young, and now that I am old, and have watched it and noted its results, I mourn more than ever the extinction of the household arts. Cold storage, deplorable as it is, has done far less harm to the home than the Higher Education.[93]

This passage stands as a compact articulation of Wharton's politics, neatly expressing her opposition to democratic modernity and the technologies, emancipations and educations that enable it. Less obviously, the racial categories at play here serve to reiterate what we have seen Wharton say before: it is Anglo-Saxons who disruptively embrace modernity, and, implicitly, Latin and most specifically French who conservatively resist it. The exception to that Anglo-Saxon disruptiveness lays itself out on the splendid Dutch table of Wharton's own gourmandising antecedents, who convivially devour what their Black servants make.

Wharton, like Wendell, thus embraces a racial makeup that is 'purely Anglo-Saxon', but disaffiliates from the 'Puritan' strand of Anglo-Saxonry represented by Puritan liberals like Eliot. That grimly self-righteous Puritan strand fanatically advocates for democracy, education, political equality and the duty of service. Distancing themselves from the Puritans, Wendell and Wharton describe a different white heritage: writing at a time when whiteness and democracy are closely associated, they tell stories of their own bloodlines that claim whiteness without claiming democracy.

Colonial Mansions: Wharton and the Genteel Tradition

The narrative about the genteel tells a story preoccupied with New England, and 'Puritanism' figures importantly in its early iterations. Given that ideas about New England and its Puritans are ideas about whiteness, we should not be surprised to recognise that this narrative follows the contours of one of white supremacism's favourite myths, even as it later circulates in works that do not advocate white supremacism. This final section of the chapter takes up several of the early twentieth-century texts that help to form the narrative about the genteel in order to show how Wharton (among others) contributes to the early formation of that narrative in ways that have gone unremarked. Attending to neocolonial affinities and invocations of Old New England, we can see how thinking about Anglo-Saxon racial decline feeds directly into influential articulations of the narrative about the genteel.

The neocolonial notably appears in George Santayana's foundational 'The Genteel Tradition in American Philosophy' (1911). Santayana (Hyde Professor in 1905–6) sees the pathological divide of the US manifest in its architecture:

> a neat reproduction of the colonial mansion – with some modern comforts introduced surreptitiously – stands beside the sky-scraper. The American Will inhabits the sky-scraper; the American Intellect inhabits the colonial mansion. The one is the sphere of the American man; the other, at least predominantly, of the American woman. The one is all progressive enterprise; the other is all genteel tradition.[94]

Wharton's Mount, built in 1905, resembles the mansion Santayana describes here; in a 1907 letter to Sally Norton, she associates sky-scrapers derisively with Eliot and his new business school.[95] We might ponder at length how to map Wharton's Mount and Eliot's business school on to Santayana's famous gendered binary; what I wish to note here instead is that Wharton's real mansion and figurative skyscraper precede Santayana's famous address by several years. This is not the only instance in which we can observe Wharton anticipate the tropes and ideas that become part of the narrative about the genteel that then sometimes serves to disparage her.

In order to observe Wharton's role in the formation of this narrative, it is useful to consider two essays published shortly after *French Ways* (1919) and *Age of Innocence* (1920): Vernon Louis Parrington's 'Our Literary Aristocrat' (1921) – in which the eponymous aristocrat is Wharton herself – and Van Wyck Brooks's 'Literary Life' (1922). Both of these refer to the scene in *Age of Innocence* in which Ned Winsett talks to Newland Archer about going 'down into the muck'. That Brooks and Parrington both attend to this exchange makes sense: Michael Nowlin, noting that *French Ways* and *Age of Innocence* 'are in fact complementary cultural nationalist texts', perceptively observes Wharton's 'anachronistic' inclusion, in her novel of Old New York, the arguments of later 'New York intellectual radicals' who oppose 'a besieged genteel tradition'.[96] Both Parrington and Brooks treat the scene from Wharton's novel as if she had presented it by accident: focusing on her characters rather than her arguments, they decline to engage fully with her as a thinker.

Like the Professor in her 'Descent of Man', Wharton's Winsett is a writer beset and thwarted by the forces of a huge, stupid, mostly female readership: 'a pure man of letters, untimely born in a world that had no need of letters', he is forced to work at a 'women's weekly, where fashion-plates and paper patterns alternated with New England love-stories and advertisements of temperance drinks'. He manifests 'the sterile bitterness of the still young man who has tried and given up'.[97] Brooks quotes this and comments: 'sterile bitterness, a bright futility, a beginning without a future: that is the story of Ned Winsett'. He notes 'how symbolic this is of the literary life in America'.[98] Here we can see Brooks drawing directly from Wharton as he develops his iteration of narrative about the genteel, which especially emphasises sterility. Though his aims and outlook differ significantly from Wharton's, her evocation of idiot women readers, a thwarted male and an overwhelming sterility offers him useful materials.

In his use of this same scene from *Age of Innocence*, Parrington attributes to Wharton the qualities that she represents in her characters. In *Main Currents* (1927–30), Winsett's feeling of being untimely born belongs to Wharton herself: Her 'attitude', Parrington writes, is 'expressed in the words '*Je suis venue trop tard dans un monde trop vulgaire.*' He and Brooks both make such feelings of belatedness characteristic of the genteel. Earlier, in 'Our Literary Aristocrat', Parrington quotes Winsett's remark about going 'down into the muck' in order to cast Wharton herself as an Archer who retreats from that muck and writes about 'rich nobodies' instead of real working Americans.[99]

Wharton responds to this sort of criticism in 'The Great American Novel' (1927), rejecting the idea that novelists must represent 'the man with the dinner-pail'. In a letter of the preceding year, she links this idea to Brooks's own comments about realism in *The Pilgrimage of Henry James*. She objects to Brooks's insistence 'that human relations in America are intrinsically as interesting as in the old centres of civilization & social life'. As early as 1904, Wharton had expressed her dismay at 'the assumption that the people I write about are not "real" because they are not navvies & char-women'.[100]

Although Wharton, like Brooks and Parrington, advocates realism over idealism, she and these young men diverge on the question of what realism should represent. This divergence points to the different political orientations of their respective responses to the sort of idealism they observe in Boston. Parrington characterises both Wharton and James as false realists and locates them within the genteel tradition. Making the 'genteel' roughly equivalent to 'Brahminism', he aligns the Brahmins with 'Edith Wharton's contemporary Knickerbockers', and describes these elites retreating from rough reality. Wharton, Parrington writes, is 'the last of our literary aristocrats of the genteel tradition', and James is 'the last subtle expression of the genteel', marking 'the last refinement of the genteel tradition'.[101]

These 'lasts' anticipate the title of Santayana's novel *The Last Puritan* (1935), which follows a doomed young New England man, last of his race. Along with belatedness, being the last of something is characteristic of the genteel: to be part of this tradition is to stand, dusty and exhausted, on the verge of extinction. Wendell, as we shall see, performs overtly this sort of imminent vanishing. And here it is useful to recall: Wendell taught both Brooks and Parrington at Harvard. When Parrington describes James and Wharton as the 'last' of the genteel tradition, he is not reciting a white supremacist narrative of racial replacement. But Wendell, in the source material he offers for this story of decline and extinction, most certainly is.

In his 1921 essay, Parrington links Wharton not just to the aristocratic but to the Puritanical – both categories from which, as we have seen, she excepts herself explicitly. Pointing to 'the severe ethical code which Puritanism has bequeathed her', Parrington makes that code part of a larger set of associations with Old New England. Parrington's Wharton manifests the antiquarian aesthetic of the colonial revival: 'She is as finished as a Sheraton sideboard, and with her poise, grace, high standards, and perfect breeding, she suggests as inevitably old wine and slender decanters.'[102] Parrington's language echoes Brooks's earlier imagery in *Wine of the Puritans* (1908), which pictures such decanters shattered. Brooks develops similar associations in *Indian Summer* (1940), when he reports on Wendell's sense that 'good old families had good old glass, Hepplewhite chairs and good Madeira... they had been English and should have remained so'.[103]

Parrington and Brooks are not wrong to associate these thinkers with fine antiques. Kassanoff points to a 1913 letter in which Wendell describes to Wharton the 1789 house in Portsmouth, New Hampshire, that he has inherited, 'a pleasant brick old home which has been in the family for a hundred years or so'. He adds: 'The things in it – furniture, china, glass, what-not – have never been dispersed, and there are countless unimportant old papers, interesting to me because by and by they revive what little past we know in America, as little else can. So I plunge back into olden times.'[104] Earlier, he expresses delight at finding that the house contains 'admirable examples of American Chippendale, of Hepplewhite, and of Sheraton'. To the same correspondent, he writes that he finds in the house 'more of our old times left than I dared hope'; having listed its notable contents, he adds, 'In New England the old order passes so swiftly that I know hardly any other place so wholly of the olden time.'[105]

While Wendell dedicated himself to preserving his familial portal to the olden time, Wharton had built for herself a mansion inspired by a seventeenth-century English country house and named after the Long Island estate ('in what is now the dreary waste of Astoria') of her own Revolution-era antecedent, Ebenezer Stevens.[106] Though hers is new and his is old, Wendell's and Wharton's large, white, neoclassical residences both boast lines and ornament that comport with the Georgian style of the colonial revival. Just as Wendell prizes the undispersed inheritance contained in his Portsmouth house, Wharton cherishes the andirons in the form of eagles that she inherits from Stevens. Kassanoff observes that Wharton finds at the house she names after his estate a 'feudal civility' – a pleasure present in the deferent dedication of her head gardener as well as the 'antiquarian refuge' offered by the New England countryside, which became a destination for many nostalgic tourists during the period.[107] Though

The Mount boasts commodious modernities, Wharton, like Wendell, has ways of plunging back into olden times.

The vocabulary of the colonial revival and its penchant for Georgian furniture appears in the undated manuscript where Kassanoff finds Wharton using the phrase 'Pure English': in that story, 'Sheraton' is a magazine editor seeking to defend 'Pure English' from its sad fate in 'our poor polyglot country'.[108] The fictional Sheraton may have an analogue in *Atlantic* editor Bliss Perry (Hyde Professor 1909–10). Inviting Perry in 1905 to visit and mourn with her 'The Republic of Letters', Wharton praises him for 'maintaining the tradition of what a good magazine should be, in the face of our howling mob of critics & readers', and adds: 'I hope the Atlantic will long continue to nurse its little flame of sweetness & light in the chaotic darkness of American "literary" conditions.' Presenting this letter, Wharton's biographer comments: 'in the 1900s, her letters are full of attacks on American culture and literary declines'.[109]

Stories of decline from this period frequently feature New England. Kassanoff documents Wharton's sustained engagement across multiple works with a discourse of native decline and Anglo-Saxon extinction that finds in New England 'the last outpost of Anglo-Saxon purity'. In her treatment of rural New England, Kassanoff notes, 'Wharton was participating in an ideologically charged contest over the changing face of America itself . . . The region's transformation into a national fetish came in response to the perceived threat of Anglo-American decline.'[110] While Eliot's New England past serves a story of progress, Wharton's, like Wendell's, figures in a story more concerned with decline and extinction. Both this extinction and this progress are white: when Eliot admonishes Wendell for telling a story of New England decline, what he says is that, quite to the contrary, 'all race qualities are wonderfully persistent' in their region.[111]

Albeit in different ways, Eliot and Wendell both contribute to a broader 'mania for the region of New England', which manifests not just in colonial revival architecture and a lively market for antiques, but also in a burgeoning tourism trade, the proliferation of 'New England Societies' and other organisations devoted to New England (or 'Puritan') heritage, and a large body of cultural production about New England: fiction, tourist guides, local histories, and an abundance of visual art representing landscapes and persons (often Pilgrims or Puritans) associated with the region. This period also sees the rise of organised efforts to preserve the material remains of the colonial era, most especially its domestic architecture. As the devotees of Old New England worry over the decline, extinction and racial replacement of the Puritans' descendants, they can dedicate themselves to saving old buildings: the desire to conserve, preserve and regenerate extends to both old houses and the race of those who once walked their corridors.[112]

This narrative of dispossession, extinction and replacement is one in which Wendell gives himself a leading role. Referring to his own people as 'native Americans', and 'the elder race', he writes in *Liberty, Union, and Democracy* of a 'despairing sense that we of the elder tradition are a race peacefully conquered, overwhelmed as surely as if the invasion had been emphasized by all the circumstance of war'. Elsewhere he affirms, 'I feel that we Yankees are as much things of the past as any race can be. America has swept from our grasp. The future is beyond us.'[113] This role is one that Wendell seems to savour. He detects, as Kassanoff notes, distinct aesthetic opportunities in decadence: in *Literary History* (1900) he remarks, 'Artistic expression is apt to be the final fruit of a society about to wither'; earlier, in his *Stelligeri* (1893), he had declared, 'The songs that live are the swan-songs'.[114] He repeatedly tells Horace Kallen (a correspondent and a former student) that he intends to write 'a queerly personal book ... a plain record of how New England, American tradition, has appealed to me, and sunk into me, all my life'; or about the fascination of his old house, not 'quite history nor yet quite fiction – rather a record of what tradition makes old New England seem to have been'.[115]

Kallen takes up the tale Wendell tells about himself. In 'Democracy Versus the Melting Pot' (1915), he quotes a 'great American man of letters', generally identified as Wendell, who intones: 'we are submerged beneath a conquest so complete that the very name of us means something not ourselves ... I feel as I should think an Indian might feel, in the face of ourselves that were.'[116] Others too accept Wendell's account of himself. H. L. Mencken's derisive 1925 assessment of Wendell bears the title 'The Last New Englander' and refers to its subject as 'the last flower of the Puritan *Kultur*'.[117] Mencken's title notably echoes a letter (to William James) in which Wendell refers to himself as 'the last of the Calvinists'.[118] We might recall here as well Wharton's remark to Bernard Berenson that Wendell represents 'the last of the tradition we care for'.[119] Like the 'lasts' that James and Wharton represent for Parrington, these 'lasts' evoke the imminent extinction that is one of the genteel tradition's defining traits.

Amongst Wendell's students, it is Brooks who most influentially adopts his teacher's story of New England decline. Brooks effectively recites Wendell's swan song in his own work: as the Conclusion that follows will suggest, his iteration of the narrative about the genteel draws heavily and directly from the drama of racial extinction performed personally by his teacher. Brooks also draws directly from Wendell's friends Adams and Wharton. This is clear in 'Literary Life', which not only works from Ned Winsett's 'sterile bitterness', but also suggests that Adams fails in the same way that Ned Winsett does. Quoting Adams's early letter about forming a *'school'*, Brooks assails him for his 'passivity'; he also quotes William James's 'Social Value of the College-Bred'. Pointing to the absence of such a school and the impotence of such men, Brooks agonises over the failure of the US to produce a *'grand écrivain'*; though he launches his essay by borrowing the ideas of a *grande écrivaine*, he drops Wharton after the first paragraph.[120]

Brooks is able to use Adams's and Wharton's own ideas against them in this essay partly because he erases their intellectual agency in his text. Without mentioning Adams's name (though he appears elsewhere in the essay), Brooks draws from his *Life of George Cabot Lodge* (1911), quoting a 1904 letter by Lodge that Adams includes in that book. Adams also includes long passages from Wharton's 1910 essay on Lodge, who was her friend as well as Adams's; Wharton haunts Brooks's essay as an unacknowledged interlocutor in this respect too.[121] In the passage just before the words Brooks quotes, Lodge writes:

> fifty years ago . . . [the American man] was the unquestioned head of his family, the master of his house, the father of as many children as he wanted to have. His wife's business was to bear his children and manage his household to suit him, and she never questioned it. To-day he is absolutely dethroned. A woman rules in his stead.

Brooks begins quoting just after that dire declaration, as Lodge continues to despair over his 'dying race'; he offers Lodge's observation that 'the American man' is mostly a 'sentimental idiot' incapable of 'independent thought'. He is also apparently incapable of other things: 'His wife finds him so sexually inapt that she refuses to bear him children and so drivelling in every way except as a money-getter that she compels him to expend his energies solely in that direction while she leads a discontented, sterile, stunted life.' Brooks asks: 'Is this to be denied?'[122]

This vision of white sterility appears in Brooks's later work too. Some twenty years after 'Literary Life', in *Indian Summer*, he refers again to Lodge's letters as he describes the declining Boston of the

1890s. There, he links Lodge's perspective explicitly to Wendell's, and quotes from Wendell's letters (by then published) a remark about the vanishing Yankee race being a thing of the past. Wendell, Brooks writes, 'expressed a general feeling that the days of the Yankee folk were numbered'; he names Lodge, Adams, Godkin and Norton among the 'New England men of letters who echoed and amplified this note of Wendell's'. Elsewhere in the same chapter, he remarks: 'Wendell's leading thought was much the same as Henry Adams's – that the world had been steadily going to the dogs ever since the time of Dante.' In this 1940 text, when he quotes from Lodge ('we are a dying race'), Brooks does cite his source and name Adams as its author. He adds: 'Lodge's argument was based on biological grounds. It followed the line of Theodore Roosevelt, apropos of "race-suicide."'[123]

As this last comment suggests, *Indian Summer* sets itself at some remove from the perspectives of these earlier thinkers. As Brooks refers to Wendell's feelings of belatedness and imminent extinction, he asks repeatedly: 'Was New England really dying? Or did it merely wish to think so?' Brooks offers an ambivalent answer, noting that 'if, as these authors believed, New England was a failure, New England was a tragic failure, truly'. But Wendell's swan-song drama of extinction was always suffused with that sort of glamour. Even as Brooks distances himself in this later work from the overt racism and conservatism of his sources, his own account of declining, exhausted, sterile cultural production follows the contours of their story of Anglo-Saxon decline and extinction. In the rougher, angrier essay of 1922, the fidelity of that following is self-aware and explicit; there, rather than distancing himself from Lodge's argument, he suggests that it cannot be denied. Although Brooks writes in *Indian Summer* 'the New England mind repeated its tale of exhaustion', his own work participates in that repetition.[124]

Partly because Brooks and others in his generation find 'Puritan' so useful a concept as they rebel against their Victorian predecessors, it is easy to read any attack on the 'Puritan' as a progressive attack on something conservative: all the more so, given that reactionary white supremacists like Wendell claim Old New England as their terrain and describe themselves as the attenuated, expiring end of its racial purity. So it is useful to remind ourselves that 'Puritan' is an unstable concept embedded in stories that are themselves contested and constantly changing. Attacks on the 'Puritan' can be sallies for sensory and aesthetic pleasure and sexual emancipation; they can also can be royalist, reactionary attacks on something liberal and democratic.

The Puritan may be the dour opponent of *volupté*; but the Puritan may also be the radical abolitionist, the smug partisan of the Union cause, or the liberal Unitarian doggedly advocating education and political (but not social) equality. Not least because that advocacy of education is inseparable from the logic of development that also informs eugenicism, the snowbound fanaticism of the Puritan is easy to dislike. But we should not forget: in imaginative renderings of the American past, the contrary of this rigid, self-righteous Puritan iciness may be a temperate warmth in which the elect pursue leisurely pleasure rather than service, and systems like feudalism, oligarchy or slavery sink deep roots into fertile land, stable and uninterrupted.

Conclusion

The Reign of the Genteel

Henry Adams, Henry James and Edith Wharton all contribute to a body of thought that disparages something from New England, something variously 'Puritan', serenely certain, ascetic, anhedonic, dour, calm, complacent and cold; that thing, as they criticise it, includes a historically specific liberalism centred at Harvard and in Boston, one that venerates with peculiar fervour the ideals of education and democracy. To its grim sincerity, they bring irony and detached observation; to its rigid idealism, they bring a realist attention to local particulars; to its claims that humans are teachable and must be taught, they bring the perception that humans are in fact often stupid, bestial or depraved; to its serene certainty and commitment to action, they bring a receptivity to doubt and hesitation; to its stern call to service, they bring a sense that leisure, pleasure and luxury surely have their value. In this Boston liberalism and their responses to it, we see two different ethics for inhabiting privilege and power, two different ways of being a cultivated elite. Both this liberalism and their responses to it are elitist, and both of these elitisms are also racisms.

As the twentieth century proceeds, these authors' responses to this liberalism become less legible because this liberalism itself becomes mischaracterised or obscured by a set of ideas about the 'genteel' and 'the genteel tradition'. Although individual scholars and critics usually know exactly what they mean when they use these words, usage overall is incoherent and shifting. Perhaps partly because of that amorphous pliancy, this set of ideas powerfully influences twentieth-century criticism and scholarship. Broadly speaking, the narrative about the genteel makes this serenely certain, sternly cold New England thing an effeminate sterility that blights American culture. Over time, this blight becomes more consistently associated with political attitudes that are antidemocratic or nativist, or both. When this blighting New England force is cast as a grim old conservative malignity, it becomes easier to forget or disregard the exchanges in which it speaks for democracy – especially when democratic thought is understood normatively as antiracist and anti-elitist, rather than historically as a set of ideas sometimes profoundly embedded in racism and elitism. As the elitist, racist liberalism that argues forcefully for democracy and education fades from view, so too do the counter-arguments about democracy and education that Adams, James and Wharton offer in response to it.

How does this happen? How does the narrative about the genteel form, develop, mutate and travel? Several scholars have suggested some answers these questions. Linda Dowling's study of Charles Eliot Norton notes that 'the Norton of Santayana's so-called genteel tradition – pallid, Puritan, sapless, moribund' – perfectly suits the purposes of Progressive historians; she implicates in particular Van Wyck Brooks and Richard Hofstadter, deploring 'Hofstadter's unrelenting reduction of civic idealism to a bewildered anxiety about status and social dominance'. Jackson Lears, among others, questions that '"displaced patrician" view', which he too attributes primarily to Brooks and Hofstadter. More recently, Leslie Butler and Andrew L. Slap have also worked to revise that account of liberal reformers as a 'displaced elite class trying to regain power'.[1] Articles by Joan Shelley Rubin and Elizabeth Renker crucially complement the work of those historians by attending to the more specifically literary applications of the term 'genteel'.[2]

Taking cues from these reassessments, this Conclusion sketches out in rough, sweeping strokes some key episodes in the development of the narrative about the genteel. I focus on Brooks, Norton and Barrett Wendell, whose role in this development remains insufficiently noticed. First, I note Wendell's influence on Brooks and examine the distortions in Brooks's portrait of him and Norton. I then close with a brief discussion of the sterile, bookish womanhood that so often figures the genteel. In twentieth-century texts, this womanhood represents a vapid Victorian oppressiveness unsettled by a righteous (sometimes democratic, usually male, usually young) rebellion. But we can trace this desiccated femininity back to a politically loaded nineteenth-century schoolmarm type, and also to narratives of Anglo-Saxon racial decline, where the coldly sterile white woman abets her race's extinction.

The phrase 'genteel tradition' comes from George Santayana. When he first offers this crisp articulation in a 1911 address, Santayana works with a robust body of existing thought; and, after he coins it, the phrase takes on a life of its own, one in which it acquires meanings not just detached from his arguments but effectively opposed to them. If we try to understand the meaning of 'genteel tradition' by looking to Santayana's texts, we miss entirely the applications of that phrase beyond his work, as well as the relationship between those applications and the body of thought that precedes and feeds into Santayana's arguments. Here my subject is that body of thought and that broader pattern of usage, rather than the (also very rich) question of what Santayana meant.

In the broader story about the genteel, Brooks plays a major role. Both he and Santayana develop their ideas about the genteel at President Eliot's Harvard, where Brooks studied from 1904 to 1908; Santayana did not personally teach Brooks, but Wendell did.[3] As Eric Aronoff notes, Brooks's *America's Coming-of-Age* (1915) 'articulates what would become the classic formulation of "Young America's" critique of the "genteel tradition" of the nineteenth century'.[4] Brooks describes a pathological binary in which a lifeless, idealising, moribund American culture and a crude, practical, business-minded American reality exist in total isolation from one another: the 'Highbrow' and the 'Lowbrow' manifest 'two main currents in the American mind running side by side but rarely mingling'.[5] This early formulation notably names the binary form itself as the pathology; in most later iterations of the narrative about the genteel, the pathology inheres in one side of the binary, which is gendered. Brooks develops his critique in other early works too, including *Wine of the Puritans* (1908) and, as discussed in the preceding chapter, 'Literary Life' (1922). In his later works, especially *New England: Indian Summer* (1940), he revises and extends some of his early thinking about the genteel. Though Brooks's leaps and elisions have long been recognised, his arguments – many of which are overtly framed as polemic rather than scholarship – persisted in shaping scholars' assumptions during the twentieth century.[6]

Brooks's ideas find an especially influential extension in the work of Vernon Louis Parrington, who also studied under Wendell at Harvard. Parrington's three-volume *Main Currents in American Thought* (1927–30) takes up Brooks's 'currents' and develops a nuanced, visionary expression of the binary formation he describes. 'Parrington's accomplishment', notes Randall Fuller, 'was in effect the crowning achievement of the critical movement begun by Brooks.'[7] Parrington's attack on the genteel, like Brooks's, makes an argument for realism, objecting to a genteel 'retreat' from rough reality – or, as Brooks puts it, with reference to Norton, a 'denial of life, a denial that was sterile and complacent'.[8]

Parrington portrays 'The Reign of the Genteel' as a prudish, idealising blight that originates amongst the 'Brahmins' of Cambridge and Boston's Back Bay, a kind of dry mould generated by a 'New England in Decay'. He names Stoddard, Stedman, Aldrich and *The Atlantic* as chief upholders of the genteel, but notes: 'the genteel tradition, as Professor Santayana has pointed out, has long been a disease in New England. Some of the finest minds of the Renaissance – Emerson and Hawthorne in particular – had suffered from it'. Parrington quotes at length from Santayana's 1911 address, and elsewhere in his study names Wharton and James among those contaminated by this New England disease.[9] As Nancy Glazener and Claudia Stokes both observe, *Main Currents* offers a powerful account of a gendered dichotomy in which manly realism and democracy oppose conservative, effeminate idealism. Both Glazener and Stokes treat the 'genteel' separately, associating it primarily with Santayana; yet the gendered dichotomy of Santayana's 'genteel tradition' does not separate itself neatly from the dichotomy evoked by Parrington, whom Rubin identifies as one of the thinkers who help to define and promulgate the ubiquitous phrase.[10]

Parrington's sources for thinking about the genteel tradition go beyond Santayana, and also beyond Brooks. Showing that 'the origins of Parrington's literary history emerged decades before the end of the nineteenth century, and its constituent parts were already in wide circulation by the 1880s', Stokes locates sources for Parrington's narrative of 'aristocratic overthrow and democratic ascent' in the copyright wars of the late nineteenth century, where copyright activists develop the idea of 'the writer as a vigorous, manly, and patriotic labourer' instead of an effete, elite, un-American intellectual.[11] What I want to suggest is that Santayana too – along with Brooks and others – draws from a teeming abundance of already-circulating ideas about manliness, potency and intellectual elites as he formulates his own arguments about the genteel.

Decades before Santayana gives the fateful address in California that launches the twentieth-century career of 'the genteel tradition', the word 'genteel' already had negative connotations.[12] And, during the years before he utters the phrase, multiple writers are already handling the ideas that it later invokes. Ellery Sedgwick notices a 1902 *Atlantic* article about capitalism and effeminate culture 'anticipating Santayana's critique of the genteel tradition'. In his *Future in America* (1906), H. G. Wells disparages 'genteel remoteness' and opines, 'culture, as it is conceived in Boston, is no contribution to the future of America'. Casey Nelson Blake and Fuller both suggest that

Santayana's 1911 address draws from Brooks's *Wine of the Puritans* (1908).[13] So, again, to understand 'the genteel tradition' as something that begins and ends with Santayana is to adopt a limited account of how these ideas operate. When Santayana makes his argument about the genteel, he draws from a body of existing material; and, importantly, he is not the only one to do so. Brooks's development of the 'classic formulation' of the critique of the 'genteel' is roughly simultaneous; he draws from Santayana, and he also draws from the body of existing material from which Santayana is drawing.

That material includes a broad old set of misogynist tropes, as well as the observations of the earlier visitors to the US – including Henry James, Oscar Wilde and Paul Bourget – who had noted a peculiarly sharp distinction between the sexes there.[14] Brooks and other theorists of the genteel also draw from the robust tradition of feminising attacks on New England mugwumpery and anti-imperialism. That tradition offers ample resources for writers ascribing an aridly effeminate infertility to New England thinkers. Consider, for example, a hostile 1898 newspaper article about Norton that calls him 'a true type of that fine flower of culture which is worshipped with extravagant and idolatrous rites in Boston and Cambridge. It is eminently graceful and generally sterile.'[15] This sounds a lot like Brooks, but this article does not attack Norton for sapping the vitality of art: it attacks him for denouncing the Spanish American war and telling his students not to enlist. The language used by advocates of imperialism and strenuous masculinity serves Brooks helpfully as he advocates for art and literature. Obviously, Santayana's derision for the effeminate qualities of the genteel sounds very different from, for example, Theodore Roosevelt's calls for manly action; but both of these strands of opposition to aspects of Boston liberalism offer Brooks versatile misogynist imagery as he opposes the same.

The cleanly confined definition of 'the genteel tradition' as a literary phenomenon associated with a particular set of New York poets tends to obscure the fact that it is Harvard and the liberalism of thinkers like Norton and (even more so) Eliot that provoke both Santayana's and Brooks's critiques. That problematically neat definition also tends to hamper recognition of the significant overlap between the (never consistently defined) groups of 'genteel reformers' who tend to interest historians and of authors of the 'genteel tradition' who tend to interest literary critics. Similarly, the promiscuous, opportunistic usage of 'genteel' and 'the genteel tradition' makes it easy to forget that Brooks's and Santayana's early critiques do very different things. Wilfred McClay notes that 'chroniclers of the period's literary and intellectual history . . . have generally implied that Santayana . . . was a spiritual fellow-traveller in the tens' and twenties' radical ferment'. As McClay and other scholars of Santayana affirm, this is a gross misperception. Pointing to the uses of Santayana's ideas in *America's Coming-of-Age*, Robert Dawidoff notes that Brooks, 'like most Americanists, recast Santayana's analysis as cultural activism, as if it were an agenda for reform'; and yet, 'the essence of Santayana's understanding of American civilization remains its unapologetic quietism'.[16]

Although both Santayana and Brooks have in their sights a complacent liberalism that belongs to Harvard and Boston, Brooks's critique is more immanent and Santayana's less so. As Brooks attacks Boston liberalism, he conspicuously carries forward its agendas. McClay, observing in Brooks an 'unconscious allegiance to the genteel tradition', suggests that he and his fellow revolutionaries 'embodied and perpetuated its fundamental premises – even as they believed themselves to be its mortal enemies'; Fuller, who traces Brooks's lifelong grappling with Emerson's thought, notes that he 'reenacts the very cultural program of "The American Scholar" he publicly derides'; Rubin notes that Brooks 'shared with Norton and Godkin an Arnoldian understanding of the critic's responsibility to invent a usable past and create a discerning audience'.[17] And indeed, in his agonised, bitterly admonitory, relentlessly complaining texts, the young writer more than once sounds very much like Norton in full-on Victorian jeremiad mode. Brooks shares Boston liberalism's goal of redeeming modern democracy through culture, and attacks it for failing to achieve that goal. Santayana's critique of the same is not especially democratic nor especially interested in political action. In those respects, Santayana's critique shares certain attitudes and ideas with the critical responses to Boston liberalism that this book has identified in the work of Adams, James and Wharton, as well as their more reactionary friend Wendell.

Adams is a flagrantly obvious source for Brooks's thinking about gendered dichotomy, sapped vitality and Bostonian calm. Brooks makes this debt to Adams explicit, hailing him as a twentieth-century thinker born before his time:

> The *Education,* with its acrid flavour, struck, during the war-years, the note of the moment. It appealed to the younger generation, who felt themselves adrift, and who were in revolt against their past, against puritanism and its restrictions, the sexlessness of American art . . . Adams, for many, seemed an older brother, who had shared their disillusionments long before them.[18]

This all sounds pleasantly insubordinate and liberatory. But, as I have argued, when Adams assails 'puritanism' and other Bostonian tendencies, his attack opposes not just 'sexlessness': it opposes a liberalism committed to education and democratic ideals. And, moreover, Adams's opposition to 'sexlessness' is a veneration of primitive sexual vitality that celebrates the absence of rational intellect in womanhood and non-whiteness. Chapter 1 examined that celebration, and Chapter 6 noted how Brooks took up the some of the nastier elements of Adams's material as he drew from him: in 'Literary Life', the 'sexlessness' that Brooks objects to is the sexlessness of an Anglo-Saxon woman who declines to have sex with her weak Anglo-Saxon husband, and thus bitchily hastens the extinction of the race. Brooks and Adams may indeed be modern brothers united across time by their rebellion against an oppressive Victorian unsexiness. But their rebellion liberates rather selectively.

Ideas about Anglo-Saxon extinction also feed into Brooks's thinking via Wendell, who is profoundly committed to the story of a declining white race living out its last days in a New England formerly more pure.[19] Wendell gets harsh treatment in Brooks's *Autobiography* (1965) as well as *Indian Summer*, where Brooks notably slights him by remarking that 'his best book' is his *English Composition*, not his works of criticism and literary history.[20] Recalling his college professors, Brooks writes that he 'probably learned most from Irving Babbitt', though he dislikes him and his 'curiously inhuman brand of humanism'.[21] As the preceding chapter noted, Babbitt himself echoes Wendell in his response to President Eliot's liberalism.

Brooks is not the only thinker whom Wendell influences. Largely due to his teaching at Harvard, Wendell's focus on New England shapes literary-historical scholarship for decades after his death, as Stokes observes.[22] Glazener points specifically to the link between Wendell and the narrative about the genteel when she writes that Wendell, in his emphasis on New England, 'unwittingly provided groundwork for countless subsequent literary historians to castigate Boston for fostering what has often been called, in a phrase George Santayana frames for a slightly different purpose, a "genteel tradition" in literature, the product of a complacent, repressed, and self-congratulatory elite'.[23] Santayana's purposes do indeed differ from those of the literary historians who adopt his phrase. But they are more closely aligned with those of Wendell, with whom he shares a distaste for the self-righteous, anti-imperialist, moralistic, democracy- and education-obsessed ideology that pervades their institution and drives the 'Puritan liberal' at its helm. Santayana has little respect for Wendell's intellect ('his force spent itself in foam'), but feels amicably that they are 'on the same side of the barricade' at President Eliot's Harvard, where he feels, as he puts it, a 'divergence between me and my environment'.[24]

Brooks's early articulations of the narrative about the genteel tradition carry forward Wendell's and Santayana's assessments of Emerson, New England and the serene liberalism regnant at Harvard. Brooks's Emerson resembles Santayana's and Wendell's: in emanating weakly from a worn-out Calvinism and in feeding on ideas in books rather than life, he is (as Henry Adams too will be for Brooks) 'essentially passive', and he effuses what Brooks memorably calls 'the peculiar flavor of that old New England culture, so dry, so crisp, so dogmatic, so irritating'.[25]

Brooks reproduces elements of Wendell's literary-historical writing with remarkable fidelity. One of the things he reproduces is Wendell's articulation of a dualistic logic – which, it should be noted, precedes Santayana's by over a decade. In 'American Literature' (1893), an early, compressed iteration of the ideas in *Literary History of America*, Wendell identifies two 'lines of thought', one based on 'theology' or 'theoretical principles' and the other on 'experience' or a 'practical principle', which, he says, may 'account for the two Americans of the Eighteenth Century whose names most certainly survive in the history of American literature... These are Jonathan Edwards and Benjamin Franklin.'[26] Six years later, *Literary History* more fully articulates a narrative in which Emerson and Transcendentalism form a modern misgrowth of the Puritan tendency to idealism; it juxtaposes chapters on Edwards and Franklin (taking care to observe that the latter was 'not technically a gentleman').[27] As Brooks's biographer, James Hoopes, has noted, his 'two main currents' replicate Wendell's two 'lines of thought': one current contains Puritan piety, Edwards, Emerson, idealism and Transcendentalism, and then 'the unreality of most contemporary American literature'; the other starts in 'the practical shifts of Puritan life', and develops in Franklin and then 'contemporary business life'.[28]

In Brooks's work, this dichotomy serves progressive, democratic argument about art, truth and renewal. In Wendell's work, this dichotomy assists in a diagnosis of Boston liberalism's fundamental error: it helps Wendell, the self-professed last Calvinist, explain that egalitarian democracy is neither desirable nor possible, and that all but the elect are unfit. Wendell is generally placed within a 'genteel tradition' committed to aesthetic idealism; Stokes and others treat him as an 'antirealist'.[29] That classification is not false, but it threatens to obscure important elements of Wendell's political thinking. He admires one strain of Puritan idealism, the 'orderly idealism' he finds in the Calvinist Doctrine of Election; but he vehemently opposes the other strain of Puritan idealism, which (in his account) degenerates into Unitarianism and liberalism.[30] Against that sort of idealism, he advocates a realism that recognises that humans are not perfectible and thus not suited for democratic governance. In his antidemocratic latter-day Calvinism, he contributes to the conservative realist critique of democratic liberalism to which (as this book has argued) Adams, James and Wharton also contribute. His argument for realism shows up substantially transmuted in the work of his students, who put it to different uses.

Though Wendell's literary-historical writing influenced Brooks significantly, Wendell may have influenced Brooks still more powerfully through his manner and person. Brooks's account of late nineteenth- and early twentieth-century New England portrays Wendell negatively, but also places him centrally, making him an emblematic figure of a pervasive atmosphere of decay, exhaustion and Anglophilia. When Brooks writes about New England, he rather credulously transcribes Wendell's ongoing personal dramatisation of Anglo-Saxon extinction, his long dandiacal one-man melodrama of decadent whiteness. As the preceding chapter noted, Wendell's student, Horace Kallen, too transcribes his teacher's performance. But Wendell's colleagues at Harvard watch his show with more scepticism. Santayana offers a canny and circumspect account of it in his memoir. President Eliot and William James both apparently push back against Wendell's sense that he personally embodies the vanishing Yankee tribe: each suggests to Wendell that the feeling of decline and extinction belong to himself alone, rather than to the whole region and race.[31]

Brooks's understanding of Wendell shapes his representation of Norton. He makes Wendell's self-conscious experience of Anglo-Saxon extinction and vapid reactionary nostalgia the mode of Norton too, and the dominant note of Harvard and New England at large. In Brooks's account, Wendell and Norton merge as more or less uniform Harvard exemplars of what ails the US. The two professors, he writes in *Indian Summer*, share a 'mood of retrospection, so closely allied to the moods of regret and defeat'; this mood, he writes, 'expressed itself most fully in Barrett Wendell', who 'shared Norton's feeling, – he was born too late in a world too old; and he could not find his way back to the earlier Boston'.[32] Brooks had evoked this sort of belatedness in 'Literary Life', as he quoted Wharton's description of the 'untimely born' Ned Winsett, and Parrington had he attributed such belatedness to Wharton herself. That attribution corresponds with Brooks's characterisation of Norton's and Wendell's conservative nostalgia; for both Parrington and Brooks, such belatedness is a marker of the genteel.[33]

Norton, Wendell and Wharton do indeed share a conservative nostalgia; there is much that binds them together, and much that they agree on. Norton and Wendell are chief among Wharton's friends in the literary professoriate, and they are friends with each other. Norton had been Wendell's cherished teacher, and Santayana regards them both as allies in humanism at an institution governed by an 'anti-humanist'.[34] There is, moreover, specific evidence that would seem to show Norton and Wendell sharing a political outlook. In a 1901 letter, Norton recommends Wendell's new *Literary History*, declaring it 'far the best book on the subject, full of excellent literary criticism, and with some admirable & novel points of view' (at the time there were very few books on the subject, so this comment is not as fulsome as it may now sound). Earlier in the same letter, Norton engages implicitly with *Literary History*'s ideas as he writes:

> I reach one conclusion – that I have been too much of an idealist about America, had set my hopes too high, had formed too fair an image of what she might become. Never had nation such an opportunity, she was the hope of the world. Never again will any nation have her chance to raise the standard of civilization. My error was a natural one for a New Englander born when and where I was.

Pointing to the 'moral forces at work' in the nation, Norton confesses: 'I saw mainly the good, I did not recognize how strong were the bad.'[35] In these comments, Norton locates himself within the story told by *Literary History*, which describes at length, and with much derision, this New England 'error'. Elsewhere, Wendell attributes this error to the Unitarian Puritan tradition that he associates with Eliot, and clarifies that his disagreement with this tradition is 'constant'. His *Literary History* indicates explicitly the political implications of that disagreement: 'What is good merits freedom; what is bad demands control'.[36]

So we might see Norton's comment about coming belatedly to see 'the bad' as an avowal of Wendell's views on democracy. We might also see in Norton's 'error' an anticipation of the 'Mistake' identified by James.[37] Indeed, Norton would seem to articulate as early as the 1870s the sort of realist critique of democratic idealism that James ambivalently expresses, and that Norton's own students Wendell and Babbitt would develop in their opposition to Eliot. In 1873, having visited Emerson in Concord to collect Carlyle's letters to him, Norton writes to Carlyle himself that Emerson's 'serene confidence in the order of the universe, his joy in life, his hopefulness, put to shame my weaker faith in the actual and instant supremacy of good. He reflects himself in the world; – and if men were but all Emersons one might share his confidence!' Norton describes a version of the error that *Literary History* describes: the serene New Englander projects himself and his own limited experience – an experience of white homogeneity – on to all humanity, and thus draws mistaken conclusions. Two years later, he writes again to Carlyle of Emerson's 'invincible optimism', noting, 'he rebukes me for my doubts'.[38]

Given Norton's rejection of this optimism, his criticism of his own idealism and his dismay at modern US democracy, it is perhaps not surprising that his thinking blurs so entirely with Wendell's in Brooks's account. Decisions about what to include in Norton's archive and what to publish from his correspondence further facilitate this blurring: as Dowling notes, Norton '[took] care to eliminate from the personal papers he left to Harvard' much evidence of his own Emersonian leanings around the time of the Civil War.[39] The editors of his letters, moreover, censor in a manner that obscures his disagreements with Wendell, probably because Wendell is still alive when they publish in 1913. One of the things they choose not to print is the latter part of the letter in which Norton declares that he has been 'too much of an idealist' and recommends *Literary History*.

In the censored portion of the letter, Norton continues to discuss Wendell's book, observing that 'on the ground of pure literature his judgments are generally distinguished by good sense, independence, and wide scope of vision in the lower ranges of thought'. But Norton sees Wendell falter in the higher ranges, the ground where literature mingles with the spiritual: he describes failures to see clearly the authors central to the New England tradition at the heart of his book. Wendell, Norton writes, 'is deficient in spiritual insight, & consequently some of his appreciations are strikingly incompetent. His talk about Emerson, tho' in part acute, is curiously deficient in comprehension; in a less degree the same is true in what he says of Lowell.'[40]

These unpublished sentences point to a divergence on Emerson that is indicative of a bigger rift. For both men (as for many others), Emerson stands for a New England idealism that is optimistic about democracy. Norton distances himself from that optimism, but holds grimly to that idealism, even as he recognises himself in the erroneous New England idealists of Wendell's history. In his address for Emerson's 1903 centenary, Norton works in same hagiographic mode with which treats his other dead friends, hailing their commitments to culture and to public service.[41] As Kermit Vanderbilt notes, this address restates the sort of commentary that Norton had been offering for years: it objects to Emerson's refusal to recognise anything but the good in nature and in men, and it also celebrates his 'idealism'. Norton, Vanderbilt writes, 'never lost that youthful vision of America which for shorthand purposes he labelled "Emersonian"'.[42]

By his own account both an idealist – or 'too much of an idealist' – and a pessimist, Norton yields on neither of those fronts.[43] In his own subtle and rich essay about Norton, William Dean Howells too calls him an 'idealist' and comments: 'Although he had been so often disappointed, I do not believe he ever ceased to expect beautiful and true things from the future which he was so apt to deny any promise.' Howells explains: 'He saw the America of his ideal still practicable, and however she disappointed him, he could not leave to love her, though doubtless if she could have been sensibly personified to him he would have told her some home truths that would have done her good.'[44] Santayana, like Howells, talks about love when he talks about Norton's politics, referring to 'love of home and country (which was profound in Norton, and the cause of his melancholy)'. He describes Norton as 'sad'.[45] Norton's sad, disappointed, pessimistic idealism is an easily misread stance, one that Amanda Anderson's account of 'bleak liberalism' helpfully explains: she argues not just that liberalism eagerly welcomes critique, but also that liberalism encompasses doubt and profound sadness about the difficulty of realising its ideals.[46] Norton is an exemplary bleak liberal.

Brooks's mischaracterisation of Norton's views, however, arises not just from good-faith misreading but also from sloppiness or manipulation of evidence. Like many thinkers critical of Norton, Brooks quotes disproportionately from his despondent letters of the late 1890s, written when he was especially distressed by the Venezuela crisis and then the Spanish–American War. The April 1896 letter from which Brooks quotes selectively to document Norton's feeling of belatedness actually documents the opposite: noting with 'satisfaction' (as he does in published work too) the unprecedented general material well-being of humanity in his own modern moment, Norton muses, 'there is no period at which we would rather have lived', and exclaims: 'How interesting our times have been and still are! None ever so interesting, or so full of change and of problems!'[47] Brooks's claims about Norton's and Wendell's shared sense of belatedness also elide the fact that Wendell was, in fact, born much later than Norton, by nearly three decades.

The differences between Wendell and Norton are evident to anyone who takes the time to read their work and their letters – starting with their views on Emerson or imperialism and going on from there. When Wendell sends William James a copy of his *Literary History* (along with a friendly greeting for Henry), he confesses: 'in sentiment it is Tory, pro-slavery, and imperialistic; all of which I fear I am myself'.[48] This remark (addressed to a noted anti-imperialist) is flip, but it is also precisely true. Both Wendell and Norton express and participate in racism, and both regard the uncultivated mass of Americans with alarm; but the gleefully provocative doctrine of election that Wendell professes differs starkly from the anguished faith in an ideal democracy that Norton nurses up to the end of his life. Nevertheless, in Brooks's account, Wendell effectively serves to smear Norton; and then, while Wendell remains relatively obscure, Norton rises as the derided emblem of the genteel. But all the intellectual vapidity, fastidious prudery, antidemocratic classism and racist nativism with which Norton comes to be associated belong more properly to his friend in the English department.

Just as the similarity between Norton's and Wendell's outlooks has been overstated, the similarity between Norton's and Eliot's outlooks has been understated. That is understandable, given their obvious differences, which Santayana's portrait of Harvard accentuates elegantly. It is easy to see these cousins as a study in contrast. Eliot is a philistine scientist administrator who presides over an expansionist university, founding schools and raising buildings, his extraordinarily successful career an apparently unstoppable force for professionalisation and 'efficiency'; his eye is on progress and the future, and he is friendly with capitalism and business. Meanwhile, Norton, passionate scholar of art and literature, holds court with aesthete acolytes in his library at Shady Hill; translating Dante, editing his dead friends and lecturing undergraduates about medieval art, he looks to the past and to the Old World. In this contrasting portrait, which is not inaccurate, Eliot looks like a liberal heralding neoliberalism, and Norton does not look very liberal at all. And yet, as John Jay Chapman observes, the two men are in fact similar.[49] What they agree about is liberal culture or liberal education, to which both are profoundly and vocally committed. In expressing this commitment, both draw quite overtly from the same sources: Emerson, Arnold and Mill. Henry May's 1959 account portrays these cousins perceptively. Identifying them as 'the best examples of the two types of American transmitters of nineteenth-century culture', May (echoing Santayana's 'sad') makes Norton representative of 'the sadder group of custodians of culture' and Eliot representative of 'the cheerful custodians'; he refers to 'Yea-sayers like President Eliot and Nay-sayers like Professor Norton'.[50] As May's account suggests, we can see Norton and Eliot speak for variant strands of Victorian liberalism, each of which values liberal culture.

In the same 1915 essay that notes these cousins' similarity, Chapman also describes Norton as 'a beaming little old gentleman with a note as sweet as an eighteenth-century organ', and refers to his 'old-maidish whimsicalities of opinion'.[51] In *Indian Summer*, Brooks quotes this remark from Chapman, and also quotes Santayana; like them, he disparages Norton him by feminising him. Santayana's 'Genteel American Poetry' (1915) describes a 'simple, sweet, humane, Protestant literature, grandmotherly in that sedate spectacled wonder with which it gazed at this terrible world and said how beautiful and how interesting it all was'.[52] Brooks makes Norton himself into the gazing grandmother of Santayana's description, with a dash of Chapman's beamer: he describes a 'sweetly, sadly beaming little Norton, with his habit of shaking his head as he smiled and sighed'. A few pages later, he quotes in a footnote Santayana's remark, 'Old Harvard men will remember the sweet sadness of Professor Norton. He would tell his classes, shaking his head with a slight sigh, that the Greeks did not play football.' Alongside this sweet, sighing, grandmotherly Norton, Brooks also mentions 'the great-grandmotherly Mrs Howe', endlessly reciting her Battle Hymn.[53]

'Sweet' acquires a special sting during the twentieth century, lending Arnold's 'sweetness and light' a cloying quality. But, as Stefan Collini's reading suggests, that phrase probably used to sound different.[54] Before saccharine is ubiquitously familiar, 'sweet' can denote something serious and precious; Norton uses it frequently in his letters to describe the character of people whom he likes and admires, both men and women. Later, though, 'sweet' more frequently connotes a vitiating femininity and an Arnoldian snobbishness. As for 'grandmotherly' (or, indeed, 'great-grandmotherly'), that this adjective should function to belittle was apparently self-evident to many twentieth-century literary thinkers. Douglas L. Wilson observes in 1967 that 'Santayana's description-indictment is at its most devastating when . . . the feminine and the superannuated . . . are fused and the genteel tradition is personified as a kind of senile femininity.'[55]

Such devastation is not confined to Santayana's texts. Much more broadly, the genteel is associated with the effeminate, blamed on female readers and represented with imagery of women.⁵⁶ Variously maidenish, old, old-maidenish, cold, ugly, prudish, lesbian, or, too incestuously, an aunt or a grandmother, the female figures that represent the genteel have something in common: they do not have sex. Or, more specifically, they do not have sex with men and (therefore) do not reproduce. They thus form a useful sign not just for a 'Puritan' rejection of sensuousness and sex but also for the sterility of American cultural production. But, as Chapter 6 shows, when this sterile woman comes into Brooks's developing critique of the genteel, via Adams, she is not just coldly sterile but white, and her sexlessness is a problem because it abets the decline and extinction of the Anglo-Saxon race. The story of that decline and extinction also enters Brooks's account in his transcription of Wendell's dramatic performance as the last of the vanishing Yankee tribe. As the twentieth century advances, this sort of impolitely overt racism fades from the narrative about the genteel. But the useful figure of the unacceptably unsexy, unsexual woman lingers; and, though she never needs to be labelled as such, she stays unmistakably white.

The unsexy, unsexual white femininity that figures the genteel also has origins in the type of the New England schoolmarm. As Chapter 2 notes, Harriet Beecher Stowe fashions an especially influential antebellum incarnation of this New England type in her ambivalent portrait of Aunt Ophelia; and one of Ophelia's most notable successors is James's Olive Chancellor, who shares her granitic New England spinster–educator qualities. In making Olive a New England schoolmarm figure, James links her educational project to the educational endeavours of Reconstruction. James's portrayal of Olive and her milieu notably features a specific pattern of imagery that reappears later in invocations of the genteel: 'culture' materialised into a woman's domestic décor, including books or other commodities displayed on shelves or 'brackets', and texts or images nailed to walls. Basil Ransom observes: 'He had always heard Boston was a city of culture, and now there was culture in Miss Chancellor's tables and sofas, in the books that were everywhere, on little shelves like brackets (as if a book were a statuette) in the photographs and water-colours that covered the walls, in the curtains that were festooned rather stiffly in the doorways.' James may have based this account of a Charles Street parlour on the Charles Street 'drawing-room' of the *Atlantic* editor and his wife, which, in 1915, he remembers for its 'inscribed and figured walls', ornamented with letters and autographs and illustrations and original editions.⁵⁷

America's Coming-of-Age offers a striking echo of Olive's parlour. In a remarkable passage, Brooks describes the transformation of George William Curtis into the insipid décor of a rented house 'with little idealistic mottoes hanging from every bracket'. As in Olive's parlour, 'culture' (here in the form of Curtis's writing) becomes the debris of a bookish woman's interior: his work suffuses the decoration of the house, 'everywhere, on the shelves, in the closets, under the albums', pervading this domestic space alongside all the other clutter that constitutes the culture consumed by the female resident. The mottoes and brackets in *America's Coming-of-Age* recall the mention in *Wine of the Puritans* of 'those purveyors of an irrelevant "Sweetness and Light" we still find in the magazines and on little cardboard mottoes hung up on gas-fixtures'.[58]

Brooks's vapid, housebound Curtis is at odds with the Curtis who has appeared on the pages of this book, who argues for the duties of the educated elite in public life, polemicises during the Civil War for a racially inclusive definition of 'human', and celebrates a Puritan liberalism extending from Cromwell and Milton to the antislavery movement and the Union cause. An unusually bohemian member of the varied liberal set that also includes the more staid and scholarly Norton, Curtis did indeed write light literature and serve female readers; he did so partly because he advocated the inclusive diffusion of culture to broad audiences, including women and girls. The fictional Olive and the real George William Curtis are both feminists, and both are committed to a vision of culture that valorises both education and democracy. Both *The Bostonians* and *America's Coming-of-Age* question that vision by describing the cluttered domestic interiors of women, where culture withers and dies.

As in the case of Adams, it is not necessarily wrong to see Brooks and James as modern allies united against a Bostonian, Victorian thing. It is wrong, however, to understand that Bostonian, Victorian thing as simply conservative and their critique as simply liberatory. And though Brooks finds useful resources for his own critique of Boston liberalism in James's critique of the same, we should not read Brooks's democratic politics back into James's text when we see them use similar imagery. Both of these 'inscribed and figured' interiors point to the hypocrisy and failure of the liberal project of culture; but their analyses of that failure's causes and implications are not identical, nor even necessarily similar.

As the twentieth century goes on, there are further, fainter echoes of Olive's gaunt New England femininity and the inscribed parlour in

Charles Street where culture materialises, desiccates and expires. Parrington describes a 'genteel tradition' that believes literature belongs 'to the library and the drawing room, and . . . must observe the drawing-room amenities'; he locates that gentility in Boston's 'Back Bay, where dwelt the authentic representatives of Brahminism', and 'Cambridge that was a lesser Back Bay'.[59] Charles Street is in Beacon Hill, not the newer, flashier Back Bay, an adjacent neighbourhood that becomes fashionable later – but the Brahmin perspective that considers that distinction significant is exactly what Parrington dislikes.

Given the vastness of the wider sea of misogynist imagery about bookish women, we might say the pattern of unsexy femininity that figures the genteel is indistinct and merely conjectural. But both Wilson and Brooks himself notice this pattern and regard it as meaningful. Wilson notices a proliferation of sterile, unsexy women in the poetry of early twentieth-century Harvard men: 'Santayana's personification – the bespectacled grandmother – continued to reappear in a multitude of reincarnations,' he observes, pointing to e. e. cummings's 'Cambridge ladies who live in furnished souls' and Wallace Stevens's 'High-toned Old Christian Woman'.[60] Brooks spots this pattern decades earlier. Rather than recognising his own contributions to it, he reads it as evidence that confirms his own argument. Pointing to cummings and also to T. S. Eliot, he writes, 'both felt as Henry Adams felt about Boston, and there were many others who shared their feeling'. Quoting scattered images from these poets and others, Brooks mentions not just 'Cambridge ladies' but also 'Boston virgins', and presents this pattern of images of unsexy, unsexual femininity as proof of Boston's artistic and spiritual death.[61]

In the 1915 poem from which Brooks quotes, T.S. Eliot writes of 'barren New England Hills' and juxtaposes a modern girl with her older aunts. The poem concludes:

> Upon the glazen shelves kept watch
> Matthew and Waldo, guardians of the faith,
> The army of unalterable law.[62]

Like those in Brooks's description of Curtis, Eliot's 'shelves' suggestively recall his distant kinsman President Eliot's 'Five-Foot Shelf' of Harvard Classics (1909). That fifty-volume set promised readers a full liberal education, but also offered a precisely measured quantity of parlour decoration. That T.S. Eliot's shelves are 'glazen' links his poem to the ubiquitous complaint that genteel art and artists are under or behind glass, separate from life.[63]

During the twentieth century, the narrative about the genteel and the white spinster–teacher type who tends to figure it are ubiquitous, and their meanings slide and shift. This female figure is part of complex, messy systems of imagery and storytelling. Within that complex messiness, though, we can trace this trajectory: before she stands simply for prudery and dusty vapidity, the spinster–teacher can stand for a New England liberalism that aims to educate for democracy; and, especially in the early years of the twentieth century, she can also stand for a white womanhood that does not reproduce. When Brooks invokes sterile femininity to make claims about artistic death, he draws from, among other sources, the ideas of his teacher Wendell, whose thinking about whiteness and decline is integral to his more general opposition to liberalism. Wendell suggests that the idealism of New England liberals is wrong because it does not take into account the actual nature of humans; Adams, James and Wharton too express versions of this realist critique.

The dogmatic idealism that Wendell attributes to Puritans and Unitarians matches the rigid fanaticism of Wharton's own Puritans; that rigidity belongs not just to her Puritans but to Fulvia, the liberal woman scholar whom she sees proceed, like modernist writers, '*à thèse*' rather than according to the local particulars that her own realist conservatism privileges. Fulvia's inflexibility corresponds in turn with the serene *crânerie* and calm complacency that both James and Adams disavow and describe as characteristic of Boston. Wharton, James and Adams all push back against this idealistic Puritan rigidity. Along with thinkers like Wendell and Santayana, they develop a body of thought that portrays Boston liberalism as wrong. Brooks draws from this body of thought as he formulates his own critique of Boston liberalism; like Parrington after him, he takes the stuff of this realist critique of liberalism and uses it to fashion another, one that is more progressive and democratic.

In contributing to the pool of ideas that furnishes Brooks with the stuff of his narrative about the genteel, which then helps to shape the study of American literature for decades, Adams, James and Wharton help to inform the discipline's assumptions and thus their own receptions. When we study these writers in the context of disciplinary history, one of the things we find is that they are part of it. This is not at all surprising, because they are part of tight social and professional networks that also contain the teachers and students who are key figures in disciplinary history. Norton, hired by his cousin President Eliot in the same wave of Reconstruction-era recruitment that brings Adams and William James to Harvard, helps to usher all three writers into print; Wendell, student of Norton, Adams and William James, is a friend of Wharton and a teacher to Brooks, whose second wife had been friendly with Adams in her youth. And this is just to describe some of the most obvious links in a densely woven web of privileged connection. American snobs know each other: especially Northern, East Coast snobs, and especially snobs affiliated with Harvard. That institution is a nexus within these networks; there, as at Newport, London or Paris, walls and gates enclose spaces where the powerful gather and exchange the ideas that then, noticed or not, help to form the stories that shape the ways we read.

Notes

Notes to Introduction

1. James, *Literary Criticism*, 1:161, 160, 161, 163, 179, 177 (hereafter cited as *LC*).
2. Adams, *Letters of Henry Adams*, ed. Levenson, 6:638.
3. James to Adams, 19 November 1903, in *Henry James: A Life in Letters*, ed. Horne, 388.
4. James, *LC*, 1:177, 160, 161, 178.
5. James, *Notes of a Son and Brother*, 318–19.
6. Wharton, *Backward Glance*, 154, 155, 154.
7. Parrington, *Main Currents*, 2:435–6.
8. Ibid. 3:50,51.
9. Gradert, *Puritan Spirits in the Abolitionist Imagination*, 11. For a succinct account of the actual shift from Calvinism to Unitarianism, and its relation to democratic liberalism, see Kittlestrom's chapter on William Ellery Channing in *Religion of Democracy*; on perceptions of 'Puritan' intensity over time, see the helpful synthesis offered by Rivett and Van Engen, 'Postexceptionalist Puritanism'. On Douglas's *Feminization* and its interest in 'the changing status of the public intellectual', see Pelletier, Stokes and Van Engen, 'The Last Cleric', 186.
10. James, *LC*, 1:654, 1:686–7.
11. Parrington, *Main Currents*, 3:51.
12. James, *LC*, 1:161, 163, 177–8.
13. See Butler, *Critical Americans*; Kittelstrom, *Religion of Democracy*; Slap, *Doom of Reconstruction*; Tucker, *Mugwumps: Public Moralists of the Gilded Age*.
14. Butler, *Critical Americans*, 11.
15. For an overview, see Goodlad, 'Literature and Liberalism'; see also Anderson, *Bleak Liberalism*, and Lecourt, *Cultivating Belief*.
16. See Aronoff, *Composing Cultures*, 33–42. Offering an incisive overview of the shifting meanings of 'culture', Aronoff points to continuities between Arnoldian culture and the culture advocated by Van Wyck Brooks, showing that anthropological and literary understandings of the term develop interdependently in an interdisciplinary modernist

milieu. On the inclusiveness of Arnold's 'culture', see Collini, *Arnold*, 85–7.
17. Turner, *Liberal Education of Charles Eliot Norton*; Dowling, *Charles Eliot Norton*; Stevens, *Mrs Gaskell & Me*.
18. See, for example, Poirier, 'The Vapor Trail of Charles Eliot Norton'; Dowling, *Charles Eliot Norton*, xii–xiv; see also her pugnacious endnotes, 168–72.
19. In a passing remark about these authors' respective anti-Semitisms, Freedman anticipates much of what this book uncovers: James's is 'garden variety', Adams's 'wildly pestiferous' and Wharton's 'cunningly snobbish'. *Temple of Culture*, 118. Ball's *False Starts* fruitfully builds upon this comment, extending to Adams and Wharton the special attention that Freedman gives to James; see 67–112.
20. Bromell's 'Reading Democratically' helpfully defines this trap and avoids it, using Wharton's text to develop progressive thought while explicitly declining to attribute that thought to Wharton herself. Claybaugh shows how writers without reformist intentions (including James) adopt reformist literary forms and represent reform; see *Novel of Purpose*, 7–8.
21. For concise summaries of scholarship on these authors' politics, see Buelens, 'Henry James and the (Un)canny American Scene', 196–8; and Fleissner, 'Wharton, Marriage, and the New Woman', 454–5.
22. 'French Ways', 241.
23. On transatlantic expatriate traditions amongst African–American writers, see Dickerson, *Dark Victorians*, especially 44–73; Edwards, *Practice of Diaspora*; and Tamarkin, *Anglophilia*, especially 178–246. On white male modernists abroad, see Zwerdling, *Improvised Europeans*.
24. Horne, 'Reinstated', 48. Amongst these three there was variation in fortune and status: the James family drew income from property in Syracuse, but Henry still needed to earn money, and Henry Sr was an eccentric paterfamilias. Adams came from one of the nation's great political families; they were very rich, but not rich enough to be impervious to financial shocks. Wharton, proud of her lineage, was much wealthier than either, and also much more commercially successful as a writer.
25. To name a few of Wharton's Harvard men: Walter Berry '81, Teddy Wharton '73, Bernard Berenson '87, Morton Fullerton '86, Gaillard Lapsley '93 and Bay Lodge '95.
26. Stokes, *Writers in Retrospect*, 184.
27. Along with Stokes's work, several studies document the important role in disciplinary history played by Norton and Wendell; see Graff, *Professing Literature*; Shumway, *Creating American Civilization*; Vanderbilt, *American Literature and the Academy*.
28. Samuels, *Henry Adams: The Major Phase*, 429; see 425–30; Adams to James, 18 November 1903, *Henry Adams: Selected Letters*, 441; James, *Complete Notebooks*, 214.

29. Wharton to Sara Norton, 5 June 1903, in *Letters of Edith Wharton*, ed. Lewis and Lewis, 84.
30. Parrington, *Main Currents*, 3:382.
31. See Stokes, *Writers in Retrospect*; Glazener, *Reading for Realism*.
32. See Broaddus, *Genteel Rhetoric*; Cyganowski, *Magazine Editors and Professional Authors in Nineteenth-Century America*; Dawidoff, 'Introduction', and *The Genteel Tradition and the Sacred Rage*; Dowling, *Charles Eliot Norton*, xii–xix; Glazener, *Reading for Realism*, 229–51; Howe, 'The Genteel Tradition'; McClay, 'Two Versions of the Genteel Tradition: Santayana and Brooks'; Renker, 'The "Genteel Tradition" and Its Discontents'; Rubin, 'The Genteel Tradition at Large', 11–13; Sedgwick, 'The American Genteel Tradition'; Stokes, *Writers in Retrospect*; and Wilson, 'Introductory.'
33. Santayana, *The Genteel Tradition in American Philosophy*, 4–20; Kazin qtd Wilson, 'Introductory', 24; Trilling, 'Smile of Parmenides', 32.
34. See Hall, 'The Victorian Connection'; Blodgett, 'The Mugwump Reputation'; May, *The End of American Innocence*; Schneirov, *The Dream of a New Social Order*; Rubin, *The Making of Middlebrow Culture*, 1–33; Lears, *No Place of Grace*.
35. Lears, 'Managerial Revitalization of the Rich', 184; see also *No Place of Grace*, 358n70, 360n1.
36. Fleissner, *Women, Compulsion, Modernity*; Ball, *False Starts*, 28; see 27–65. See also Chapman and Hendler's Introduction to *Sentimental Men*.
37. See Glazener, *Reading for Realism*, and Warren, *Black and White Strangers*.
38. Warren, *Black and White Strangers*, 15.
39. See May, *The End of American Innocence*. For helpful examinations of culture, democracy, social control, and the relationship between 'high' and 'low' culture, see Bentley, *Frantic Panoramas*; Dowling, *The Vulgarization of Art*; and Levine, *Highbrow/Lowbrow*.
40. See Bentley, *Frantic Panoramas*; Cooper, *The Autobiography of Citizenship*; Fisher, *Reading for Reform*; Speicher, *Schooling Readers*; Raber, *Progressivism's Aesthetic Education*.
41. On the political functions of liberal education and liberalism's logic of development in the US, see Levander, *Cradle of Liberty* and Schmidt, *Sitting in Darkness*. For critical accounts of liberalism more broadly, see Lowe, *The Intimacies of Four Continents*; Mehta, *Liberalism and Empire*; Mills, *Black Rights/White Wrongs*; and Losurdo, *Liberalism*.
42. See Wilson, *Specters of Democracy*; Bromell, *The Time Is Always Now*; Margolis, *Fictions of Mass Democracy in Nineteenth-Century America*; Nelson, *Commons Democracy*; Laski, *Untimely Democracy*; and Pratt, *The Strangers Book*. A set of earlier works take a similar approach: see *Materializing Democracy*, ed. Castronovo and Nelson; Castronovo, *Beautiful Democracy*; Salazar, *Bodies of Reform*. In contrast, During, *Against Democracy*, finds in antidemocratic thought

resources for resisting a liberal democracy that becomes indistinguishable from liberal capitalism.
43. Anderson notes: 'within American democracy ... there have been essential relationships between popular education and the politics of oppression. Both schooling for democratic citizenship and schooling for second-class citizenship have been basic traditions in American education' (*The Education of Blacks in the South*, 1). On the fundamentally exclusionary nature of US citizenship, see Smith, *Civic Ideals*, and Foner, *Story of American Freedom*. On embodiment in the US context, see Karen Sánchez-Eppler, *Touching Liberty*; in the British context, see Hadley, *Living Liberalism*.

Notes to Chapter 1

1. On Adams and vocation, see Decker, *The Literary Vocation of Henry Adams*, and Banta, 'Being a "Begonia"'; on his early liberalism, see Butler, 'Investigating the "Great American Mystery"', and Gustafson, 'Henry Adams'. For a concise account of Adams's changing thought over time, see Levenson's examination of his anti-Semitism, 'The Etiology of Israel Adams'.
2. Georgini, *Household Gods*, shows how Adams rejects his family's traditional commitments to Christianity and republicanism. Lears's *No Place of Grace* describes Adams as an 'antimodern modernist', whose embrace of a matriarchal 'vitalist cult of domesticity' rejects the patriarchal, liberal, optimist, individualist, positivist, Spencerian thinking of modernity. As many scholars have noted, Adams socialised with women and travelled south in order to come into contact with the qualities he liked. Banta discusses Adams's adoption of female roles and notes that the men who interest Adams are themselves feminine men, or 'tropical birds' ('Being a "Begonia"', 60). Orr, '"I measured her as they did with pigs"', insightfully examines Adams's response to the bodies and epistemologies he encounters during his South Seas travels.
3. Lowe, *Intimacies of Four Continents*, 7, 3, 15.
4. Ibid. 15; Schuller, *The Biopolitics of Feeling*, 5–6.
5. For for a summary of this conversation, see Moreland, *The Medievalist Impulse*, 77–117. See also Sommer, 'The Feminine Perspectives of Henry Adams' *Esther*'. Banta offfers an important broader discussion of Adams and gender in 'Being a "Begonia"'. Biographies of Marion Hooper Adams also address these issues: see Dykstra, *Clover Adams*, and Kaledin, *The Education of Mrs. Henry Adams*.
6. Rauchway, 'Regarding Henry', 55; Moreland, *The Medievalist Impulse*, 114–16; Weinstein, 'From True Woman to New Woman to Virgin', 309.
7. Bederman, *Manliness & Civilization*, 25, 23.

8. Herman writes that 'Adams turned his seminar ... into a laboratory for investigating the Anglo-Saxon thesis' (160); see *The Idea of Decline*, 157–65. On Anglo-Saxonism and the Teutonic origins theory in Adams's circle, see Gossett, *Race*, 84–122; on Adams, 103–6. Gossett observes that 'the tone of Adams's contribution to [*Essays in Anglo-Saxon Law*] is favorable to democracy, and there are no appeals to racism'. Gossett also writes of the Teutonic origins theory in the US: 'the theory began as a justification for representative government ... As it developed, however, it came more and more to mean that the "old Americans" – those of English and northern European antecedents – were the "real Americans." As time passed, it lost its strong and simple pride in democratic institutions and drew its racial lines more exclusively.' See also Horsman, *Race and Manifest Destiny*; Dyer, *Theodore Roosevelt and the Idea of Race*, 45–68; and Painter, *History of White People*, 247–50.
9. Comley, 'Henry Adams' Feminine Fiction', suggests that 'Primitive Rights' is 'an Ur-text to Adams's novels' (6). Partenheimer, 'Henry Adams's "Primitive Rights of Women"', helpfully examines the address's sources.
10. 'Lectures', 1. Samuels notes that the summary offered in the paper is too insubstantial to indicate whether the original address differs significantly from the version published several decades later in *Historical Essays* (*Young Henry Adams*, 349n7).
11. Rauchway, 'Regarding Henry', 62.
12. On the reception of *Subjection* in the US, see Pugh, 'John Stuart Mill, Harriet Taylor, and Women's Rights in America', and Habegger, *Henry James and the "Woman Business"*, 47–53, which discusses William James's review of *Subjection* in the *North American Review* in 1869.
13. Samuels, *Young Henry Adams*, 261–2.
14. Mill, *Collected Works* 21:272–3 (hereafter cited as CW).
15. Ibid. 21:274.
16. Ibid. 21:273–4.
17. Ibid. 21:264, 283–4.
18. Collini, 'Introduction', in Mill, CW, 21:xv.
19. Mill, CW 21:281–2, 290, 282, 271.
20. Adams, *Democracy*, 160. Subsequent citations in the text refer to this edition.
21. Bay, *Wives of the Leopard*, 1–3; on the 'Dahomey Village', see Bederman, *Manliness & Civilization*, 31–41; Curtis, *Orations*, 1:119.
22. Mill, CW, 21:290.
23. Adams to John Hay, 18 October 1893, *Henry Adams: Selected Letters*, 293; Georgini, *Household Gods*, 158.
24. On Adams and Darwin, see Fleissner, 'The Ordering Power of Disorder' and the Introduction to *Women, Compulsion, and Modernity*; Levenson, 'Henry Adams, U.S. Grant, and Evolution'; and (on Lyell) Smith and Higginson, 'No Traces of a Beginning'.

25. Boggs, *Animalia Americana*, 9–10, 19, 24. Boggs notes that animals are 'a recent invention . . . that goes hand in hand with the emergence of colonial modernity' and function as 'the grounds on which colonial and domestic power relations get negotiated' (24). Ellis, *Antebellum Posthuman*, discusses the relationship between Darwinian biology and liberalism's 'human' in the antebellum US.
26. Seitler, *Atavistic Tendencies*, 7, 9, 16.
27. Paul and Day, 'John Stuart Mill', 226, 227.
28. The *North American Review* reviews Edward H. Clarke's *Sex in Education* in 1874. Kaledin, *Education of Mrs. Henry Adams*, analyses the review as Adams's own (135–7), but Samuels suggests it was not written by him; see *Young Henry Adams*, 244, 320. The review echoes *Subjection* when it asserts: 'a woman, however charming to the eye, is but half fitted to be the companion of an educated man' ('Review of *Sex in Education*', 151).
29. Mill, CW, 21:269, 270, 277.
30. Ibid. 2:319.
31. Ibid. 1:270.
32. Adams, *Esther*, 116. Subsequent citations in the text refer to this edition.
33. Adams, 'King', 172–3.
34. Mill, CW, 21:300–1.
35. This failure of compassion speaks to a strand of liberal thinking about the human. Noting that 'the liberal subject emerges through its properly affective engagement with animals', Boggs observes a Lockean liberal pedagogy that operates by locating cruelty to humans and to animals on a 'continuum'. Boggs, 'Animals and the Formation of Liberal Subjectivity', 202, 201.
36. The mention of a Newfoundland here is interesting because Melville specifies this breed in a line of *Benito Cereno* that compares Black people to dogs.
37. Mill, CW, 21:325, 324, 335, 326. Dowling discusses the centrality of companionate marriage within transatlantic liberalism during this period, with reference to Mill, in *Charles Eliot Norton*, 109–19.
38. Ibid. 21:288, 293, 294–5.
39. Ibid. 21:295, 334, 290, 336.
40. Ibid. 21:249–50, 244.
41. Adams to Henry Cabot Lodge, 2 January 1873, *The Letters of Henry Adams*, ed. Levenson, 2:155 (hereafter cited as *LHA*).
42. Adams, 'Harvard College', 136–8.
43. Adams, *The Education of Henry Adams*, 283.
44. Adams to Charles Milnes Gaskell, 4 October 1875, *LHA*, 2:239.
45. Adams to Robert Cunliffe, 31 August 1875, *LHA* 2:234.
46. Kaledin, *The Education of Mrs. Henry Adams*, 140.
47. Vandersee, 'The Pursuit of Culture'.

48. The Petrarch plot is suggestive, given Harvard liberals' focus on Italian literature. Van Wyck Brooks recalled: 'Italian studies ... were a part of the atmosphere that all men breathed. Dante, Petrarch, Ruskin and Browning were Boston citizens in their way' (*New England: Indian Summer*, 435). Thomas Wentworth Higginson's translations of Petrarch appear in *The Atlantic* in 1867 and in book form in 1900.

Notes to Chapter 2

1. Perry, 'An American on American Humour', 5.
2. James to Thomas Sergeant Perry, June 1883, in *Henry James: A Life in Letters*, ed. Horne, 149 (hereafter cited as *Life in Letters*).
3. See Blair, *Henry James*; Warren, *Black and White Strangers*; and, more recently, Noonan, *Reading The Century Illustrated Monthly Magazine*. Hochman sensitively reads *The Bostonians* in *The Century* in 'Reading Historically/Reading Selectively'.
4. Trilling's 'The Princess Casamassima' and Nussbaum's 'Perception and Revolution' observe *Princess* express liberalism; they are mostly interested in their own liberalisms, not the historically specific liberalism with which the novel engages.
5. See Stone, *Communications with the Future*, 26, 179n31; 139–40; and Lustig's magisterial 'James, Arnold, "Culture," and "Modernity"'.
6. See James, *Life in Letters*, 53n4.
7. Butler, *Critical Americans*, 120, 124, 126. The realm of print that Butler describes is discussed in more theoretical terms as a Habermasian public sphere: both Bentley (*Frantic Panoramas*, 113–22) and Salmon (*Henry James and the Culture of Publicity*, 14–45) argue that *The Bostonians* speaks to and of a Habermasian transformation. Henry (*Liberalism and the Culture of Security*, 126–63) also uses Habermas to discuss *The Bostonians*' engagement with liberalism.
8. On the partly simultaneous composition and publication of these novels, see Anesko, *"Friction with the Market"*, 79–118, 470–5. On the differences between the two magazines, see Noonan, *Reading The Century Illustrated Monthly Magazine*, xii, and Butler, *Critical Americans*, 144–5.
9. See *Atlantic*, vols 87–9, and Sedgwick, *The Atlantic Monthly*, 307.
10. James to Grace Norton, 3 November 1884, in *Henry James Letters*, ed. Edel, 3:54.
11. Claybaugh, *Novel of Purpose*, 140; see 134–51.
12. James, *Princess Casamassima*, 331; *The Bostonians*, 28. Subsequent citations in the text refer to these editions.
13. Several readings of the novel that notice the debate treat them separately; see Henry, *Liberalism and the Culture of Security*; Warren, *Black and White Strangers*; Noonan, *Reading The Century Illustrated Monthly Magazine*.

14. Cable, 'Freedman's Case', 412.
15. See Grady, 'In Plain Black and White'; Kendi, *Stamped from the Beginning*, 265; Blight, *Race and Reunion*, 174–84, 294–5; Hartman, *Scenes of Subjection*, 165; see 164–9.
16. Hochman, 'Reading Historically/Reading Selectively', 275, 270. Duquette argues too that 'in *The Bostonians* James expresses his deep scepticism about the terms being dictated in reconciliation fiction' (*Loyal Subjects*, 106).
17. Cable, 'Freedman's Case', 413.
18. Dudley, 'How Shall We Help the Negro?', 273, 276.
19. Ibid. 277.
20. Ibid. 278, 275.
21. Jenkins, 'A Plea', 811; 'Prejudice and Progress', 966.
22. I find no indication that the simultaneous publication of the debate and the novel is deliberate. Others have suggested that James modified the novel (making Basil the Westerner into a Southerner) to complement the Civil War series; see Smith and Peinovich, '*The Bostonians*', 300.
23. Shaheen, '"The Social Dusk of That Mysterious Democracy"', 285, 283, 287.
24. James, *Literary Criticism* 1:641 (hereafter cited as *LC*). See Schmidt, *Sitting in Darkness*, 51–4.
25. Stowe, *Uncle Tom's Cabin*, 164–5. Farrell notes Stowe's engagement with a 'cross-racial evangelical pedagogy' (or 'Puritan Pedagogy') that aims for 'the cultivation of citizens' ('Dying Instruction', 243–4).
26. James, *LC*, 1:259.
27. Halpern, 'Searching for Sentimentality', 63. Noting Olive's similarity with Ophelia, Halpern identifies *The Bostonians* (along with novels by Twain and Howells) as one of several simultaneously serialised critical responses to sentimentalism in *The Century*.
28. Warren, *Black and White Strangers*, 92–3.
29. Butchart, *Schooling the Freed People*, ix–x, x; see also Faulkner, *Women's Radical Reconstruction*.
30. Du Bois, *Writings*, 380, 432; Du Bois also, however, dismissively mentions 'Aunt Ophelia's word, "Shiftless!"', 469; Butchart, *Schooling the Freed People*, x. See also Warren, *Black and White Strangers*, 103–4.
31. Warren, *Black and White Strangers*, 92.
32. 'Degradation of Politics', 460–1.
33. See Eliot, 'What is a Liberal Education?'
34. Waldstein, 'The Lesson of Greek Art', 262, 269.
35. 'A Broad View of Art', 474–5.
36. Noonan, *Reading The Century*, 108.
37. Habegger discusses the reception of *Subjection* in the James family, *Henry James*, 27–62.
38. Bollinger, '"Poor Isabel"', 170.
39. Butler, *Critical Americans*, 101. Butler notes that Carlyle became for American liberals a 'symbol of a corrupting and dehumanizing racism',

and, in his opposition to democracy and the expansion of suffrage, their 'perfect foil' – but they valued the 'vindication of cultivated duty and aesthetic truth' in his earlier work (107, 109); see 100–9, 138–40.

40. Hall, *Civilising Subjects*, 25.
41. Blair, 'Realism, Culture, and the Place of the Literary', 158, 161.
42. James, *LC*, 1:242.
43. James, *LC*, 1:242–3.
44. See Norton, *Letters of Charles Eliot Norton*, 1:502–8; 2:143, 2:484–6.
45. James, *LC*, 1:244, 245. Norton's 1903 speech about Emerson refers similarly to his 'ready responsiveness to every claim of thought or word of another' ('Address of Charles Eliot Norton', 51).
46. Du Bois, *Writings*, 432.
47. James, *LC*, 1:245.
48. Habegger argues that *The Bostonians* expresses Carlyle's position as interpreted by Henry Sr: 'both James and his father', he observes, '*loved* his ferocious assault on popular optimistic liberalism far more than they admitted' (*Henry James*, 197).
49. James, *LC*, 1:254.
50. Bollinger, '"Poor Isabel"', 165.
51. Arnold, *Culture and Anarchy*, 88.
52. Blair, 'Realism', 156.
53. James, *Portrait of a Lady*, 358.
54. Blair, 'Realism', 156.
55. James is sensitive to these nuances; see, for example, his passing remark about 'what "culture" is getting to mean', *LC*, 1:695. See also Habegger, *Henry James*, 184–6; and Smith and Peinovich, '*The Bostonians*', 304.
56. Cf. Wharton's comments that a ship is '"demoralizingly comfortable," as H. James says of England'; and that 'after six months of eye-starving' in the US, Paris's beauty provokes 'demoralizing happiness'. Wharton to Eunice Maynard, 7 January 1907, and Wharton to Sara Norton, 18 December 1907, in *Letters of Edith Wharton*, 111, 125.
57. See Turner, *Liberal Education*, 277, 316–19; and Dowling, *Charles Eliot Norton*, 134–43.
58. Vanderbilt, *Charles Eliot Norton*, 128.
59. See Freedman, *Professions of Taste*, 86–93, 115–16, 134.
60. Bailkin, *Culture of Property*, 26.
61. Noting the role of illustration in *The Atlantic*'s 'mission to educate and elevate the tastes' of readers, Tucker discusses an 1870 article that refers to 'vast populations . . . out of the reach of museums and art galleries' (*The Illustration of the Master*, 6).
62. John, *Best Years of the Century*, 188–90.
63. James, *LC*, 2:1087.
64. James, *Life in Letters*, 149.
65. Anesko, *Letters, Fictions, Lives*, 242.
66. James, *Complete Notebooks*, 233.

67. James to Norton, 6 December 1886, *Letters of Henry James*, ed. Lubbock, 1:124. James alludes suggestively to *Hamlet*.
68. Qtd in Bell, 'James, The Audience of the Nineties, and The Spoils of Poynton', 225.
69. James, *Henry James on Culture*, 176.
70. James puts the phrase 'representative of culture' in quotation marks when he first uses it in this essay; see *American Essays*, 120–1.

Notes to Chapter 3

1. James to Wharton, 17 August 1902, in *Henry James: A Life in Letters*, ed. Horne, 368 (hereafter cited as *Life in Letters*).
2. Rattray reads the novel differently, suggesting that by representing poverty here and elsewhere, Wharton manifests 'radicalism'. 'Edith Wharton's Unprivileged Lives', 114.
3. Wharton, *Backward Glance*, 128–9 (hereafter cited as *BG*).
4. Wharton to William Crary Brownell, 7 January 1902, in *Letters of Edith Wharton*, ed. Lewis and Lewis, 42n2, 49 (hereafter cited as *LEW*).
5. Lewis, *Edith Wharton*, 138–9; Goodman, *Edith Wharton's Women*, 29, 33.
6. Lee, *Edith Wharton*, 136–7 (hereafter cited as *EW*); Wharton, *BG*, 154.
7. Wharton, *BG*, 154–6; Lewis, *Edith Wharton*, 139; see also Lee, *EW*, 95–6.
8. Norton's daughter Lily reported that Wharton's 'houses were all perfect, but cold; there was never the sound of young and ardent feet, of romping dogs': always 'Papillons or Pekinese', Wharton's dogs apparently did not romp like those at Ashfield, where, Lily declares, 'life was as informal as it was the reverse at Lenox'. Lubbock, *Portrait of Edith Wharton*, 46–7.
9. Wegener, '"Rabid Imperialist"', 784.
10. Wharton to Sara Norton, 12 March 1901, in *LEW*, 45.
11. Wharton to Sara Norton, 29 August 1902 and 5 September 1902, *LEW*, 67, 68n2.
12. Lewis, *Edith Wharton*, 145.
13. Kassanoff, *Edith Wharton*, 14–15.
14. See Blazek, '"The Very Beginning of Things"'.
15. Norton, 'Introduction', iii, vii, viii.
16. Turner, *Liberal Education*, 356.
17. Butler, *Critical Americans*, 124.
18. Petit documents a 'literacy test debate' that is 'long, dynamic, and consequential', extending from the mid-1890s to World War I. See *The Men and Women We Want*, 5.
19. Butler, *Critical Americans*, 124. See also Turner, *Liberal Education*, 357–8.

20. Norton goes on: 'If the Chinese and Japanese civilization were in one scale, and the British and American in another, it is likely that they would more nearly balance each other than the missionaries and the Christians generally have supposed. I have no such liking for our civilization that I want to see it prevail in Asia, and I cannot but hope that the Chinese have drawn back only *pour mieux sauter.*' Norton to Samuel Gray Ward, 7 October 1901, in *Letters of Charles Eliot Norton*, 2:311–12 (hereafter cited as *LCEN*).
21. Norton, 'Some Aspects of Civilisation in America', 643; Norton to Leslie Stephen, 8 January 1896, in *LCEN*, 2:237; Norton to Samuel G. Ward, 26 April 1896, in *LCEN*, 2:243. Eliot directly contradicts Norton's comments about what is possible in 'a single generation'; see Eliot, *Charles W. Eliot: The Man and His Beliefs*, ed. Neilson, 2:739–40.
22. Norton, 'Introduction', vii.
23. Wilson, 'University Training', 112–13.
24. Norton, 'Introduction', v.
25. Qtd in Emerson, 'Charles Eliot Norton', 31.
26. Wharton, *Uncollected Critical Writings*, 99–100, 103, 101 (hereafter cited as *UCW*).
27. Ibid. 99.
28. Ibid. 100.
29. Wharton, *Collected Stories, 1891–1910*, 404, 402, 403 (hereafter cited as *CS*).
30. Ibid. 403.
31. Ibid. 397.
32. Norton, 'The Intellectual Life', 324, 313.
33. Wharton, *CS*, 398, 405–6, 412.
34. Ibid. 409.
35. Wharton, *BG*, 155–6.
36. Lee, *EW*, 110.
37. Wharton, *BG*, 127.
38. Qtd Blazek, '"Very Beginning"', 63.
39. Norton to Henry B. Fuller, 30 May 1895, in *LCEN*, 2:225.
40. See, for example, Norton, 'True Patriotism', in *LCEN*, 2:262–3.
41. Vance, 'Edith Wharton's Italian Mask', offers an insightful reading of the novel, helpfully explaining the multiple genres it incorporates and identifying readers (including Norton) for whom Wharton wrote.
42. Wharton, *Valley of Decision*, 2:277, 280. Subsequent parenthetical citations refer to this text.
43. Wharton to Sara Norton, 13 February 1902, in *LEW*, 57; Wharton to William Crary Brownell, 14 February 1902, in *LEW*, 58.
44. Norton to S. G. Ward, 10 March 1902, *LCEN*, 2:319. Lee, *EW*, 96, 770n39.
45. Qtd Blazek, '"Very Beginning"', 63–4.
46. Norton to Ward, 2 March 1902, in *LCEN*, 2:319.

47. Wharton, *Fruit of the Tree*, 624.
48. Tuttleton, 'The Fruit of the Tree', 165. See also Wharton's 'The Quicksand' (1902), included with 'Descent' in *Descent of Man* (1904), which makes a more ambivalent statement on these matters, but similarly juxtaposes 'theories, ideas, abstract conceptions of life' against 'the actual . . . the particular way in which life presents itself' and objects to making decisions according to 'beautiful theories' (Wharton, *Descent*, 121–2).
49. Norton, 'Female Suffrage', 152.
50. Norton disparages Harriet and Helen Taylor, attributes Mill's feminism to excessive deference towards these pushy women, observes that Mill himself has salient feminine qualities, and gossips with Carlyle about Mill's love life. See Norton to Chauncey Wright, 1 May 1869, in *LCEN*, 1:329–30; Norton to Chauncey Wright, 13 September 1870, in *LCEN*, 1:398–402; 1873 Journal, in *LCEN*, 1:492, 495–8; Norton to Thomas Carlyle, 16 November 1873, in *LCEN*, 2:18.
51. Norton, 'Bryn Mawr College: Commencement Address', June 1896, bMS Am 1088.5 (Box 1), Houghton Library, Harvard University (hereafter cited as 'Bryn Mawr'); John Morley, 'Matthew Arnold', 1052.
52. Norton, 'Bryn Mawr'.
53. Norton, 'Address to Radcliffe Graduates', 45.
54. Wharton, *CS*, 395.
55. Ibid. 394.
56. Wharton, *CS*, 82–3. 'The Pelican' also links to 'Descent' in its references to Darwin, Spencer, 'The Fall of Man' and a vapid 'reconciliation of science and religion' (*CS*, 84–5).
57. Bourget, *Outre-mer*, 1:130.
58. Vance, 'Edith Wharton's Italian Mask', 170.
59. Wharton, *BG*, 128.
60. Norton, 'Bryn Mawr'.
61. Wharton, *UCW*, 200–1.
62. Lee, *EW*, 613. Wharton's correspondent here is Minnie Jones, to whom, Lee notes, Wharton addressed racist, sexist and anti-Semitic remarks that she would not make to others.
63. Wharton, *BG*, 155. She mentions this fondly in a 1902 letter to Norton as well; see *LEW*, 61.
64. See Norton, *LCEN*, 2:387.
65. See, for example, the conclusion to Norton, 'Culture of the Imagination'.
66. Lee, *EW*, 110.
67. Wegener, 'Form, "Selection," and Ideology', 133. Dale Bauer argues otherwise, pointing to a 'brave new politics' manifest in Wharton's 'immersion in mass culture' after World War I (*Edith Wharton's Brave New Politics*, xii). See also Haytock, *Edith Wharton and the Conversations of Literary Modernism*; and Peel, *Apart from Modernism*.
68. EW to Bernard Berenson, 6 January 1923, *LEW*, 461.

69. Wegener, 'Form, "Selection," and Ideology', 135n18.
70. EW to William Crary Brownell, 14 February 1902, *LEW*, 58.
71. Wharton, *BG*, 127.

Notes to Chapter 4

1. See Hammond, 'The Enclosure of the Harvard Yard'. In 1886, James writes of Harvard as 'a space reserved by means of a low rustic fence, rather than inclosed (for Harvard knows nothing either of the jealousy or the dignity of high walls and guarded gateways)'. *Bostonians*, 210.
2. Barrett Wendell to William James, 4 October 1900, in Howe, 'A Packet of Wendell–James Letters', 677.
3. Norton, 'A Criticism of Harvard Architecture', 360.
4. James, *American Scene*, 49, 46 (hereafter cited as *AS*).
5. Accounts that see James's decision to represent urban poverty as bravely exceptional or indicative of progressive politics disregard his conspicuous debts to the robust literary traditions of slumming and flânerie. On the conversation about James's politics and *The American Scene*, see Haviland, *Henry James's Last Romance*, 12–18; Buelens, 'Henry James and the (Un)canny American Scene', 196–8; and Freedman, *Temple of Culture*, 117–23. Fluck, 'Power Relations in the Novels of James', argues incisively that the 'liberal' and the 'radical' James can complement each other.
6. Anesko, 'James in America', 11.
7. Aldrich, *Unguarded Gates*, 13; Lazarus, *Poems*, 202.
8. Wendell, *Stelligeri*, front matter, 8, 16.
9. Qtd Hoogenboom, *Outlawing the Spoils*, 99.
10. Posnock (*Trial of Curiosity*, 158) quotes this line from Bender (*New York Intellect*, 183), who quotes from Hofstadter (*Anti-Intellectualism*, 174), who is in turn quoting from Hoogenboom (*Outlawing the Spoils*, 99). Graff (*Professing Literature*, 83) offers it too, quoting from Trachtenberg (*Incorporation of America*, 155). Trachtenberg does not a cite a source, but may also be quoting from Hoogenboom.
11. See *Letters of Charles Eliot Norton*, 2:254, 1:116–17 (hereafter cited as *LCEN*).
12. See also Dawidoff, *The Genteel Tradition and the Sacred Rage*.
13. See Posnock, *Trial of Curiosity*, 145; and 'Henry James', 'Affirming the Alien' and '1904'.
14. Posnock, '1904', 490, 492.
15. Posnock, 'Henry James', 276; 'Affirming the Alien', 225; '1904', 489.
16. Walker, 'Introduction', x; Haviland, *Henry James's Last Romance*; see Blair, *Henry James*.
17. Warren, 'Race', 283.

18. Blair, *Henry James*, 2, 71; 'Henry James, Race, and Empire', 122.
19. Posnock, '1904', 490.
20. Buelens, *Henry James and the 'Aliens'*, 28.
21. James, *Notes of a Son and Brother*, 281.
22. Warren, 'Still Reading Henry James?', 284.
23. Posnock, 'Affirming the Alien', 228.
24. Posnock, 'Henry James', 276.
25. Posnock, '1904', 491, 489.
26. Posnock, 'Henry James', 276.
27. Posnock, *Trial of Curiosity*, 9. As Walker notes, James also writes about politics for *The Nation* in 1878–9. See *Henry James on Culture*.
28. Maher, *Biography of Broken Fortunes*, 45–6.
29. The literature on these questions is vast; Castronovo offers an incisive recent intervention in 'What are the Politics of Critique?'; see also Castronovo and Castiglia, 'A "Hive of Subtlety"'.
30. See Levine, *Forms*; Kornbluh, 'The Realist Blueprint', 199, and *The Order of Forms*.
31. James, *AS*, 22.
32. Arnold, *Culture and Anarchy*, 33.
33. See Menand, *Metaphysical Club*, 61–7.
34. Buelens develops this argument across several works; see 'Henry James's Oblique Possession', *Henry James and the 'Aliens'*, 'Henry James and the (Un)canny American Scene'.
35. Hoogenboom, *Outlawing the Spoils*, 99.
36. Turner, *Liberal Education*, 242–3, 253.
37. Norton, 'Intellectual Life', 324, 323.
38. Norton, 'Harvard', 4. Reprinted in 1895, this essay first appeared in *Harper's* in 1890.
39. Qtd Vanderbilt, *Charles Eliot Norton*, 264–5n64.
40. 'Exercises at Memorial Hall', 283.
41. See Records of the President of Harvard University, Charles W. Eliot, 1869–1930. UAI 5.150. Harvard University Archives, Cambridge, MA. Box 158, Letterbook, p. 109.
42. Norton, 'Intellectual Life', 321.
43. Mill, *Collected Works*, 18:269.
44. James to Norton, 31 March 1873, *Henry James: A Life in Letters*, ed. Horne, 53 (hereafter cited as *Life in Letters*). James discusses the 'religion of doing' and the relationship between writing and action in the Preface to *The Golden Bowl*. See *Literary Criticism*, 2:1340 (hereafter cited as *LC*).
45. Solomon observes that during the 1880s 'the responsibilities of native youth became the major focus of all thinking citizens [. . .] All over the country, the education of the native college man was a watchword in the cause of good citizenship.' She notes that 'Harvard College excelled in the new civic education' of this decade, and names Norton, Eliot and Wendell among those who pursued this aim 'most conspicuously'.

Ancestors and Immigrants, 88–9. Because the educated elite is generally white and male, conversations about its functions and powers are a key part of this period's racialised discourse of masculinity. See, for example, Townsend, *Manhood at Harvard*; Hoganson, *Fighting for American Manhood* and 'Harvard Men'; and Murphy, *Political Manhood*. From a slightly different angle, Jackson Lears fruitfully considers interventions in this conversation as part of a 'revitalization' of the ruling class; see Lears, 'Managerial Revitalization'.

46. See Kent, *Brains and Numbers*; Knights, *The Idea of the Clerisy*; Collini, *Public Moralists*; Harvie, *Lights of Liberalism*; on the US, see also Kloppenberg, *Uncertain Victory*, 160–70, and Herman, *Idea of Decline*, 158–60.
47. James to Howells, 4 May 1898, *Letters, Fictions, Lives: Henry James and William Dean Howells*, ed. Anesko, 309 (hereafter cited as *Letters, Fictions, Lives*).
48. See Lustig, 'James, Arnold, "Culture"'; Stone, *Communications*, 11–44; Adams, 'Uses of Distinction'; and Raleigh, *Matthew Arnold*.
49. 'American Letter', 264; see also, for example, the issues of 27 November 1897, 6 February 1898 and 16 April 1898.
50. James, *LC*, 1:695.
51. Godkin, *Unforeseen Tendencies*, 75–6, 196, 213.
52. James, *LC*, 1:653–4.
53. 'What Maisie Knew', 19.
54. James to Howells, 19 August 1898, *Letters, Fictions, Lives*, 312.
55. James, *LC*, 1:651–3.
56. Arnold, *Civilization in the United States*, 76.
57. Morley, 'Young England', 492.
58. Arnold, *Civilization*, 76–7; *Discourses*, 22, 25–6, 68, 69.
59. Emerson, 'Aspects of Culture', 95, 93, 95, 90, 93. Meehan discusses Emerson as 'America's first public intellectual' (*A Liberal Education*, 7); Teichgraeber emphasises his role as 'public moralist' (*Building Culture*, 24–47); see also Dolan, *Emerson's Liberalism*.
60. See Raleigh, *Matthew Arnold*, 78–81; Arnold, *Civilization*, 170.
61. Norton, 'Intellectual Life', 313–14.
62. Ibid. 323, 313.
63. Norton, 'Some Aspects of Civilization in America', 644, 642, 644, 651. Butler observes that this 'hand-wringing over immigration was fairly uncharacteristic' for Norton, noting that he, like Eliot, 'remained aloof from the nativist attitudes of many of his peers'. *Critical Americans*, 302n96.
64. James, *LC*, 1:652, 654.
65. See Godkin, 'Duty of Educated Men'; Roosevelt, 'Manly Virtues', 'College Graduate'.
66. Roosevelt, *American Ideals*, 21, 24.
67. James, *LC*, 1:665. On James and Roosevelt, see Horne, '"Reinstated"' and 'Poodle and Bull Moose'.

68. Godkin, 'Duty of Educated Men', 50, 45.
69. Roosevelt, *American Ideals*, 42, 37, 54, 61, 49, 37.
70. Ibid. 48, 49–50.
71. James, *LC*, 1:665.
72. James, *American Essays*, 120, 124.
73. James, *LC*, 1:670.
74. Rowe has examined James's attitudes towards imperialism in multiple works; a useful summary is his 'Nationalism and Imperialism'. Horne notes that James's thinking about imperialism is shaped by his 'complex sense of high civilisation as only ever achieved for the few at a tragic cost of guilt, blood, and ugliness for the many, a grim consciousness he had developed in Europe' ('"Reinstated"', 62n54).
75. James to Frances Morse, 19 October 1898, *Letters of Henry James*, 1:303; James to Henry James III, 24 February 1899, *Letters of Henry James*, 1:318. Cf. James in 1892: 'I haven't – thank heaven – a single political opinion' (qtd Horne, 'Poodle and Bull Moose', 15).
76. James to Howells, 4 May 1898, *Letters, Fictions, Lives*, 308–9.
77. James to Howells, 19 August 1898, *Letters, Fictions, Lives*, 313.
78. James to Henry James III, 24 February 1899, *Letters of Henry James*, 1:318.
79. Posnock, *Trial of Curiosity*, 157, 145.
80. Godkin, 'Duty of Educated Men', 45; James, *LC*, 1:689; see Posnock, *Trial of Curiosity*, 153.
81. Posnock, *Trial of Curiosity*, 158.
82. James, *LC*, 1:690, 665.
83. Ibid. 1:694, 690, 691, 688.
84. James, *AS*, 93, 92, 99, 93.
85. With attention to thinkers like William James and Randolph Bourne, Bramen shows that there is a 'cultural pattern' around the turn of the century in which 'the rhetoric of variety (and domesticated heterogeneity) provided an important means of refashioning Americanism in modern terms' (*Uses of Variety*, 10).
86. Warren summarises his argument and that of Michaels in 'Race', 283–6.
87. James, *Complete Notebooks*, 234–5.
88. Ibid. 237.
89. James, *AS*, 49.
90. See Johnson, 'Henry James and the China Trade'. Noting James's friendship with Hay, Johnson concludes that James is probably aware of political upheavals affecting China during the period, but does not treat them in his fiction. Hsu, 'Post-American James', discusses the 'open door' and notes James's 'aesthetic of circumscription'.
91. James, *AS*, 49.
92. James, *Complete Notebooks*, 235; Arnold, *Civilization*, 170.
93. Arnold, *Civilization*, 121, 145, 147.
94. Ibid. 170, 172, 177.

95. Howells, 'Editor's Study', 315.
96. Lustig, 'James, Arnold, "Culture"'.
97. James, *AS*, 53, 45–6, 225–6.
98. James, *Henry James on Culture*, 52, 47, 48, 54.
99. James, *LC*, 2:1138.
100. James, *Henry James on Culture*, 49–50; Pater, *Renaissance*, 152.
101. Norton, 'Harvard', 6.
102. Eliot, *Charles W. Eliot: The Man and his Beliefs*, ed. Neilson, 1:88 (hereafter cited as *CWEMB*).
103. Norton, 'Harvard', 15.
104. Eliot, *CWEMB*, 1:82.
105. Norton, 'Harvard', 5–6, 15.
106. Eliot, 'Diversity', 1, 8. Lears notes that a different address by Eliot figures in the 'lineage' of 'the contemporary rhetoric of "diversity"'; this unpublished address even more conspicuously does so ('Managerial Revitalization', 195). On that rhetoric, see Ahmed, *On Being Included*.
107. Synnott, *Half-Opened Door*, 34, 29.
108. Norton, 'Harvard', 15; Eliot, *CWEMB*, 1:80.
109. Eliot, *CWEMB*, 1:88. Wagoner, in 'Charles W. Eliot' and 'American Compromise', offers a helpful overview of Eliot's thinking about race and immigration. See also Solomon, *Ancestors and Immigrants*, 180–8; Hawkins, *Between Harvard and America*, 181–93.
110. James, *AS*, 50, 92.
111. James, *Complete Notebooks*, 236.
112. James, *AS*, 52, 333, 334.
113. Norton, 'Intellectual Life', 321, 324.
114. James, *AS*, 335.
115. Ibid. 46.
116. Ibid. 260.
117. Ibid. 286.
118. Ibid. 45, 234, 46, 53, 234.
119. James, *Princess Casamassima*, 308.
120. James, *AS*, 152.
121. Ibid. 185.
122. Ibid. 186.
123. Ibid. 125.
124. Ibid. 126.
125. Ibid. 21, 22.
126. Warren, *Black and White Strangers*, 97.
127. Wharton and Codman, *Decoration of Houses*, 22–3, 126; *Uncollected Critical Writings*, 61, 62 (hereafter cited as *UCW*).
128. James, *Henry James on Culture*, 55.
129. Wharton, *French Ways*, 50.
130. Wharton, *Backward Glance*, 51.

131. Wegener, 'Form, "Selection," and Ideology', 133–4.
132. Wharton, *Uncollected Critical Writings*, 154–5.
133. Mill, *Collected Works*, 18:190.
134. Ibid. 18:275.
135. Norton, 'Intellectual Life', 319, 320, 321; see Mill, *Collected Works*, 18:274.
136. Norton, 'Intellectual Life', 319, 320.
137. Ibid. 320.
138. Arnold, *Civilization*, 122.
139. Bourne, 'Trans-National', 87–8.
140. James, *AS*, 98. See Bourne, 'Trans-National', 90, 96.
141. James, *AS*, 97.
142. Ibid. 225, 226.
143. Ibid. 335.
144. James, *LC*, 2:145. James writes here on Balzac, who had been the subject of one of his lectures during the US tour.
145. James, *AS*, 44.
146. Ibid. 171–2.
147. Norton, 'Intellectual Life', 312. See also Norton to Samuel G. Ward, 14 July 1897, in *LCEN*, 254.
148. James, *AS*, 172.
149. James, *LC*, 1:688; *American Essays*, 127.
150. Santayana, *The Genteel Tradition in American Philosophy*, 13.
151. Adams to James, 18 November 1903, *Henry Adams: Selected Letters*, 441.
152. James to Adams, 21 March 1914, *Life in Letters*, 533. Herford grapples productively with the questions these letters raise. He warns: 'In the late personal writings James is committed to kindness, and to intelligence, and to style, equally and simultaneously, and the resulting complexity is hard to describe or account for.' See *Henry James's Style of Retrospect*, 54–6.
153. William James to Henry James, 24 January 1909, *Correspondence of William James*, 3:376–7.
154. Eliot, 'In Memory of Henry James', 649.
155. Poirier, 'The Vapor Trail', 29, 28.
156. Posnock, *Trial of Curiosity*, 158.
157. For a succinct and perceptive account of relations between Norton and the Jameses, see Turner, *Liberal Education*, 440n71.
158. James, *American Essays*, 127, 123, 127.
159. Parrington, *Main Currents*, 3:54, 2:435–6; 3:239, 240, 241. Parrington also, however, names James, along with Adams, as one of 'the more daring children of Boston' who 'sought congenial atmosphere elsewhere' (3:54).
160. Posnock, *Trial of Curiosity*, 158, 146, 197. Posnock describes the formation of this account of James, pointing to the influence of Van

Wyck Brooks and noting that 'political pressures helped shape strategically partial portraits' of the novelist. Observing that, over time, 'James is praised by liberals for fleeing from modern life yet damned for it by leftists', he argues that James does no such fleeing and that both liberals and leftists fail to see 'James's critique of bourgeois, genteel culture' (55, 77, 76). For his discussion of James and 'Puritanism', see 56–8.

161. Ibid. 197. See 196–200; Posnock compares Norton's performance of masculinity with that of James, Santayana and Howard Sturgis.
162. Norton, 'Intellectual Life', 321.
163. James, *American Essays*, 122.
164. Ibid. 124.
165. Bollinger, '"Poor Isabel"', 167.
166. James, *The American*, 110–11. See also James's revisions to this passage for the New York edition.
167. Henry James to William James, 22 September 1872. *William and Henry James: Selected Letters*, 83.
168. James, *American Essays*, 127. Howells strikes a similar note: 'his make was essentially religious, Biblical, Puritanical, and, however he would have imagined himself Hellenic, he was in his heart Hebraic. That is, when he thought he was supremely loving beauty, he was supremely loving duty, the truth which is in beauty, and is inseparably one with it' ('Charles Eliot Norton', 841).
169. James, *American Essays*, 121–2.
170. Parrington, *Main Currents*, 3:54.
171. James, *American Essays*, 122, 123.
172. James, *American Essays*, 124.
173. Posnock, *Trial of Curiosity*, 145–6.
174. Chapman, *Memories and Milestones*, 132, 133, 139.
175. Gradert, *Puritan Spirits in the Abolitionist Imagination*, 58. Gradert observes: 'we have overlooked the Puritans' usefulness within a rebellious abolitionist imagination because we have presumed their influence to be a conservative one' (*Puritan Spirits*, 10).
176. Curtis, *Orations*, 1:256–7, 1:388.
177. Fuller, *Emerson's Ghosts*, 53, 54.
178. Norton to Carlyle, 22 December 1873, *LCEN*, 2:27 (see also Norton to Carlyle, 6 May 1875, *LCEN*, 2:52); James to Norton, 31 March 1873, *Life in Letters*, 52, 52n4.
179. Howells, 'Editor's Study', 315.
180. James, *LC*, 1:239, 244, 245.
181. Ibid. 1:254, 269, 243.
182. Wendell, *Stelligeri*, 12–13. Wendell's student, Horace Kallen, refers in his article on US democracy to 'Emerson, who ... expresses the culmination of that movement ... from the agonized conscience of colonial and Puritan New England ... to serene and optimistic assurance'

('Democracy Versus the Melting Pot', 192). This sort of serenity is also associated with President Eliot; see Brooks, *New England: Indian Summer*, 102–7, 410; and Perry, *And Gladly Teach*, ix.
183. Wendell, *Literary History of America* 313, 327.
184. Wendell, 'Charles Eliot Norton', 88.
185. Turner, *Liberal Education*, 399.
186. Wendell, 'Charles Eliot Norton', 84.

Notes to Chapter 5

1. Adams to Roosevelt, 11 March 1907, *The Letters of Henry Adams*, ed. Levenson, 6:51–2 (hereafter cited as *LHA*).
2. See Samuels, *Henry Adams: The Major Phase*, 332–4 (hereafter cited as *Major Phase*).
3. Perry, 'The Adamses', 382. Perry adds that Eliot went on to speak well of Adams's work at Harvard and his *History of the United States, 1801–1816*; 'what he disliked in the "Education," evidently, was the affectation of futilitarianism, the manner of a Stendhal'.
4. Qtd Solomon, *Ancestors and Immigrants*, 176.
5. Konstantinou, *Cool Characters*, xi.
6. Stratton, *The Politics of Irony*, 19.
7. Santayana, *Persons and Places*, 392.
8. Zamir, *Dark Voices*, 8.
9. Warren, *What Was African American Literature?*, 10.
10. Du Bois, *Writings*, 1000.
11. Du Bois, *Writings*, 581. Eliot writes a letter of recommendation for Du Bois in 1891, describing him as an exceptionally capable member of his race, a young man who 'would be considered a very promising student if he were white'; see 'W. E. B. Du Bois: The Activist Life'. Du Bois calls Eliot 'cold, precise but exceedingly just and efficient' (*Writings*, 581).
12. Adams, *Education of Henry Adams*, 7. Subsequent citations in the text refer to this edition.
13. Cantiello, 'Educators', 30, 35, 37, 42.
14. Decker, 'Autobiography, Education', 48–9, 54, 62n11.
15. See Lewis, *W. E. B. Du Bois: Biography of a Race*, 79–116, 380; Du Bois, 'A Negro Student at Harvard'; *Writings*, 578–86, 602–3.
16. These pieces were part of Perry's extended 1901–2 series on Reconstruction and disenfranchisement.
17. Cantiello, 'Educators', 42, 44n14.
18. Field, 'The Souls of Henry Adams', 64.
19. On Black intellectuals in the US, see James, *Transcending the Talented Tenth*; Cooper, *Beyond Respectability*; and Posnock, *Color and Culture*, which argues that 'black writers circa 1900 were arguably the first modern American intellectuals' (2).

20. Du Bois, *Writings*, 603.
21. Du Bois, 'The Philosophy of Mr. Dole', 26.
22. Henry Adams to Charles Francis Adams, 21 November 1862, *LHA*, 1:315–16.
23. Emerson, 'Aspects of Culture', 93, 95.
24. Curtis, *Orations*, 1:35, 34; see 1:95–122. Hofstadter notes that Curtis was 'one of the most prominent advocates of a more aggressive role in politics for educated men' (*Anti-Intellectualism*, 188). See, for example, his 'The Public Duty of Educated Men' (1877), 'The Leadership of Educated Men' (1882) and 'The Spirit and Influence of Higher Education' (1884). Butler discusses Curtis and the 'problem of vocation' (*Critical Americans*, 17–19; 39).
25. Phillips, *Scholar in a Republic*, 22.
26. See Norton, *Letters of Charles Eliot Norton*, 2:126–7 (hereafter cited as *LCEN*); and Perry, *And Gladly Teach*, 68n1.
27. Arnold, *Discourses*, 9–10, 14.
28. Henry Adams to Charles Francis Adams, 21 November 1862, *LHA*, 1:315–16.
29. William James, 'Social Value', 420, 421.
30. Du Bois, *Writings*, 847.
31. Godkin, 'Duty of Educated Men', 45; see Roosevelt, 'Manly Virtues', 'College Graduate', and Townshend, *Manhood at Harvard*, 277–278.
32. 'University Notes', 207.
33. 'The Great Minds of America', 323. The article draws from several pieces by Eliot, mostly his much-reprinted 'Five American Contributions to Civilization' and also 'The Working of American Democracy' and 'The Function of Education in Democratic Society'.
34. Eliot, *Charles W. Eliot: The Man and His Beliefs*, ed. Neilson, 2:735.
35. Ibid. 2:736.
36. Letter of 30 April 1909, in James, *Charles W. Eliot, President of Harvard University, 1869–1909*, 2:166; 'Address of President Eliot', 13, 9, 12. Eliot's unnamed correspondent in this 1909 letter is W. Monroe Trotter, who initiates their remarkable exchange; see Records of the President of Harvard University, Charles W. Eliot, 1869–1930. UAI 5.150. Harvard University Archives, Cambridge, MA (Box 114).
37. Atlanta University Brochure qtd Lewis, *W. E. B. Du Bois*, 379. Du Bois introduces Eliot when he speaks at the university in 1909.
38. Du Bois, *Writings*, 434.
39. Ibid. 852, 856, 857.
40. Anderson, *The Education of Blacks in the South*, 248.
41. On Du Bois's elitism, see Dickerson, *Dark Victorians*, 95–106; James, *Transcending*, 15–33; and Warren, 'An Inevitable Drift?' On his eugenic thinking, see English, *Unnatural Selections*, 35–64. On the conservative functions of 'uplift', see Gaines, *Uplifting the Race*.
42. Lewis, *W. E. B. Du Bois*, 108.

43. Meehan locates Du Bois, Eliot and William James among the 'students' of Emerson who redefine liberal education in the twentieth century; see *A Liberal Education in Late Emerson*.
44. Eliot, *Charles W. Eliot, The Man and His Beliefs*, ed. Neilson, 1:189–90, 191. Norton quotes Arnold similarly in his *Forum* article 'Some Aspects of Civilization in America', 651.
45. Du Bois, *Writings*, 842, 846, 861.
46. Ibid. 581, 602.
47. Ibid. 861, 420; see also 510.
48. Cooper, *Beyond Respectability*, 15.
49. Emerson, 'American Scholar', 49.
50. Du Bois, *Writings*, 603.
51. Adams to Henry James, 18 November 1903, *LHA*, 6:524.
52. Henry Adams to Charles Francis Adams, 21 November 1862, *LHA*, 1:315–16.
53. Adams, *Democracy*, 6–7.
54. Adams to Cunliffe, 31 August 1875, *LHA*, 2:234.
55. Henry Adams to Charles Francis Adams, 21 November 1862, *LHA*, 1:315.
56. Vandersee, 'The Hamlet in Henry Adams', 188–90. Decker, *Literary Vocation*, notes that Adams points to these tendencies in himself early on.
57. Adams to Whitelaw Reid, 9 September 1903, *LHA*, 6:177.
58. Bollinger, '"Poor Isabel"', 176n4, 162; Raleigh, *Matthew Arnold*, 68.
59. Vandersee, 'Hamlet', 190.
60. Cantiello points to the elitism of Adams's endorsement of informal education, and notes that the chapter entitled 'Failure' 'stands, in both title and content, in direct opposition to the dominant (if lesser read) narrative of teaching put forth in the memoirs of the period'. She also notes that readers of *Atlantic* would have had access to many abbreviated teacher-memoirs in the late 1800s, along with Du Bois's ('Educators as Autobiographers', 30, 32).
61. Du Bois, *Writings*, 408.
62. Ibid. 854.
63. Adams to Charles Milnes Gaskell, 4 March 1907, *LHA*, 6:48.
64. Adams's boldest experiments with physics come in his *Letter to American Teachers of History*, which does elicit some resistance from experts. The record of that resistance compiled by his biographer shows that Adams had an attentive audience of eminent thinkers. See Samuels, *Major Phase*, 485–96.
65. Adams to Gaskell, 29 September 1870, *LHA*, 6:81.
66. Samuels, *Major Phase*, 91–2.
67. Adams to Charles W. Eliot, 12 June 1892, *LHA*, 4:21.
68. Adams to Gaskell, 2 August 1910, *LHA*, 6:354–5.
69. Du Bois, *College-Bred Negro*, 48, 46, 51, 53–4.
70. Evans, *Black Women in the Ivory Tower*, 55.

71. Ball, *False Starts*, 92. Ball's examination of anti-Semitism and the 'rhetoric of failure' in the work of Adams and Wharton shows that such rhetoric does far more than merely bolster prestige; see 67–112.
72. Lubbock, *Portrait of Edith Wharton*, 30.
73. Brooks, 'The Literary Life', 196. Brooks presumably quotes from Ford's 1920 edition.
74. See Parrington, *Main Currents*, 3:54; 3:214–27; 3:239–41; and Dawidoff, *The Genteel Tradition and the Sacred Rage*; Sproat, *The Best Men*; Posnock, *Trial of Curiosity*, 157.
75. Slap, *Doom of Reconstruction*, xiv. See also Butler, *Critical Americans*.
76. Hofstadter, *Anti-Intellectualism*, 174.
77. Ibid. 174, 175–6, 177. As Jackson Lears has pointed out, this story of dispossession is false and useful; see Lears, 'Managerial Revitalization'.

Notes to Chapter 6

1. Wharton to Wendell, 19 July 1919, in *Letters of Edith Wharton*, ed. Lewis and Lewis, 424 (hereafter cited as *LEW*).
2. Kassanoff, *Edith Wharton*, 22. See also Lee, *Edith Wharton*, 267–71 (hereafter cited as *EW*).
3. Among Hyde Professors, Wharton knew Archibald C. ('Archie') Coolidge (1906–7) and Bliss Perry (1909–10). Wendell corresponded with William James about his taking the post in 1905–6, but it ultimately went to Santayana. Wendell wrote to Hyde: 'The lectures begin with astonishing success ... The hall seats eight hundred; the aisles were packed with people standing.' He added: 'Meanwhile, I am assiduously attending to the social duties involved,' noting that he and his wife see 'the Paul Bourgets, whom we knew through their intimate friends, Henry James and Mrs. Wharton'. Howe, *Barrett Wendell and His Letters*, 158–9 (hereafter cited as *BWL*).
4. See Olin-Ammentorp, *Edith Wharton's Writings from the Great War*.
5. Wharton gives this address in February 1918; it is published the following month in the *Revue hebdomadaire* as part of a series. I am grateful to Virginia Ricard for drawing attention to and translating this address.
6. Qtd Olin-Ammentorp, *Edith Wharton's Writings from the Great War*, 79.
7. Kassanoff, *Edith Wharton*, 28–30; Wharton, *Backward Glance*, 119 (hereafter cited as *BG*); Lee, *EW*, 173.
8. Gossett, *Race*, 123–43; Graff, *Professing Literature*, 69–72; Shumway, *Creating American Civilization*. See also Renker, *The Origins of American Literary Studies*, and Stokes, *Writers in Retrospect*.
9. See Perry, *And Gladly Teach*, 218. Roosevelt had multiple links to the Hyde Professorship; in 1906 Wendell writes of plans to go to DC with

Coolidge 'to lunch . . . with the President, and talk about the Sorbonne lectures' (Howe, *BWL*, 180).
10. Wharton, *Age of Innocence*, 88–9.
11. See Kirsch, 'Innocence and the Arena'.
12. Wharton, *BG*, 95–6.
13. See Schuller, *Biopolitics of Feeling*.
14. Canby, 'Literature', 206.
15. Wharton, *BG*, 10–11.
16. Wendell, *France of Today*, 55–6.
17. Sollors, *Beyond Ethnicity*, 6–7, 4, 88.
18. Wendell, *Liberty, Union, and Democracy*, 10 (hereafter cited as *LUD*); Wendell to Robert White-Thomson, 31 March 1917, in Howe, *BWL*, 282; Wendell to G. F. Cherry, 27 May 1913, in Howe, *BWL*, 254.
19. Wendell, *Literary History of America*, 482, 342 (hereafter cited as *LHA*).
20. Eliot to Dean Briggs, 13 March 1901, in James, *Charles W. Eliot*, 2:134.
21. Eliot, *Charles William Eliot: The Man and His Beliefs*, ed. Neilson, 1:20 (hereafter cited as *CWEMB*).
22. Eliot to Dean Briggs, 13 March 1901, in James, *Charles W. Eliot*, 2:135.
23. Stokes, *Writers in Retrospect*, 176. Parrington treats 'quality' as snobbish by putting it in scare quotes when he remarks that Wharton 'belongs to the "quality" and the grand manner is hers by right of birth' ('Our Literary Aristocrat', 151).
24. Eliot, *CWEMB*, 1:21.
25. See, for example, Eliot, *American Contributions to Civilization*, 135–57.
26. James, *Charles W. Eliot*, 2:167. Eliot expresses this idea repeatedly. The best summary of his thinking about race and segregation in the US is Wagoner, 'The American Compromise'.
27. See 'Address of President Eliot', 14. In this 1904 address he also recommends militarised police; that is somewhat unusual in his œuvre, where education is the more constant refrain.
28. Wharton, *French Ways*, 18, 80, 16, x (hereafter cited as *FW*).
29. Ibid. viii, ix, x.
30. Ibid. 71, 66.
31. Ibid. 39, 133, 67.
32. Lee, *EW*, 675.
33. See Tocqueville, *Démocratie en Amérique*, 2:171.
34. Wharton, 'Amérique en Guerre', 8; *FW*, 32, 54–5, 72. Translations are my own, prepared in consultation with Virginia Ricard's important work on this text. See Wharton, 'America at War'.
35. Wharton, *FW*, 68–9, 55.
36. Ibid. 74, 113, 72, 75.
37. See Bourdieu, *Distinction*, 1–7.
38. Wharton, *Uncollected Critical Writings*, 156 (hereafter cited as *UCW*).
39. Wendell, *Privileged Classes*, 266.

40. Wharton, *BG*, 49–50.
41. Ibid. 179–80, 311–12.
42. Ibid. 157.
43. Ibid. 5.
44. Wharton, 'Amérique en Guerre', 8, 10.
45. My discussion of the uses of 'Puritan' is indebted to Blight, *Race and Reunion*; Conforti, *Imagining New England*; Dawson, *The Unusable Past*; Gradert, *Puritan Spirits in the Abolitionist Imagination*; Kammen, *Mystic Chords of Memory*; Lindgren, *Preserving Historic New England*; Seelye, *Memory's Nation*; Reynolds, *John Brown, Abolitionist*; Rivett and Van Engen, 'Postexceptionalist Puritanism'; and Rosenbaum, *Visions of Belonging*. Rivett and Van Engen summarise how the Puritan origins theory has operated in twentieth- and twenty-first-century scholarship and give a brief account of its earlier developments; see 678–81.
46. Stokes discuses this antagonism in her chapter on Wendell, which offers the best and most sustained scholarly treatment of him and his work. *Writers in Retrospect*, 139–86.
47. Reynolds, *John Brown*, 16; see 14–19, 27–8.
48. Gradert, *Puritan Spirits*, 76, 75.
49. Ibid. 43–73; Seelye, *Memory's Nation*, 361–95.
50. Bancroft qtd Dawson, *The Unusable Past*, 74; see 61–75. See also Reynolds, *John Brown*, 17–18.
51. Gradert, *Puritan Spirits*, 11.
52. Curtis, *Orations*, 1:388, 1:256–7, 1:245, 1:369, 1:385 (see also 1:393–7); 1:99, 105–6. In his *Literary History*, Wendell notably presents Curtis the 'Knickerbocker' author of light literature, not Curtis the political orator (222).
53. Conforti, *Imagining New England*, 207.
54. Kammen, *Mystic Chords*, 379; see 375–92.
55. Conforti, *Imagining New England*, 204–5; see 203–62.
56. Kammen, *Mystic Chords*, 214. Important treatments of 'Puritan' in this period and after come from (among others) Charles Francis Adams, Brooks Adams, Henry Cabot Lodge, Van Wyck Brooks, H. L. Mencken and Stuart Sherman.
57. Gradert puts it pithily: 'Abolitionists' revolutionary Puritan, much like Max Weber's proto-capitalist, H. L. Mencken's Jazz Age prude, Miller's Cold War exceptionalist, and New Americanists' atom bomb imperialist, generally says more about the moment in which it originated than about the Puritans themselves.' *Puritan Spirits*, 5.
58. Kammen notes that the conversation about 'Puritans' is often imprecise about nomenclature; see *Mystic Chords*, 389.
59. See Saunderson, *Charles W. Eliot*. William Allan Neilson writes, in a biographical sketch, that Eliot has 'a Puritan's absolute candor and

a Puritan's reserve' (*CWEMB*, xxv). Brooks calls him a 'Channing Unitarian of the Boston–Puritan–Roman type, serene as Cato, cheerful as a boy' and notes (echoing Wendell's account with characteristic fidelity): 'he shared Emerson's faith in human nature' (*New England: Indian Summer*, 102–7). When a memorial gate for Eliot goes up at Harvard in 1935, its metalwork includes little Puritan hats.
60. Bliss Perry recalls him saying 'I am not interested in the past. I am interested in the future,' and adds: 'when he was on his feet and facing a public audience, his favorite themes were the education and religion and society of the future' (*And Gladly Teach*, viii–ix).
61. Eliot, 'Address at the Dedication of the Provincetown Monument to the Pilgrims, 1910'; Seelye, *Memory's Nation*, discusses this event (561–2).
62. On the relationships between actual Puritanism, Calvinism, religious liberalism and political liberalism in New England, see Kittelstrom, *Religion of Democracy*.
63. Wendell, *LUD*, 65, 62, 63–4.
64. Wendell, *LHA*, 286.
65. Wendell to Robert White-Thomson, 9 November 1909, in Howe, *BWL*, 202.
66. Wendell, *LHA*, 286.
67. See Self, *Barrett Wendell*, 90–2; Babbitt, 'President Eliot'.
68. Wendell, *Stelligeri*, 119; *LHA*, 16–17.
69. Singley, *Edith Wharton: Matters of Mind and Spirit*, 93; see 89–126.
70. Wharton, 'Amérique en Guerre', 22.
71. See Eliot, *CWEMB*, 1:191; Lee, *Edith Wharton*, 172; Wharton, *UCW*, 156.
72. Tocqueville, *Démocratie en Amérique*, 2:171–4; Ramsden, *Edith Wharton's Library*, 125.
73. Gradert, *Puritan Spirits*, 4.
74. Wharton, *FW*, 71, 84. Later, Wharton writes: 'Like all Anglo-Saxons, the old-time Americans came of a wandering, an exploring stock; unlike the Latins, we have never been sedentary except when it was too difficult to get about' (*UCW*, 256).
75. Wharton, 'Amérique en Guerre', 8.
76. Ibid. 14–16. Wharton's account of Puritans may draw from Brooks Adams's *Emancipation of Massachusetts* (1887); her library includes a marked-up 1899 edition (Ramsden, *Edith Wharton's Library*, 1). That book is also among Wendell's sources for *LHA*.
77. Eliot, *American Contributions*, 362.
78. Wharton, *FW*, 80–1; 'Amérique en Guerre', 13, 16–17.
79. Wharton, 'Amérique en Guerre', 17.
80. Wharton, *FW*, 85–6.
81. Wendell, *LUD*, 147–8; *LHA*, 483.
82. Howe, 'A Packet', 674; Howe, *BWL*, 7.

83. This appreciation for Cavalier types corresponds with Wendell's account of the US Civil War. Both Wendell and Wharton offer accounts that are largely reconciliationist; Wharton (in 'Amérique en Guerre') leans slightly towards an emancipationist account, Wendell towards a white supremacist one. Wharton offers standard reconciliationist ideas: she emphasises the noble principle that drives each side of the conflict; she does not condemn the Confederacy; and she suggests that slavery was regrettable because it caused the war and the economic ruin of the South, rather than because it was slavery. But the fact that she mentions slavery at all sets her account apart from many reconciliationist narratives of the war, which work to erase entirely from the record slavery, race and African–Americans themselves. (I use here terms from Blight, *Race and Reunion*.)
84. See Roosevelt, 'Address of President Roosevelt', 8.
85. Seelye, *Memory's Nation*, 490. On Dutch or 'Knickerbocker' heritage, see Kassanoff, *Edith Wharton*, 168m12; and Dyer, *Theodore Roosevelt*, 28–9.
86. Wharton, 'Amérique en Guerre', 5.
87. Ibid. 12.
88. Ibid. 11–12.
89. Wharton, *BG*, 9–10, 14.
90. Ibid. 58–9.
91. Ammons, 'Edith Wharton and Race', 77; see 74–7. See also Haytock, 'Edith Wharton and the Writing of Whiteness'.
92. Wharton, *BG*, 59; Wharton quotes Sydney Smith's 'A Recipe for Salad'.
93. Wharton, *BG*, 59–60.
94. Santayana, *The Genteel Tradition in American Philosophy*, 4.
95. Wharton to Sally Norton, 23 June 1907. Edith Wharton Collection. Yale Collection of American Literature, Beinecke Rare Book and Manuscript Library, Yale University. YCAL MSS 42 (Box 29, Folder 901).
96. Nowlin, 'Edith Wharton's Higher Provincialism', 90.
97. Wharton, *Age of Innocence*, 87–8.
98. Brooks, 'Literary Life', 179.
99. Parrington, *Main Currents*, 3:382 (Parrington paraphrases Musset's *Rolla*); 'Our Literary Aristocrat', 154, 153.
100. Wharton, *UCW*, 155; *LEW*, 493n3; Wharton to Brownell, 25 June 1904, in *LEW*, 91.
101. Parrington, *Main Currents*, 2:435, 3:382, 3:240. Parrington also suggests that James, like Adams, escapes the scene of the genteel (3:54).
102. Parrington, 'Our Literary Aristocrat', 151.

103. Brooks, *Wine of the Puritans*, 17–18; *New England: Indian Summer*, 427.
104. Qtd Kassanoff, *Edith Wharton*, 185n9.
105. Wendell to Robert White-Thompson, 16 October 1910 and 5 November 1910, in *BWL*, 209, 207.
106. Wharton, *BG*, 13.
107. Kassanoff, *Edith Wharton*, 120–1.
108. Ibid. 28–9.
109. Qtd Lee, *Edith Wharton*, 172–3.
110. Kassanoff, *Edith Wharton*, 122, 123; see 119–25.
111. See Stokes, *Writers in Retrospect*, 176–7.
112. Rosenbaum, *Visions of Belonging*, 1; see also Conforti, *Imagining New England*; Kammen, *Mystic Chords*; and Seelye, *Memory's Nation*. On the historic preservation movement, see Lindgren, *Preserving Historic New England*.
113. Wendell, *LUD*, 5, 8–9; Wendell to Robert Thomson, 17 December 1893, in *BWL*, 108.
114. Qtd Kassanoff, *Edith Wharton*, 56; Wendell, *Stelligeri*, 113; *LHA*, 462. Kassanoff discusses Ralph Marvell's 'identification with the doomed aborigine'; see 20, 26.
115. Wendell to H. M. Kallen, 15 December 1910 and 23 August 1912, in Howe, *BWL*, 210, 251.
116. Kallen, 'Democracy Versus the Melting Pot', 194.
117. Mencken, *Prejudices*, 323. Mencken notably associates Wendell derisively with Wharton: 'Wendell's actual books, I believe, are now all dead ... His volume on Shakespeare, published in 1894, is admired by Sir Arthur Quiller-Couch and Mrs. Edith Wharton, but no one else seems to remember it' (325). Mencken apparently draws this association from Wendell himself; see Howe, *BWL*, 326.
118. Howe, 'A Packet', 674.
119. Lewis, *Edith Wharton*, 436.
120. Brooks, 'Literary Life', 179, 196, 193–4, 180.
121. See Adams, *Life of George Cabot Lodge*, 142–4, 146; and Wharton, *UCW*, 188–97, 195n2. Adams and Wharton discussed (in Paris) her article on Lodge, and Adams praised it; see Samuels, *Major Phase*, 497. Wharton attended Phi Beta Kappa Day at Harvard in 1906 to see Bay Lodge read his poem; she and Sally Norton did not especially like it. See Lewis, *Edith Wharton*, 171.
122. Adams, *Life of George Cabot Lodge*, 129–30; Brooks, 'Literary Life', 183–4.
123. Brooks, *New England: Indian Summer*, 411, 409, 428, 411.
124. Ibid. 411, 431, 432, 411.

Notes to Conclusion

1. Dowling, *Charles Eliot Norton*, xiii; Lears, *No Place of Grace*, 358n70, 360n1; Slap, *Doom of Reconstruction*, xiv. Butler, *Critical Americans*, 6, 11. Butler and Slap both work to revise Sproat, whose *The Best Men: Liberal Reformers in the Gilded Age*, as Slap notes, works from Hofstadter's iteration of the narrative about the genteel. Slap and Cmiel both question Sproat's conclusions as well as his use of 'best men'. Slap notes that Sproat nowhere cites a contemporary source for it (xxv, n5). Cmiel, who notes that Emerson uses the phrase too, suggests that Sproat does not see that it is 'a time-honored usage, closely associated with Cicero's *liberales*' (*Democratic Eloquence*, 114, 296n3).
2. See Renker, 'The "Genteel Tradition" and Its Discontents', and Rubin, 'The Genteel Tradition at Large'.
3. Hoopes, *Van Wyck Brooks*, 61.
4. Aronoff, *Composing Cultures*, 24.
5. Brooks, *America's Coming-of-Age*, 9.
6. Anesko offers a helpful discussion of Brooks's 'slipshod' work (and Parrington's use of it), with a focus on Henry James, in *Monopolizing the Master*; see 123–7.
7. Fuller, *Emerson's Ghosts*, 69.
8. Brooks, *New England: Indian Summer*, 421 (hereafter cited as *Indian Summer*).
9. See Parrington, *Main Currents*, 3:53. Parrington discusses 'The Reign of the Genteel' in *Main Currents*, 2:435–41; with reference to Santayana, he takes up the 'genteel tradition' again as he discusses 'New England in Decay' during the 1870s, 3:50–4; he describes Henry James as a failed realist, associating him with "the genteel tradition," 3:239–41; and associates Wharton with the same, 3:381–2. Parrington excepts Henry Adams from the contamination of the genteel, and suggests in passing that James escapes it too; see 3:54; for more on Adams, see 3:214–27.
10. See Glazener, *Reading for Realism*, 231–2; Stokes, *Writers in Retrospect*, 27–8; Rubin, 'The Genteel Tradition', 11–13.
11. Stokes, *Writers in Retrospect*, 77–8.
12. Tomsich, *A Genteel Endeavor*, 2; Cmiel notes: '*Genteel* and *gentility* took on negative connotations after 1850 ... The terms referred to false and pretentious efforts at refinement, or attempts of "low" people to affect cultivation. Women were often cited as the main offenders' (*Democratic Eloquence*, 132).
13. Blake, *Beloved Community*, 116; Fuller, *Emerson's Ghosts*, 74n19; Sedgwick, *A History of the Atlantic Monthly*, 304; Wells, *Future in America*, 176, 175.

14. Hoopes points to James's *American Scene* and Matthew Arnold's *Civilization in the United States* as influences on Brooks's early work (*Van Wyck Brooks*, 62).
15. Qtd Hoganson, 'Harvard Men', 121.
16. McClay, 'Two Versions of the Genteel Tradition', 369–70; Dawidoff, 'Introduction', xvi, xviii; see also Wilson, 'Introductory', 22.
17. McClay, 'Two Versions of the Genteel Tradition', 386; Fuller, *Emerson's Ghosts*, 57; Rubin, 'The Genteel Tradition', 13.
18. Brooks, *Indian Summer*, 490. Lears notes this consonance as he discusses Adams's and Brooks's antimodernisms in *No Place of Grace*.
19. Hoopes describes Wendell's teaching and influence on Brooks's early works in *Van Wyck Brooks*, 46–8, 61–2, 101.
20. Brooks, *Indian Summer*, 450.
21. Brooks, *Autobiography*, 122.
22. Stokes, *Writers in Retrospect*, 184–6.
23. Glazener, *Reading for Realism*, 231–2.
24. Santayana, *Persons and Places*, 405, 406, 392.
25. Brooks, *America's Coming-of-Age*, 81, 73.
26. Wendell, *Stelligeri*, 120–1.
27. Wendell, *Literary History of America*, 93.
28. Brooks, *America's Coming-of-Age*, 9–10. See Hoopes, *Van Wyck Brooks*, 101.
29. See Stokes, *Writers in Retrospect*, 27–8.
30. See Wendell, *Liberty, Union, and Democracy*, 72, 79, 90, 310.
31. See Santayana, *Persons and Places*, 405–6; Stokes, *Writers in Retrospect*, 176–7; Howe, 'A Packet of Wendell–James Letters', 678.
32. Brooks, *Indian Summer*, 424–5.
33. Wharton, *Age of Innocence*, 87–8; see Brooks, 'Literary Life', 179; Parrington, *Main Currents*, 3:382.
34. Santayana, *Persons and Places*, 392.
35. Norton, *Letters of Charles Eliot Norton*, 2:303–4 (hereafter cited as *LCEN*).
36. Howe, *Barrett Wendell and His Letters*, 202. Wendell, *Literary History of America*, 286.
37. James, *LC*, 1:178.
38. Norton to Carlyle, 22 December 1873, *LCEN*, 2:27; Norton to Carlyle, 6 May 1875, *LCEN*, 2:52. On Norton's distance from Emerson, see Dowling, *Charles Eliot Norton*, 85, 96–7, 133–4.
39. Dowling, *Charles Eliot Norton*, 38.
40. Norton to Samuel Gray Ward, 13 March 1901. Charles Eliot Norton Letters, ca. 1830–1908 (MS Am 1088.2). Houghton Library, Harvard University (Box 7). Ward, like Norton himself, had known Emerson personally.
41. See Norton, 'Address of Charles Eliot Norton'; 'The Life and Character of George William Curtis'; and 'James Russell Lowell'.
42. Vanderbilt, *Charles Eliot Norton*, 231.

43. Norton to Carlyle, 22 December 1873, *LCEN*, 2:27. See also 1:502–8; 2:127–8; 2:167–8; 2:225.
44. Howells, 'Charles Eliot Norton', 844, 846–7.
45. Santayana, *Persons and Places*, 400.
46. See Anderson, *Bleak Liberalism*.
47. Brooks, *Indian Summer*, 425; Norton to Samuel Gray Ward, 26 April 1896, *LCEN*, 2:243–4.
48. Howe, 'Packet', 677.
49. Chapman, *Memories and Milestones*, 139.
50. May, *The End of American Innocence*, 35, 36, 37, 58.
51. Chapman, *Memories and Milestones*, 142, 140; Brooks, *Indian Summer*, 420–1.
52. Santayana, *The Genteel Tradition: Nine Essays by George Santayana*, 73.
53. Brooks, *Indian Summer*, 420–1, 417–18. Brooks may adapt this image from James; see *LC*, 1:176.
54. See Collini, *Arnold*, 83–4.
55. Wilson, 'Introductory', 14.
56. Glazener observes: 'The recourse to feminization as a way of discrediting an ideological opponent ... accounts for the slippage from women's being constructed by a male-dominated literary establishment as needing protection, on the one hand, to women's being blamed for the establishment's taboos, on the other' (*Reading for Realism*, 235).
57. James, *Bostonians*, 17; *Literary Criticism*, 1:165. Historic New England offers fascinating photographs of this parlour at 148 Charles Street in its online digital collections; see <historicnewengland.org>.
58. Brooks, *America's Coming-of-Age*, 86; *Wine of the Puritans*, 96.
59. Parrington, *Main Currents*, 2:436, 435.
60. Wilson, 'Introductory', 15.
61. Brooks, *Indian Summer*, 515. Suggestively, James Baldwin too mentions 'mottoes' in connection with the moral certainties of Stowe and Aunt Ophelia. 'Everybody's Protest Novel', 13.
62. T. S. Eliot, *Poems of T. S. Eliot*, 1:24.
63. See, for example, Santayana, *Genteel Tradition in American Philosophy*, 42; Parrington, 'Our Literary Aristocrat', 153.

Bibliography

'A Broad View of Art'. *Century* 31, no. 3 (January 1886): 474–5, <https://babel.hathitrust.org/cgi/pt?id=coo.31924079633321&view=1up&seq=484> (last accessed 5 July 2020).
Adams, Amanda. 'The Uses of Distinction: Matthew Arnold and American Literary Realism'. *American Literary Realism* 37, no. 1 (2004): 37–49.
Adams, Henry. *Democracy: An American Novel*. New York and London: Penguin, 2008.
—. *The Education of Henry Adams*. New York: Library of America, 2010.
—. *Esther*. New York and London: Penguin, 1999.
—. 'Harvard College'. *North American Review* CXIV (January 1872): 110–47, <https://babel.hathitrust.org/cgi/pt?id=chi.78009399&view=1up&seq=120> (last accessed 5 July 2020).
—. *Henry Adams: Selected Letters*. Ed. Ernest Samuels. Cambridge, MA, and London: Belknap Press of Harvard University Press, 1992.
—. 'King'. In *Clarence King Memoirs: The Helmet of Mambrino*. New York: Putnam's, 1904, <http://archive.org/details/clarencekingmemo00cent> (last accessed 5 July 2020).
—. *The Letters of Henry Adams*. Ed. J. C. Levenson. 6 vols. Cambridge, MA, and London: Belknap Press of Harvard University Press, 1982.
—. *The Life of George Cabot Lodge*. Boston: Houghton Mifflin, 1911, <https://archive.org/details/lifegeorgecabot00adamgoog/page/n11/mode/2up> (last accessed 5 July 2020).
—. Review of *Old Cambridge and New; College Life: An Autobiographical Fragment*, by Thomas C. Amory and Edward Everett. *The North American Review* 114, no. 234 (1872): 110–47, <https://www.jstor.org/stable/25109658> (last accessed 5 July 2020).
Ahmed, Sara. *On Being Included: Racism and Diversity in Institutional Life*. Durham, NC: Duke University Press, 2012.
Aldrich, Thomas Bailey. *Unguarded Gates and Other Poems*. New York: Houghton, Mifflin, 1895, <http://archive.org/details/unguardedgatesa01aldrgoog> (last accessed 5 July 2020).
'American Letter'. *Literature* 2, no. 20 (5 March 1898): 263–4.
Ammons, Elizabeth. *Edith Wharton's Argument with America*. Athens: University of Georgia Press, 1980.

—. 'Edith Wharton and Race'. In *The Cambridge Companion to Edith Wharton*. Ed. Millicent Bell, 68–86. Cambridge: Cambridge University Press, 1995.
Anderson, Amanda. *Bleak Liberalism*. Chicago: University of Chicago Press, 2016.
Anderson, James D. *The Education of Blacks in the South, 1860–1935*. Chapel Hill and London: University of North Carolina Press, 1988.
Anesko, Michael, *'Friction with the Market': Henry James and the Profession of Authorship*. New York: Oxford University Press, 1986.
—. 'James in America: In Quest of (the) Material'. *The Cambridge Quarterly* 37, no. 1 (2008): 3–15, <https://www.muse.jhu.edu/article/233409> (last accessed 5 July 2020).
—. ed. *Letters, Fictions, Lives: Henry James and William Dean Howells*. New York: Oxford University Press, 1997.
—. *Monopolizing the Master: Henry James and the Politics of Modern Literary Scholarship*. Stanford: Stanford University Press, 2012.
Arnold, Matthew. *Civilization in the United States: First and Last Impressions of America*. Boston: Cupples and Hurd, 1888, <http://archive.org/details/civilizationinun00arno> (last accessed 5 July 2020).
—. *Culture and Anarchy*. New Haven: Yale University Press, 1994.
—. *Discourses in America*. London: Macmillan, 1885, <http://archive.org/details/discoursesiname03arnogoog> (last accessed 5 July 2020).
Aronoff, Eric Paul Wallach. *Composing Cultures: Modernism, American Literary Studies, and the Problem of Culture*. Charlottesville: University of Virginia Press, 2013. ProQuest Ebook Central.
Babbitt, Irving. 'President Eliot and American Education'. In *Character and Culture: Essays on East and West*, 198–224. New Brunswick, NJ: Transaction, 1995.
Bailkin, Jordanna. *The Culture of Property: The Crisis of Liberalism in Modern Britain*. Chicago: University of Chicago Press, 2004.
Baldwin, James. 'Everybody's Protest Novel'. In *Notes of a Native Son*. New York: Penguin, 2017.
Ball, David M. *False Starts: The Rhetoric of Failure and the Making of American Modernism*. Evanston: Northwestern University Press, 2014.
Banta, Martha. 'Being a "Begonia" in a Man's World'. In *New Essays on the Education of Henry Adams*. Ed. John Carlos Rowe, 49–86. Cambridge: Cambridge University Press, 1996.
Bauer, Dale M. *Edith Wharton's Brave New Politics*. Madison: University of Wisconsin Press, 1994.
Bay, Edna G. *Wives of the Leopard: Gender, Politics, and Culture in the Kingdom of Dahomey*. Charlottesville: University of Virginia Press, 1998.
Bederman, Gail. *Manliness & Civilization: A Cultural History of Gender and Race in the United States, 1880–1917*. Chicago: University of Chicago Press, 1995.

Bell, Millicent. 'James, The Audience of the Nineties, and *The Spoils of Poynton*'. *The Henry James Review* 20, no. 3 (1 November 1999): 217–26.
Bender, Thomas. *New York Intellect: A History of Intellectual Life in New York City, from 1750 to the Beginnings of Our Own Time*. New York: A. A. Knopf, 1987.
Bentley, Nancy. *Frantic Panoramas: American Literature and Mass Culture, 1870–1920*. Philadelphia: University of Pennsylvania Press, 2009.
Blair, Sara. 'Henry James, Race, and Empire'. In *A Historical Guide to Henry James*. Ed. John Carlos Rowe and Eric Haralson, 121–53. New York: Oxford University Press, 2012. Oxford Scholarship Online.
—. *Henry James and the Writing of Race and Nation*. Cambridge: Cambridge University Press, 1996.
—. 'Realism, Culture, and the Place of the Literary: Henry James and *The Bostonians*'. *The Cambridge Companion to Henry James*. Ed. Jonathan Freedman, 151–68. Cambridge: Cambridge University Press, 1998.
Blake, Casey Nelson. *Beloved Community: The Cultural Criticism of Randolph Bourne, Van Wyck Brooks, Waldo Frank, and Lewis Mumford*. Chapel Hill: University of North Carolina Press, 1990.
Blazek, William. '"The Very Beginning of Things": Reading Wharton through Charles Eliot Norton's Life and Writings on Italy'. In *Edith Wharton and Cosmopolitanism*, 62–86. Gainesville: University Press of Florida, 2016.
Blight, David W. *Race and Reunion: The Civil War in American Memory*. Cambridge, MA: Belknap Press of Harvard University Press, 2001.
Blodgett, Geoffrey. 'The Mugwump Reputation, 1870 to the Present'. *Journal of American History* 66, no. 4 (1980): 867–87, <www.jstor.org/stable/1887641> (last accessed 5 July 2020).
Boggs, Colleen Glenney. *Animalia Americana*. New York: Columbia University Press, 2013. University Press Scholarship Online, 2015.
—. 'Animals and the Formation of Liberal Subjectivity in Nineteenth-Century American Literature'. In *Oxford Handbook of Nineteenth-Century American Literature*. Ed. Russ Castronovo. Oxford: Oxford University Press, 2012.
Bollinger, Laurel Anne. '"Poor Isabel, Who Had Never Been Able to Understand Unitarianism!": Denominational Identity and Moral Character in Henry James's The Portrait of a Lady'. *Henry James Review* 32, no. 2 (2011): 160–77.
Bourdieu, Pierre. *Distinction: A Social Critique of the Judgement of Taste*. Trans. Richard Nice. Cambridge, MA: Harvard University Press, 1984.
Bourget, Paul. *Outre-mer: notes sur l'Amérique*. 2 vols. Paris: A. Lemerre, 1895, <http://gallica.bnf.fr/ark:/12148/bpt6k1116780> (last accessed 5 July 2020).

Bourne, Randolph. 'Trans-National America'. *The Atlantic Monthly* 118 (July 1916): 86–97, <https://babel.hathitrust.org/cgi/pt?id=chi.50824634&view=1up&seq=98> (last accessed 5 July 2020).

Bramen, Carrie Tirado. *The Uses of Variety: Modern Americanism and the Quest for National Distinctiveness*. Cambridge, MA: Harvard University Press, 2000.

Broaddus, Dorothy C. *Genteel Rhetoric: Writing High Culture in Nineteenth-Century Boston*. Columbia: University of South Carolina Press, 1999.

Bromell, Nicholas Knowles. 'Reading Democratically: Pedagogies of Difference and Practices of Listening in *The House of Mirth* and *Passing*'. *American Literature* 81, no. 2 (2009): 281–303.

—. *The Time Is Always Now: Black Political Thought and the Transformation of US Democracy*. Oxford: Oxford University Press, 2013. Oxford Scholarship Online, 2013.

Brooks, Van Wyck. *America's Coming-of-Age*. New York: B. W. Huebsch, 1915, <https://archive.org/details/americascomingo00broogoog/page/n9/mode/2up> (last accessed 5 July 2020).

—. *An Autobiography*. New York: E. P. Dutton, 1965.

—. 'The Literary Life'. In *Civilization in the United States, an Inquiry by Thirty Americans*. Ed. Harold Stearns, 179–98. New York: Harcourt, Brace, 1922, <https://archive.org/details/civilizationinun00stea/page/n6/mode/2up> (last accessed 5 July 2020).

—. *New England: Indian Summer, 1865–1915*. Chicago: University of Chicago Press, 1984.

—. *The Wine of the Puritans: A Study of Present-Day America*. London: Sisley's, 1908, <http://archive.org/details/winepuritansast00broogoog> (last accessed 5 July 2020).

Buelens, Gert. *Henry James and the 'Aliens': In Possession of the American Scene*. Amsterdam and New York: Rodopi, 2002.

—. 'Henry James's Oblique Possession: Plottings of Desire and Mastery in The American Scene'. *PMLA* 116, no. 2 (2001): 300–13, <www.jstor.org/stable/463518> (last accessed 5 July 2020).

—. 'Henry James and the (Un)Canny American Scene'. In *A Companion to Henry James*, 193–207. Oxford: John Wiley & Sons, 2009, <https://doi.org/10.1002/9781444304978.ch11> (last accessed 6 July 2020).

—. 'Possessing the American Scene: Race and Vulgarity, Seduction and Judgment'. In *Enacting History in Henry James: Narrative, Power, and Ethics*. Ed. Gert Buelens, 166–92. Cambridge: Cambridge University Press, 1997, <https://doi.org/10.1017/CBO9780511553660.011> (last accessed 5 July 2020).

Butchart, Ronald E. *Schooling the Freed People: Teaching, Learning, and the Struggle for Black Freedom, 1861–1876*. Chapel Hill: University of North Carolina, 2010.

Butler, Leslie. *Critical Americans: Victorian Intellectuals and Transatlantic Liberal Reform*. Chapel Hill: University of North Carolina Press, 2007.

—. 'Investigating the "Great American Mystery": Theory and Style in Henry Adams's Political Reform Moment'. In *Henry Adams & the Need to Know*. Ed. William Merrill Decker and Earl N. Harbert, 80–103. Boston: Massachusetts Historical Society, 2005.

Cable, George Washington. 'The Freedman's Case in Equity'. *Century* 29, no. 3 (January 1885): 409–18, <https://babel.hathitrust.org/cgi/pt?id=coo.31924079633339&view=1up&seq=419> (last accessed 5 July 2020).

Canby, Henry Seidel. 'Literature in Contemporary America'. In *The America of Today: Being Lectures Delivered at the Local Lectures Summer Meeting of the University of Cambridge, 1918*. Ed. Gaillard Lapsley, 199–212. Cambridge: Cambridge University Press, 1919.

Cantiello, Jessica Wells. 'Educators as Autobiographers: Henry Adams and Teacher-Memoirists of the Nineteenth Century'. *A/b: Auto/Biography Studies* 33, no. 1 (2018): 29–46.

Castiglia, Christopher, and Russ Castronovo. 'A "Hive of Subtlety": Aesthetics and the End(s) of Cultural Studies'. *American Literature* 76, no. 3 (8 September 2004): 423–35.

Castronovo, Russ. *Beautiful Democracy: Aesthetics and Anarchy in a Global Era*. Chicago: University of Chicago Press, 2007.

—. 'What Are the Politics of Critique?: The Function of Criticism at a Different Time'. In *Critique and Postcritique*. Ed. Elizabeth S. Anker and Rita Felski, 230–51. Durham, NC: Duke University Press, 2017.

Castronovo, Russ, and Dana D. Nelson, eds. *Materializing Democracy: Toward a Revitalized Cultural Politics*. Durham, NC: Duke University Press, 2002.

Chapman, John Jay. *Memories and Milestones*. New York: Moffat, Yard, 1915, <http://archive.org/details/memoriesandmile02chapgoog> (last accessed 5 July 2020).

Chapman, Mary, and Glenn Hendler, eds. *Sentimental Men: Masculinity and the Politics of Affect in American Culture*. London: University of California Press, 1999.

Claybaugh, Amanda. *The Novel of Purpose: Literature and Social Reform in the Anglo-American World*. Ithaca: Cornell University Press, 2007.

Cmiel, Kenneth. *Democratic Eloquence: The Fight over Popular Speech in Nineteenth-Century America*. New York: William Morrow, 1990.

Collini, Stefan. *Arnold*. New York: Oxford University Press, 1988.

—. *Public Moralists: Political Thought and Intellectual Life in Britain, 1850–1930*. Oxford and New York: Oxford University Press, 1991.

Comley, Nancy R. 'Henry Adams' Feminine Fictions: The Economics of Maternity'. *American Literary Realism, 1870–1910* 22, no. 1 (1989): 3–16, <www.jstor.org/stable/27746372> (last accessed 5 July 2020).

Conforti, Joseph A. *Imagining New England: Explorations of Regional Identity from the Pilgrims to the Mid-Twentieth Century*. Chapel Hill and London: University of North Carolina Press, 2001.

Cooper, Brittney C. *Beyond Respectability: The Intellectual Thought of Race Women*. Urbana: University of Illinois Press, 2017.

Cooper, Tova. *The Autobiography of Citizenship: Assimilation and Resistance in U.S. Education*. New Brunswick, NJ: Rutgers University Press, 2015.

Curtis, George William. *Orations and Addresses of George William Curtis*. Ed. Charles Eliot Norton. 3 vols. New York: Harper & Brothers, 1894, <http://archive.org/details/orationsandaddr03curtgoog> (last accessed 5 July 2020).

Cyganowski, Carol Klimick. *Magazine Editors and Professional Authors in Nineteenth-Century America: The Genteel Tradition and the American Dream*. New York: Garland, 1988.

Dawidoff, Robert. *The Genteel Tradition and the Sacred Rage: High Culture vs. Democracy in Adams, James, and Santayana*. Chapel Hill: University of North Carolina Press, 1992.

—. 'Introduction to the Bison Books Edition'. In *The Genteel Tradition: Nine Essays by George Santayana*. Ed. Douglas L. Wilson, vii–xx. Lincoln: University of Nebraska Press, 1998.

Dawson, Jan Carletta. *The Unusable Past: America's Puritan Tradition, 1830 to 1930*. Chico, CA: Scholars Press, 1984.

Decker, William Merrill. 'Autobiography, Education: Henry Adams and the Definition of a Genre'. *A/b: Auto/Biography Studies* 33, no. 1 (2018): 47–63.

—. *The Literary Vocation of Henry Adams*. Chapel Hill, NC, and London: University of North Carolina Press, 1990.

'The Degradation of Politics'. *Century* 29, no. 3 (January 1885): 460–1, <https://babel.hathitrust.org/cgi/pt?id=coo.31924079633339&view=1up&seq=470> (last accessed 5 July 2020).

Dickerson, Vanessa D. *Dark Victorians*. Urbana: University of Illinois Press, 2008.

Dolan, Neal. *Emerson's Liberalism*. Madison: University of Wisconsin Press, 2009.

Dowling, Linda C. *Charles Eliot Norton: The Art of Reform in Nineteenth-Century America*. Hanover, NH: University Press of New England, 2007.

—. *The Vulgarization of Art: The Victorians and Aesthetic Democracy*. Charlottesville: University Press of Virginia, 1996.

Du Bois, W. E. B., ed. *The College-Bred Negro*. Atlanta: Atlanta University Press, 1900, <http://archive.org/details/collegebrednegr00univgoog> (last accessed 5 July 2020).

—. 'A Negro Student at Harvard at the End of the 19th Century'. *The Massachusetts Review* 1, no. 3 (Spring 1960): 439–58, <www.jstor.org/stable/24494510> (last accessed 5 July 2020).

—. 'The Philosophy of Mr. Dole'. *The Crisis* 8 (May 1914): 24–6, <https://onlinebooks.library.upenn.edu/webbin/serial?id=crisisnaacp> (last accessed 5 July 2020).

—. *Writings*. New York: The Library of America, 1986.

Dudley, T. U. 'How Shall We Help the Negro?' *Century* 28 (June 1885): 273–80, <https://babel.hathitrust.org/cgi/pt?id=coo.31924079630327&view=1up&seq=283> (last accessed 5 July 2020).

Duquette, Elizabeth. *Loyal Subjects: Bonds of Nation, Race, and Allegiance in Nineteenth-Century America*. New Brunswick, NJ: Rutgers University Press, 2010, <https://www.jstor.org/stable/j.ctt5hhxqs> (last accessed 5 July 2020).

During, Simon. *Against Democracy: Literary Experience in the Era of Emancipations*. New York: Fordham University Press, 2012.

Dyer, Thomas G. *Theodore Roosevelt and the Idea of Race*. Baton Rouge: Louisiana State University Press, 1980.

Dykstra, Natalie. *Clover Adams: A Gilded and Heartbreaking Life*. Boston: Houghton Mifflin Harcourt, 2012.

Edwards, Brent Hayes. *The Practice of Diaspora: Literature, Translation, and the Rise of Black Internationalism*. Cambridge, MA: Harvard University Press, 2003.

Eliot, Charles William. 'Address at the Dedication of the Provincetown Monument to the Pilgrims, 1910' (Box 224, Folder 349). Records of the President of Harvard University, Charles W. Eliot, 1869–1930. UAI 5.150. Harvard University Archives, Cambridge, MA.

—. 'Address of President Eliot'. In *The Work and Influence of Hampton*, 562–6. New York: Armstrong Association, 1904.

—. *American Contributions to Civilization*. New York: Century, 1897, <http://archive.org/details/americancontrib00unkngoog> (last accessed 5 July 2020).

—. *Charles W. Eliot, the Man and His Beliefs*. Ed. William Allan Neilson. 2 vols. New York and London: Harper & Brothers, 1926.

—. 'Diversity and Unity in Family, College, and State,' 20 March 1911 (Box 24, Folder 364). Records of the President of Harvard University, Charles W. Eliot, 1869–1930. UAI 5.150. Harvard University Archives, Cambridge, MA.

—. 'What Is a Liberal Education?' *Century* 28 (June 1885): 203–12, <https://babel.hathitrust.org/cgi/pt?id=coo.31924079630343&view=1up&seq=213> (last accessed 5 July 2020).

Eliot, T. S. 'In Memory of Henry James'. In *The Complete Prose of T. S. Eliot: The Critical Edition: Apprentice Years, 1905–1918*. Ed. T. S. Eliot, Jewel Spears Brooker and Ronald Schuchard, 648–52. Baltimore: Johns Hopkins University Press and Faber & Faber, 2014.

—. *The Poems of T. S. Eliot*. 2 vols. London: Faber & Faber, 2015.

Ellis, Cristin. *Antebellum Posthuman: Race and Materiality in the Mid-Nineteenth Century*. New York: Fordham University Press, 2018.

Emerson, Edward Waldo. 'Charles Eliot Norton: The Man and the Scholar'. In *Charles Eliot Norton: Two Addresses*, 3–40. Boston and New York: Houghton Mifflin, 1912, <https://archive.org/details/cu31924022030237/page/n12> (last accessed 5 July 2020).

Emerson, Ralph Waldo. 'The American Scholar'. In *Ralph Waldo Emerson*. Ed. Richard Poirier, 37–52. New York: Oxford University Press.
—. 'Aspects of Culture'. *Atlantic Monthly* 21 (January 1868): 87–95, <https://babel.hathitrust.org/cgi/pt?id=hvd.hny8wa&view=1up&seq=97> (last accessed 5 July 2020).
English, Daylanne K. *Unnatural Selections: Eugenics in American Modernism and the Harlem Renaissance*. Chapel Hill: University of North Carolina Press, 2004. ProQuest Ebook Central.
Evans, Stephanie Y. *Black Women in the Ivory Tower, 1850–1954: An Intellectual History*. Gainesville: University Press of Florida, 2007. ProQuest Ebook Central.
'Exercises at Memorial Hall'. *Harvard Graduate's Magazine* 18 (December 1909): 282–4, <https://babel.hathitrust.org/cgi/pt?id=hvd.32044092663343&view=1up&seq=332> (last accessed 5 July 2020).
Farrell, Molly. 'Dying Instruction: Puritan Pedagogy in Uncle Tom's Cabin'. *American Literature* 82, no. 2 (1 June 2010): 243–69.
Faulkner, Carol. *Women's Radical Reconstruction: The Freedmen's Aid Movement*. Philadelphia: University of Pennsylvania Press, 2007.
Field, Emily Donaldson. 'The Souls of Henry Adams: Du Boisian Aspects of The Education'. *Arizona Quarterly: A Journal of American Literature, Culture, and Theory* 67, no. 3 (2011): 61–90.
Fisher, Laura R. *Reading for Reform: The Social Work of Literature in the Progressive Era*. Minneapolis: University of Minnesota Press, 2018.
Fleissner, Jennifer. 'The Ordering Power of Disorder: Henry Adams and the Return of the Darwinian Era'. *American Literature* 84, no. 1 (2012): 31.
—. 'Wharton, Marriage, and the New Woman'. In *The Cambridge History of the American Novel*. Ed. Leonard Cassuto, Clare Virginia Eby and Benjamin Reiss, 452–69. Cambridge: Cambridge University Press, 2011.
—. *Women, Compulsion, Modernity: The Moment of American Naturalism*. Chicago: University of Chicago Press, 2004.
Fluck, Winfried. 'Power Relations in the Novels of James: The "Liberal" and the "Radical" Version'. In *Enacting History in Henry James: Narrative, Power, and Ethics*. Ed. Gert Buelens, 16–39. Cambridge: Cambridge University Press, 1997.
Foner, Eric. *The Story of American Freedom*. New York: W. W. Norton, 1998.
Freedman, Jonathan L. *Professions of Taste: Henry James, British Aestheticism and Commodity Culture*. Stanford: Stanford University Press, 1990.
—. *The Temple of Culture: Assimilation and Anti-Semitism in Literary Anglo-America*. New York: Oxford University Press, 2000.
'French Ways and Their Meaning'. *The New Republic* 20, no. 255 (24 September 1919): 241, <https://babel.hathitrust.org/cgi/pt?id=hvd.hxqfnm&view=1up&seq=263> (last accessed 5 July 2020).
Fuller, Randall. *Emerson's Ghosts: Literature, Politics, and the Making of Americanists*. New York: Oxford University Press, 2007. Oxford Scholarship Online.

Gaines, Kevin Kelly. *Uplifting the Race: Black Leadership, Politics, and Culture in the Twentieth Century*. Chapel Hill: University of North Carolina Press, 1996.

Georgini, Sara. *Household Gods: The Religious Lives of the Adams Family*. New York: Oxford University Press, 2019.

Glazener, Nancy. *Reading for Realism: The History of a U.S. Literary Institution, 1850–1910*. Durham, NC: Duke University Press, 1997.

Godkin, Edwin Lawrence. 'The Duty of Educated Men in a Democracy'. *The Forum* 17 (March 1894): 39–51, <https://babel.hathitrust.org/cgi/pt?id=mdp.39015030768959&view=1up&seq=47> (last accessed 5 July 2020).

—. *Unforeseen Tendencies of Democracy*. Boston and New York: Houghton, Mifflin, 1898.

Goodlad, Lauren M. E. 'Liberalism and Literature'. In *The Oxford Handbook of Victorian Literary Culture*. Ed. Juliet John. Oxford: Oxford University Press, 2016, <https://doi.org/10.1093/oxfordhb/9780199593736.013.22> (last accessed 27 July 2020).

Goodman, Susan. *Edith Wharton's Women: Friends & Rivals*. Hanover, NH: University Press of New England, 1990.

Gossett, Thomas F. *Race: The History of an Idea in America*. New York: Oxford University Press, 1997.

Gradert, Kenyon. *Puritan Spirits in the Abolitionist Imagination*. Chicago: University of Chicago Press, 2020.

Grady, Henry W. 'In Plain Black and White'. *Century* 29, no. 7 (1885): 909–17, <https://babel.hathitrust.org/cgi/pt?id=coo.31924079633339&view=1up&seq=919> (last accessed 5 July 2020).

Graff, Gerald. *Professing Literature: An Institutional History*. Chicago: University of Chicago Press, 1987.

'The Great Minds of America. II. Charles William Eliot'. *The North American Review* 186, no. 624 (1907): 321–6, <www.jstor.org/stable/25106017> (last accessed 5 July 2020).

Gustafson, Sandra M. 'Henry Adams, Political Reform, and the Legacy of the Republican Roman Senate'. *Classical Receptions Journal* 7, no. 1 (2015): 97–112, <https://doi.org/10.1093/crj/clu010> (last accessed 5 July 2020).

Habegger, Alfred. *Henry James and the 'Woman Business'*. Cambridge: Cambridge University Press, 1989.

Hadley, Elaine. *Living Liberalism: Practical Citizenship in Mid-Victorian Britain*. Chicago: University of Chicago Press, 2010.

Hall, Catherine. *Civilising Subjects: Metropole and Colony in the English Imagination, 1830–1867*. Oxford: Polity, 2002.

Hall, David D. 'The Victorian Connection'. *American Quarterly* 27, no. 5 (1975): 561–74.

Halpern, Faye. 'Searching for Sentimentality in Henry James's *The Bostonians*'. *The Henry James Review* 39, no. 1 (Winter 2018): 62–80.

Hammond, Mason. 'The Enclosure of the Harvard Yard'. *Harvard Library Bulletin* 31, no. 4 (1 October 1983): 340–83.

Hartman, Saidiya V. *Scenes of Subjection: Terror, Slavery, and Self-Making in Nineteenth-Century America*. New York: Oxford University Press, 1997.

Harvie, Christopher. *The Lights of Liberalism: University Liberals and the Challenge of Democracy, 1860–86*. London: Allen Lane, 1976.

Haviland, Beverly. *Henry James's Last Romance: Making Sense of the Past and the American Scene*. Cambridge and New York: Cambridge University Press, 1997.

Hawkins, Hugh. *Between Harvard and America: The Educational Leadership of Charles W. Eliot*. New York: Oxford University Press, 1972.

Haytock, Jennifer. *Edith Wharton and the Conversations of Literary Modernism*. New York and Basingstoke: Palgrave Macmillan, 2008.

—. 'Edith Wharton and the Writing of Whiteness'. In *The New Edith Wharton Studies*. Ed. Jennifer Haytock, 158–72. Cambridge: Cambridge University Press, 2019, <https://doi.org/10.1017/9781108525275> (last accessed 5 July 2020).

Henry, Katherine. *Liberalism and the Culture of Security: The Nineteenth-Century Rhetoric of Reform*. Tuscaloosa: University of Alabama Press, 2011.

Herford, Oliver. *Henry James's Style of Retrospect: Late Personal Writings, 1890–1915*. Oxford: Oxford University Press, 2016.

Herman, Arthur. *The Idea of Decline in Western History*. New York: Free Press, 1997.

Higginson, Thomas Wentworth. 'Americanism in Literature'. *Atlantic Monthly*, January 1870, <https://babel.hathitrust.org/cgi/pt?id=chi.78035620&view=1up&seq=68> (last accessed 5 July 2020).

Hochman, Barbara. 'Reading Historically/Reading Selectively: *The Bostonians* in the *Century*, 1885–1886'. *The Henry James Review* 34, no. 3 (Fall 2013): 270–8.

Hofstadter, Richard. *Anti-Intellectualism in American Life*. New York: Vintage, 1962.

Hoganson, Kristin L. *Fighting for American Manhood: How Gender Politics Provoked the Spanish–American and Philippine–American Wars*. New Haven: Yale University Press, 1998.

—. 'Harvard Men: From Dudes to Rough Riders'. In *Yards and Gates*. Ed. Laurel Thatcher Ulrich, 117–28. New York: Palgrave Macmillan, 2004.

Hoogenboom, Ari Arthur. *Outlawing the Spoils: A History of the Civil Service Reform Movement, 1865–1883*. Chicago: University of Illinois Press, 1968.

Hoopes, James. *Van Wyck Brooks: In Search of American Culture*. Amherst: University of Massachusetts Press, 1977.

Horne, Philip. 'Poodle and Bull Moose'. *TLS* (11 June 2014): 13–15.

—. '"Reinstated": James in Roosevelt's Washington'. *The Cambridge Quarterly* 37, no. 1 (2008): 47–63, <https://www.muse.jhu.edu/article/233418> (last accessed 5 July 2020).
Horsman, Reginald. *Race and Manifest Destiny: The Origins of American Racial Anglo-Saxonism*. Cambridge, MA: Harvard University Press, 1981.
The 'How I Was Educated' Papers: From the Forum Magazine. New York: Appleton, 1888, <https://archive.org/details/howiwaseducatedp00newy/page/n6/mode/2up> (last accessed 5 July 2020).
Howe, Daniel Walker. 'The Genteel Tradition'. *Reviews in American History* 2, no. 2 (1974): 243–8.
Howe, M. A. DeWolfe. *Barrett Wendell and His Letters*. Boston: Atlantic Monthly Press, 1924.
—. 'A Packet of Wendell–James Letters'. *Scribner's* (December 1928): 674–87.
Howells, William Dean. 'Charles Eliot Norton: A Reminiscence'. *North American Review* 198 (December 1913): 836–48, <https://www.jstor.org/stable/25151010> (last accessed 5 July 2020).
—. 'Editor's Study'. *Harper's*, July 1888, <https://babel.hathitrust.org/cgi/pt?id=hvd.hnybin&view=1up&seq=326> (last accessed 5 July 2020).
Hsu, Hsuan. 'Post-American James and the Question of Scale'. *The Henry James Review* 24, no. 3 (2003): 233–43.
James III, Henry. *Charles W. Eliot, President of Harvard University, 1869–1909*. 2 vols. London: Constable, 1930.
James, Henry. *The American*. New York: Penguin, 1986.
—. *The American Essays*. Ed. Leon Edel. Princeton: Princeton University Press, 1989.
—. *The American Scene*. New York: Penguin, 1994.
—. *The Bostonians*. Ed. Daniel Karlin. Cambridge: Cambridge University Press, 2019.
—. *The Complete Notebooks of Henry James*. Ed. Leon Edel and Lyall H. Powers. New York: Oxford University Press, 1987.
—. *Henry James on Culture: Collected Essays on Politics and the American Social Scene*. Ed. Pierre A. Walker. Lincoln: University of Nebraska Press, 1999.
—. *Henry James Letters*. Ed. Leon Edel. 4 vols. London: Macmillan, 1974.
—. *Henry James: A Life in Letters*. Ed. Philip Horne. New York: Viking Penguin, 1999.
—. *The Letters of Henry James*. Ed. Percy Lubbock. 2 vols. London: Macmillan, 1920, <http://archive.org/details/lettersofhenryja01jamerich> (last accessed 5 July 2020).
—. *Literary Criticism*. 2 vols. New York: Library of America, 1984.
—. *Notes of a Son and Brother, and The Middle Years: A Critical Edition*. Charlottesville: University of Virginia Press, 2011.
—. *Portrait of a Lady*. New York: Oxford World's Classics, 2009.
—. *The Princess Casamassima*. Ed. Adrian Poole. Cambridge: Cambridge University Press, 2019.

—. *The Spoils of Poynton*. New York: Penguin, 1987.
James, Joy. *Transcending the Talented Tenth: Black Leaders and American Intellectuals*. New York and London: Routledge, 1997.
James, William. *Correspondence of William James*. 3 vols. Ed. Ignas K. Skrupskelis and Elizabeth M. Berkeley. Charlottesville: University of Virginia Press, 1992–4.
—. 'The Social Value of the College-Bred'. *McClure's* 30, no. 4 (February 1908): 419–22.
James, William, and Henry James. *William and Henry James: Selected Letters*. Ed. Ignas K. Skrupskelis and Elizabeth M. Berkeley. Charlottesville: University of Virginia Press, 1997.
Jenkins, C. N. 'A Plea for National Aid to Education'. *Century* 30 (September 1885): 810–11, <https://babel.hathitrust.org/cgi/pt?id=coo.31924079630327&view=1up&seq=820> (last accessed 5 July 2020).
John, Arthur. *The Best Years of the Century: Richard Watson Gilder, Scribner's Monthly, and the Century Magazine, 1870–1909*. Urbana: University of Illinois Press, 1981.
Johnson, Kendall. 'Henry James and the China Trade'. *Modern Fiction Studies* 60, no. 4 (29 December 2014): 677–710.
Kaledin, Eugenia. *The Education of Mrs. Henry Adams*. Philadelphia: Temple University Press, 1981.
Kallen, Horace. 'Democracy Versus the Melting Pot (Part I)'. *The Nation*, 18 February 1915, 190–4.
Kammen, Michael G. *Mystic Chords of Memory: The Transformation of Tradition in American Culture*. New York: Knopf, 1991.
Kassanoff, Jennie A. *Edith Wharton and the Politics of Race*. Cambridge: Cambridge University Press, 2004.
Kendi, Ibram X. *Stamped from the Beginning: The Definitive History of Racist Ideas in America*. New York: Nation Books, 2016.
Kent, Christopher. *Brains and Numbers: Elitism, Comtism, and Democracy in Mid-Victorian England*. Buffalo: University of Toronto Press, 1978.
Kirsch, Geoffrey R. 'Innocence and the Arena: Wharton, Roosevelt, and Good Citizenship'. *American Literary Realism* 51, no. 3 (2019): 200–19, <https://www.muse.jhu.edu/article/721145> (last accessed 5 July 2020).
Kittelstrom, Amy. *The Religion of Democracy: Seven Liberals and the American Moral Tradition*. New York: Penguin, 2015.
Kloppenberg, James T. *Uncertain Victory: Social Democracy and Progressivism in European and American Thought, 1870–1920*. New York and Oxford: Oxford University Press, 1986.
Knights, Ben. *The Idea of the Clerisy in the Nineteenth Century*. New York: Cambridge University Press, 1978.
Konstantinou, Lee. *Cool Characters: Irony and American Fiction*. Cambridge, MA: Harvard University Press, 2016.
Kornbluh, Anna. *The Order of Forms: Realism, Formalism, and Social Space*. Chicago: University of Chicago Press, 2019.

—. 'The Realist Blueprint'. *The Henry James Review* 36, no. 3 (11 November 2015): 199–211.
Lapsley, Gaillard. *The America of Today*. Cambridge: Cambridge University Press, 1919.
Laski, Gregory. *Untimely Democracy: The Politics of Progress after Slavery*. New York: Oxford University Press, 2017. Oxford Scholarship Online, 2017.
Lazarus, Emma. *The Poems of Emma Lazarus*. Boston: Houghton, Mifflin, 1889, <http://archive.org/details/poemsemmalazaru04lazagoog> (last accessed 5 July 2020).
Lears, T. J. Jackson. 'The Managerial Revitalization of the Rich'. In *Ruling America: A History of Wealth and Power in a Democracy*. Ed. Steve Fraser and Gary Gerstle, 181–214. Cambridge, MA: Harvard University Press, 2005.
—. *No Place of Grace: Antimodernism and the Transformation of American Culture, 1880–1920*. New York: Pantheon, 1981.
Lecourt, Sebastian. *Cultivating Belief: Victorian Anthropology, Liberal Aesthetics, and the Secular Imagination*. Oxford: Oxford University Press, 2018.
'Lectures'. *Boston Evening Transcript*, 11 December 1876, <https://news.google.com/newspapers?nid=sArNgO4T4MoC&dat=18761211&printsec=frontpage&hl=en> (last accessed 5 July 2020).
Lee, Hermione. *Edith Wharton*. New York: Alfred A. Knopf, 2007.
Levander, Caroline. *Cradle of Liberty: Race, the Child, and National Belonging from Thomas Jefferson to W. E. B. Du Bois*. Durham, NC: Duke University Press, 2006.
Levenson, J. C. 'The Etiology of Israel Adams: The Onset, Waning, and Relevance of Henry Adams's Anti-Semitism'. *New Literary History* 25, no. 3 (1 July 1994): 569–600.
—. 'Henry Adams, U.S. Grant, and Evolution: Practicing History in the Age of Darwin'. In *Henry Adams & the Need to Know*. Ed. William Merrill Decker and Earl N. Harbert, 104–37. Charlottesville: University of Virginia Press, 2005.
Levine, Caroline. *Forms: Whole, Rhythm, Hierarchy, Network*. Princeton: Princeton University Press, 2015.
Levine, Lawrence W. *Highbrow/Lowbrow: The Emergence of Cultural Hierarchy in America*. New Haven: Harvard University Press, 1988.
Lewis, David L. *W. E. B. DuBois: Biography of a Race, 1868–1919*. New York: Henry Holt, 1993.
Lewis, R. W. B. *Edith Wharton: A Biography*. New York: Fromm International, 1985.
Lindgren, James Michael. *Preserving Historic New England: Preservation, Progressivism, and the Remaking of Memory*. New York: Oxford University Press, 1995.
Losurdo, Domenico. *Liberalism: A Counter-History*. Trans. Gregory Elliott. London and New York: Verso, 2011.

Lowe, Lisa. *The Intimacies of Four Continents*. Durham, NC: Duke University Press, 2015.
Lubbock, Percy. *Portrait of Edith Wharton*. London: Jonathan Cape, 1947.
Lustig, T. J. 'James, Arnold, "Culture," and "Modernity"; or, A Tale of Two Dachshunds'. *The Cambridge Quarterly* 37, no. 1 (2008): 164–93.
McClay, Wilfred M. 'Two Versions of the Genteel Tradition: Santayana and Brooks'. *New England Quarterly* 55, no. 3 (1982): 368–91.
Maher, Jane. *Biography of Broken Fortunes: Wilkie and Bob, Brothers of William, Henry, and Alice James*. Hamden, CT: Archon, 1986, <http://archive.org/details/biographyofbroke00mahe> (last accessed 5 July 2020).
Margolis, Stacey. *Fictions of Mass Democracy in Nineteenth-Century America*. Cambridge: Cambridge University Press, 2015.
May, Henry F. *The End of American Innocence: A Study of the First Years of Our Own Time, 1912–1917*. New York: Knopf, 1959.
Meehan, Sean Ross. *A Liberal Education in Late Emerson: Readings in the Rhetoric of Mind*. Rochester, NY: Camden House, 2019, <https://www.jstor.org/stable/j.ctv6jmbd3> (last accessed 5 July 2020).
Mehta, Uday Singh. *Liberalism and Empire: A Study in Nineteenth-Century British Liberal Thought*. Chicago: University of Chicago Press, 1999.
Menand, Louis. *The Metaphysical Club*. New York: Farrar, Straus, and Giroux, 2001.
Mencken, H. L. *Prejudices: Fourth, Fifth, and Sixth Series*. New York: Library of America, 2010.
Mill, John Stuart. *Collected Works of John Stuart Mill*. 33 vols. Ed. John M. Robson. Toronto: University of Toronto Press, 1963–1991.
Mills, Charles W. *Black Rights/White Wrongs: The Critique of Racial Liberalism*. New York: Oxford University Press, 2017.
Moreland, Kim Ileen. *The Medievalist Impulse in American Literature: Twain, Adams, Fitzgerald, and Hemingway*. Charlottesville: University Press of Virginia, 1996.
Morley, John. 'Matthew Arnold'. *The Nineteenth Century* (December 1895): 1041–55. ProQuest British Periodicals.
—. 'Young England and the Political Future'. *Fortnightly Review* (April 1867): 491–6. ProQuest British Periodicals.
Murphy, Kevin P. *Political Manhood: Red Bloods, Mollycoddles, & the Politics of Progressive Era Reform*. New York: Columbia University Press, 2008.
Nelson, Dana D. *Commons Democracy: Reading the Politics of Participation in the Early United States*. New York: Fordham University Press, 2016.
Noonan, Mark J. *Reading The Century Illustrated Monthly Magazine: American Literature and Culture, 1870–1893*. Kent, OH: Kent State University Press, 2010.
Norton, Charles Eliot. 'Address of Charles Eliot Norton'. In *The Centenary of the Birth of Ralph Waldo Emerson as Observed in Concord, May*

25, 1903, 45–58. Concord, MA: Riverside Press, 1903, <https://archive.org/details/emersoncentenary00concrich/page/n8> (last accessed 5 July 2020).
—. 'Address to Radcliffe Graduates'. *Harvard Graduate's Magazine* 10 (September 1901): 38–45, <https://babel.hathitrust.org/cgi/pt?id=hvd.32044107292609&view=2up&seq=54> (last accessed 5 July 2020).
—. 'Bryn Mawr College: Commencement Address'. bMS Am 1088.5 (Box 1). Houghton Library, Harvard University.
—. 'A Criticism of Harvard Architecture Made to the Board of Overseers'. *Harvard Graduate's Magazine* 12 (March 1904): 359–62, <https://babel.hathitrust.org/cgi/pt?id=hvd.32044107292583&view=1up&seq=407> (last accessed 5 July 2020).
—. 'The Culture of the Imagination'. bMS Am 1088.5 (Box 1). Houghton Library, Harvard University.
—. 'Female Suffrage and Education'. *The Nation* 5 (22 August 1867): 152.
—. 'Harvard'. In *Four American Universities*, 3–43. New York: Harper & Brothers, 1895, <https://archive.org/details/fouramericaniv02nort/page/14> (last accessed 5 July 2020).
—. 'The Intellectual Life of America'. *New Princeton Review* (November 1888): 312–24, <https://babel.hathitrust.org/cgi/pt?id=nyp.33433081665337&view=1up&seq=320> (last accessed 5 July 2020).
—, ed. 'Introduction'. In *First Book*, Heart of Oak Books, rev. edn, 6 vols. Boston: D. C. Heath, 1903, <https://archive.org/details/heartoakbooks-06nortgoog/page/n10> (last accessed 5 July 2020).
—. 'James Russell Lowell'. *Harper's* 86 (May 1893): 846–57, <https://babel.hathitrust.org/cgi/pt?id=uc1.31210010305728&view=1up&seq=852> (last accessed 5 July 2020).
—. *Letters of Charles Eliot Norton*. 2 vols. Ed. Sara Norton and M. A. DeWolfe Howe. Boston: Houghton Mifflin, 1913.
—. 'The Life and Character of George William Curtis'. In *Memorials of Two Friends, James Russell Lowell: 1819–1891, George William Curtis: 1824–1892*. New York: Privately printed, 1902, <http://archive.org/details/memorialsoftwofr00curt> (last accessed 5 July 2020).
—. 'Some Aspects of Civilization in America'. *The Forum* 20 (February 1896): 641–51, <https://babel.hathitrust.org/cgi/pt?id=mdp.39015013275154&view=2up&seq=650> (last accessed 5 July 2020).
Nowlin, Michael. 'Edith Wharton's Higher Provincialism: *French Ways* for Americans and the Ends of *The Age of Innocence*'. *Journal of American Studies* 38, no. 1 (2004): 89–108, <www.jstor.org/stable/27557465> (last accessed 5 July 2020).
Nussbaum, Martha C. 'Perception and Revolution: *The Princess Casamassima* and the Political Imagination'. In *Love's Knowledge: Essays on Philosophy and Literature*. 195–219. New York: Oxford University Press, 1990.
Olin-Ammentorp, Julie. *Edith Wharton's Writings from the Great War*. Gainesville: University Press of Florida, 2004.

Orr, John C. '"I Measured Her as They Did with Pigs": Henry Adams as Other'. In *Henry Adams & the Need to Know*. Ed. William Merrill Decker and Earl N. Harbert, 273–99. Boston and Chartotteville: Massachusetts Historical Society; distributed by the University of Virginia Press, 2005.

Painter, Nell Irvin. *The History of White People*. New York: W. W. Norton, 2010.

Parrington, Vernon Louis. *Main Currents in American Thought*. 3 vols. New Brunswick, NJ: Transaction, 2011–13.

—. 'Our Literary Aristocrat'. In *Edith Wharton: A Collection of Critical Essays*. Ed. Irving Howe, 151–4. Englewood Cliffs, NJ: Prentice-Hall, 1962.

Partenheimer, David. 'Henry Adams's "Primitive Rights of Women": An Offense against Church, the Patriarchal State, Progressive Evolution, and the Women's Liberation Movement'. *The New England Quarterly* 71, no. 4 (1998): 635–42.

Pater, Walter. *The Renaissance*. New York: Oxford University Press, 1998. Oxford World's Classics.

Paul, Diane B., and Benjamin Day. 'John Stuart Mill, Innate Differences, and the Regulation of Reproduction'. *Studies in History and Philosophy of Biological and Biomedical Sciences* 39, no. 2 (2008): 222–31.

Peel, Robin. *Apart from Modernism: Edith Wharton, Politics, and Fiction before World War I*. Madison, NJ: Fairleigh Dickinson University Press, 2005.

Pelletier, Kevin, Claudia Stokes and Abram Van Engen. 'The Last Cleric: Ann Douglas, Intellectual Authority, and the Legacy of *Feminization*'. *J19* 7, no. 1 (Spring 2019): 185–208.

Perry, Bliss. 'The Adamses'. *The Yale Review* 20 (Winter 1931): 380–3.

—. *And Gladly Teach*. Boston and New York: Houghton, Mifflin, 1935.

Perry, Thomas Sergeant. 'An American on American Humour'. *St James's Gazette*, 5 July 1883, 5–6.

Petit, Jeanne D. *The Men and Women We Want: Gender, Race, and the Progressive Era Literacy Test Debate*. Rochester, NY: University of Rochester Press, 2010, <https://www.jstor.org/stable/10.7722/j.ctt81ns7> (last accessed 5 July 2020).

Phillips, Wendell. *The Scholar in a Republic*. Boston: Lee and Shepard, 1881, <http://archive.org/details/scholarinrepubli01phil> (last accessed 5 July 2020).

Poirier, Richard. 'The Vapor Trail of Charles Eliot Norton'. *New Republic* 222, no. 19 (2000): 25–33.

Posnock, Ross. '1904: Henry James in America'. In *A New Literary History of America*. Ed. Greil Marcus and Werner Sollors, 488–93. Cambridge, MA: Harvard University Press, 2009.

—. 'Affirming the Alien: The Pragmatist Pluralism of The American Scene'. In *The Cambridge Companion to Henry James*. Ed. Jonathan Freedman, 224–46. Cambridge: Cambridge University Press, 1998.

—. *Color and Culture: Black Writers and the Making of the Modern Intellectual*. Cambridge, MA: Harvard University Press, 1998.
—. 'Henry James and the Limits of Historicism'. *The Henry James Review* 16, no. 3 (1 November 1995): 273–7.
—. *The Trial of Curiosity: Henry James, William James, and the Challenge of Modernity*. New York: Oxford University Press, 1991.
Pratt, Lloyd. *The Strangers Book: The Human of African American Literature*. Philadelphia: University of Pennsylvania Press, 2016.
'Prejudice and Progress'. *Century* 30 (October 1885): 965–7, <https://babel.hathitrust.org/cgi/pt?id=coo.31924079630327&view=1up&seq=975> (last accessed 5 July 2020).
Pugh, Evelyn. 'John Stuart Mill, Harriet Taylor, and Women's Rights in America, 1850–1873'. *Canadian Journal of History/Annales Canadiennes d'Histoire* 13, no. 3 (1978): 423–42.
Raber, Jesse. *Progressivism's Aesthetic Education: The Bildungsroman and the American School, 1890–1920*. New York: Palgrave Macmillan, 2018.
Raleigh, John Henry. *Matthew Arnold and American Culture*. Berkeley: University of California Press, 1957.
Ramsden, George. *Edith Wharton's Library: A Catalogue*. York: Stone Trough, 1999.
Rattray, Laura. 'Edith Wharton's Unprivileged Lives'. In *The New Edith Wharton Studies*. Ed. Jennifer Haytock, 113–28. Cambridge: Cambridge University Press, 2019, <https://doi.org/10.1017/9781108525275> (last accessed 5 July 2020).
Rauchway, Eric. 'Regarding Henry: The Feminist Henry Adams'. *American Studies* 40, no. 3 (1999): 53–73.
Renker, Elizabeth. 'The "Genteel Tradition" and Its Discontents'. In *The Cambridge History of American Poetry*. Ed. Alfred Bendixen and Stephen Burt, 403–24. Cambridge: Cambridge University Press, 2014, <http://dx.doi.org/10.1017/CHO9780511762284> (last accessed 5 July 2020).
—. *The Origins of American Literature Studies: An Institutional History*. Cambridge: Cambridge University Press, 2007.
'Review of *Sex in Education; Or, a Fair Chance for the Girls*, by Edward H. Clarke'. *The North American Review* 118, no. 242 (1874): 140–52, <https://www.jstor.org/stable/25109791> (last accessed 5 July 2020).
Reynolds, David S. *John Brown, Abolitionist: The Man Who Killed Slavery, Sparked the Civil War, and Seeded Civil Rights*. New York: Vintage, 2005.
Riss, Arthur. *Race, Slavery, and Liberalism in Nineteenth-Century American Literature*. New York: Cambridge University Press, 2006.
Rivett, Sarah, and Abram Van Engen. 'Postexceptionalist Puritanism'. *American Literature* 90, no. 4 (1 December 2018): 675–92.
Roosevelt, Theodore. *Address of President Roosevelt on the Occasion of the Laying of the Corner Stone of the Pilgrim Memorial Monument*. Washington, DC: Government Printing Office, 1907, <https://catalog.hathitrust.org/Record/009560073> (last accessed 5 July 2020).

—. *American Ideals*. New York: G. P. Putnam, 1897, <https://archive.org/details/americanidealsa00roosgoog/page/n11> (last accessed 5 July 2020).

—. 'The College Graduate and Public Life'. *Atlantic Monthly* 74 (August 1894): 255–60, <https://babel.hathitrust.org/cgi/pt?id=chi.78024063&view=1up&seq=267> (last accessed 5 July 2020).

—. 'The Manly Virtues and Practical Politics'. *The Forum* 17 (July 1894): 551–7, <https://babel.hathitrust.org/cgi/pt?id=uc1.31210014861213&view=1up&seq=273> (last accessed 5 July 2020).

Rosenbaum, Julia B. *Visions of Belonging: New England Art and the Making of American Identity*. Ithaca: Cornell University Press, 2006.

Rowe, John Carlos. 'Nationalism and Imperialism'. In *Henry James in Context*. Ed. David McWhirter, 246–57. Cambridge: Cambridge University Press, 2010.

Rubin, Joan Shelley. 'The Genteel Tradition at Large'. In *Cultural Considerations: Essays on Readers, Writers, and Musicians in Postwar America*, 11–28. Amherst: University of Massachusetts Press, 2013. ProQuest Ebook Central.

—. *The Making of Middlebrow Culture*. Chapel Hill: University of North Carolina Press, 1992.

Salazar, James B. *Bodies of Reform: The Rhetoric of Character in Gilded Age America*. New York: New York University Press, 2010.

Salmon, Richard. *Henry James and the Culture of Publicity*. Cambridge: Cambridge University Press, 1997.

Samuels, Ernest. *Henry Adams: The Major Phase*. Cambridge, MA: Belknap Press of Harvard University Press, 1964.

—. *The Young Henry Adams*. Cambridge, MA: Harvard University Press, 1965.

Sánchez-Eppler, Karen. *Touching Liberty: Abolition, Feminism, and the Politics of the Body*. Berkeley: University of California Press, 1993.

Santayana, George. *The Genteel Tradition in American Philosophy; and Character and Opinion in the United States*. New Haven: Yale University Press, 2009.

—. *The Genteel Tradition: Nine Essays by George Santayana*. Ed. Douglas L. Wilson. Lincoln: University of Nebraska Press, 1998.

—. *Persons and Places: Fragments of Autobiography*. Ed. William G. Holzberger and Herman J. Saatkamp Jr. Cambridge, MA: MIT Press, 1986.

Saunderson, Henry Hallam. *Charles W. Eliot, Puritan Liberal*. New York and London: Harper & Brothers, 1928.

Schmidt, Peter. *Sitting in Darkness: New South Fiction, Education, and the Rise of Jim Crow Colonialism, 1865–1920*. Jackson: University Press of Mississippi, 2008.

Schneirov, Matthew. *The Dream of a New Social Order: Popular Magazines in America, 1893–1914*. New York: Columbia University Press, 1994.

Schuller, Kyla. *The Biopolitics of Feeling: Race, Sex, and Science in the Nineteenth Century*. Durham, NC: Duke University Press, 2018.
Sedgwick, Ellery. 'The American Genteel Tradition in the Early Twentieth Century'. *American Studies* 25, no. 1 (1984): 49–67, <https://journals.ku.edu/amerstud/article/view/2575> (last accessed 5 July 2020).
—. *A History of the Atlantic Monthly, 1857–1909: Yankee Humanism at High Tide and Ebb*. Amherst: University of Massachusetts Press, 1994.
—. 'Henry James and the "Atlantic Monthly": Editorial Perspectives on James' "Friction with the Market"'. *Studies in Bibliography* 45 (1 January 1992): 311–32, <www.jstor.org/stable/40371971> (last accessed 5 July 2020).
Seelye, John D. *Memory's Nation: The Place of Plymouth Rock*. Chapel Hill: University of North Carolina Press, 1998.
Seitler, Dana. *Atavistic Tendencies: The Culture of Science in American Modernity*. Minneapolis: University of Minnesota Press, 2008. ProQuest Ebook Central.
Self, Robert T. *Barrett Wendell*. Boston: Twayne, 1975.
Shaheen, Aaron. '"The Social Dusk of That Mysterious Democracy": Race, Sexology, and the New Woman in Henry James's *The Bostonians*'. *American Transcendental Quarterly* 19, no. 4 (2005): 281–99.
Shumway, David R. *Creating American Civilization: A Genealogy of American Literature as an Academic Discipline*. Minneapolis: University of Minnesota Press, 1994.
Singley, Carol J. *Edith Wharton: Matters of Mind and Spirit*. Cambridge: Cambridge University Press, 1995.
Slap, Andrew L. *The Doom of Reconstruction: The Liberal Republicans in the Civil War Era*. New York: Fordham University Press, 2007.
Smith, Crosbie, and Ian Higginson. '"No Traces of a Beginning, No Prospect of an End": Henry Adams, Charles Lyell, & the Politics of Uniformity'. In *Henry Adams & the Need to Know*. Ed. William Merrill Decker and Earl N. Harbert, 104–37. Boston: Massachusetts Historical Society, 2005.
Smith, Herbert F., and Michael Peinovich. '*The Bostonians*: Creation and Revision'. *Bulletin of the New York Public Library* 72 (May 1969): 298–308.
Smith, Rogers M. *Civic Ideals: Conflicting Visions of Citizenship in U.S. History*. New Haven: Yale University Press, 1997.
Sollors, Werner. *Beyond Ethnicity: Consent and Descent in American Culture*. New York: Oxford University Press, 1986.
Solomon, Barbara Miller. *Ancestors and Immigrants: A Changing New England Tradition*. Chicago: University of Chicago Press, 1972.
Sommer, Robert F. 'The Feminine Perspectives of Henry Adams' *Esther*'. *Studies in American Fiction* 18, no. 2 (1990): 131–44.
Speicher, Allison. *Schooling Readers: Reading Common Schools in Nineteenth-Century American Fiction*. Tuscaloosa: University of Alabama Press, 2016.

Sproat, John G. *The Best Men: Liberal Reformers in the Gilded Age*. New York: Oxford University Press, 1968.

Stevens, Nell. *Mrs Gaskell & Me: Two Women, Two Love Stories, Two Centuries Apart*. New York: Picador, 2018.

Stokes, Claudia. *Writers in Retrospect: The Rise of American Literary History, 1875–1910*. Chapel Hill: University of North Carolina Press, 2006.

Stone, Donald David. *Communications with the Future: Matthew Arnold in Dialogue*. Ann Arbor: University of Michigan Press, 1997.

Stowe, Harriet Beecher. *Uncle Tom's Cabin*. New York: Oxford World's Classics, 2008.

Stratton, Matthew. *The Politics of Irony in American Modernism*. New York: Fordham University Press, 2014.

Synnott, Marcia Graham. *The Half-Opened Door: Discrimination and Admissions at Harvard, Yale, and Princeton, 1900–1970*. Westport, CT: Greenwood Press, 1979.

Tamarkin, Elisa. *Anglophilia: Deference, Devotion, and Antebellum America*. Chicago: University of Chicago Press, 2008.

Teichgraeber, Richard F. *Building Culture: Studies in the Intellectual History of Industrializing America, 1867–1910*. Columbia: University of South Carolina Press, 2010.

Tocqueville, Alexis de. *De la démocratie en Amérique*. 2 vols. Paris: Garnier Flammarion, 1981.

Tomsich, John. *A Genteel Endeavor: American Culture and Politics in the Gilded Age*. Stanford: Stanford University Press, 1971.

Townsend, Kim. *Manhood at Harvard: William James and Others*. New York: W. W. Norton, 1996.

Trachtenberg, Alan. *The Incorporation of America: Culture and Society in the Gilded Age*. New York: Hill and Wang, 2007.

Trilling, Lionel. 'The Princess Casamassima'. In *The Liberal Imagination: Essays on Literature and Society*, 58–92. New York: Scribner's, 1976.

—. 'The Smile of Parmenides: George Santayana in His Letters'. *Encounter* (December 1956): 30–7.

Tucker, Amy. *The Illustration of the Master: Henry James and the Magazine Revolution*. Stanford: Stanford University Press, 2010.

Tucker, David M. *Mugwumps: Public Moralists of the Gilded Age*. Columbia: University of Missouri Press, 1998.

Turner, James C. *The Liberal Education of Charles Eliot Norton*. Baltimore: Johns Hopkins University Press, 1999.

Tuttleton, James W. '"The Fruit of the Tree": Justine and the Perils of Abstract Idealism'. In *The Cambridge Companion to Edith Wharton*. Ed. Millicent Bell, 157–68. Cambridge: Cambridge University Press, 1995.

'University Notes'. *Harvard Graduate's Magazine* 16 (September 1907): 205–8, <https://babel.hathitrust.org/cgi/pt?id=hvd.32044107292518&view=1up&seq=231> (last accessed 5 July 2020).

Vance, William L. 'Edith Wharton's Italian Mask: *The Valley of Decision*'. In *The Cambridge Companion to Edith Wharton*. Ed. Millicent Bell, 169–98. New York and Cambridge: Cambridge University Press, 1995.

Vanderbilt, Kermit. *American Literature and the Academy: The Roots, Growth, and Maturity of a Profession*. Philadelphia: University of Pennsylvania Press, 1986.

—. *Charles Eliot Norton: Apostle of Culture in a Democracy*. Cambridge, MA: Belknap Press, 1959.

Vandersee, Charles. 'The Hamlet in Henry Adams'. In *Critical Essays on Henry Adams*. Ed. Earl N. Harbert, 187–210. Boston: G. K. Hall, 1981.

—. 'The Pursuit of Culture in Adams' *Democracy*'. *American Quarterly* 19, no. 2 (1967): 239–48.

'W. E. B. Du Bois: The Activist Life (Online Exhibit)', <http://scua.library.umass.edu/exhibits/dubois/page3.htm> (last accessed 8 December 2019).

Wagoner, Jennings L. 'The American Compromise: Charles W. Eliot, Black Education, and the New South'. In *Education and the Rise of the New South*, 26–46. Boston: G. K. Hall, 1981.

—. 'Charles W. Eliot, Immigrants, and the Decline of American Idealism'. *Biography* 8, no. 1 (1985): 25–36.

Waldstein, Charles. 'The Lesson of Greek Art, Part I, The Education of the People'. *Century* 31, no. 9 (December 1885): 259–71, <https://babel.hathitrust.org/cgi/pt?id=coo.31924079633321&view=1up&seq=269> (last accessed 5 July 2020).

Walker, Pierre A. 'Introduction'. In *Henry James on Culture: Collected Essays on Politics and the American Social Scene*. Ed. Pierre A. Walker, ix–xliv. Lincoln: University of Nebraska Press, 1999.

Warren, Kenneth W. *Black and White Strangers: Race and American Literary Realism*. Chicago: University of Chicago Press, 1993.

—. 'An Inevitable Drift? Oligarchy, Du Bois, and the Politics of Race between the Wars'. *Boundary 2* 27, no. 3 (2000): 153–69, <https://www.muse.jhu.edu/article/3318> (last accessed 5 July 2020).

—. 'Race'. In *Henry James in Context*. Ed. David McWhirter, 280–91. Cambridge: Cambridge University Press, 2010.

—. 'Still Reading Henry James?' *The Henry James Review* 16, no. 3 (1995): 282–5.

—. *What Was African American Literature?* Cambridge, MA: Harvard University Press, 2011.

Wegener, Frederick. 'Form, "Selection," and Ideology in Edith Wharton's Antimodernist Aesthetic'. In *A Forward Glance: New Essays on Edith Wharton*. Ed. Clare Colquitt, Susan Goodman and Candace Waid, 116–38. London: Associated University Presses, 1999.

—. '"Rabid Imperialist": Edith Wharton and the Obligations of Empire in Modern American Fiction'. *American Literature* 72, no. 4 (2000): 783–812.

Weinstein, Cindy. 'From True Woman to New Woman to Virgin'. In *Henry Adams & the Need to Know*. Ed. William Merrill Decker and Earl N. Harbert, 300–14. Massachusetts Historical Society Studies in American History and Culture, no. 8. Boston: Massachusetts Historical Society, 2005.

Wells, H. G. *The Future in America: A Search after Realities*. New York and London: Harper & Brothers, 1906.

Wendell, Barrett. 'Charles Eliot Norton'. *The Atlantic Monthly* 103 (January 1909): 82–8, <https://babel.hathitrust.org/cgi/pt?id=uc1.b000556089&view=1up&seq=96> (last accessed 5 July 2020).

—. *The France of Today*. New York: Scribner's, 1907.

—. *Liberty, Union and Democracy: The National Ideals of America*. New York: Scribner's, 1906.

—. *A Literary History of America*. New York: Scribner's, 1900.

—. *The Privileged Classes*. New York: Scribner's, 1908.

—. *Stelligeri: And Other Essays Concerning America*. New York: Scribner's, 1893.

Wharton, Edith. *The Age of Innocence*. New York: Oxford University Press, 2008.

—. 'America at War: Explaining National Character in 1918'. Trans. Virginia Ricard. *TLS*, 16 February 2018.

—. 'L'Amérique en Guerre'. *La Revue hebdomadaire*, March 1918, <https://gallica.bnf.fr/ark:/12148/bpt6k5814225z> (last accessed 5 July 2020).

—. *A Backward Glance: An Autobiography*. New York: Simon & Schuster, 1998.

—. *Collected Stories, 1891–1910*. New York: Library of America, 2001.

—. *Descent of Man*. New York: Scribner's, 1904, <https://archive.org/details/descentofman00wharrich/page/n7> (last accessed 5 July 2020).

—. *French Ways and Their Meaning*. New York and London: D. Appleton, 1919, <http://archive.org/details/frenchwaystheirm00whar> (last accessed 5 July 2020).

—. *The Fruit of the Tree*. New York: Scribner's, 1907.

—. *The Letters of Edith Wharton*. Ed. R. W. B. Lewis and Nancy Lewis. New York: Charles Scribner's Sons, 1988.

—. *The Uncollected Critical Writings*. Ed. Frederick Wegener. Princeton: Princeton University Press, 1996.

—. *The Valley of Decision*. 2 vols. New York: Scribner's, 1902.

Wharton, Edith, and Ogden Codman. *The Decoration of Houses*. New York: Charles Scribner's Sons, 1897, <http://archive.org/details/decorationofhous00wharrich> (last accessed 5 July 2020).

'What Maisie Knew' (Review). *Literature* 1, no. 1 (23 October 1897): 19.

Wilson, Douglas L. 'Introductory'. In *The Genteel Tradition: Nine Essays by George Santayana*. Ed. Douglas L. Wilson, 1–25. Lincoln: University of Nebraska Press, 1998.

Wilson, Ivy G. *Specters of Democracy: Blackness and the Aesthetics of Politics in the Antebellum U.S.* New York and Oxford: Oxford University Press, 2011.

Wilson, Woodrow. 'University Training and Citizenship'. *The Forum* (September 1894): 107–16, <https://babel.hathitrust.org/cgi/pt?id=uc1.31210015302340&view=2up&seq=134> (last accessed 5 July 2020).

Zacharias, Greg. 'Liberal London, Home, and Henry James's Letters from the Later 1870s'. *Henry James Review* 35, no. 2 (2014): 127–40.

Zamir, Shamoon. *Dark Voices: W. E. B. Du Bois and American Thought, 1888–1903.* Chicago: University of Chicago Press, 1995.

Zwerdling, Alex. *Improvised Europeans: American Literary Expatriates and the Siege of London.* New York: Basic Books, 1998.

Index

abolitionism, 31, 59–60, 146, 157, 212; *see also* antislavery activism
Adams, Brooks, 276n, 277n
Adams, Henry
  Boston, Bostonians and Harvard, criticism of, 1, 43–5, 152, 163–90
  on 'culture' or education as exercise of power, 24–5, 44–7, 183–93
  and Darwinian thought, 27–8, 34–8, 180
  and Du Bois, 163–8, 170, 173–5, 184–7, 190–1
  and Eliot, Charles William, 24, 162–5, 171–3, 174–5, 177, 183, 188–9
  and Emerson, 169, 176, 182
  formal education, criticism of, 182–93
  the 'genteel', associated with, 12, 114–15, 193–5
  the 'genteel', excepted from, 193, 278n, 280n
  the 'genteel', source for narrative about, 193–4, 230–1, 238–9, 247, 249
  and Harvard, 28, 43–5, 183, 186–90, 192, 256n
  interest in the undeveloped or savage, 10, 23–4, 26, 31–40, 178–9, 239, 255n
  early liberalism of, 23, 178–81
  and Mill, 23–36, 40–7, 180, 187
  in Paris, 9, 10, 194, 279n
  on pedagogy, 43–4, 187–8
  publication practices of, 23, 24
  on women, sex, and marriage, 23–40, 44–7, 230, 239, 257n
Adams, Henry, works of
  Democracy, 16, 24, 31–3, 37–9, 45–8, 179
  The Education of Henry Adams, 1, 44, 48, 160, 162–7, 170, 175, 176–95, 238
  Essays in Anglo-Saxon Law, 28, 256n
  Esther, 16, 24, 27, 33, 36–7, 39–40, 45–7
  Letter to Teachers of American History, 189, 273n
  Life of George Cabot Lodge, 230, 279n
  'The Primitive Rights of Women', 28–30, 256n
Adams, Marion 'Clover', 27
Aldrich, Thomas Bailey, 12, 53, 114, 236
Ammons, Elizabeth, 223
Anderson, Amanda, 244
Anderson, James D., 174, 255n
'Anglo-Saxon race'
  Adams, Henry, Harvard teaching and, 28, 265n
  affinity for democracy and liberty, 86–8, 212
  racial decline and extinction of, 228–32, 234, 239, 241, 247
  tendency to conquest and *inquiétude*, 217–19
  Wharton on, 206–7, 210, 212, 217–24
  see also 'English-speaking race'; Teutonic origins theory; whiteness
Anthony, Susan B., 28
anti-imperialism, 130, 237, 239, 245; *see also* Spanish-American War; Venezuela crisis

anti-Semitism, 8, 114, 253n, 255n, 274n
antislavery activism, 17, 31, 157–8,
    212, 248; *see also* abolitionism
Arnold, Matthew
    Arnoldian 'culture', 7, 68, 119, 168,
        174, 252–3n
    as Boston liberals' influencer
        and interlocutor, 6, 68, 118–19,
        121, 127–8, 139, 168, 174, 217,
        238, 245
    'genteel tradition', accomplice to,
        7–8, 246
    and Howells, 136–7, 158
    and James, Henry, 52, 68, 121, 124,
        126, 128, 133, 136–7, 148
    on 'the remnant', 16–17, 118–19,
        121–2, 124, 126, 164, 170,
        173, 194
    'sweetness and light', 7, 168, 217, 246
    tour of US, 52, 182
    and Wharton, 68, 217
Arnold, Matthew, works by
    Civilization in the United States,
        127, 136
    'Civilization in the United States', 136
    Culture and Anarchy, 68, 119
    'Numbers; or, the Majority and the
        Remnant', 126, 170
    'A Word about America', 126
    'A Word More about America', 149
Aronoff, Eric, 7, 235, 252–3n
assimilation, 87, 129, 133–5,
    140–1, 147–8, 202–3; *see also*
    immigration; nativism
Atlanta University, 122, 166, 173
The Atlantic Monthly
    Aldrich as editor of, 53
    Arnold on, 52
    'Atlantic group' periodicals, 13
    Du Bois in, 59, 122, 166,
        184, 273n
    Eliot, Charles William in, 172
    as 'genteel' periodical, 12, 236
    Higginson in, 258n
    and James, Henry, 1, 4, 160, 247
    liberal discourse, site for, 6, 50, 53,
        121, 260n
    Perry, Bliss as editor of, 162, 166, 228
    Roosevelt in, 128
    Wharton on, 228

Babbitt, Irving, 51, 68, 159, 160,
    215–16, 239, 242
Bailkin, Jordanna, 76
Ball, David, 13, 192, 253n, 274n
Bancroft, George, 212
Bederman, Gail, 27–8
Bentley, Nancy, 14, 254n, 258n
Berenson, Bernard, 110, 229, 253n
Blair, Sara, 65, 70–2, 115–16
Blake, Casey Nelson, 236–7
Blazek, William, 84
Blight, David, 56
Boggs, Colleen Glenney, 34, 257n
Bollinger, Laurel, 62, 68, 155, 182
Boston *see* New England
Bourdieu, Pierre, 209–10
Bourget, Paul, 103–5, 237
Bourne, Randolph, 115, 147–8,
    149, 267n
'Brahmins' of Boston, 3, 154, 205, 226,
    236, 249; *see also* New England
Bramen, Carrie Tirado, 267n
Breuil, Jean du, 108
Bright, John, 212
Bromell, Nicholas, 15, 253n
Brooks, Van Wyck
    and Adams, Henry, 193–4, 230,
        238–9, 247
    and Emerson, 158, 240
    at Harvard, 5, 193, 237
    'genteel tradition', develops
        narrative about, 5, 51, 153–4,
        193–4, 224–31, 234–51
    and James, Henry, 226, 248
    and Norton, Charles Eliot, 235,
        238, 241–2
    Victorian thinkers and Arnoldian
        culture, affinities with, 238, 252n
    and Wendell, 5, 226–7, 229–31,
        235, 239–42, 247
    and Wharton, 225–7, 230
Brooks, Van Wyck, works by
    America's Coming-of-Age, 235,
        238, 248
    Autobiography, 239
    'Literary Life', 193, 225, 230, 235,
        239, 241–2
    New England: Indian Summer, 227,
        230–1, 235, 238, 239, 241, 246
    The Pilgrimage of Henry James, 226

Brooks, Van Wyck (*cont.*)
Wine of the Puritans, 227, 235, 237, 248
Brown, John, 119, 157, 169
Bryn Mawr College, 101, 105
Buelens, Gert, 116, 119
Butler, Leslie, 6, 52–3, 64, 85–6, 234, 259–60n, 266n
Butler, Nicholas Murray, *Meaning of Education*, 124-5, 132

Cable, George Washington, 'The Freedman's Case in Equity', 56–7
Calvinism *see* 'Puritan'
Canby, Henry Seidel, 196, 198, 201
Cantiello, Jessica Wells, 165–6, 185, 190, 191–2, 273n
Carlyle, Thomas
 on 'Aristocracy of Talent', 121
 on democracy and education, 61, 64–7
 James, Henry on, 61, 64–7, 78–9, 158–9, 260n
 Norton, Charles Eliot, edited by, 1, 52, 158–9, 243
 as pessimist in correspondence with optimist Emerson, 52, 65, 158–9, 243
 racism of, 64, 259–60n
The Century Illustrated, 12, 50, 53, 56–7, 60–1, 65, 73, 77, 259n
Channing, William Ellery, 213, 252n
Chapman, John Jay, 157, 160, 245–6
Civil War (US), 34, 53, 56, 64, 117, 155, 212, 248, 278n
civilisation
 civilising mission as brutal domination, 24, 45, 63, 130
 as development from barbarism, 63, 68, 75–6, 86, 130, 136–7, 149, 174, 196, 200–1, 203–8, 219, 262n
 racial differentiation in development from barbarism, 26, 27–8, 31, 86, 174, 196, 200–1, 203–8, 219, 262n
 as repository of art and culture threatened by democratisation, 50, 68–9, 71–2, 74, 75–6, 136–7, 267n

Clarke, Edward, 35, 257n
Claybaugh, Amanda, 54, 253n
Cmiel, Kenneth, 280n
Collini, Stefan, 30, 246, 252–3n
colonial revival, 83, 213, 224–5, 227–8; *see also* New England
Conforti, Joseph, 211, 213
Coolidge, Archibald, 274n, 274–5n
Cooper, Brittney, 175
Cooper, Tova, 14
Cowley, Malcolm, 153–4
culture
 Adams, Henry on, 44–7, 179
 as crucial to democracy, 6, 69, 75–6, 79, 118–19, 120–1, 124–5, 238
 James, Henry on, 52–79, 260n, 261n
 as material debris of woman's home, 62, 73, 247–9
 as means of exercising power, 14, 24–5, 44–7, 66, 209–10
 multiple and shifting definitions of term, 7, 252–3n, 260n
 as ongoing practice and process of development, 6, 68, 119, 174–5, 203, 245–6
 as separate from reality and manly roughness, 7, 11, 168, 235
 as source of pleasure dependent on ease, 68, 70–1, 208–9
 as threatened by democratisation, 54, 76–9, 91–2, 208
 Wharton on, 68, 208–9
 see also Arnold, Matthew; civilisation; education
'cultural custodianship' *see* 'custodians of culture'
cummings, e. e., 249
Curtis, George William
 antislavery oratory of, 31, 169, 212
 at Ashfield with Norton, 83
 as 'genteel' thinker, 12, 248
 on leadership by educated elite, 17, 122, 169, 272n
 as liberal thinker, 6
 light literature, writer of, 248, 276n
 on 'Puritan spirit' and 'English-speaking race', 87, 157–8, 212, 213, 214

Curtis, George William, works by
  'American Doctrine of Liberty', 31, 169
  'The Duty of the American Scholar to Politics and the Times', 122, 169
  'The Leadership of Educated Men', 122
  'The Public Duty of Educated Men', 122
  'The Puritan Principle and Puritan Pluck', 158, 212
  'The Puritan Spirit', 158, 212
'custodians of culture', 12–14, 50, 246

Dante, 1, 245, 258n
Darwin, Charles, 24, 34–7, 100, 103, 256n, 263n
Darwinian thought *see* evolutionary science
Davis, Jefferson, 217
Dawidoff, Robert, 193, 238
Day, Benjamin, 34
Decker, William, 165–6, 255n, 273n
'diversity', 134, 139–42, 147–50, 268n
Douglas, Ann, *The Feminization of American Culture*, 4, 252n
Dowling, Linda, 7, 234, 243, 257n
Dreyfus affair, 122, 170
Du Bois, W. E. B.
  and Arnold, 164, 168, 173–4
  and Eliot, Charles William, 164–5, 173, 271n
  elitism and eugenicism of, 164, 272n
  and Emerson, 164, 168, 173–4, 273n
  and evolutionary science, 180
  on leadership by educated elite, 17, 122, 173–5
  as New England liberal and Harvard man, 164–5, 174–5
  New England schoolmarm, account of, 59, 66–7
  and Norton, Charles Eliot, 174
  on political agency of artists and intellectuals, 163–4, 168
  and pragmatism, 115
  on teachers and teaching, 173–4, 184, 185

Du Bois, W. E. B., works by
  Autobiography of W. E. B. Du Bois, 166
  The College-Bred Negro, 122, 166, 173–4, 190–1
  'Criteria of Negro Art', 164
  Dusk of Dawn, 168
  'Negro Schoolmaster in the New South', 184–5
  Souls of Black Folk, 53, 59, 122, 163–4, 166–7, 174–5, 184–5
  'The Talented Tenth', 17, 122, 166, 170–1, 173–5, 187
Dudley, Bishop T. U., 57
Dunning, William Archibald, *Essays on the Civil War and Reconstruction*, 132
Dutch race and lineage, 220–3

educated elite
  action and agency of, 121, 129, 167, 168–75, 193–4
  conversation about, 121–2
  and 'numbers', 126–8
  pleasure and leisure, committed to, 128, 132–3, 142–4, 161, 175, 199
  racial composition of, 122, 126, 173–4, 206–7
  service and duty, committed to, 121–2, 126–8, 129, 138–40, 142, 164–5, 169–74, 177, 199, 200
education
  as control or domination, 14, 24–5, 45–7, 61, 63–4, 66–7, 255n
  democratisation of, doubt about or opposition to, 64–5, 67, 76–7, 88–92, 97–8, 108–9, 190–2, 205, 207–11, 223
  of freedmen, 53, 56–60, 66–7, 247
  liberalism, core value of, 6, 23, 26, 35–6, 40–1, 49, 50, 60, 62–3, 68, 85–8, 119–22, 124–5, 138–40, 171–5, 176–7, 200–1, 204–5, 214, 232, 245–6
  pedagogy, teachers and teaching, 40–5, 173–4, 182–8
  and pleasure, 68–75, 143–4, 183–4
  of women, 34–5, 45–6, 53, 83, 100–2, 103–5, 141
  see also culture; educated elite

Edwards, Jonathan, 240
Eliot, Charles William
 and Adams, Henry, 28, 43, 162, 166, 176–7, 183, 188–90
 and Arnold, 68, 168, 174, 217
 democracy, faith in, 138–9, 142, 162–3, 199
 development, perfectibility, and progress, faith in, 88, 174, 203–5, 216, 228, 262n
 on 'diversity', 139–40, 142, 149, 268n
 and Du Bois, 164–5, 166, 167, 168–9, 173–5, 271n
 as educated citizen, model of, 138, 171–2
 on educated elite, duties and powers of, 120–3, 128, 169, 172–5, 199
 education qualification for suffrage, support for, 85, 205
 and Emerson, 168, 174, 182, 271n, 273n, 277–8n
 eugenicism of, 140, 164, 174, 200, 203–4
 and evolutionary science, 88, 149, 174, 180, 200, 216
 the 'genteel', associated with, 12
 Harvard, reforming President of, 10, 60, 113, 177, 189, 224–5, 245
 on immigration, 85, 266n, 268n
 as liberal thinker, 6, 60, 163, 237, 239, 245–6
 as 'Puritan', 157, 163, 176, 213–14, 276–7n, 213–16, 218–19, 220, 224, 277–8n
 on race and segregation, 86, 139–40, 173, 199–201, 202, 203–5, 228, 268n, 272n, 275n
 Unitarianism of, 176, 214–15
 and Wendell, 196, 203–5, 215–16, 239, 241, 242
Eliot, Charles William, works by
 'Diversity and Unity in Family, College, and State', 139–40
 'The Function of Education in Democratic Society', 122
 The Harvard Classics, 85, 207–8, 249
 'New Definition of a Cultivated Man', 174
 'What is a Liberal Education?', 60
 'Why We Honor the Puritans', 218–19
Eliot, T. S., 9, 152, 216, 249
Emerson, Ralph Waldo
 and Adams, Henry, 176, 179
 'The American Scholar', 122, 169, 176, 182
 'Aspects of Culture', 122, 127, 169
 Brooks, Van Wyck on, 238, 240
 and Carlyle, 52, 65–6, 158, 243
 on the educated elite, 17, 122, 124, 127–8, 169, 173, 266n, 280n
 and Eliot, Charles William, 164, 168, 174, 182
 and Du Bois, 122, 164, 168, 174
 the 'genteel', associated with, 158, 236
 James, Henry on, 4, 52, 65–6, 68, 158
 as liberal thinker, 6, 52, 62, 266n
 and Norton, Charles Eliot, 1, 52, 65, 242–4, 260n
 serene optimism of, 52, 62, 158–9, 243, 270–1n, 276–7n
 Wendell on, 240, 243
English-speaking race, 86–8, 212; see also 'Anglo-Saxon race'
eugenicism, 26, 140, 164, 174, 200, 203–5, 216, 232
Evans, Stephanie, 191
evolutionary science, 24, 27–8, 33–8, 174, 180, 200, 216, 256n, 257n

Field, Emily Donaldson, 166–7, 185
Fisher, Laura R., 14
Fleissner, Jennifer, 13
'forms', 118, 137–8, 145–7
The Forum, 121, 128–9, 165
Franklin, Benjamin, 165, 240
Freedman, Jonathan, 75, 253n
Freedmen's Bureau, 53, 58–9, 253n; see also Reconstruction
Fuller, Randall, 158, 235, 236–7, 238

Garrison, William Lloyd, 158, 212
Gaskell, Elizabeth, 7
Gaskell, Charles Milnes, 188, 189

'genteel tradition'
  and Adams, Henry, 8, 167, 193–5, 230, 238–9
  and Arnold, 7, 246
  and Brooks, Van Wyck, 5, 51, 153, 193, 225–6, 229–32, 235–42, 244
  effeminacy and unsexy white womanhood, 11, 33, 234, 237, 246–50
  historiography of, 11–14, 233–4, 237–8, 280n
  and James, Henry, 4, 50–1, 61, 66, 115, 116, 117, 118, 151–61, 238
  and Norton, Charles Eliot, 7, 151–61, 241–6
  and Parrington, 3–5, 11, 51, 154, 225–7, 235–6
  and Santayana, 4, 11, 153, 224, 226, 234–40, 246
  and Wendell, 51, 159–60, 201, 216, 227–31, 235, 238, 239–45
  and Wharton, 11, 81, 201, 224–32, 238, 241–2
  white sterility and racial decline, 194, 224, 226–31, 239, 241, 247, 249, 250
Gilder, Richard Watson, 6, 12, 53, 77
Glazener, Nancy, 11, 13, 236, 239, 282n
Godkin, Edwin Lawrence, 12, 17, 114–15, 129, 130–3, 151, 160, 193, 231, 238
  Unforeseen Tendencies of Democracy, 124–6, 132–3, 152–3
  'The Duty of Educated Men in a Democracy', 122, 128–9, 171
Gossett, Thomas, 256n
Gradert, Kenyon, 4, 211, 212, 217, 270n
Grady, Henry, 56–7

Hall, Catherine, 64
Halpern, Faye, 59
Hamlet, 176, 179–82, 261n
Harper's, 12, 265n
Harrison, J. B., 84
Hartman, Saidiya V., 56–7
Harvard University
  and Adams, Henry, 25, 28, 43–5, 183, 186–90, 192, 256n
  and Brooks, Van Wyck, 5, 193, 237
  and Eliot, Charles William, 10, 60, 113, 138–40, 142, 149, 177, 189, 224–5, 245
  and James, Henry, 10, 62, 70, 75, 113, 135–6, 137, 140–3, 264n
  and James, William, 9, 10, 117, 141, 250–1
  and Norton, Charles Eliot, 1, 10, 75, 90, 113, 114, 119, 134, 138–40, 142, 154, 155, 157, 265n
  and Parrington, 5, 235
  Phi Beta Kappa proceedings at, 31, 122, 127, 169–70, 279n
  and Wendell, 10, 113, 114, 197–8, 226, 229–30, 235, 239, 241, 265n
  and Wharton, 2, 9, 10, 90, 196–8, 253n
  see also Radcliffe College
Haviland, Barbara, 115
Hawthorne, Nathaniel, 159, 236
Hay, John, 135–6, 188, 194, 267n
Herford, Oliver, 269n
Higginson, Thomas Wentworth, 4, 6, 258n
Hochman, Barbara, 57
Hofstadter, Richard, 13, 193–4, 234, 272n
Holmes, Oliver Wendell, 205
Horne, Phillip, 9, 267n
Howe, Julia Ward, 157, 246
Howells, William Dean, 6, 12, 78, 123, 125, 130–1, 136–7, 158, 244, 259n, 270n
Hyde, James Hazen, 197, 274n
Hyde Professorship, 197–8, 224, 228, 274–5n

idealism
  literary, as attribute of 'genteel', 2, 3, 13–14, 18–19, 33, 81, 93, 153–4, 226, 234, 236, 240–1
  political, 2, 13–14, 16, 18–19, 33, 51, 59–60, 68, 81, 93, 94, 96–100, 108, 158, 160, 214–17, 240–1, 242–4, 250

immigration, 85–6, 114–15, 128, 133–4, 139–41, 202–5, 266n; *see also* assimilation; nativism
imperialism, 28, 45, 63, 83, 117, 124, 130–1, 237, 245, 267n; *see also* Spanish-American War; Venezuela crisis

James, Henry
  and Arnold, 52, 68, 118–19, 122, 124, 126, 136–7
  on asceticism and pleasure, 54–5, 62–3, 68–75, 122–3, 133, 143, 155–6
  on Boston, Bostonians, and New England, 4, 13, 49–79, 123, 150–61
  on Carlyle, 65–6, 67, 158–9, 260n
  and Eliot, Charles William, 113, 120, 123, 124, 134, 138–40, 142
  and Emerson, 68, 122, 124, 127, 158–9
  the 'genteel', associated with, 12, 116, 154, 236, 280n
  the 'genteel', excepted from, 151–2, 278n, 280n
  the 'genteel', source for narrative about, 4, 51, 153–4, 237, 247–9
  and Godkin, 118–19, 122, 124, 128–33, 152–3, 160
  and Harvard, 10, 62, 70, 75, 113, 135–6, 137, 140–3, 264n
  and the literary marketplace, 78–9, 125–6
  and Norton, Charles Eliot, 1–3, 10, 52, 65, 68–9, 75, 79, 118–21, 122–4, 127–8, 134, 138–40, 142, 148–9, 151–61
  and Paterian aestheticism, 54, 69–70, 71, 75, 138, 143
  politics of, scholarly conversation about, 115–17, 264n, 267n, 269–70n
  and Roosevelt, 122, 124, 128–30
  on social democracy as unfavourable to culture, civilisation and artmaking, 76–8, 144–51
  and Wharton, 80, 146–7, 201, 210

James, Henry, works by
  The American, 155
  'An American Art-Scholar: Charles Eliot Norton', 151–61, 176
  'American Letters' from *Literature*, 4, 117, 123–33
  The American Scene, 113, 115–17, 134–51
  The Bostonians, 4, 13, 49–76, 138, 146, 155, 175, 247–8, 260n
  The Europeans, 155
  'The Founding of the "Nation"', 1, 4–5, 160, 242
  'The Long Wards', 79
  'Mr. and Mrs. James T. Fields', 1, 4–5, 160, 247, 282n
  Notes of a Son and Brother, 2
  The Princess Casamassima, 49–56, 69–70, 73–9, 143–4, 258n
  'The Question of our Speech', 123, 134, 137–8, 146
  What Maisie Knew, 125
James, Henry, III, 131
James, Henry, Sr, 4, 253n
James, Wilky, 117
James, William
  'genteel tradition', excepted from (with Henry) by Santayana, 151–2
  at Harvard, 9, 10, 119, 141, 250–1
  James, Henry, correspondent of, 155
  as liberal thinker, 6, 273n
  on leadership by educated elite, 117, 122, 170–1, 174
  pragmatism of, 115
  as public intellectual, 117
  'The Social Value of the College-Bred', 122, 170–1, 193, 230
  Subjection of Women, review of, 256n
  on variety, 267n
  Wendell, correspondent of, 113, 220, 229, 241, 245, 274n

Kaledin, Eugenia, 44
Kallen, Horace, 229, 241, 270–1n
Kammen, Michael, 211, 213
Karlin, Daniel, 62
Kassanoff, Jennie, 84, 197, 198, 218, 227–9, 279n

Kazin, Alfred, 12
Kendi, Ibram X., 56
King, Clarence, 36
Kirsch, Geoffrey R., 199
Konstantinou, Lee, 163
Kornbluh, Anna, 118

Lapsley, Gaillard, 196, 253n
Laski, Gregory, 15
Lazarus, Emma, 114
Lears, Jackson, 13, 234, 255n, 266n, 268n, 274n
Levine, Caroline, 117–18
liberalism
   antiracist and leftist critiques of, 14, 16, 24–5
   conservative realist critiques of, 2, 5–6, 14–15, 23–5, 33, 47–8, 51, 54, 67–8, 81, 92–100, 153–4, 159, 215–16, 240–1, 250
   liberal subject, embodiment of, 15–16, 23–4, 26, 54, 57, 81–2, 96, 100–3, 105–8
   of New England, 6–7, 15, 23, 33, 52, 62, 66, 68, 75–6, 138–40, 157–8, 160–1, 163, 164–5, 167, 175, 180, 182, 196, 213–14, 233, 236–9, 240, 244, 250
   see also civilisation; culture
Literature magazine, 117, 123–5, 128, 130
Lodge, George 'Bay' Cabot, 230–1, 253n, 279n
Lodge, Henry Cabot, 28, 43, 276n
Lowe, Lisa, 24–5
Lowell, James Russell, 6, 10, 243
Lustig, T. J., 137

McClay, Wilfred, 237–8
McKim, Mead and White, 113, 144
Maine, Henry, 29, 30
Margolis, Stacey, 15
May, Henry, 14, 245–6
Menand, Louis, 119
Mencken, H. L., 12, 229, 279n
Michaels, Walter Benn, 134
Mill, Harriet Taylor, 24, 263n

Mill, John Stuart
   and Adams, Henry, 23–37, 40–7, 169, 180, 187
   Autobiography, 35–6, 41
   as Boston liberals' influencer and interlocutor, 6, 52–3, 101, 118, 148, 245, 263n
   Considerations on Representative Government, 25
   'Inaugural Address', 42–3
   On Liberty, 121–2, 148
   Principles of Political Economy, 35
   Subjection of Women, 24–6, 28–30, 32, 33, 34–7, 40–3, 62, 64, 101, 256n, 257n, 259n
Moreland, Kim, 27
Morley, John, 101, 126
Mount, the see Wharton, Edith
Mugwumps, 12, 52, 60, 237
Munsterberg, Hugo, 141

The Nation, 1, 6, 12, 101, 114, 132, 154, 160
nativism, 85–6, 113–16, 123, 148, 202, 213, 233, 245, 266n; see also assimilation; immigration
Neilson, William Allan, 276–7n
Nelson, Dana, 15
New England
   Boston disliked and criticised, 4, 9–10, 17, 44, 73, 152, 155, 176–80, 222, 247
   implicated in narrative about 'genteel', 1–6, 14, 51, 61, 153–4, 224–31, 236–8, 240, 241, 247–50
   liberalism of, 6, 15, 23, 33, 52, 62, 66, 68, 75–6, 138–40, 157–8, 160–1, 163, 164–5, 167, 175, 180, 182, 196, 213–14, 233, 236–9, 240, 244, 250
   narrative of decline about, 4, 51, 226–31, 236, 241
   New York, contrasted unfavourably with, 70, 155, 220–4
   'Old New England' and the colonial revival, 227–9
   political idealism of, 13–14, 67–8, 159–60, 215–16, 242–4

New England (*cont.*)
  regional antagonism during Civil War, Reconstruction and 'second civil war', 58–60, 155, 157–8, 211–13, 219–20
  as site of white racial purity and Anglo-Saxon extinction, 114, 151, 204, 226, 228–31, 239, 241
  see also Brahmins; Harvard University; Puritans; schoolmarm figure; Unitarianism
New Humanism, 160, 215–16, 239; *see also* Babbitt, Irving
Nicolay, John George, *Life of Lincoln*, 188
Noonan, Mark J., 61
North American Review, 85, 171–2, 256n, 257n
Norton, Charles Eliot
  and Adams, Henry, 1, 3, 10
  anti-imperialism of, 83–4, 86, 128, 130
  and Arnold, 68, 127–8, 136
  Ashfield, summer residence at, 82–3, 84, 109, 261n
  Brooks, Van Wyck, portrayal by, 231, 235, 238, 241–6
  and Carlyle, 52, 65, 158–9, 243
  on culture and democracy, 52, 68–9, 79, 85–6, 91–2, 93–4, 95–6, 118, 119–21, 127–8, 138–9, 142, 144, 151, 158–60, 174–5, 245–6
  and Du Bois, 174–5
  and Eliot, Charles William, 134, 138–40, 142, 149, 157, 245–6
  and Emerson, 52, 65, 127–8, 158–9, 243–4, 260n
  the 'genteel', associated with, 3, 7–9, 12–13, 80, 114–15, 153–4, 234, 237, 246
  and Harvard, 1, 10, 75, 90, 113, 114, 119, 134, 138–40, 142, 154, 155, 157, 265n
  Heart of Oak books, 85–8
  idealism of, 81, 92–4, 95–6, 160, 242–4
  and immigration, 114, 119, 128, 148, 266n
  'Intellectual Life of America', 91, 119–21, 127–8, 148, 155
  and James, Henry, 1–3, 52, 65–6, 68–9, 79, 123, 124, 128, 130, 134–44, 151–61, 157n, 176
  liberalism of, 6, 52–3, 75–6, 95–6, 118–19, 121, 148–9, 244
  as New England 'Puritan' type, 153, 155–60
  on race and civilisation, 68, 86–8, 99, 262n
  and Ruskin, 75, 101, 138
  Shady Hill, Cambridge residence at, 2, 90, 245
  'Some Aspects of Civilisation in America', 86, 128
  and Wendell, 10, 159–60, 241–5
  and Wharton, 2–3, 10, 80–5, 88, 90–6, 99, 100–2, 105, 109–10, 198, 261n
  on women's education and suffrage, 101–2, 105, 263n
Norton, Elizabeth 'Lily', 261n
Norton, Grace, 10, 53–4, 162–3
Norton, Sara 'Sally', 10, 11, 82–4, 90–1, 94, 224, 279n
Nowlin, Michael, 225

Olin-Ammentorp, Julie, 197
Olmstead, Frederick Law, 65

Parrington, Vernon Louis
  on Adams, Henry, 193, 269n, 280n
  on 'Brahmins' and New England's decline, 3–5, 51, 154, 156, 236, 280n
  'genteel tradition', develops narrative about, 3–5, 51, 153–4, 225–7, 235–6, 241–2, 249, 250, 280n
  on James, Henry, 154, 193, 229, 269n, 280n
  Main Currents in American Thought, 3–5, 154, 156, 225–6, 235–6, 249, 269n, 280n
  'Our Literary Aristocrat', 11, 225–7, 241–2, 275n
  and Wendell, 5, 235
  on Wharton, 11, 225–7, 229, 241–2, 275n, 280n

Pater, Walter, 54, 69–71, 75, 138, 143
Paul, Diane B., 34
Perry, Bliss, 53, 162–3, 166, 198, 228, 274n, 277n
Perry, Thomas Sergeant, 49–50, 52, 55, 56, 77
Petrarch, 45–6, 258n
Phelps, William Lyon, 198
Phillips, Wendell, 'The Scholar in a Republic', 122, 169–70, 172
Poirier, Richard, 152
Posnock, Ross, 115–18, 131–2, 147, 152–3, 154, 157, 193, 264n, 270n, 271n
Pound, Ezra, 9
pragmatism, 115–16, 119
Pratt, Lloyd, 15
'Puritan'
  Calvinism and, 214–16, 240–1, 252n
  Civil Wars (English, US, and 'second' US), role within, 212–13
  education, democracy and liberty, associated with, 58, 123, 157–8, 159, 163, 201, 212–14, 248, 259n
  'genteel tradition' and prudery, associated with, 3, 123, 153, 156, 227, 234, 238–9, 247
  inflexible certainty and idealism of, 58, 119, 123, 157, 158–60, 176, 211–12, 217–18, 240–1, 250
  'Knickerbocker' Dutch, contrasted against, 220–4
  placing duty and morality over pleasure and art, 58, 123, 155–6, 161, 206, 218–19, 270n
  radical abolitionism, associated with, 157–8, 211–12, 248, 270n
  shifting meanings of term, 153–4, 157, 211–14, 231–2, 276n
  Unitarianism and, 4, 62, 213–15, 242, 252n
  see also 'Anglo-Saxon race'; New England; whiteness

Raber, Jesse, 14
race, 23–6, 27–8, 32–3, 35–6, 85–8, 98–9, 139–40, 173–4, 198, 200–3, 205–6, 211, 259–60n;
  see also 'Anglo-Saxon race'; civilisation; culture; 'English-speaking race'; evolutionary science; whiteness
Radcliffe College, 101–2, 170, 193
Rauchway, Eric, 27, 28–9
reading
  democracy, literacy, and the literary marketplace, 84–92, 95, 99, 125–6, 261n
  as education, 63, 70, 179, 183
  political functions of, 116, 124, 125, 129
  'reading into', practice of Henry James, 122–3, 124, 132–3
  see also culture; education
realism
  of Adams, Henry, 47–8
  conservative and critical of democracy, 5, 8, 13–14, 47, 67–8, 81, 109–10, 153–4, 159, 216–17, 226
  democratic, progressive and masculine, 5, 8, 13–14, 51, 153–4, 226, 235–6
  of James, Henry, 54, 67–8
  of Wendell, 159, 216, 240–1
  of Wharton, 80–1, 92–3, 96–100, 109–10, 216–17
Reconstruction, 15, 49, 53, 56–9, 66–7, 132, 213, 247, 250
'remnant' see educated elite
Renker, Elizabeth, 234
Richardson, H. H., 194
Roosevelt, Theodore
  and Adams, Henry, 162, 178, 194
  assimilationism of, 147
  on educated elite, 128–30, 171–2, 193
  and Hyde Professorship, 274–5n
  imperialism of, 28
  and James, Henry, 128–30
  and masculinity, 28, 237, 265–6n
  and race, 220–1, 231
  and Wharton, 83–4, 198–9, 210, 221

Roosevelt, Theodore, works by
  'Address of President Roosevelt' (at Provincetown Pilgrim Monument), 220
  American Ideals, 124, 128
  'The College Graduate and Public Life', 122, 128
  'The College Man', 171, 193
  'The Man in the Arena', 198–9
  'The Manly Virtues and Practical Politics', 128
  'True Americanism', 128
Rousseau, Jean Jacques, 165
Rowe, John Carlos, 130, 267n
Rubin, Joan Shelley, 13, 234, 236, 238
Ruskin, John, 93, 101, 138, 258n

Samuels, Ernest, 29, 188, 256n, 257n
Santayana, George
  on Eliot, Charles William and his Harvard, 163, 239–40, 242
  'genteel tradition', contributions to narrative about, 5, 11, 12, 151–2, 234–42, 249, 250, 280n
  'Genteel American Poetry', 246
  'The Genteel Tradition in American Philosophy', 11, 151, 224, 236–7
  as Hyde Professor, 224, 274n
  The Last Puritan, 226
  and Norton, Charles Eliot, 244, 245, 246, 270n
  Persons and Places, 163, 240, 241, 242, 244, 245
schoolmarm figure, 13, 32–3, 51, 58–60, 62, 81–2, 234, 246–50; *see also* genteel tradition; New England; Reconstruction
Schuller, Kyla, 26, 200
Scribner's, 85
Sedgwick, Ellery, 236
Seelye, John, 211, 212, 221
Seitler, Dana, 34
sentimentalism, 4, 13–14, 58–9, 212, 213, 259n
Shady Hill *see* Norton, Charles Eliot
Shaheen, Aaron, 58
Singley, Carol, 216
Slap, Andrew L., 193, 234, 280n
Sollors, Werner, 202

Solomon, Barbara Miller, 265–6n
Sorbonne *see* Hyde Professorship
Spanish-American War, 130–1, 237, 244
Speicher, Allison, 14
Spencer, Herbert, 35, 103
spinster *see* schoolmarm figure
Sproat, John G., *The Best Men: Liberal Reformers in the Gilded Age*, 193, 280n
Stevens, Wallace, 249
Stoddard, Richard Henry, 12, 236
Stokes, Claudia, 10, 11, 236, 239, 240, 276n
Story, William Wetmore, 152
Stowe, Harriet Beecher, 212, 247
  'New England Ministers', 4
  Uncle Tom's Cabin, 13, 58–9, 247, 259n, 282n
Stratton, Matthew, 163
Sumner, Charles, 158, 212
Synnott, Marcia Graham, 140

'Talented Tenth' *see* Du Bois, W. E. B.
Taylor, Helen, 263n
Teutonic origins theory, 8, 28, 87–8, 99, 140, 256n; *see also* 'Anglo-Saxon race'; 'English-speaking race'; whiteness
Tocqueville, Alexis de, 23, 148, 169, 180, 207, 217
Trilling, Lionel, 12, 258n
Turner, James, 7, 160, 269n
Tuttleton, James, 100

Unitarianism, 3, 4, 18, 62, 68, 155, 157, 160, 163, 176–7, 180, 181, 182, 213–15, 220, 241, 242, 250, 252n, 277n

Vance, William, 103
Vanderbilt, Kermit, 244
Vandersee, Charles, 45, 180, 182
Venezuela crisis, 86, 128, 244

Waldstein, Charles, 'The Education of the People', 60
Walker, Pierre, 115–16, 265n
Ward, Samuel, 94–5, 281n

Warren, Kenneth W., 13–14, 59–60, 116–17, 134, 146, 163–4
Wegener, Frederick, 83, 109–10, 147
Weinstein, Cindy, 27
Wells, H. G., *Future in America*, 236
Wendell, Barrett
  and Adams, Henry, 10, 230
  Brooks, Van Wyck, portrayal by, 229–30, 231, 234, 239–42
  on Calvinism, Puritanism and Unitarianism, 68, 201, 211, 214–16, 220, 240–1, 242
  on democracy, 159, 201, 214–16, 220, 240–1, 242, 243
  and Eliot, Charles William, 203–4, 211–16, 228, 239, 241, 242
  English Composition, 239
  France of Today, 197, 202
  the 'genteel', associated with, 240
  the 'genteel', source for narrative about, 229–31, 239–42
  Harvard teaching, 10, 113, 114, 197–8, 226, 229–30, 235, 239, 241, 265n
  as Hyde Professor, 197–8, 274n
  idealism, criticism of, 51, 68, 159, 214–16, 240–1, 243, 250
  on immigration, 114, 115, 120, 202–3
  and James, Henry, 10, 274n
  and James, William, 113, 220, 229, 241, 245, 274n
  Liberty, Union and Democracy, 197, 202–3, 229
  Literary History of America, 197, 203–4, 215–16, 229, 240, 242–3, 245
  and Norton, Charles Eliot, 114, 159–60, 241–5
  on slavery and 'Africans', 199–200, 203, 245, 278n
  Stelligeri, 114, 159, 240
  and Wharton, 10, 196–205, 209, 211, 216–17, 220, 224, 226–9, 241–2, 274n, 278n
  on white racial decline and extinction, 226, 228–31, 241, 247, 250
Wharton, Edith
  on the Anglo-Saxon race, 156, 206–7, 217–24, 228
  'continuity' and conservation, praise for, 146–7, 205, 217–23, 227–8
  democratic social or political order, criticism of, 96–9, 118, 146–7, 221–4
  democratisation of culture, criticism of, 88–92, 97–8, 208
  on the Dutch and New York, 220–4
  evolutionary science and, 88, 100, 200, 216
  formal education and wilful learning, criticism of, 88–9, 103–5, 205, 206–10
  on the French and France, 205–9, 218–19
  the 'genteel', associated with, 11, 12, 225–6, 236, 241–2
  the 'genteel', source for narrative about, 81, 224–6, 230, 238, 241–2
  and Harvard, 2, 9, 10, 90, 196–8, 253n
  and James, Henry, 118, 123, 146–7, 156
  idealism, criticism of, 92–101, 109–10, 216–17, 263n
  The Mount, 82–3, 109, 224–5, 227–8, 261n
  and Norton, Charles Eliot, 3, 80–8, 90–1, 92–6, 100–2, 109–10
  on 'Puritans' and New England, 160, 176, 211, 216–21, 224, 226–9
  on race, 98, 198, 199–201, 206–7, 210–11
  Roosevelt and, 83–4, 198–9, 210, 221
  Wendell and, 10, 196–205, 209, 211, 216–17, 220, 224, 226–9, 241–2, 278n
  on women and feminism, 96–8, 100–9

Wharton, Edith, works by
  The Age of Innocence, 198–9, 225–6, 230, 241
  'L'Amérique en Guerre', 197–8, 207, 211, 217–19, 221–2, 278n
  'Angel at the Grave', 90–1
  A Backward Glance, 109, 110, 146, 199, 201–2, 211, 222–4
  The Book of the Homeless, 199
  Decoration of Houses, 146
  'The Descent of Man', 85, 89–92, 102–3, 208, 225, 263n
  French Ways and Their Meaning, 146, 196–7, 205–8, 217–19, 225
  The Fruit of the Tree, 100
  'The Great American Novel', 147, 226
  'High Pasture', 109
  The House of Mirth, 80
  'Impoverishing the Language', 146
  'The Pelican', 90, 103, 263n
  'The Pretext', 90
  The Valley of Decision, 80–3, 94–108, 160
  'The Vice of Reading', 84–5, 88–9, 92, 103–4, 207
Wharton, Teddy, 192–3, 210, 253n
whiteness, 15, 23–6, 36, 87–8, 134–5, 140, 149–51, 173, 220–4, 228–31, 239, 241, 250; *see also* 'Anglo-Saxon race'; 'English-speaking race'
Wilde, Oscar, 237
Williams College, 84, 90
Wilson, Douglas L., 246, 249
Wilson, Ivy, 15
Wilson, Woodrow, 86, 168
Woolson, Constance Fenimore, 58, 155
World War I, 1, 5, 79, 117, 197–8, 199, 217

Yale University, 108, 114, 119, 140, 154, 196, 198, 204

Zamir, Shamoon, 163–4, 166

EU representative:
Easy Access System Europe
Mustamäe tee 50, 10621 Tallinn, Estonia
Gpsr.requests@easproject.com

www.ingramcontent.com/pod-product-compliance
Lightning Source LLC
Chambersburg PA
CBHW051559230426
43668CB00013B/1911